How Ottawa Spends, .

MW01178960

THE SCHOOL OF PUBLIC POLICY AND ADMINISTRATION
at Carleton University is a national center for the study of public
policy and public management.

The School's Centre for Policy and Program Assessment provides
research services and courses to interest groups, businesses, unions,
and governments in the evaluation of public policies, programs
and activities.

School of Public Policy and Administration
Carleton University
10th Floor Dunton Tower
1125 Colonel By Drive
Ottawa, ON
Canada K1S 5B6
www.carleton.ca/sppa

How Ottawa Spends, 2011–2012

Trimming Fat or Slicing Pork?

Edited by

CHRISTOPHER STONEY

and

G. BRUCE DOERN

Published for
The School of Public Policy and Administration
Carleton University
by
McGill-Queen's University Press
Montreal & Kingston · London · Ithaca

© McGill-Queen's University Press 2011
ISBN 978-0-7735-3918-1

Legal deposit third quarter 2011
Bibliothèque nationale du Québec

Printed in Canada on acid-free paper that is 100% ancient forest free
(100% post-consumer recycled), processed chlorine free.

McGill-Queen's University Press acknowledges the support of the Canada
Council for the Arts for our publishing program. We also acknowledge
the financial support of the Government of Canada through the Canada
Book Fund for our publishing activities.

Library and Archives Canada has catalogued this publication as follows:

How Ottawa spends.
    1983–
    Imprint varies.
    Includes bibliographical references.
    Continues: How Ottawa spends your tax dollars, ISSN 0711-4990.
    ISSN 0822-6482
    ISBN 978-0-7735-3918-1 (2011/2012 edition)

    1. Canada – Appropriations and expenditures – Periodicals.
    I. Carleton University. School of Public Policy and Administration

HJ7663.H69   354.710072'2   C84-030303-3

This book was typeset by Interscript in 10/12 Minion.

Contents

Preface

This is the 32nd edition of *How Ottawa Spends*. As always, we are especially indebted to our roster of contributing academic and other expert authors from across Canada and abroad for their insights and for their willingness to contribute to public debate in Canada.*

Thanks are also due to Brittney Fritsch and Mary Au at the School of Public Administration for their excellent research and technical support and to Joan McGilvray and her colleagues at McGill-Queen's University Press for their always professional editorial and publishing services and expertise.

None of this work would have been possible without the continuing support and scholarly stimulation provided by our colleagues at the School of Public Policy and Administration at Carleton University and in the Politics Department at Exeter University.

Christopher Stoney and Bruce Doern
Ottawa,
May 2011

---

* The opinions expressed by the contributing authors to this volume are the personal views of the authors of individual chapters and do not necessarily reflect the views of the editors or of the School of Public Policy and Administration at Carleton University.

How Ottawa Spends, 2011–2012

1 Harper Budgeting in a New Majority Government: Trimming Fat or Slicing Pork?

CHRISTOPHER STONEY AND G. BRUCE DOERN

INTRODUCTION

The May 2nd 2011 election results gave the Harper Conservatives their long sought majority government and in the process produced a major realignment of Canadian politics. The Tories won 167 seats, the NPD 102, the Liberals 34, the Bloc Quebecois 4, and the Green Party 1 (the election of Elizabeth May as its first elected Member of Parliament). In the popular vote the Tories gained 39.6 percent, the NPD 30.6 percent, the Liberals 18.9 percent, the Bloc 4 percent and the Green Party 3.9 percent.

Enough Canadians supported the Tories and Harper's leadership at least to the extent of agreeing that he represented a safe pair of hands regarding the economy and reducing the deficit. Voter support for a majority government occurred despite a mistrust of the Harper Tories regarding their less than stellar record on the basics of Canadian democracy and accountability. These were the twin contending narratives that preceded the election and the Harper government's March 22nd Budget and they continued during the election as the main touchstones of fiscal policy and electoral politics.

The election, however, produced a greatly changed political context for Harper to deal with since voters punished the Liberal Party and the Bloc Quebecois and rewarded Jack Layton and the NPD elevating Layton to be Leader of the Opposition with a level of support the NPD has never enjoyed in federal politics, both nationally and in Quebec where it won 58 of the 75 Quebec seats and garnered 43 percent of the vote. Both Liberal leader Michael Ignatieff and Bloc leader, Gilles Duceppe were defeated in their own ridings and resigned as party leaders. Harper's Conservatives also have a considerably reduced electoral presence in Quebec due to losses to the NPD.

In 2011 and beyond Canadians as citizens, taxpayers, and recipients of public money enter a new era of overt fiscal austerity as initial measures are announced, and others are promised both in Budget 2011 and in the Tory election platform. The trimming and slicing is being carried out and defended by a Harper Conservative government that successfully trumpeted its competence as an economic manager. But it is also a government that made ill-advised cuts to the GST and has increased federal spending significantly since it came to power in 2006. Its 2011 Budget and election platform contained new spending even as it reiterated its plan to eliminate the deficit by 2014–2015.

In this edition of *How Ottawa Spends*, we cast the policy and budgetary choices in terms of the political arts of both trimming fat and slicing pork, political strategies practiced by previous Liberal governments as well.[1] Life under serious deficits and austerity last occurred in the mid 1990s under the auspices of the Chretien Liberals as a majority government.[2] It began what would turn out to be a decade in power. With Paul Martin as Minister of Finance, the austerity strategy and its underlying math calculus was to reduce the then 13 year long huge federal deficit by cutting spending by 20 percent with by far the largest component coming from core federal-provincial established health and social transfers. It was also relying on, and hoping for, a growing economy and thus increasing federal revenues. By 1997 the federal budget shifted to surpluses for the next 8 years. Job done, but not without pain in the 1993–1996 period and beyond in some program areas where cuts ranged much more widely and deeply, including cuts in defence and research and development (R&D) spending.

This time an even larger Harper era deficit is different, occurring in the wake of the global recession and banking crisis and the soon to end federal stimulus program. Budget 2011, and the subsequent May 2nd federal election results partly reveal this but the differences in strategy compared to the mid-1990s Liberal approach were already fully in evidence. First Harper had already stressed in Budget 2010 that, unlike the Chretien Liberal cuts, the Tories would protect the main federal-provincial and largely social and medicare program transfers but without clearly specifying whether this meant the existing base of these programs, the current 6 percent annual growth rate formula or some other defined number now to be determined in a majority Parliament context. They would also seek to ensure that national defence, law and order spending and programs for Canada's seniors would not be harmed by cuts. Second, the fiscal implication of this protective stance is that the bulk of the cuts would have to come eventually from an array of mainly smaller federal government programs, thus helping the Tories work towards their goal of a reduced federal presence in a federal system which the Harper government has cast as open federalism. Third, the Harper austerity strategy had to be co-ordinated to a significant extent with the larger global aspects of the recession and its aftermath as discussed and planned through the G-20.

The Harper austerity strategy as revealed in the 2011 Budget and in the 2011 election campaign is also centered on planned and hoped for economic growth and thus healthy increases in tax revenues as potentially an even greater contributor to future balanced budgets or small surpluses by 2015–2016. But it was the overall Harper five year record in office that became pivotal in the May 2nd, 2011 election that was forced three days after the Budget Speech by a Parliamentary vote that defeated the government on a historic contempt of Parliament motion.

This record includes the persona and tactics of the Prime Minister as Canada's longest serving minority government prime minister whose strongest political goal other than that of securing a majority government is to make the Conservatives his new hoped for "natural" governing party to replace the Liberals.[3] The election results with the Liberals now the third largest federal party may well allow Harper to claim victory on this larger goal, although it is not at all impossible that discussions about a possible NPD-Liberal merger may be heard so that the center-left can unite much as Canada's political right united under the merger of the Canadian Alliance and the former Progressive Conservatives to produce Harper's Conservative Party.

It is not surprising that austerity-era fiscal priority-setting involves both trimming fat and slicing pork, with the former aimed at finding real or imagined efficiencies. The pork is short for "pork barrel" spending. It is often an extremely negative term implying spending not aimed at the broad public or general interest but rather at narrow, specific, or partisan interests, including spending initiatives calibrated to favor the governing party's core voting support or regional base. Slicing pork implies cuts but it can also imply slicing in the form of carving and dicing for maximum partisan and electoral benefit. These culinary metaphors in political craft can thus refer to the design and implementation, and the winding down, of the Harper government's stimulus program but also to other parts of its own past expenditures and new initiatives in the 2011 Budget and election promises to further forge a center-right government (see more below). Both fat trimming and pork slicing are useful dual descriptors and analytical entry points when dealing with: a) minority government that has now become a majority government; b) a fiscal crisis and its austerity aftermath; and c) an era when the penchant for practicing the arts of politics has gone well beyond "spin" to one of continuous unrelenting verbal partisan warfare lubricated by increased spending since 2006 both before and during the recession.

Our account in this chapter looks first at the forces and factors that have produced the austerity era and how they reveal the underlying stated and unstated Harper record. The second section then sets out the Harper Conservative agenda as set out in the March 22, 2011, Budget and in the 2011 election. The agendas of the Opposition parties, the Liberals, the NPD and the Bloc Quebecois are also examined particularly as revealed in their 2011 election campaign platforms and rhetoric. They too were offering their own versions of trimming fat and slicing pork, but they also revealed other narratives, successfully or not. The NPD emulated Harper's 2006 election platform by focusing on a short compact list of priorities and budgetary promises that resonated in Quebec and then nationally. As we see further below, The Bloc Quebecois stuck to its familiar Quebec only messages which massively misjudged the mood of many parts of the soft-nationalist Quebec electorate. The Liberals revealed a platform that was family focused but read like a mirror image of the Harper platform in some key respects.

We then preview our authors' chapters in this edition. These cover fiscal, policy and political issues and realms ranging from the economic stimulus program, health care, environment, and northern strategy to governance realms such as immigration, regulatory agencies, and the uses of new media. Finally, with these analyzes fully in mind, we offer our concluding views of a related set of five immediate future national policy and fiscal agenda challenges and choices. These include: Harper era social policy; immigration policy and politics as a pivotal Harper strategy both to emulate and defeat the Liberal Party; Parliamentary and democratic institutional independence, broader governance reform issues and approaches; and environment policy and climate change.

THE DRIVING FORCES OF AUSTERITY POLITICS, PRIORITIES AND BUDGETING

As countries have begun to emerge from the economic turmoil of global recession, it is increasingly apparent that Canada has fared better than many others (Greece Ireland, Spain, the UK and US for example) and the reasons for this were analyzed in several of last year's chapters in *How Ottawa Spends 2010-11*.[4] However, as global stimulus packages have begun to wind down austerity deficit reduction packages are now being prepared and implemented to deal with unsustainable levels of national debt and fiscal deficits while promoting economic growth and employment. To accommodate the different economic standing of individual countries, the G20 advocated a flexible approach whereby countries with less severe financial problems could tackle recovery at their own pace. A flexible approach makes sense, but the degree to which Canada can use its autonomy is limited given its close ties to the US economy and also the continuation of federal politics conducted on a knife edge of partisanship.

In this section we consider the record of the Harper government over the past five years and the impact of its spending, economic and fiscal policies on the size and management of the current deficit. We also focus on the impact of minority government on policy-making and the constrained policy choices available to the Harper government for reducing the fiscal deficit and size of the overall debt. Current economic conditions, in some respects, appear to be not that different from those encountered in the mid1990s. However a protracted period of minority government has created a topsy-turvy era in Canadian federal politics. No longer was it possible to assume that a party's policies, particularly fiscal and economic, would correspond to its traditional ideological position along the left-right spectrum of Canadian politics. For example, reflecting on the adoption of the federal stimulus package, Drummond states succinctly that "the Conservatives took the Liberal position and the gap between the parties disappeared."[5] This may well be true regarding fiscal policy overall but, as we see below, other differences certainly emerged in the 2011 election battle, regarding both social policy and some aspects of tax policy.

Having effectively forced the Conservative government's hand in embracing a Keynesian style stimulus package to reflate a flagging economy, the Liberal and NPD parties have nonetheless not missed the opportunity to berate the government for incurring record levels of debt and for mismanaging the nation's finances. For its part, the Harper government, having been reluctant initially to turn on the stimulus tap, quickly appreciated the political capital that government spending on this scale brings, particularly when it is directed, as Les Pal's analysis in chapter 2 shows, towards highly visible ribbon cutting infrastructure projects. Having adopted and extended a massive spending program that helped to create Canada's deficit, many would have predicted that a Conservative government would embark on a severe cost cutting program to rival or even surpass that of the Liberals during the early-mid 1990s.[6] However, its approach in a minority government and 2011 election context has been tactical and subtle.

Severe cuts were not introduced before the 2011 Budget and election but major ones will have to be in the wake of election. Prior to the election the Harper government continued to increase spending, particularly in such priority areas as defence, security and prisons. Thus, even without the spending burst of the economic stimulus program, which took program spending from 13 to 16% of GDP, in his five years in office Prime Minister Stephen Harper has substantially boosted federal government expenditures.[7] Federal program spending during the Martin Liberal's final year in power – 2005–06 – stood at $175-billion. By 2009–10, under Harper, it had climbed to $245-billion.

Even after taking into account the relative growth in the Canadian economy over the same period, program expenses – which include departmental program spending as well as major transfers of money to individuals and other levels of government – increased more than 25% over five years.[8] Some of this increase resulted from the revised equalization payments established under Harper, though some of the provincial transfer increases were established under the Martin Government.

Predictably, spending grew sharply in specific departments prioritized by the Harper government. For example, the central food-and consumer-safety departments – the Public Health Agency, Health Canada, the Canadian

Institutes for Health Research, and the Canadian Food Inspection Agency – increased their spending by 77.5%, 16%, 10% and 9.6% respectively between 2005–06 and 2009–10. During that time, spending at the RCMP increased by more than 45%, and the Department of National Defence boosted its expenditures by 21%.[9]

The number of federal government employees has also grown markedly in a number of departments not identified as priorities – and in some cases more sharply. For example, Fisheries and Oceans spending increased by nearly 19% from 2005–06 to 2009–10; Indian and Northern Affairs Canada increased by 14%; Citizenship and Immigration increased by more than 52%; Human Resources and Skills Development Canada grew by nearly 18%.[10] While some departments reduced their spending over the same period (Justice 4%; Finance 11%; Canadian Heritage 6%) these were fairly modest in comparison to the levels of the above budget increases.[11]

In addition to the increases in program spending, the Harper era has added thousands of staff for a variety of reasons to the federal public service. Since the Conservative government came to power the Canadian Forces have added 7,754 people to their regular forces and reserves.[12] That's an expansion of 8.7%, bringing the total to 96,675 people at the end of the 2009–10 fiscal year. Over the same period, the number of RCMP officers increased more than 16%, climbing to 24,445 from 20,936. In addition, employment in the departments receiving funding for federal food-and consumer-safety initiativesalso grew slightly, namely Health Canada (1,212 full-time jobs added),the Canadian Food Inspection Agency (833 jobs added), the Public Health Agency of Canada (757 jobs added), and the Canadian Institutes for Health Research (72 jobs added).[13]

Although it could be argued that increases in the number of public servants in these areas are consistent with the Tory agenda, Minsky believes they "defy conventional thinking about Conservative devotion to smaller government" and also points to significant growth beyond these priority areas. For example: Human Resources and Skills Development Canada increased its full-time equivalents (FTEs) by more than 8,000 (a growth of 47%); the Canada Border Service Agency took on nearly 2,662 FTEs (22% growth); Indian Affairs and Northern Development got 1,280 (32% growth); Citizenship and Immigration added 969 (28% growth).[14] Overall, the federal public service – which includes civilian employees at National Defence and the RCMP, but not the military members and police officers already counted – swelled by 33,023 people, slightly more than 13%, over five years. Relative to the growth in Canadian population under the Harper government, the federal public service grew by 7.8%, a pace of growth described by Poschmann as "obviously unsustainable."[15]

On the other side of the fiscal balance sheet the government has announced plans, as a part of its low tax economy objective (see more below) to further reduce levels of corporate income tax from 16.5% to 15% which could further limit fiscal capacity unless expected growth in employment and profits can offset the reduction in taxes. Although cutting taxes is consistent with Conservative ideology, critics argue that it will mean sustaining the debt for longer especially if spending continues to grow.[16]

The Harper record leaves some in the Conservative base bemused, given that it has been generated by a government publicly committed to smaller government, lower taxes and a "tough on crime" agenda.[17] Terence Corcoran, the National Post's conservative columnist, recently voiced his disapproval of the party's perceived largesse since coming into office: "I challenge anyone to come up with five economically 'conservative' achievements ... Federal program spending over the five years rose 43 per cent ... Measured in constant un-inflated dollars per capita, the bite amounts to an increase of $1,298 in new federal spending for every man, woman and child."[18]

Of course this is not the first government to see its ideological instincts and ambitions trumped by the political realities of the day, not to mention the actual responsibilities of governing, but there can be little doubt that the current political climate in Canada is pushing the parties toward the centre and having a pronounced impact on their policies. In terms of spending Drummond describes the convergence as follows:

> If I showed you a chart of government expenditure from 1997 and I asked you to mark when the government changed, you wouldn't have a hope of getting it right. They're indistinguishable. The Liberals cut expenditures for three years then they let the barn door fly wide open. And the Conservatives just kept it wide open. Both parties ran program spending at about six-per-cent growth until the recession, then the Conservatives put it up to double digits. But the Liberals probably would have done the same thing.[19]

While the Conservative's apparent embrace of Liberal, centrist spending habits and promotion of 'big' government surprised many, its tolerance for debt and adoption of limited debt reduction measures, is described by Simpson as "leisurely, to say the least."[20]

The Conservative plan prior to the 2011 Budget to erase the $55.6-billion deficit consists mainly of ending stimulus spending, freezing operational budgets, and trimming 5% from departmental budgets through a process of departmental review intended to identify 5% of low priority spending for reallocating to other purposes However, the government's efforts to demonstrate fiscal prudence are largely made possible by a $7.4-billion decrease in transfer payments, including a $2.6-billion reduction in employment insurance transfers to individuals largely because of improving economic conditions. Another big factor in the spending decrease is a $3.4-billion drop in debt charges as a result of lower-than-expected interest rates.[21] In addition to exercising modest restraint in spending, the government is pinning its hopes on the resumption of economic growth to eventually balance the budget. As Curry suggests "It's a far cry from the deficit-fighting drama of the mid-1990s, when the then-Liberal government prompted howls of outrage across the country with painful cuts that closed military bases and slashed provincial transfers."[22]

What really characterised Martin's austerity plan was a very heavy reliance on spending cuts in federal-provincial social transfer payments to eliminate the deficit and then run budget surpluses. As Jackson argues, this policy decision carried enormous political and social significance:

> Putting the burden of debt reduction on social spending cuts rather than on taxation meant that the burden of Canadian deficit reduction fell on the lower end of the income distribution, and this was a significant factor behind the pronounced increase in Canadian income inequality over the 1990s. Between 1993 and 2001, the after-tax and transfer income share of the bottom 80% of families fell as the share of the top 20% rose from 36.9% to 39.2%.[23]

The irony is that when right wing governments cut social expenditure it often exacts a greater political price on them than it does on left of centre parties – as the Conservatives found when they made minor cuts to Quebec cultural grants prior to the last election; a decision that some commentators felt cost them Quebec seats and a possible majority. Instead, the Conservatives say that they will rely on relatively benign remedies to reduce the deficit such as public service attrition rates and quite limited across the board cuts.

Our point then is not a party political one but rather reflects our concern that sustained minority government has imposed significant constraints on the all the parties and, in particular, it drives short-term partisan thinking whereby policies must be able to deliver short-term political capital (read "pork") with minimal risk. In a minority government context, the main parties become highly risk averse and tend to adopt policies mainly on their ability to deliver quick wins, maximise votes in key electoral constituencies and outmanoeuvre opposition parties and, when necessary, Parliament, government watchdogs and the media. As the analysis by Castle and Phillips in chapter 8 shows, longer term economic issues such as innovation gaps and productivity traps operate below the radar of fiscal and policy attention.

It could be argued that a more ruthless approach is necessary to govern and cling to power in an era of minority politics. However, the price for this in respect of transparency, accountability, and democratic procedures should not be underestimated. Access to information and respect for the institutions and processes of government have provided two recurring and controversial themes during Harper's tenure in office. House of Commons' Speaker Peter Milliken ruled recently that the Liberals have a case in arguing the government breached the parliamentary privileges of MPs by refusing to disclose sufficient details about corporate tax cuts and the costs of Conservative crime bills. To both requests, the Finance department returned a one paragraph answer: such data was "a matter of cabinet confidence and, as such, the government is not in a position to provide such information."[24] It was the passage of an eventual contempt of Parliament motion that brought down the Harper Government on March 25th 2011 and triggered the 2011 election.

To use cabinet confidentiality as a means of keeping secret basic information about the anticipated costs of its policies sets a disturbing precedent. According to Ibbitson the Harper government uses "cabinet confidence" the way the Nixon administration used "executive privilege." [25] He also points out that since the Liberals provided projections of corporate profits when they were in government "it is ridiculous for the Conservatives to maintain that the cost of their law-and-order legislation is a state secret. How is Parliament to judge the wisdom of that legislation if it can't measure its projected impact in prisons built and guards hired?"[26]

The Speaker also ruled that there is a case to be made that International Co-operation Minister Bev Oda breached privilege by making conflicting statements about her role in the denial of funding to an international aid group and which appeared to be an attempt to deliberately mislead Parliament. Both rulings have helped to place the government in contempt of parliament and continue a long running dispute between the executive and the legislature which has also required the Speaker to rule on parliamentary access to the Afghan detainee records.

Motions for contempt of parliament have only happened on five occasions since confederation.[27] However, the prime minister seems to feel that the ends justify the means commenting that "our focus can't become on parliamentary procedure, our focus has to be on the big interests of Canadians, and in my judgment, that is the economy."[28] The Harper government has also taken promotion and advertising to new levels. For example, controversy surrounds the public funds the government is spending on partisan-style backdrops, billboards, and site visit promotions and raises serious questions about where the divide is between government and party interests and between communication and political advertising.

The so-called "in-and-out" affair on election spending provides further evidence of the importance attached to advertising in the modern era and the lengths that the Conservative Party went to maximise its campaign advertising budget. While it is ironic that the Conservative Party's main campaign platform was to clean up government after the Chretien Liberal's sponsorship scandal – also advertising related – but it now faces charges that it too was circumventing the rules during the 2006 campaign. It also reinforces the impression that the Harper government regards the rules as an inconvenience in its attempt to govern, to stay in power and win his majority government mandate from voters. Ethics and respect for due process were compromised in favour of short-term political advantage and, in terms of public debate, attack politics rhetoric will continue to dominate substance.

BUDGET 2011, THE 2011 ELECTION AND THE HARPER CONSERVATIVE AND OPPOSITION PARTY AGENDAS

The 2011 Conservative Budget and Election Platform

Finance Minister James Flaherty's 2011 Tory Budget of March 22nd was prepared with a high expectation of an election soon to follow and it did. As a political and economic election platform document it followed earlier scripts in the Tory run-up to the Budget and thus, in our terms, it was thin and oblique on any overt cutting and trimming (that would come in later years and few details were provided) but chock full of sliced pork with numerous highly visible gesture items to hoped for grateful voters. The latter were aimed both at the Tory's own political support base but also it's hoped for majority-producing swing voters in winnable swing electoral ridings, especially in Ontario.

Flaherty's *Budget Speech* is the best political expression of the electoral Budget and its agenda themes but details also emerge in the *Budget in Brief* and *Budget Plan* documents.[29] Headlined in the Budget Speech as "the next phase of Canada's economic action plan: a low tax plan for jobs and growth," Flaherty sought to place his sixth budget in the context of the Harper era record since 2006 and the government as one that has made "responsible choices."[30] It also stressed that, though Canada has done well in the recession compared to other countries, "the global economy is still fragile", hence the need to "secure our economic recovery" and to "stay on track." He reiterates early on that "We will keep taxes low. We will undertake additional targeted investments to support jobs and growth. We will control government spending, and stay on track to eliminate the deficit."[31]

New spending is thus referred to as "targeted investment" and budget cuts as the "controlling" of spending in part so that cuts in general or particular cuts do not gain political notoriety and visibility in an election campaign. No attention whatsoever is drawn in the Budget Speech to big-ticket spending on new jet aircraft or new or extended prisons that are a part of Harper defence and law and order agenda. The highlighted items in the Budget Speech include the following selected examples under some of its main thematic sections:

- Hiring Credit for Small Business (a one year Employment Insurance break for some 525,00 Canadian small businesses)
- Extend the 50% straight-line accelerated Capital Cost Allowance for manufacturing or processing machinery and equipment by an additional two years.
- Extend the current Forest Innovation and Market Development programs
- Establish a Family Caregiver Tax Credit (an amount of $2000 that will benefit more than 500,000 Canadians caring for loved ones with an annual tax reduction of $300)
- Establish a Children's Arts Tax Credit (up to $500 per child in qualifying expenses for eligible arts or cultural activities representing a maximum of $75 in federal income tax savings)
- Extend for one year the EcoEnergy Retrofit Homes program
- Provision of targeted top-up benefit to the Guaranteed Income Supplement (up to $600 per year for single seniors and $840 per year for senior couples)
- Introduce legislation to confirm permanent funding for municipal infrastructure through the Gas Tax Fund
- Forgive a portion of federal student loans for new doctors, nurses and nurse practitioners who agree to practice in under-served rural or remote areas
- Establish a new Volunteer Firefighters Tax Credit
- Establish additional Canada Excellence Research Chairs
- Support for Perimeter Institute, Brain Canada and Institut National D'Optique
- 30 Industrial Research Chairs at colleges and polytechnics across Canada[32]

Little or no mention of budget cuts and austerity as such is made until the final section of the Budget Speech. This crucial reality is discussed then under the label of "returning to balanced budgets." Here, Finance Minister Flaherty notes that the return to balanced budgets by 2015–2016 will be achieved in three ways:

- First, we will complete our stimulus package, as promised.
- Second, we will continue specific measures to restrain the growth of government program spending.
- Third, we will complete, within the next year, a comprehensive review of government spending[33] (the strategic and operating review).

Even in the much more voluminous Budget Plan document, the details of any savings already achieved, are buried in an appendix and the narrative about actual cuts is subdued and oblique.[34] But there is a graph in chapter 5 of the Budget Plan which plots the Program Expenses to GDP Ratio and shows it returning to pre-recession levels by 2015–16.[35] So Canadians will only find out about what kinds of program cuts will occur after the Strategic and Operating Review is carried out under majority government conditions and its outcomes are known.

Harper spending and low tax agenda plans were further revealed in its 2011 election platform released less than three weeks after the Budget Speech and also in the two televised party leader debates and in other particular campaign announcements across the country. In general terms the Tory platform document, *Here For Canada*, reiterated the main Budget 2011 themes including the low-tax plan for jobs and economic growth but with the additional commitment to eliminate the deficit one year earlier, by 2014–15.[36] Among the further spending and tax credit items and promises are:

· The creation of a new national park in eastern Rouge Valley of the greater Toronto area;
· A $4.2 billion loan guarantee for a Newfoundland and Labrador hydro-electric project;
· A commitment to Quebec of $2.2 billion to compensate it for harmonizing its sales tax with the federal GST;
· Several new tax breaks for individuals but with the proviso that these would not come into effect until the deficit is eliminated;
· An enhanced guaranteed income supplement for low income seniors;
· The establishment of a $5 million Office of Religious Freedom to monitor religious freedom around the world.[37]

In the leadership debates and in campaign speeches Harper presented his government as a source of economic and political stability in uncertain times and contrasted this with the Ignatieff Liberals and its "coalition" which he characterized as being a risky and high spending option for Canadians. When the NPD began to surge in the polls during the election, Harper cast the NPD as the even riskier option for Canadians. Unlike the 2006 and 2008 elections, Harper now felt confident enough to call openly for a majority government mandate.

The Liberal Party Election Platform

The Liberal Party platform document, *Your Family, Your Future, Your Canada* provided Canadians with their first look at a broad Ignatieff-led agenda on the federal budget and related policies and priorities.[38] The Liberals had of course revealed before the election some of their key stances including its opposition to "jets and jails", the Tory plans for new jet aircraft for the air force and for expanded jails which anchored the Tory law and order agenda. The Liberals also opposed the planned further Tory reductions in the corporation tax rate.

These positions featured again in the Liberal campaign platform but the Liberal strategy mapped out a series of measures on: the economy as a whole, families, clean resources and a healthy environment, bringing Canadians together, and Canada in the world.[39] Among the more specific policies and priorities in the Ignatieff Liberal agenda are to:

- Reduce the deficit to one percent of GDP within two years, down from 3.6 percent in 2009–10.
- Establish a Prudence Reserve to manage any unforeseen events
- Champion three key business sectors expected to be sources of growth
- (clean resources, health and biosciences, and digital technologies)
- Create a Youth Hiring Incentive for small and medium-sized businesses
- Family care support for those caring for sick loved ones at home ($1 billion)
- Establish a Learning Passport: a program of direct support to families for higher education ($1 billion)
- Create a Secure Retirement Option to help Canadians save
- Establish a Green Innovation Tax Credit ($400 million)
- Put in place a Canadian Transportation and Infrastructure Strategy [40]

During the election campaign, particularly towards its latter stages, the Liberals also aggressively sought to present themselves as the more trusted defender of federal health care spending compared to the Harper Tories. This included Liberal support for maintaining the current levels of 6 percent annual increase beyond its current 2014 federal-provincial agreement end date.

The NPD Election Platform

The Jack Layton-led New Democratic Party platform *Giving Your Family a Break* set out a set of "practical first steps" centered on seven thematic priorities.[41] Characterizing his plan for new spending as being less than the Conservative plans, the Layton agenda was based on measures that would increase taxation on big business and on carbon-emitting industries, and from tax cheaters. Layton, however, drew particular attention in his "affordable plan to get Ottawa working for your family" and to his immediate commitment to "improving your health services, rewarding the job creators, strengthening your pension, and making your life a little more affordable."[42]

On health care, the NPD promised a new 10 year federal-provincial accord, increased investments in more doctors and nurses, making medicines more affordable and on its climate change theme, the party promised the adoption of a new Climate Change Accountability Act and also the establishment of green bonds to fund research and development.[43] During the election campaign Layton's Quebec strategy also emerged and garnered remarkable success in Quebec seats and votes, not only because the above policies and priorities already resonated in a province whose political culture is already quite left of center but also because Layton was reaching out to the soft nationalist vote. In particular he was offering an approach which would offer "the winning conditions" for Quebec to fully join the Canadian constitution, and hence opening up the risky pandora's box of constitutional reform politics.

The Bloc Quebecois Platform

The Bloc Quebecois platform, *Parlons Qc*, reflects its basic Quebec only focus with its agenda being expressed as "demands" on Ottawa, and its leader Gilles Duceppe asserting from the outset that "we've been plunged into an election campaign because Stephen Harper has written off Quebec."[44] Duceppe argues again that "Quebec will only be free once it has decided to create a sovereign nation."[45]

The Bloc's demands in their platform relate mainly to their sense of what regions in Quebec involve and therefore that "all federal programs be assessed for their impact on regions", including federal policies that promote industries in Quebec's regions, such as forestry, agriculture supply management, and fishermen, but also quality infrastructure.[46]

Since the Bloc was confident during the early election stages that it would maintain its dominant majority among federal parties competing for votes and seats in Quebec, its platform did not engage in aggressive overt separatist discourse, even though it and others were already speculating on the probability of the next Quebec provincial election resulting in the defeat of the current Quebec Liberal government led by Jean Charest and a victory for the separatist Parti Quebecois.

Prime Minister Harper, however, in the final stages of the 2011 election campaign did raise the spectre of such a renewed separatist threat as being yet another reason for a strong federal Tory majority government. The Bloc's low key and often stale campaign became unraveled when the Layton-led NPD got serious traction in Quebec and resulted in the Bloc being decimated and reduced to a rump of 4 MPs in the House of Commons.

A Harper majority government is likely to adopt an "austerity and return to budgetary surplus plan" that is not much different than that revealed in the Budget 2011 and in the election, depending of course on what happens to the global and the US economy and these broader deficit reduction plans and outcomes. Harper sought to reassure Canadians about his support for health care spending and investment but there are still strong fears about what a Harper majority will do with even more unfettered power. Some federal programs will be cut but will these be programs that offend the Tory political base or will other criteria govern both cuts and the redesign of some programs after the promised strategic expenditure review? And, since the Harper Tories escaped the wrath of voters for their undemocratic and "attack politics" practices, there are valid and understandable fears among many Canadians that these practices will only escalate now that majority status is secured.

AN OVERVIEW OF THE CHAPTERS

LESLIE PAL examines the politics and content of the Harper government's economic stimulus program by arguing that in the management of recessions by conservative parties they can "walk in the wild" and return. He argues that recession of this magnitude can actually create political opportunities that run against the instinctive grain of a conservative government like Canada's. Five rules of recession politics and public policy are posited: 1. Spending quickly to boost employment means "shovel-ready" programs that are visible and tangible to voters; 2. The emphasis on small, quick projects means a wide regional disbursement (even though there was a special and large package to deal with the automotive industry), and again, visibility and local impact; 3. These two factors provide an unparalleled platform for government advertising and publicity; 4. A conservative government can plausibly project disinclination, caution, and even grim strength in the face of spending challenges – they are reluctant virgins dragged to the altar of stimulus; and 5. The return to fiscal discipline has two key virtues or reaffirmations. First, it is a reaffirmation for the political base of its party's true colours. Second, it is a reaffirmation of the evils of deficits, and plays strongly into a narrative of sin (limited deficit financing) and redemption (getting back to "fiscal balance").

RUTH HUBBARD AND GILLES PAQUET make the case for a fundamental governance review as a needed basic feature of austerity and renewal. They argue that imposing the same shock treatment as was used in the 1990s is unlikely to work (given minority governments, revived acrimonious federal-provincial relations, and the level of indebtedness of lower order governments). Politically, it would be immeasurably more costly to resolve fiscal problems by autocratically cutting transfers to provinces and savaging federal programs, while leaving the governing system untouched. They argue that a new setting calls for a new paradigm – the shift from big 'G' Government to small 'g' governance – not simply doing the same with less, but finding ways to do things differently, if at all, and doing it collectively. The analysis shows the value of a shift in the unit of analysis towards issue domains as a new approach, and a new strategy. The chapter then illustrates in two case studies that opportunities exist for such an approach, and indicates how it might work. The authors also indicate under which circumstances this approach is likely to be adopted, and what barriers would appear to exist to it being carried out successfully.

JAMES LAHEY analyzes trends in federal public service compensation over the past twenty years and describes how this compensation is "normally" determined, and assesses measures to control these expenditures. He recommends changes to how federal compensation is managed that could better sustain the confidence and understanding of public servants and Canadians generally. The arguments advanced are that: a) the existing system tends to fluctuate between rapid increases and arbitrary constraints, inflating costs in "good" times and alienating employees in "bad"; b) this system "works" in that the federal public service has a stable employee base and, broadly speaking, serves Canadians well: c) however, the system is likely more expensive than necessary and would benefit from greater comparability with the private sector, increased transparency, and an expanded scope for negotiations that fosters realistic tradeoffs. He concludes as well that getting compensation in the public service "right" is critical. People, or more precisely their capacities and engagement, determine the success of modern knowledge-based organizations. To attract and motivate its fair share of talent as experienced leaders retire, the federal public service needs to offer compensation that compares reasonably with the private sector. Times of restraint invite economy measures that can save money in the short run, but may destabilize employee commitment, and therefore results. Understanding better how the system works, or could work, in the longer term can help balance fairness to taxpayers and employees.

DEREK IRELAND, ERIC MULLIGAN, KERNAGHAN WEBB AND WEI XIE assess the issue of how possible regulatory agency budget cuts might still support the public interest by developing a better approach to understanding regulator-regulatee relations and industry characteristics. They argue that regulatory budget cutbacks are less likely to result in serious reductions in compliance and performance when: products and transactions are less complex; industries are more stable and mature; corporate reputation for product quality and social responsibility is important to competitive advantage; well governed global supply chains and large retailers and other business customers with buyer power discipline company behaviour; larger trading partners have the regulatory resources and will to maintain high compliance levels during a period of fiscal restraint; and competitive markets and co-regulation provide voice and exit opportunities to consumers and other stakeholders. In contrast, the risks for compliance and performance are higher for markets and industries with the opposite characteristics such as: social norms and a business history and culture that favour non-compliance; substantial instability, entry, exit and "churning"; large imports from emerging market economies; significant information asymmetries, switching costs, and buyer inertia; and, public and merit goods and common pool resources that are less subject to market discipline. The chapter illustrates why and how similar regulatory agency budget cutbacks can have different consequences for compliance and performance depending on the characteristics of the regulatory regime.

DOUGLAS MACDONALD assesses the Harper government's energy and climate change policy. He argues that the Harper government is failing to address all three of the main policy challenges. It is ignoring the environmental implications of energy development; is making no effort to address the problem of differing provincial interests with respect to climate change mitigation; and has abandoned, with one exception, climate change policy sovereignty. He shows how federal government must change the trajectory of environment-energy policy by engaging with the provinces as equal partners and how it must work with them to develop a national energy policy which addresses these three basic challenges and thus contributes to Canadian unity and autonomy. Given their constitutional and political powers, the provinces must be accepted as full partners in the process of developing a new, coherent national (federal-provincial) energy policy which balances both economic and environmental implications. Canadian climate change targets must be set through federal-provincial negotiation, not in Washington or by the international regime. The cost of the total Canadian emission reduction thus agreed upon must be allocated amongst sectors and provinces using the established procedures of intergovernmental relations and equitable cost sharing. If that can be done (admittedly a tall challenge) the federal government will then be in a strong position to negotiate both with our American partner and the other members of the international climate-change regime.

FRANCOIS BREGHA explores federal policies and approaches regarding strategic environmental assessment (SEA) of government policies and plans, as distinct from assessing environmental projects. He argues that after twenty years of practice at the federal level, SEA's promise remains largely unfulfilled: the theoretical benefits listed in the Cabinet Directive on SEA, are still just that. While this chapter identifies methodological, informational, management and political barriers which have hampered SEA's effective implementation, Bregha shows that the absence of a sustained government commitment to environmental sustainability remains the single most important explanation for the current situation. While successive governments have acknowledged the importance of sustainable development, fighting climate change and considering environmental factors in decision-making, they have also:

· provided tax write-offs (now expired) to accelerate the development of the Alberta oil sands;
· repeatedly invested in the automobile industry, whose products are one of the chief causes of greenhouse gas emissions;
· continued to encourage population and undifferentiated economic growth, both of which are likely to lead to greater material throughput and increased production of wastes, making environmentally sustainability harder to achieve.

These initiatives are all legitimate and can be defended, but each raises major environmental issues. An effective SEA process would have highlighted the environmental implications of these decisions and helped identify alternatives that reduced adverse environmental effects. Instead, environmental consider-ations are often an after-thought in such decisions, when they figure at all. As a result, SEA has not furthered more environmentally-sustainable forms of development nor visibly increased the coherence of federal policies. The costs of an ineffective SEA process can be substantial. The current inadequacies of the federal SEA process ensure that Canada will continue to pay a heavy, yet largely avoidable, environmental price for many future government decisions.

DAVID CASTLE AND PETER W.B. PHILLIPS examine Canadian science and technology spending and its long present innovation gaps and productivity traps. They argue that, in many ways, Canada has already gone through a lost decade, the term used to describe Japan's slump in the 1980s, and it faces an-other. While public investments in S&T have increased to some extent, more could have been invested and more could have been achieved. The impres-sive gains in scientific knowledge and technological know-how are not being translated into socio-economic benefit in Canada by innovators, and innova-tion is not translating into productivity gains. There is a rising level of angst in the public sector and elsewhere that Canada has not got the right strategy for realizing the benefits of a knowledge-intensive economy. One sign is that while the OECD is encouraging governments to work on developing strategically coordinated policy frameworks, Canada has become increasingly focused on tactical manoeuvres like the Centres of Excellence for Commercialization and Research – alarmingly close to the disregarded tactic of picking or replicat-ing winners. How many Research in Motion's can Canada create and sustain, one might ask, and would it not be better to think of something new? While the government is trying to put a positive spin on its policy and the economy, there are unambiguous signs that change is in the wind.

VANDNA BHATTIA assesses federal-provincial health care spending charac-terizing it overall as exhibiting the politics of drift. She argues that notwith-standing its endorsement of the Liberal's earlier 10-Year Plan, the Harper government has demonstrated a profound indifference to Medicare, and has repeatedly asserted that health care is a provincial jurisdiction. Short of pro-moting a complete federal withdrawal, it has declared its commitment to a publicly funded system but also advocated "a flexible and sustainable system that allows for innovation and reform" within the Canada Health Act. Apart from similar anodyne statements, there has been an impenetrable federal si-lence on the issue for the past few years. In the meantime, health care expen-ditures continue to rise, exceeding inflation and population growth. Fuelled by a robust 6% annual increase in the cash portion of the CHT, health spending is currently averaging about 40% of provincial program expenditures. The sustainability of this level of and growth in spending is increasingly being called into question as the effects of the recent recession reverberate through government coffers. With the imminent expiry in 2014 of the *10-Year Plan*, the negotiation of new targets for the CHT has become the focal point of debate about the future of the health care system in Canada. Even as Ottawa quietly seeks input into future health transfer negotiations with the provinces, the temporal and fiscal imperatives impelled by its ambitious deficit-slaying targets have laid the ground rules: federal health care spending will be ring-fenced in the coming austerity program. There will be no health care cuts but there will be little or no new money either. For provinces faced with equally, if not more, ruthless budgetary dilemmas the negotiations, such as they are, promise to be less than satisfying. A plausible basis for consensus is a watered-down – more flexible – Canada Health Act. This may take the form of an actual amendment to the Act to modify the principles and/or the enforcement requirements, or it may simply be an implicit agreement to continue to allow the Act to drift and ultimately become irrelevant and obsolete.

RICHARD SCHULTZ examines the role of Industry Canada as an economic regulator through an analysis of Globalive case and the lessons of political licensing. He shows that most of the debate over the Globalive licensing decisions has focused on either the positive effects it will have on broadening competition in the cellular sector or on the loosening of the current restrictions on foreign investment in Canadian telecommunications. He argues, however, that the attractiveness of the policy outcome must be balanced against the decision-making process that public policy-makers employ in reaching that outcome. The Globalive process was fundamentally flawed. In assessing the original ministerial licensing proposed in the 1992 version of the Telecommunications Act, Schultz argued that with a political licensing system, "… we will not know if the Minister and the Cabinet have been consistent, prudent, honest, or indeed lawful in its implementation of the law. We will not know if the Minister or cabinet has been arbitrary or capricious in its decision-making. We will not know if the Minister or Cabinet has been subject to, and a participant in, manipulation by politically effective groups or individuals." Absent a negative court decision that overturns the Cabinet decision, the licensing of Globalive is now irreversible. That said, the larger issues of the political licensing and the role of Industry Canada as an economic regulator need to be addressed. This is particularly true because the department has issued a consultative document prior to the next round of spectrum licensing. Schultz believes there is a simple solution to ameliorate the problems of unstructured political decision-making and the concomitant absence of transparency and due process. Canada should consider adopting the approach common to most other members of the OECD, namely to assign spectrum licensing to an independent regulatory agency.

FRANCES ABELE probes and assesses the Conservatives' vision for northern Canada as expressed in Throne and other speeches, their northern policy statements (the Northern Strategy and the Statement on Northern Foreign Policy) and selected social, economic, environmental and political measures. These are measured against the very large northern challenges that concern all Canadians. She concludes that, while there have been some important steps in the right direction related to infrastructure, knowledge about the North and foreign policy, two deeply important policy challenges have been virtually ignored. These are the need for: first, measures to sustain social and political development and democratization in northern institutions, and second, implementation of an effective Canadian response to global warming. The chapter shows that a close analysis of the Conservatives' use of political rhetoric and the concrete measures that they have taken reveals a pronounced shift from the path followed by previous (Liberal) governments. In areas of exclusive federal jurisdiction, the Conservative government has been willing to spend – or at least to make large spending commitments. To a degree not seen since the 1950s, the Conservative government claims the North as a territory to be developed in the national interest, defining that interest, and consequently federal policy, almost entirely in terms of defense and economic development. With this stance, the federal power is poised to override – or at best ignore – the process of political and social development that reflects the purposes of northerners themselves, and of other Canadians who support them, in building the basis of a just society in the territorial North. Northern community and regional interests risk being superseded by federal purposes in national defence and economic development. At the same time, the dynamic system of intergovernmental relationships and practices built up over the last three decades by northern Aboriginal and public governments and previous federal governments is being largely ignored. Indeed, the delicate balancing and negotiation that has enabled so much cooperation and progress towards new governing arrangements which feature a more equitable role for Aboriginal people is being replaced by a much less resilient "command and control" approach.

NICK FALVO examines the housing situation in the Northwest Territories (NWT), especially as it affects low-income residents. The chapter examines how government-assisted housing is administered in the NWT, as well as the uniqueness of government-assisted housing in the NWT. What is uniquely challenging to the NWT vis-à-vis the rest of Canada, however, is high unemployment, especially amongst members of Aboriginal groups, and most especially in small communities. Indeed, the small communities are where housing problems – especially with respect to overcrowding and the need for major repairs – are the most acute. The chapter shows that while recent federal funding announcements, along with matching contributions from the GWNT, have allowed the Housing Corporation to replace old housing stock with newer units, the overall number of government-assisted units remains unchanged, which does not bode well for the 400 NWT households currently sitting on waiting lists for public housing. But, as the annual federal contributions diminish, it ought to be emphasized that this represents an opportunity to recommit. Indeed, if the federal government chooses to see its reduced annual expenditures on social housing as net savings and then invests this savings into supporting already-existing public housing in the NWT, those very units can remain viable. In the post-World War II era, the federal government was embarrassed into helping NWT residents meet basic social needs, as the international spotlight highlighted the fact that Ottawa was neglecting the North. The federal government had little choice but to step up its efforts to meet social needs. As the Harper government vies for a physical presence in the North in an effort to make the most of geopolitical opportunity, history may repeat itself. Overcrowded housing and units in disrepair can exist when nobody is watching, but they can become glaringly obvious in the spotlight of an international race for access to northern oil and minerals.

NEIL BRADFORD AND CAROLINE ANDREW review the Harper immigration agenda set in the context of the history of immigration policy and politics. They argue that immigration represents a policy field of particular significance and complexity in Canada. It speaks to central questions about the country's national identity as well as its prospects for economic and social development. Its design and delivery is truly a multi-level, collaborative undertaking with policy performance relying on the combined and aligned efforts of all levels of government, settlement sector agencies, mainstream organizations, business associations, and newcomers themselves. The chapter also shows that 'politics of immigration policy' have become a major axis of federal electoral competition both under Harper and under earlier Liberal governments. The authors argue that policy fields of such complexity and significance are likely also to feature daunting tasks of coordination and continuity. They analyze these under the concept of metagovernance so as to capture how central governments manage devolved policy systems through framing multiple deliberations and steering diffuse interactions. Metagovernance involves governments tackling complex policy problems and decision processes through combinations of tools quite removed from the traditional reliance on hierarchy *or* networks *or* markets. When governments confront complexity, "it's the mix that matters", rather than the application of a single governance logic or pure policy instrument. This approach helps make sense of the Conservative government's simultaneous mix of values-based centralization as reflected in the revamped citizenship guide; the open federalism decentralization that frames the provincial nominee program; and the community-driven devolution now inspiring the Local Immigration Partnerships (LIPs) implementation. In all of this activity, the Conservatives are "steering at a distance", bringing a variety of governance logics to bear on the different elements of their overall immigration agenda.

MARY FRANCOLI examines the barriers to new media adoption in Canada's Public Service. She highlights how people today have a wealth of information available at their fingertips and the tools to interact with government on a regular basis. They are demonstrating a greater desire to have a voice and to have access to even more information and knowledge, but our politicians and members of the bureaucracy – the guardians of much of our knowledge – often seem uncertain about how to share. This uncertainty stems in part from a tension that exists within the Canadian political and bureaucratic landscape. On the one hand, we have political and bureaucratic rhetoric espousing the benefits of increased access to information and citizen engagement, coupled with the belief that information and communication technology can achieve this. On the other hand, we see a lack of a clear policy and legal framework governing the use of technology for such purposes and a political environment that has not always demonstrated willingness for transparency and the sharing of information. The chapter identifies both the potential benefits and barriers to adopting social media as a means of engaging citizens, providing information and delivering services. She argues that social media has become so widely used that it is impossible to ignore and, as such, must be embraced. In order for the public service to maximize the benefits of such technology, three things need to happen. First, a clear policy framework, aimed at both public servants and Canadians, has to be developed and communicated as a means of guiding online conduct and managing the expectations of the different actors who are becoming more engaged and connected. Second, members of the public service need to better understand social media and be ready and willing to use it properly. Third, broad cultural change is needed within the public service to allow employees greater freedom to engage in direct communication with citizens. This sort of cultural change is difficult and requires high-level support. While implementing such recommendations is not easy, they are important first steps for the government and public service when it comes to embracing a new and more interactive relationship with Canadians. Such a new relationship has the potential to improve government transparency and strengthen democracy.

In addition to the core fiscal arts of trimming fat and slicing pork as examined earlier in the chapter our authors' chapters raise key related political and economic issues and challenges that face the newHarper majority government, the hugely changed opposition party configuration , and Canadians as a whole. We draw upon and extend these analyses as we look briefly in conclusion at five related challenges and choices.

Harper Era Social Policy

One of the main concerns of Canadians opposed to the election of a Harper-led Conservative government was the expected attack on the welfare state and anticipated cuts to social policy, including health care. In truth, cuts to social spending have so far been limited by the government's minority status, leading opponents, as in the 2006 and 2008 elections, to warn Canadians of a "hidden agenda" should Harper gain a majority. The minority status afforded the government has meant that it has had to broker deals, in order to stay in power and this has tempered major cuts or reforms in social policy. The Conservatives have also been careful not to alienate groups such as new immigrants who depend heavily on social services or Quebec voters where social and cultural spending remain politically salient and sensitive issues.

In addition, pensions and health care are increasingly important to many Canadians as the population continues to age and health care costs continue to rise above the rate of inflation. Tempting as it might be to restructure both these areas the reality is that older Canadians are still the people who tend to vote in elections making them a disproportionately powerful section of the electorate. Given this, we should not be surprised to hear the Finance minister recently reiterate his commitment to social spending: "We need to have a reasonable budget for Canadians ... [w]e want to maintain social transfers in Canada. That's clear. We don't want to repeat the actions of the Liberal government in Canada 15 years ago when they reduced transfers."[47] This is a remarkable but clear statement from a Conservative finance minister overseeing a record deficit and a gross national debt that at 82 per cent of GDP is up from 65 per cent in 2007 and stands higher than at any time since the early 1980s.

As we have seen earlier, during the 1990's recession, Liberal Finance Minister, Paul Martin, cut deeply into federal transfers to the provinces, which fell by 1.9 percentage points of GDP, from 1992 to 2000. Most of the burden fell on social programs under provincial jurisdiction, notably public health insurance (which covers physician and hospital care) and welfare or social assistance which provides basic income support.[48] The old formula under which the federal government paid one half of welfare costs was scrapped, and welfare rates were slashed in real terms in almost every province. Because of cuts to unemployment insurance and welfare, poverty rates remained at near recession levels through most of the 1990s, and the incomes of the bottom half of households rose very modestly, despite falling unemployment.[49]

According to Jackson, Martin's cuts stopped the Liberal government from implementing their promise to introduce a national child care and early learning program, "leaving working families pretty much on their own in seeking care arrangements. Worse, his fiscal revolution and abdication of federal leadership in social policy made Canada a much more market-dependent society, moving it much closer to the US model."[50] Between 1993 and 2002, the difference between the level of non-defence program spending in Canada and the US fell from "a huge 13.2 percentage points of GDP to just 5.7 percentage points."[51]

In spite of their professed commitment to more parsimonious government, Mr. Flaherty's comments both before and in Budget 2011 are intended to reassure voters that the scale of cuts exercised under the Liberals will not be repeated this time around. In terms of health care, the government remains at best ambivalent about the Canada Health Act, but Bhattia (chapter 9) believes that spending will nevertheless be ring fenced in some fashion in the Conservative's austerity program. However, she also points out that there will be little or no new money either which will, in effect, pass along the tough choices and much of the political fallout for cuts to services, to the provinces.

Furthermore, with the imminent expiry in 2014 of the *10-Year Plan*, the negotiation of new targets for the CHT has become the focal point of debate about the future of the health care system in Canada. However even as Ottawa quietly seeks input into future health transfer negotiations with the provinces, Bhattia argues that the government's ambitious deficit-slaying targets have laid the ground rules. Minsky contends that, "[i]f government would like to avoid growing debt and deficit, it's going to have to reign in its spending faster than the current plans indicate, and they should take a long, hard look at transfers to provinces and growth in the public service."[52] The Conservatives may see the 2014 negotiations as an opportunity to freeze or effectively cut provincial transfers and their best chance of reducing the deficit without the kind of direct political costs that increasing taxes, raising the retirement age or cutting the public service would inevitably impose.

In order to avoid the more unpopular austerity measures the government will be hoping that predicted growth is achieved and that rising house and commodity prices can offset the financial costs of carrying the added debt. Rising house prices and the increasing extraction of commodities, particularly oil from the tar sands, have added enormously to Canada's GDP in recent years and helped to insulate the country from the need to introduce harsher austerity measures. Growing reliance on commodities has also helped to disguise

Canada's relatively poor record on productivity and innovation and while this is considered a mixed blessing by many, greater exploration and investment allied to technological advances and a more liberal approach to land use are clear indications that Canada will continue to be increasingly dependent on exporting its natural resources.

As Abele discusses in chapter 11, this has particular significance for Canada's North where its natural resources are increasingly the focus of Canadian and international investors. While the Conservative government has been willing to make large spending commitments in the North she points out that this has largely focused on defence and economic development as opposed to spending on social policies and the needs of Northern and aboriginal communities. Falvo's examination of key economic and social challenges facing aboriginal communities in the NWT (chapter 12) complements Abele's thesis by illustrating the importance of social policy to the region. In particular, he focuses on housing policy, especially as it affects low-income residents who rely on government-assisted housing. His research reveals that small communities are where housing problems – especially with respect to overcrowding and the need for major repairs – are the most acute, underlining the importance of targeted, well funded housing and social policies that focus on the needs of a specific place.

While both these chapters demonstrate the dangers of conflating the various forms of government spending in a region (defence, economic development and social), the abundance of natural resources provide opportunities as well as threats for Northern communities. In particular, local jobs and enterprise could provide a means for tackling the dependency culture that federal government policies have helped to create over many decades. However, in order to facilitate such a shift and provide an appropriate mix of policies, the federal government will need to develop its policies through the local and intergovernmental processes and relationships that have slowly helped to foster trust and cooperation over many years. The danger is that if the federal government chooses to override or ignore established processes of political and social development in the North, as Abele fears, the goal of creating a just and sustainable society for aboriginal people and northerners generally will continue to elude policymakers. Moreover, if the development of the North is allowed to proceed outside of an appropriate governance and policy framework, the impacts on aboriginal communities and the environment could be devastating.

Parliamentary and Institutional Independence

Both our earlier discussion in this chapter, and the Richard Schultz analysis in chapter 3 of Industry Canada and its decisions on the Globealive case show the continuing penchant for Harper era mistrust of independent regulators, agencies and watchdogs and their officials.

The Globealive case shows the dangers of what Schultz calls "political licensing" where reasonable and legitimate law-based practices and processes were not followed. This is also part of Harper's highly selective view of accountability and ministerial responsibility. At times, ministers are said to be responsible and are merely taking decisions but in other contexts, the Harper era has become especially known as one characterized by centralized court government where only a small handful of ministers are actually trusted and where prime ministerial tentacles are everywhere. There is also little doubt that the aggressive partisan personality of Harper comes through as he practices the permanent arts of political warfare.

All prime ministers have practiced some of these sins of omission and commission but the Harper era record is quite sustained on this score. Harper won power in 2006 largely on the need for greater accountability as he rode the wave of the Liberal Sponsorship scandal to electoral victory, albeit of the minority government kind. His first new law was the Accountability Act. Under this legislative program he established several new independent watchdog agencies, including the Parliamentary Budget Officer.

But almost immediately an array of examples emerged where the Harper government in its first five years became anything but the government of accountability. These ranged from the firing of the head of the federal Nuclear Regulatory Commission, the apparently neutered minimal enforcement activity of Harper-created bodies such as the Integrity Commissioner but also the increased bureaucratization of the long established Access to Information regime. It also included the resignation of the head of Statistics Canada after the Conservatives sought for highly dubious political reasons to end the more complete and statistically valid long form census. And then came battles and controversy regarding the CRTC with internet billing decisions and the document doctoring accountability issues regarding Bev Oda the Minister of International Development with direct links to Harper's convoluted defence of his minister. Add to this the Conservative Government's disputes with the Parliamentary Budgetary Officer, a body it created, and his frequent questioning of their data and fiscal projections, and it is clear that transparent accountability is hardly the hallmark of the Harper era.

Immigration Policy and Politics as Pivotal Harper Strategy: Both to Emulate and Defeat the Liberal Party

Immigration policy and politics will continue to be a pivotal part of the Harper Government strategy both to emulate past historical Liberal Party success with earlier immigrant groups and to help defeat and weaken the Liberal Party on what the Tories hope will be a permanent long term basis. The Harper record on immigration policy under Immigration Minister Jason Kenney, a Minister whom Harper trusts, has sought to put a more visible Tory brand on the field overall such as by changing the citizenship story given to applicants by stressing Canada's historical military record rather than its peace-keeping record. It has also linked some of immigration policy to its law and order enforcement agenda and communication strategies. It has also taken long overdue steps to reduce immigration application backlogs.

The Harper government has also unambiguously seen immigration as an engine of the economy and in 2010 alone, 280,636 immigrants were admitted, the highest intake in 57 years.[53] Their view has also been reinforced by studies which argue that immigrants are a key to Canada's current and future capacity for innovation.[54] Canada's intake of immigrants compared to other countries as a percentage of population has always been high and has not provoked a serious anti-immigrant backlash as in other countries. The Tories have also massively increased the number of temporary foreign workers (283, 322 in 2010) a category of contract labour that have few rights or access to services. As the Harper Tories look ahead they are focusing on the design of a new point system regarding who should qualify for the federal skilled worker program. Their preference is for a system that favours young people, tradespeople and immigrants fluent in English or French. But this focus would likely come at the expense of a more socially centred immigration system centred more on family class immigrants.

As Neil Bradford and Caroline Andrew's analysis in chapter 13 shows, immigration represents a policy field of particular significance and complexity in Canada, dealing as it does with national identity as well as with economic and social imperatives. They also stress that the immigration policy field is quintessentially a realm of multi-level governance, involving joint jurisdiction with the provinces but also involving ever more complex coordination with local government, settlement sector agencies, mainstream organizations, business associations, and new and established immigrants themselves. Thus the Harper agenda must ultimately wend its way carefully through an intricate set of players most of whom it cannot directly or reliably control.

Broader Governance Reform Issues and Approaches

Economic crises inevitably place governments under close political scrutiny with regards to spending priorities, governance and value for money. This is understandable as transparency, access to information and due process are often superseded by expediency, confidentiality, and tighter controls as governments attempt to govern in the face of growing criticism. These issues come up in various chapters in this edition of How Ottawa Spends and help to inform the current debates about aspects of governance and possible reform.

In Pal's chapter 2 he discusses a number of concerns that have been raised with respect to the race to get stimulus money out of the door and into infrastructure projects. A recent review by the Auditor General suggests that in spite of the haste with which the money has been transferred throughout the country it appears to have been competently administered.[55] That said, there are lingering complaints that the stimulus fund was subject to direct political influence, was not properly evaluated in terms of jobs and was not reported as transparently as stimulus packages were in other countries such as Australia and the US. Another concern is that while the stimulus money is being spread across the country into thousands of shovel ready projects it represents a missed opportunity in failing to address Canada's pressing and strategic infrastructure needs.

In Hubbard and Paquet's chapter 3 analysis they also question the government's lack of strategic focus but, as opposed to targeting spending, they examine spending cuts. In particular they are skeptical of the value of traditional across the board cuts, especially in respect of provincial transfers, and argue for a paradigm shift from big 'G' Government to small 'g' governance - not simply doing the same with less, but finding ways to do things differently, if at all, and doing it collectively. In criticising the use of this big G blanket approach in the 1990s they argue that by partitioning issue domains into programs, governance concerns were unwittingly evacuated and attention was focused on managerial plumbing even where governance failures loomed large. Such silo based thinking tends to reduce government's ability to think strategically and holistically about issues as 'domains' that are often the locus of densely integrated and overlapping jurisdictions.

This taps into a growing body of literature that calls for governments to play more of an enabling role in which they facilitate dialogue and cooperation between stakeholders, often at the local level. In order to focus more collectively and effectively on issue domains Hubbard and Paquet argue that governance systems will be need to be more modular, network-like, and integrated by informal moral contracts, building on a process of social learning through a critical "multilogue" among the stakeholders. Such reforms make a lot of sense from a policy perspective, but within the current context of hyper-partisan, risk averse and short-term thinking it remains to be seen what progress will be in this direction.

Lahey's analysis in chapter 4 also focuses on public service costs and questions the effectiveness of the compensation process used to pay public servants and control these expenditures while trying to maintain and improve employee performance, motivation and recruitment. These are clearly important challenges as the government looks to reduce the costs of the public service in the face of alarming reports about declining employee morale and a looming 'war for talent' as up to 17,000 public servants become eligible to retire each year, many of them in senior and leadership positions. Lahey believes that a reward system that better reflects individual capacities and engagement could help address the issues of costs, motivation and recruitment. In order to attract and motivate its fair share of talent as experienced leaders retire, he maintains that the federal public service also needs to offer compensation that compares reasonably with the private sector.

Although reforming public sector compensation along these lines has long been the subject of research, debate and reports, it remains a seemingly intractable problem. A centralized structure, collective bargaining, inflexible career paths and a strong emphasis on equity, fairness and representation are just some of the factors that place constraints on how far the system can be reformed and wholesale changes will first require a change in culture as well as committed leadership. However, given that the demographic profile of the public service is about to change dramatically over the coming years, renewal along these lines could well be timely. A new generation of younger public servants will likely be more amenable and responsive to the kind of reforms Lahey proposes.

In chapter 14 Francoli criticizes the lack of public engagement between government and citizens and, in particular the still very limited use of social and internet media which has enormous potential to engage with the public as well as to deliver information and services. This is a crucial and timely debate in the context of public service renewal particularly in the context of demographic changes taking place. Francoli points out a number of legal and policy- related challenges that need to be addressed before technology can be more fully embraced, but it is the apparent political and bureaucratic ambivalence that appears to provide the main constraint. At every level of government, access to and control over information has become a crucial issue.

Ironically, the more transparency measures that are introduced, the more adept our governments become in restricting access to information. This tension results in an ongoing struggle over information that manifests itself in an elaborate cycle of game playing between the controllers of information and those who seek access to it. These tensions become most apparent through flashpoints, attempted cover ups and scandals, several of which gradually eroded parliament's confidence in the government instigating its defeat in Parliament on March 25th, 2011.

In many ways social media and the internet intensify these struggles over access to accurate and meaningful information which is crucial in any deliberative democracy. Pal's examination of the reporting of the stimulus fund revealed how limited the information was on the government's Action Plan website and this further illustrates the need for meaningful, substantive data to be made available if Canada's declining international transparency ranking is to be halted. Flashy websites with partisan branding and partial, biased reporting of the facts information will do nothing to advance democracy and engagement but will simply compound cynicism and further erode trust. As the chapters by Francoli, Pal, Lahey and Hubbard and Paquet demonstrate, governance reform presents a number of pressing challenges that will help to define the integrity of our overall governance structures as well as the quality and effectiveness of Canada's public service.

Environment Policy and Climate Change

Both the Harper record to date and future probabilities in environment policy and climate change are unambiguously gloomy. Douglas Macdonald's assessment in chapter 6 shows convincingly that the Harper government is failing to address all three of the main policy challenges it and Canadians face. By ignoring the environmental implications of energy development, by making no effort to address the problem of differing provincial interests with respect to climate change mitigation and by abandoning, with one exception, climate change policy sovereignty it has virtually abandoned the field.

Francois Bregha's analysis in chapter 7 shows that the Harper Tories as well as previous Liberal governments had also made precious little progress in implementing federal policies and approaches regarding strategic environmental assessment (SEA) of government policies and plans, as distinct from assessing environmental projects. Bregha concludes that while successive governments have acknowledged the importance of sustainable development, fighting climate change and considering environmental factors in decision-making, they have not walked the talk and therefore the current inadequacies of the federal SEA process ensure that Canada will continue to pay a heavy, yet largely avoidable, environmental price for many future government decisions.

The government's own National Roundtable on the Environment and Economy (NRTEE) has again argued that Canada should proceed with "made in Canada" climate change regulations rather than a defacto made in the USA policy based on broadly harmonizing eventual US regulations.[56] Frances Abele's analysis in chapter 11 of the Tory's Northern Strategy also shows that climate change gets short shrift compared to energy development and also to southern Canadian Harper rhetoric since 2006 about Canada being a global energy superpower.

If anything, Harper environmental policy as it relates to energy and climate change plays even more to an appeal to its core Alberta and western Canadian base. This was especially the case when Harper's newly appointed Environment Minister, Peter Kent, went out of his way to agree with the newly inspired policy discourse vis a vis the US concerns about the oil sands by asserting that Canada was a source of "ethical oil."[57] This is a discourse that virtually ignores the environmental issues and stresses instead that Canada as a democratic country was a close by and reliable source of energy for the US compared to Middle East and other foreign sources of energy supply.

NOTES

1 Special thanks are owed to our colleagues, Les Pal, Allan Maslove, and Michael Prince, for helpful critical comments on an earlier draft of this chapter.

2 See Gene Swimmer, ed. *How Ottawa Spends 1996–97: Life Under the Knife* (Carleton University Press, 1996) and Bruce Doern, "Evolving Budgetary Policies and Experiments: 1980 to 2009–2010", in Allan Maslove, ed., *How Ottawa Spends 2009–2010: Economic Upheaval and Political Dysfunction* (McGill-Queen's University Press, 2009) 14–46.

3 See Lawrence Martin, Harperland: *The Politics of Control* (Viking Canada, 2010).

4 Bruce Doern and Christopher Stoney, eds. *How Ottawa Spends 2010–2011: Recession, Realignment, and the New Deficit Era* (McGill-Queen's University Press, 2010)

5 Drummond, Don cited in Dan Gardner: "The economy doesn't care who wins: In the big picture, Liberal and Conservative economic policies are almost indistinguishable", *Ottawa Citizen March 1, 2011,*available at: http://www.ottawacitizen.com/business/economy+doesn+care+wins/4369474/story.html

6 Indeed, in February 2011, the conservative think tank, the Fraser Institute advocated something close to the Liberal's 1995 strategy as the best way for a Conservative government to proceed, advice that the Harper Government did not agree with. See Niels Veldhuis, Jason Clemens, and Milagros Palacios, *Budget Blueprint: How Lessons From Canada's 1995 Budget Can be Applied Today* (Fraser Institute, 2011)

7 See Amy Minsky, *National Post, Feb 6th 2011,* "Stimulus, defence fuelling federal public-service growth", available at: http://www.nationalpost.com/news/canada/politics/Stimulus+defence+fuelling+federal+public+service+growth/4233233/story.html

8 See "Postmedia" research in Amy Minsky, ibid.

9 Ibid.

10 Ibid.

11 Ibid.

12 Ibid.

13 Ibid.

14 Ibid.

15 Finn Poschmann, research executive at the C.D. Howe Institute quoted in Amy Minsky, *Ibid.*

16 Jeffrey Simpson, "Uncertainty over the US means a shadow over Canada", *Globe and Mail, February 25th 2011,* available at: http://www.theglobeandmail.com/news/opinions/opinion/uncertainty-over-the-us-means-a-shadow-over-canada/article1919397/

17 Jeffrey Simpson, Waiting for smaller government? Don't hold your breath, *Globe and Mail, February 11, 2011,* available at: http://www.theglobeandmail.com/news/opinions/jeffrey-simpson/waiting-for-smaller-government-dont-hold-your-breath/article1902704/

18 William Johnson, "Harper legacy will transcend Jekyll and Hyde analysis", *The Ottawa Citizen January 22, 2011,* available at: http://www.ottawacitizen.com/news/Harper+legacy+will+transcend+Jekyll+Hyde+analysis/4149302/story.html

19 Drummond, Don cited in Dan Gardner: "The economy doesn't care who wins: In the big picture, Liberal and Conservative economic policies are almost indistinguishable", *Ottawa Citizen March 1, 2011,* available at:http://www.ottawacitizen.com/business/economy+doesn+care+wins/4369474/story.html

20 Op. cit, February 11 2011.

21 Andrew Mayeda, Mike de Souza and Amy Minsky, "Federal spending to drop $10.4B", *Ottawa Citizen, March 1, 2011*, available at: http://www.ottawacitizen.com/news/Federal+spending+drop/4368731/story.html

22 Bill Curry, "Tories cagey about cuts to the budget", *Globe and Mail, February 8th 2011*, available at http://www.theglobeandmail.com/news/politics/tories-cagey-about-cuts-to-the-budget/article1899857/

23 Op. cit, Andrew Jackson

24 John Ibbitson, "Harper keeps Canada in dark at his own peril", February 14, 2011, available at: http://www.theglobeandmail.com/news/politics/ottawa-notebook/harper-keeps-canada-in-dark-at-his-own-peril/article1905785/

25 Ibid.

26 Ibid.

27 Andrew Mayeda, "Liberals will push for election over Tories' disrespect for democracy", *The Ottawa Citizen, March 10, 2011*, available at http://www.ottawacitizen.com/business/Harper+downplays+Speaker+ruling+says+government+focused+economy/4417860/story.html

28 *Ibid.*

29 See Canada, *The Budget Speech 2011* (Government of Canada, March 22, 2011), Canada, *Budget in Brief* (Government of Canada, March 22, 2011) and Canada, *The Budget Plan* (Government of Canada, March 22, 2011).

30 Canada, *Budget Speech*, 1.

31 Ibid., 1.

32 Ibid., 2–9.

33 Ibid., 8

34 Canada, *The Budget Plan*, Chapter 5.

35 Ibid., Chart 5.3

36 Conservative Party of Canada, *Here for Canada* (Conservative Party of Canada) 22.

37 Ibid.

38 Liberal Party of Canada, *Your Family, Your Future, Your Canada* (Liberal Party of Canada, 2011)

39 Ibid.

40 Ibid., discussed variously from p 5–73.

41 New Democratic Party, *Giving Your Family a Break: Practical First Steps* (New Democratic Party, 2011).

42 Ibid., 1.

43 Ibid., 10–14.

44 Ibid., 2.

45 Ibid., 4.

46 Ibid., 8.

47 Bill Curry, "Corporate tax cuts costlier than Tories let on, budget watchdog says", *The Globe and Mail*, February 25, 2011, available at: http://www.theglobeandmail

.com/news/politics/ottawa-notebook/corporate-tax-cuts-costlier-than-tories-let-on-budget-watchdog-says/article1920932/

48 Op. cit, Andrew Jackson.

49 Ibid.

50 Ibid.

51 Ibid.

52 Amy Minsky, "Public service, military expand under Harper government", *Postmedia News, February 6th 2011*, Available at: http://www.vancouversun.com/story_print. html?id=4233317&sponsor=

53 See John Ibbitson and Joe Friesen, "Tories Tread Carefully on Immigration Policy", *Globe and Mail*, February 14, 2011, 3 and see also Nicholas Kueng, "Canada Admits Record-High Number of Immigrants", *Toronto Star*, February 13, 2011, 4.

54 See Michelle Downie, "Immigrants as Innovators Boosting Canada's Global Competitiveness", *Conference Board of Canada, October 2010*, 1–60, available at: http://www.conferenceboard.ca/documents.aspx?did=3825

55 See 2010 Fall Report of the Auditor General of Canada Chapter 1 – Canada's Economic Action Plan, available at: http://www.oag-bvg.gc.ca/internet/English/ parl_oag_201010_01_e_34284.html

56 See National Roundtable on Environment and Economy, *Climate Prosperity* (National Roundtable on Environment and Economy, 2011) and Shawn McCarthy, "Break from U.S. and Put Price on Carbon, Ottawa Told", *Globe and Mail*, January 25, 2.

57 See Steven Chase, "Peter Kent's Green Agenda: Clean Up Oil Sands Dirty Reputation", Globe and Mail, January 6, 2011, Gloria Galloway, "Peter Kent Sees No Pressing Need for New Climate Laws", *Globe and Mail,* January 28, 2011, and Ezra Levant, *Ethical Oil: The Case For Canada's Oil Sands* (McClelland and Stewart, 2010).

PART ONE

Politics and Strategies for Restoring Fiscal Balance, Economic Growth, and Governance Renewal

2 Into the Wild: The Politics of Economic Stimulus

LESLIE A. PAL

INTRODUCTION

The "Great Recession" of the past two years has pounded Canadians and their economy, and has posed substantial policy and political challenges for the federal Conservative government. The policy challenge is evident: how to ride out the storm, prevent collapse, and restore economic growth and employment. The political challenge has been just as daunting, at least for a Stephen Harper-led government that had relentlessly branded itself as a prudent fiscal manager who would keep the lid on both spending and taxes (spending in fact increased every year the Tories were in power, but the branding exercise was still politically important).

The policy answer to the recession was spending, and in the Canadian case particularly, infrastructure spending to stimulate the economy. But spending on this scale carried the danger of generating massive deficits and thereby poisoning the brand. On the cusp of the recession, the Tories were visibly reluctant to launch a major stimulus program, then embraced it, and then had to manage it. Managing the politics of deficit spending for an ideologically conservative government is not easy. The answer – after walking into the wild – was to embrace it as a temporary journey that would soon end in safety and stability. Some background can place this strategy in context.

Like most Western countries, Canada was caught unawares by the financial crisis that had been building through 2007–2008. There were warning signs, of course, enough to indicate that some sort of recession might be on the horizon, and so the minority Conservative government headed by Stephen

Harper decided to call an election in September for October 14, 2008. The result was yet another minority government, with the Conservatives gaining 19 seats over their 2006 performance, but still short of a majority in the 308 seat legislature.

The global (and US) financial crisis blew up in the middle of the campaign. The Prime Minister was attacked by the opposition parties and challenged to articulate an economic strategy that would avoid the same meltdown in Canada. The government's responses were weak – essentially that Canada had enjoyed fiscal surpluses for a decade (even though they had been declining), that its housing market had not bubbled and burst like the US one, and that its banks were more stable and better regulated. The November 19, 2008 Speech from the Throne (SFT), for example, was nine pages long (not unusually long for a Canadian SFT, but much, much shorter than the one that was to follow in January 2009).[1]

The first mention of the economic crisis was on the second page, and largely self-congratulatory (highlighting the well-regulated banking system, public pensions, paying down the debt). There was no mention of stimulus. This state of mind was corroborated by the Economic Update that was tabled on November 27, 2008.[2] It acknowledged that, while Canada had done better than most advanced industrial countries in weathering the financial storm to date, it was likely to experience a "technical recession" in the coming year, and that policy would focus on the "fundamentals." While the Update acknowledged that deficits might occur, it pledged that these would be temporary, and moreover that it was aiming for five consecutive years of continued surplus, based in large part on a combination of prudent spending (through a new expenditure management regime) and targeted cuts. The projected surpluses were razor-thin however: $.1 billion (2009–2010 and 2010–2011), $1.1 billion (2011–2012), and $4.2 billion (2012–2013).

The Economic Update had an unfortunate passage – it proposed to eliminate the public subsidies to political parties ($1.95 per vote for a federal political party if it wins at least 2 per cent of the national vote). The opposition parties were enraged as well as frightened, and on December 1, 2008 they announced that they were prepared to work together as a coalition government and that they would vote non-confidence in the Harper Conservatives in one week. The Prime Minister, in a tense, private and lengthy conversation with the Governor-General, succeeded in persuading her to prorogue Parliament (i.e., suspend the legislature, purge pending legislation, but *not* dissolve it and require an election) until January 26, 2009.

To this point, the Tory economic policy had been steady-as-she-goes and had resisted calls for stimulus (the US, for example, had already passed the Emergency Economic Stabilization Act in October, promising US$700 billion in bailouts to the financial sector). Politics – and to some extent the sinking reality of recession – changed this dramatically. The new strategy called for unprecedented stimulus spending – by a putatively conservative government. The Tories quickly realized that this could be turned to their political advantage, but that they also had to manage the expectations that would come from turning on the fiscal taps. Those who are stimulated are reluctant to become "unstimulated", which set up an interesting if ironic dynamic for the government. It was able to harvest praise for saving the Canadian economy by pumping out money, but could cling to its conservative credentials by being firm with the endless demands for more money for evermore.

CANADA'S ECONOMIC ACTION PLAN:
POLICY DIMENSIONS

The threat of a coalition government was a near-death experience for the Conservative government. It got the message. On January 26, 2009, it tabled a SFT on January 26, 2009 that was dramatically different from the one it had issued only two months before. In terms of text, this SFT was only three and half pages long. The first page had two stark paragraphs that set a completely different tone from November 2008:

In these uncertain times, when the world is threatened by a struggling economy, it is imperative that we work together, that we stand beside one another and that we strive for greater solidarity. ...
Today we meet at a time of unprecedented economic uncertainty. The global credit crunch has dragged the world economy into a crisis whose pull we cannot escape. The nations of the world are grappling with challenges that Canada can address but not avoid.[3]

The global financial crisis had deepened since the last election, and indeed since the last SFT. This time, the SFT highlighted the issue of jobs, and referred specifically to a new "economic stimulus plan" that would be announced the next day. In addition to measures that had already been introduced in early 2008 and "re-announced" in the Economic Update in November 2008, the government now said that it would stimulate the economy, invest in infrastructure, and support key industries and the jobs dependent on them. The sombre tone of the opening paragraphs were echoed now in a statement that Canada might face several difficult years, though the stimulus would be directed to long-term growth and avoid "permanent" deficits.

This was a dramatic reversal from the government's policy stance only two months earlier. Clearly, the accelerating crisis in the United States (particularly around the automotive industry – GM and Chrysler received US17.5 billion in December 2008) had captured the Canadian government's attention. By March 2009 the Obama administration had all but nationalized the US industry (with the exception of Ford). Canada's automotive industry, along with forestry, mining, and most other exports, depend heavily on US markets, so the *fact* of recession had now replaced the *perception* two months earlier.

However, the political momentum had changed dramatically as well. The Harper Conservatives had enjoyed the surplus budget situation created by the Liberals since 1998, and though they had spent down that surplus (principally through cuts to the GST) since 2006, they continued to be ideologically committed to balanced budgets and to spending restraint. This was also a political marker – the Prime Minister had worked hard to create an image of the Conservatives as sound fiscal managers. So in all likelihood, the Economic Update of November 2008 was the product both of ideological conviction and simple incomprehension of the actual magnitude of the global financial crisis and its potential impact on Canada.

However, by January 2009, the bald facts of recession were painfully clear, and the government realized that it had to be and appear to be as active as the American administration to the south, or the Brown government in the UK. November-December 2008 changed a lot about how capitalist governments operate – the "conservative" option of doing little if nothing, or allowing market forces to prevail, of simply cutting taxes, of admiring the "titans of industry" as they gathered huge bonuses while their companies sank beneath the waves of bankruptcy and default – this was not an option any longer, no matter what the ideological proclivities of a given government in power. But the Harper conservatives realized something else. Stimulus – in the Canadian version – was politically attractive. Unlike the US, where stimulus was associated in the public mind with bail-outs and corporate bonuses, in Canada it would not. Banks were stable, and did not need bail-outs, and whatever they wished to pay to their executives was their business. The automotive industry was different of course, but unique in the Canadian case, while it formed a part of a pattern in the US, accompanying lifelines to banks and credit corporations.[4] Moreover, the iconic status of these industries (particularly GM and Chrysler) in the US mind, plus the unprecedented scope and size of expenditures, made the US (and some European) stimulus packages seem more like favours to high industry and fat banks than actual labour market stimulus.

So, just as it had been with its surpluses, low taxes, and its firm financial regulations, the Canadian government was poised for a stimulus package that could avoid the political fallout of the worst excesses of the Obama administration, and possibly reap the benefits of a soft blanket of warm money spent across the country. This section will summarize the highlights of the package – space does not allow touching on each detail.[5] A point that should be kept in mind as we review the Action Plan is that this was, and is, by recent standards, a massive stimulus package. Within one year it had contributed to placing Canada's federal government in a deficit position of over $50 billion – from a surplus the year before. The Parliamentary Budget Office, after an analysis of the budget and the economy, argued that Canada was now facing a structural deficit that would take many more years to expunge than the government projected, and with much more pain. The package had been hastily assembled – in somewhat over two months from November 2008 to January 2009. It was conceptual only, but projected hundreds of job-creating and labour market stimulus projects across the country. This posed enormous strains on the bureaucracy to ensure that due process was being followed, legal requirements met, and procurement safeguards in place. It also created opportunities, as we describe below, for political benefit.

Highlights:

- $200 billion for an Extraordinary Financing Framework that would improve credit access to individuals and businesses "to create jobs."
- $8.3 billion to assist with jobs transition.
- $7.8 billion for housing tax credits and tax relief for renovations.
- $12 billion in new infrastructure spending, "including funding for shovel-ready projects that can start this upcoming construction season, including roads, bridges, clean energy, broadband internet access and electronic health records across the country."
- $7.5 billion in sectoral adjustment funds for sectors, regions, and communities.

The sectoral adjustment funds were the most micro-policy measures. The rest worked through existing institutions or ministries. But the funds would have to be tailored to specific infrastructure and labour market needs in various parts of the country. The $12 billion in infrastructure spending, for example, claimed to be investing in more modern and greener infrastructure by (examples):

- Establishing a two-year, $4-billion Infrastructure Stimulus Fund that will provide funding to renew infrastructure.
- Providing $1 billion over five years for the Green Infrastructure Fund to support projects such as sustainable energy.
- Providing $500 million over two years to build and renew community recreation facilities across Canada.

The investment in knowledge infrastructure would involve (examples):

- Dedicating up to $2 billion to repair, retrofit and expand facilities at post-secondary institutions.
- Providing $750 million for leading-edge research infrastructure through the Canada Foundation for Innovation.
- Providing $50 million to the Institute for Quantum Computing in Waterloo, Ontario to build a new world-class research facility.

- Providing $500 million to Canada Health Infoway to encourage the greater use of electronic health records.

Investments in federal infrastructure would include (examples):

- Increasing funding to VIA Rail Canada by $407 million to support improvements to passenger rail services, including higher train frequencies and enhanced on-time performance and speed, particularly in the Montréal–Ottawa–Toronto corridor.
- Providing $72 million over five years to improve railway safety.
- Providing $130 million to Parks Canada for twinning a section of the Trans-Canada Highway through Banff National Park.
  Allocating $212 million to renew the Champlain Bridge in Montréal, Canada's busiest bridge.
- Setting aside up to $42 million for other federal bridges in need of rehabilitation throughout Canada.
- Providing up to $217 million to accelerate the construction of the Pangnirtung Harbour in Nunavut and repair core small craft harbours across Canada.
- Allocating $323 million over two years for the restoration of federally owned buildings.
- Increasing funding by $80 million over the next two years to manage and assess federal contaminated sites, facilitating remediation work totalling $165 million over two years.
- Providing funding to modernize and expand border service facilities at Prescott, Ontario; and at Huntingdon, Kingsgate, and the Pacific Highway in British Columbia.

There was more, but the point is clear: from a policy stance of modestly adjusting pre-existing programs from early 2008, and avoiding deficits, the government had gone into a mode of micro-stimulus policy, naming individual cities and institutions that would receive funding. The budget forecast, while carefully framed in terms of eventual surplus redemption, now projected deficits of $33.7 billion in 2009–2010, and $29.8 billion in 2010–2011, with balance only coming after 2014.

Before discussing details of the Action Plan, three of its broader characteristics should be noted. First, as we pointed out earlier, the Action Plan was explicitly designed as a labour market stimulus package – it was about jobs. "The main focus of the Economic Action Plan has been to help protect and create jobs during the global economic downturn. The Plan attempts to limit the number of Canadians and their families who will have to go through the experience of job loss."[6] Second, the Plan was designed to be temporary – all the monies under the Plan were to be spent by March 2011. This was based on the assumption that the financial crisis, while deep, would be short and that the world economy (and Canada's) would rebound by 2010. As well, the monies would have to be spent quickly if they were to have a stimulating effect – and this meant that hundreds of projects had to be approved and the money out the door as quickly as possible, and certainly starting early in the summer of 2009. The logic also was that a short (if intense) burst of stimulus would allow projects to be terminated or completed quickly so that the government could begin to move back towards balanced budgets and eventually, surpluses. This ran up against the natural desire of recipients for more.

The third characteristic of the Action Plan was that it had to be implemented in cooperation with provinces, municipalities, and local groups and businesses (e.g., Aboriginal communities) if it was to succeed, jurisdictions that would have to put up some of their own money for projects just as they two were being pummeled by the recession. As a federation, many of the projects would be aimed at infrastructure that was under the jurisdiction of sub-national governments and municipalities. Just as important, the stimulus package was aimed at tangible building projects ("shovel ready") like bridge reconstruction, or new buildings for universities, and only the municipalities and universities themselves would know what they needed. This in itself was an interesting departure from conventional Tory policy, which had been to get the federal government out of other jurisdictions. Suddenly, it was beaming down from the Ottawa starship into hockey rinks and community centers.

STIMULUS ACCOUNTABILITY REPORTING

Partly as a result of opposition pressure, the government promised to table quarterly reports on the Action Plan, and the first report (at time of writing there have been six) was released on March 10, 2009. It reviewed the categories of initiatives that had been outlined in the budget in January. New initiatives and programs – like the $12 billion to support infrastructure, had first to receive legal approvals, await the legislature's passing of the budget, and issue "requests for proposals" to which municipalities and provinces and other entities (e.g., universities, companies) could apply. However, some programs that were already in place could be mobilized for the Action Plan, such as the Building Canada program. With existing programs, monies could be spent immediately, so with Building Canada, the government was able to accelerate $1.5 billion in joint funding for over 480 projects in smaller communities in British Columbia, Alberta, Saskatchewan, New Brunswick and Ontario.[7]

The second report was tabled on June 11, 2009. Like the first one, the announcement of the report was made directly by the Prime Minister himself, indicative of the political importance the government place on the Action Plan. The second report argued that 80 per cent of the initiatives outlined in the plan were either flowing or had been committed (critics claimed that

Figure 1
Summary of changes to deficit position

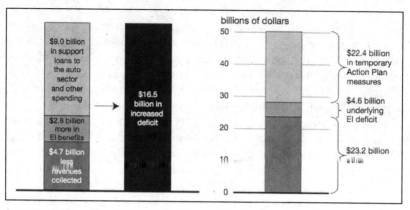

Source: *Canada's Economic Action Plan: A Second Report to Canadians* (March 10, 2009), p. 217. Retrieved on February 21, 2010 from http://www.plandaction.gc.ca/eng/index.asp

in fact very little money was being spent at this point, and the Plan consisted largely of agreements rather than tangible activities). However, the government did admit that the projected deficit for 2009–2010 would now be over $50 billion, or almost $20 billion more than it had projected only seven months earlier.[8] Almost $23 billion of that deficit would come from the stimulus package. The change in the fiscal/deficit position was largely due to falling revenues, but also to unanticipated commitments to prop up the automotive sector. When President Obama announced over US50 billion in support for GM and Chrysler (with most of the money going to GM, as the government effectively nationalized it, ousted its CEO and replaced him with another, and orchestrated union concessions), the Canadian government pledged a proportional (to its population and the size of the sector in Canada) amount to support plants north of the border. The Canadian package (co-financed by the federal and the Ontario governments) initially was to be about $4 billion, but by July had grown to $15 billion if all loans and other instruments were included.

The third report was announced by the Prime Minister on September 28, 2009, and the fourth report was released on December 2, 2009, again with an announcement by the Prime Minister. Predictably, the two reports repeated the positive conditions that had surrounded Canada's experience with the financial crisis: entering it with a well-regulated and stable financial industry, balanced budgets, lowered taxes in 2007 and 2008, and lower household debt ratios. The IMF had stated that of the G-7 countries, Canada would be the least affected by the downturn and would have the strongest recovery. Indeed, the unemployment rate in Canada by December 2009 was one full percentage point lower than the US rate – the first time that this had happened in a generation.

Figure 2
Total employment, Canada and the United States

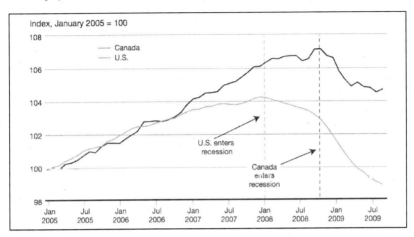

Source: *Canada's Economic Action Plan: A Third Report to Canadians* (September 28, 2009), p. 9. Retrieved on February 21, 2010 from http://www.plandaction.gc.ca/eng/index.asp

The third report stated that almost 90 per cent of the stimulus package had been spent, on a bewildering array of projects: over 4,700 provincial, territorial and municipal infrastructure projects; 1,150 projects to repair and renovate federal buildings; 447 projects to improve infrastructure at colleges and universities, and some 300 social housing projects.[9] The fourth report went further, stating that about 12,000 projects had been launched and were underway across the country. By the time the sixth report was released in September 2010, the number of projects had increased to 23,000.

Funds have been committed to more than 12,000 projects across the country, of which approximately 8,000 have begun. Projects committed include:

- Over 6,700 provincial, territorial and municipal infrastructure projects, including over 1,500 Recreational Infrastructure Canada projects.
- 1,150 projects to renovate and repair federal buildings.
- 536 projects to improve infrastructure at colleges and universities across the country.
- Over 1,800 social housing projects.
- 260 projects to improve small craft harbours.
- About 1,000 projects to assist communities hardest hit by the recession through the Community Adjustment Fund.
- Support for 56 major Canadian festivals and events.
- 80 cultural infrastructure projects.
- More than 120 projects to upgrade facilities at National Parks and National Historic Sites.
- Over 300 First Nations infrastructure and housing projects.[10]

Was the Economic Action Plan well-managed? In her 2010 Fall Report, the Auditor General of Canada concluded that "we found that the government has adequately managed these selected programs by putting in place appropriate management practices and providing programs to eligible recipients in a timely manner."[11] Did the Plan work? While there is obvious dissent, it does seem to have worked.[12] As the various reports testify, Canada seemed to have a more shallow recession than any of its G-7 partners, and certainly less sharp than the United States and the United Kingdom. The rebound was faster in 2010, and the unemployment rate did not break 10 per cent as it did in the United States. There was some debate about whether the deficits that the government was projecting could in fact be rolled back over three or four years – the Parliamentary Budget Officer argued that in fact Canada's deficit was "structural and deeper that the government's estimates.[13]

THE POLITICS OF THE ECONOMIC ACTION PLAN

We turn now to the politics or optics of the Economic Action Plan, especially its core stimulus provisions. As we mentioned earlier, there were several peculiarities about Canada's experience of the crisis and the Economic Action Plan – the speed, amount, and focus on labour markets being the most prominent. But the fact that the entire plan was temporary, and would be wound down by March 31, 2011, put a premium on speed and rapid roll-out. However, the Conservative government had invested a great deal of political capital in creating an image (even though spent as willingly as the previous government) of fiscal probity. In addition, in the 2006 election, the key Conservative message was accountability, especially for spending.

We cited the six reports on the Economic Action Plan above – these were reports or "report cards" that had been demanded by the opposition parties in exchange for supporting the budget and not defeating the government. Ironically, however, they ended up becoming useful platforms for the government to highlight all its hard work and the success of the plan. The announcements for the first four reports were made initially by the Prime Minister himself, at events and not in the House of Commons.

The government also established a dedicated web site for the Action Plan (http://www.plandaction.gc.ca/eng/index.asp). Web sites are not unusual of course, but this one had several interesting features. First, because it covered virtually every department and agency that managed any kind of labour market program, it was a "whole of government" tool that listed all projects as well as all participating departments and agencies. Second, it pulled together all press releases and advertisements regarding the Plan. There were television ads highlighting tax credits for home renovations, a basket of other tax incentives for a host of activities (e.g., renovations but also transit passes), but always with an emphasis on the impact on jobs, benefits, retraining – in short on different aspects of the Canadian labour market. Each ad urged viewers to go to the Economic Action Plan web site to see what benefits might be there for them. Third, the website used the latest social networking tools to allow visitors to share whatever they might find, but also to get regular e-mail updates on the evolution of the plan.

There were two other features to the web site that clearly highlighted the importance of ensuring that Canadians knew how beneficial this program would be for them. On the home page, at the bottom, were a series of categories entitled "What is in the Plan for Me?" There were four categories listed – individual or family; business; educational or non-profit organization, and government or aboriginal community. If one clicked on "individual or family" for example, another list appeared to its right with new sub-categories: worker, family, homeowner, and student. Clicking on one of these then revealed a colourful list of projects and programs under that category. Selecting just from the workers tab, here are five quick descriptions of new programs under the Action Plan:

> Through Canada's Economic Action Plan, the federal government has implemented the **Career Transition Assistance (CTA)** initiative to help long-tenured workers update and acquire new skills. This initiative, implemented in partnership with provinces and territories, has two components and will cost an estimated $500 million over two years. ...
> As part of Canada's Economic Action Plan, the federal government made a commitment to encourage skilled trades and apprenticeships by investing $40 million per year in a new **Apprenticeship Completion Grant (ACG)**, which complements the existing Apprenticeship Incentive Grant (AIG). ...
> On November 3, 2009 the Government of Canada tabled legislation, the **Fairness for the Self-Employed Act,** to provide Employment Insurance (EI) maternity, parental/adoption, sickness and compassionate care benefits to self-employed Canadians on a voluntary basis. This legislation, which received Royal Assent on December 15, 2009, will allow the self-employed to opt into the EI program in January 2010, while benefits will start being paid in January 2011. ...
> Through Canada's Economic Action Plan, the federal government is investing $500 million in a two-year **Strategic Training and Transition Fund (STTF)**. The fund will support provincial and territorial initiatives that help workers retrain to retain employment or transition to new jobs in communities and sectors affected by the economic downturn. ...
> Through Canada's Economic Action Plan, the federal government will freeze the **Employment Insurance (EI) premium rate** for 2010 at $1.73 per $100 of insurable earnings-the same level as in 2009 and its lowest level since 1982. Keeping the EI premium at the same level in 2009 and

2010, rather than raising it to the break-even level, will achieve a projected combined economic stimulus of $4.5 billion.

The government put special efforts into providing detailed information on not just the content of different programs and initiatives, but their regional distribution as well. The map is interactive (see Appendix). The first, national map shows the distribution of projects, the second map is the result of clicking on a group of projects, in this case in southern Ontario. The third map shows projects around the small town of Belleville in southern Ontario. Even some of the icons in map 3 represent group projects, and could keep clicking further until single projects became visible. Clicking on individual project sites brings up information about the project budget, objectives, and links to the larger program that is funding the project. The large majority of these small informational windows carry a photo of a beaming Prime Minister, framed against building signs and men in hard hats. The Prime Minister's promotion of the stimulus plan did not go unnoted: newspaper reviews in 2010 showed that he had travelled extensively in the previous year to towns and cities across the country.[14]

All this raises the issue of how the stimulus spending was used to enhance the government's popularity. There was sufficient anecdotal evidence to suggest that the Economic Action Plan was being used precisely in this way – as of course previous and similar plans under the Liberals had also been used to the same purpose. We have already discussed the government's web site as a masterful tool for political communication of the benefits of the program to specific groups and regions. Added to this was the opportunity to have "announceables" almost every week. With projects being rolled out as rapidly as possible through the summer and fall, the government had a golden opportunity to fan out its ministers and MPs to actually be at the photo-ops and unveil the cheques and the projects. This was largely innocent, but one MP took it to a new level.[15]

In the photo, Mr. Gerald Keddy, Conservative MP for South Shore-St. Margaret's in Nova Scotia, is shown handing a $300,000 cheque to the local community for the upgrading of a hockey facility in one of the communities in his riding. The cheque does not bear any evidence that it comes from the government of Canada, and in the top left sports the Conservative Party logo. As well, the cheque has Mr. Keddy's signature on it, implying that somehow the funds were coming from him personally instead of taxpayers. Once this surfaced, it appeared that at least three other Tory MPs had done similar things – identifying the project monies directly with the Conservative party. Opposition parties were outraged, and the Prime Minister admitted that this was a mistake and would not happen again. The furor died down, but it is unclear how many other examples there might have been out of thousands of projects.

Another way in which the stimulus package could have been used for political purposes was to skew the projects into Conservative as opposed to Liberal ridings. The government – despite the sophisticated web site – does not release precise information on locations and budgets, at least not together. In November 2009, a team of journalists from the Halifax Chronicle Herald, the Ottawa Citizen, and journalism students from Ottawa's Algonquin College conducted an analysis of different databases on the stimulus package, and then collated that with mapping software to see if they could pinpoint how many projects had been located in Conservative and opposition ridings, and what the correlation might be between unemployment rates and the financial size of stimulus projects.[16] The conclusion was somewhat ambivalent, but there did seem to be some anomalies.

Focusing just on the Building Canada infrastructure program, the journalists found that Conservative ridings had received almost half ($4.7 billion of a total of $8.5 billion) of total expenditures. At minimum, Conservative ridings received $3.3 million more on average per riding than did non-Conservative ridings. A complicating factor, however, was the large transit projects in major cities, many of which are in the ridings of opposition members. The single largest project under Building Canada, for example, was in the riding of a Liberal MP, but involved commitments to a metro line extension promised in 2007, well before the economic crisis. There were also some projects that, due to timing and other complications, had not been announced at the time that the study was done, and once rolled out might actually change the distribution of funding in a more even fashion.

Nonetheless, when we add the efforts around the web site, the careful staging and the sheer number of announcements, ham-handed attempts to make the stimulus look like the beneficence of either the government or individual Conservative MPs, and the visible if not overwhelming tilt in spending by ridings, it is clear (and unsurprising) that the government did try to leverage the stimulus package – something it had been reluctant to engage in – for political advantage. There were myriad and constant opportunities to engage with provincial governments, municipalities, local community groups, NGOs, trade unions, individual businesses and business associations, universities, hospitals – and all on the basis of good news. In short, there was lots of money to generate, keep and stimulate jobs, the essence of distributive politics and policy.

By March 2010, the narrative had to begin to shift towards some of the bad news – reminding Canadians that the stimulus had been temporary, and that while it would continue to operate through to mid-2011, it would be wound down and the hard work of deficit reduction would begin. This opened another interesting policy chapter – from reluctance to spend in November 2009, to its walk in the wild of deficits in 2009, the government now had to reduce expectations and design a budget that would pave the way to balance and reassert the government's reputation for fiscal firmness. That came initially with the budget of March 4, 2010.

THE THRONE SPEECH AND FEDERAL BUDGET, MARCH 2010

On December 30, 2009 the Prime Minister telephoned the Governor-General and asked her to prorogue Parliament until March 3, 2010.[17] The rationale was that the government needed to "recalibrate" its agenda, as it was switching from emergency measures to stave off recession to a longer term strategy of policies to build the economy. Prorogation suspends Parliament, and so requires a new session and a new SFT. In this instance, it also required a new budget (which traditionally in Canada is handed down in February or March). The government decided to have the SFT read on March 3, and table the budget the next day.

Like its much shorter 2009 version, this budget emphasized the continued importance of job creation, but also highlighted the successes of the Economic Action Plan, and the new need to concentrate on "fiscal balance." The government was to take this message globally in chairing the G8 and G20 summits.[18]

Our Government's first step toward restoring fiscal balance will be to wind down stimulus spending as economic activity rebounds. It will work with its provincial, territorial and municipal partners to ensure that measures under Canada's Economic Action Plan come to an end by March 31, 2011. And as chair of the G8 and G20 this year, our

Government will lead the call for a globally coordinated approach to the withdrawal of economic stimulus.

The second step toward restoring fiscal balance will be to restrain federal program spending overall, while protecting growth in transfers that directly benefit Canadians, such as pensions, health care and education.[19]

If this was the main theme of the SFT, it was accompanied by election style promises across a range of fields: innovation and building the economy; a host of family-friendly items; law-and-order provisions; measures to support retired servicemen; and some nationalistic provisions such as re-writing the national anthem.

The Budget was tabled the next day, and it was a behemoth running to over 400 pages, in part because it included a 5th report to Canadians on the Economic Action Plan.[20] An important point about the budget was that it was delivered at the beginning of the second year of the stimulus package that would continue until March 2011. So it was a somewhat unusual document – preaching austerity and frugality (in the face of a $54 billion deficit) while the money spigots were wide open and gushing for at least another twelve months, at which point they would be turned off. The budget highlights were:

· Continued stimulus spending through the next year of $25 billion, but terminated in March 2011.
· Close to $1 billion in new spending on a wide variety of projects, most connected to encouraging innovation in the economy (this was the smallest spending increase in a federal budget in over a decade).
· A reduction in the federal deficit by 50 per cent by 2011–12, and to $1.8 billion in 2014–15.
· No tax increases or cuts to transfers to provinces or to individuals.

How was this to be achieved? Almost half of the projected savings would come from ending stimulus spending, and almost half would come from freezing government department budgets for three years – again, the first time that this had been done in a decade. While public service wage increases in 2010–11 would be honoured, they would have to come from departmental operating budgets. The following two years would see freezes in pay, and possibly in hires, so that the overall public service might shrink through attrition. While military spending would continue to increase, it would grow at a slower rate (by only $.7 billion over two years on a budget base of $19 billion). Finally, all the budget numbers were based on economic growth projections (which are based on an average of 15 private sector forecasts) of 2.6 percent in 2010 and 3.2 percent in 2011, with continued stable growth thereafter, with an average of 2.1 percent from 2009 to 2014.

CONCLUSIONS

Canada has so far weathered the economic and financial crisis considerably better than its G7, G8 and G20 partners. According to the IMF, as a percentage of GDP, Canada's total government net debt is projected to grow by only 5.9 percent to 2014, the lowest of the G7 (Japan's will grow by 63.1 percent, the United Kingdom by 53.5 percent, and the United States by 42.6 percent). The United States' interest payments will increase by 170 percent in the next five years, while Canada's will stay stable. The current Canadian deficit is 3.5 percent of GDP, while the United States' is hovering at 11 percent.

The paradox, however, is that the government was reluctant to engage in stimulus spending, and only its December 2009 near-death experience converted it from a covert spender (it had increased expenditures consistently each year from 2006) to an extrovert. It focused on stimulus of the sort that would get shovels into the ground as quickly as possible. The policy context of recession should have created real liabilities for a conservative-minded government.

First, despite the massive efforts in various government statements and reports, there was some doubt that stimulus was actually working. The Fraser Institute, for example, released a report that stated: "The federal government has claimed credit for Canada's economic turnaround in the second half of 2009, but data from Statistics Canada tell a different story. The contributions from government spending and government investment to the improvement in GDP growth are negligible. Increases in private consumption and business investment were the main drivers of economic growth from the second to third quarter."[21] The Prime Minister responded sharply: "Economic theory and history is clear, governments must ... make sure [funds] are put to productive use in the economy to create jobs ... that is what we have been doing, that has been successful [and] every reputable international study says so."[22] Second, the opposition parties put up furious complaints about the politicization of the Economic Action Plan – the PMs flights, the photo-ops, even the cost of signs (some 8,500 had been sprinkled across the country).[23] None of this seemed to stick, however. Finally, the determination to end the program in March 2011 also generated predictable protests from the opposition, from municipalities,[24] and provincial premiers.[25] Ironically, these protests may have actually helped the Conservative government retain its fiscal credentials. In his Economic Update of October 2010, Finance Minister Flaherty indicated that the previous year's deficit was higher than had been predicted, but nonetheless projected a surplus of $2.6 billion in 2015–2016, in part due to the end of the stimulus package.[26]

The Tory saga shows some interesting dynamics in the management of recessions by conservative parties and how they can "walk in the wild" and return. A recession of this magnitude can actually create political opportunities that run against the instinctive grain of a conservative government like Canada's. We might term these the five rules of recession politics and public policy (the rules depend, however, on starting with a reasonably favourable position like Canada's):

1 Spending quickly to boost employment means "shovel-ready" programs that are visible and tangible to voters.
2 The emphasis on small, quick projects means a wide regional disbursement (even though there was a special and large package to deal with the automotive industry), and again, visibility and local impact.
3 These two factors provide an unparalleled platform for government advertising and publicity.
4 A conservative government can plausibly project disinclination, caution, and even grim strength in the face of spending challenges – they are reluctant virgins dragged to the altar of stimulus.
5 The return to fiscal discipline has two key virtues or reaffirmations. First, it is a reaffirmation for the political base of its party's true colours. Second, it is a reaffirmation of the evils of deficits, and plays strongly into a narrative of sin (limited deficit financing) and redemption (getting back to "fiscal balance").

We have emphasized the combination of policy and politics in this chapter – a well-managed policy initiative of economic stimulus and a well-calibrated campaign to milk political benefits from it and continue to position the Conservatives as the party of fiscal prudence. But, the recession lingers, and the stimulus has ended. Memories are short, and whatever political benefits the Tories might have reaped in 2009–2011 may easily be forgotten. They had a successful walk in the wild, but are not completely out of the woods yet.

APPENDIX: CANADA'S ECONOMIC ACTION PLAN

Geographical Distribution of Projects

Map 1: National

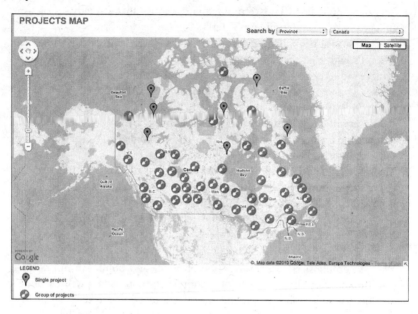

Map 2: Regional (Southeast Ontario)

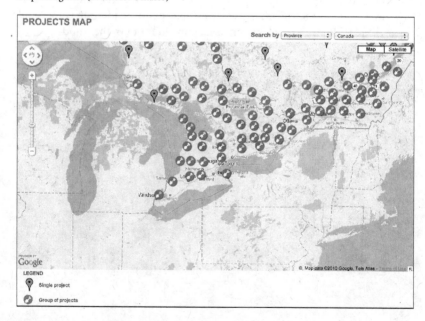

Map 3: Belleville Area (in Southeast Ontario)

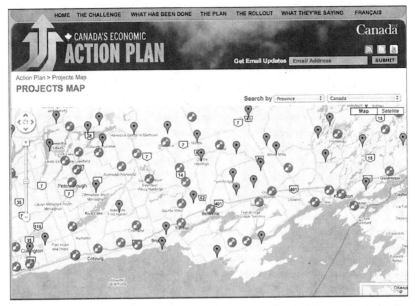

Source: Canada's Economic Action Plan. Retrieved on February 21, 2010 from http://www.actionplan.gc.ca/initiatives/eng/index.asp?mode=7

NOTES

1 Canada, Speech from the Throne, *Protecting Canada's Future*, November 19, 2008. Retrieved on February 12, 2010, from http://www.sft-ddt.gc.ca/includes/send_friend_eMail_print.asp?langFlg=e&URL=/eng/media.asp&id=1364

2 The following is taken from Canada, Economic and Fiscal Update, *Protecting Canada's Future*, November 27, 2008. Retrieved on February 15, 2010 from http://www.fin.gc.ca/ec2008/pdf/EconomicStatement2008_Eng.pdf

3 Canada, Speech from the Throne, January 26, 2009. Retrieved on February 12, 2010, from http://www.sft-ddt.gc.ca/grfx/docs/sft-ddt-2009_e.pdf

4 Christopher Waddell, "The auto industry bailout: industrial policy or job-saving social policy?," in G. Bruce Doern and Christopher Stoney, (eds), *How Ottawa Spends 2010–2011: Recession, Realignment, and the New Deficit Era* (Montreal and Kingston: McGill-Queen's University Press, 2010), 150–167.

5 *Canada's Economic Action Plan*, January 27, 2009. Retrieved on February 10, 2010 from http://www.actionplan.gc.ca/eng/index.asp

6 *Canada's Economic Action Plan*. Retrieved on February 21, 2010 from http://www.actionplan.gc.ca/eng/feature.asp?featureId=18

7 *Canada's Economic Action Plan: A First Report to Canadians*, March 10, 2009. Retrieved on February 21, 2010 from http://www.plandaction.gc.ca/eng/index.asp

8 *Canada's Economic Action Plan: A Second Report to Canadians*, June 11, 2009, p. 217. Retrieved on February 21, 2010 from http://www.plandaction.gc.ca/eng/index.asp

9 *Canada's Economic Action Plan: A Third Report to Canadians*, September 28, 2009, p. 16. Retrieved on February 21, 2010 from http://www.plandaction.gc.ca/eng/index. asp

10 *Canada's Economic Action Plan: A Fourth Report to Canadians*, December 2, 2009, p. 14. Retrieved on February 21, 2010 from http://www.plandaction.gc.ca/eng/index. asp

11 Auditor General of Canada, *2010 Fall Report: Chapter 1: Canada's Economic Action Plan*. Retrieved on November 5, 2010 from www.oag-bvg.gc.ca/internet/English/ parl_oag_201010_01_e_34284.html#hd3d

12 Philip Cross, "Year-End Review of 2009," *Canadian Economic Observer*, April 2010.

13 Canada, The Office of the Parliamentary Budget Officer, *Estimating Potential GDP and the Government's Structural Budget Balance*, January 13, 2010. Retrieved on February 21, 2010 from http://www2.parl.gc.ca/Sites/PBO-DPB/documents/ Potential_CABB_EN.pdf

14 "Harper a frequent flyer while promoting stimulus program; politics: Opposition MPS criticize travel as partisan activity," *Telegraph-Journal*, May 24, 2010.

15 CBC News, "Tory logos on federal cheques draw fire," October 14, 2009. Retrieved on February 23, 2010 from http://www.cbc.ca/canada/nova-scotia/story/2009/10/14/ ns-keddy-cheque.html The photo is in the public domain at www.chesterns.ca .

16 "Dangling dollars: Where the federal stimulus money went," *Ottawa Citizen*, November 7, 2009.

17 As we noted earlier, a prorogation suspends the legislature, purge pending legislation, but *not* dissolve it and require an election. It has been used by other Prime Ministers, but two in a row, both in December, seemed odd. Moreover, the Prime Minister traditionally visits the Governor-General personally for such matters, so a telephone call seemed an affront to regal dignity. The government had been under pressure in the House over the issue of how Canadian soldiers had handled Afghanistan detainees, and it was widely assumed that the prorogation was a ploy to shut down daily criticism in the House. There was a surprising discontent with the maneuver, but that was soon eclipsed by the Vancouver Olympics. Nonetheless, the prorogation required a new Speech from the Throne.

18 "Reduce debts, Harper tells G20 leaders; 50% or more by 2013 will seek commitments at meeting next week." *The Gazette*, June 19, 2010.

19 Canada, Speech from the Throne, *A Stronger Canada. A Stronger Economy. Now and for the Future*. March 3, 2010. Retrieved on March 5, 2010, from http://www.speech. gc.ca/grfx/docs/sft-ddt-2010_e.pdf

20 Canada, Department of Finance, *Canada's Economic Action Plan Year 2: Budget 2010: Leading the Way on Jobs and Growth*, March 4, 2010. Retrieved on March 5, 2010 from http://www.budget.gc.ca/2010/home-accueil-eng.html

21 Fraser Institute Alert, March 2010, p. 9.

22 "PM, Fraser Institute ramp up stimulus spat," CBC News, March 25, 2010. http://www. cbc.ca/canada/story/2010/03/25/harper-fraser-stimulus.html Retrieved on October 15, 2010.

23 "Signs of your tax dollars at work; 8,500 and counting. Ottawa orders civil service to document every sign promoting economic stimulus plan," The Toronto Star, September 7, 2010.

24 "Extend stimulus deal" The Ottawa Citizen, August 12, 2010.

25 "What happens if Ottawa turns off stimulus tap? Hundreds of municipalities from coast to coast could be saddled with millions in unforeseen costs," The Toronto Star, September 15, 2010.

26 "Ottawa signals slowdown in provincial payouts," Globe and Mail, October 13, 2010.

3 The Case for a Fundamental Governance Review

RUTH HUBBARD AND GILLES PAQUET

"To be meaningful and relevant, this imperative, restorative and
enhancing work of governance will need to draw from many minds,
hearts and sources, and from many ranks including the law, political
policy-makers, academics, multilateral institutions and managers."

John Dalla Costa

INTRODUCTION

The catastrophic public finance crisis in Ottawa in the early 1990s raised the
spectre of Canada having to transform its governance (effective coordination
when power, resources and information are widely distributed) because it was
showing signs of dysfunction. However, this quickly proved too daunting for
federal politicians and bureaucrats. The exercise – labelled Program Review
– instead morphed almost overnight into a public expenditures reduction
stricto sensu, without much effort at governance modification.

Putting the federal fiscal house in order (in large part on the backs of un-
suspecting provinces, with ripple effects down to municipalities) was much
easier than dealing with the governance challenges. Provincial and municipal activities were disrupted, and little was done to make governance of the
federal government or the country any more effective and innovative. In fact,
not even all the major cuts to federal government programs and operations
per se could be regarded as intelligent or defendable. Rather, being seen to
gore everyone's ox was defended as the only practical way to deal with the
precarious fiscal situation. Thus the old governing apparatus was left archi-
tecturally intact.

Consequently, as better economic times came, the refurbished margin of financial manoeuvrability generated by Program Review was merrily exploited
by successive governments. Defective structures had not been systematically
challenged, so when the next major fiscal crisis hit in the late 2000s, the governing apparatus could still be characterized as a black hole.[1]

Imposing the same shock treatment as was used in the 1990s is unlikely to work (given revived acrimonious federal-provincial relations, and the level of indebtedness of lower order governments). It would be politically immeasurably more costly to resolve fiscal problems by autocratically cutting transfers to provinces and savaging federal programs, while leaving the governing system untouched. The new setting calls for a new paradigm – the shift from big 'G' Government to small 'g' governance – not simply doing the same with less, but finding ways to do things differently, if at all, and doing it collaboratively.[2]

In the rest of the chapter, we argue that this would call for a governance review – a shift in the unit of analysis, a new approach, and a new strategy. We then illustrate in two case studies that opportunities exist for such an approach, and we indicate how it might work. Finally we indicate under which circumstances this approach is likely to be adopted, and what barriers would appear to exist to it being carried out successfully.

A NEW BASIC UNIT OF ANALYSIS

The exercise of the mid 1990s scrutinized federal government programs to see: (1) if they were still required for the public interest, (2) whether other parties (coalitions of parties) could deliver them more effectively than the federal government, and (3) finally (if programs were felt to be required and most effectively delivered by the federal government) whether they could be despatched more efficiently and economically than heretofore, and whether they were still affordable for the Canadian government.[3]

The immense advantage of this approach (imposing a single standard across the board, ensuring that no program would escape scrutiny, and using units corresponding to the Treasury Board's financial accounting template) was matched by corresponding drawbacks such as the focus on a relatively narrow unit of analysis, and avoidance of a serious scrutiny of the organizational dimension of the public sector. The priority was to make the exercise easily calculable: as a result, it allowed financial dimensions to trump all others. Unsurprisingly, the Treasury Board inherited what had been a Privy Council Office-initiated process.   .

Most unfortunate was the fact that, despite the convenience and expediency of this approach, it paid little attention to the collateral damage generated by program cuts on the issue domain within which the program was nested. In fact, the mid 1990s' experience inflicted much damage on many issue domains – damage that was momentous in many cases, even if not accurately measured by the bean counters.

The Program Review approach was also crippled by its exclusive focus on instrumental rationality (i.e. on the narrow pursuit of calculable program objectives), ignoring the broader ecological rationality (i.e. the extent to which programs cuts might be or might not be in keeping with broader contextual concerns and needs, and might cause more damage than good, even financially). By partitioning issue domains into programs, governance concerns were unwittingly evacuated, and attention was focused on managerial plumbing even where governance failures loomed large.

More importantly perhaps, the Program Review process was based on very static and stale notions of context and programs; they were analyzed as fixture of a socio-economy at a point in time, with little or no concern for the dynamics of either the context or the programs themselves, i.e. for the evolving nature of the learning socio-economy, and the learning underpinning the programs in a context that is no longer Newtonian.

These drawbacks generated a perversion of the evaluation function that thus failed to fully take into account: (1) the new evolution of the learning socio-economy as innovation-mediated and innovation-driven that transforms the context, (2) the new governance imperatives based on social learning that requires policies and programs to evolve as the context changes, and (3) the need to modify the substance and etiquette of evaluation in a context plagued with interactive complexity and 360-degree accountability which requires an *ex ante* rather than an *ex post* focus.[4]

The shift to a learning socio-economy does not entail a change of degree, but a change of kind, and governing in such a context cannot be discussed in Newtonian terms (assuming well-defined goals and a more or less placid environment, where the whole may be said to be the sum of the parts) in which the challenge could be regarded as designing control mechanisms likely to shift the organization toward certain desirable outcomes. Some problems are still tractable this way, but most are not.

In today's 'Quantum' world, a new way of thinking is required: there is no objective reality, the uncertainty principle looms large, events are at best probable, and the whole is a network of synergies and interactions among more or less self-organizing networks (i.e., the whole is quite different from the sum of the parts).[5] This has forced governance systems to become more modular, network-like, and to become integrated by informal moral contracts, building on a process of social learning through a critical multilogue among the stakeholders.[6]

In this new context, evaluation takes a new twist. It is not sufficient to operate *ex post*. What is needed is an *ex ante* appreciation of any action taken.[7] In this Quantum world, the fixation on goals and control mechanisms is unhelpful. What is required is anticipatory appraisal work, quick feedback, and ongoing negotiated efforts to make the evolving expectations with partners explicit. If the value-added by appraisal is to be substantial, much of the work has to be reframed to focus on intelligence and innovation, not simply on goals and control. The focus of evaluation must be on risk and exposure, and evaluation should not be regarded as a tool of compliance, but as a tool for change: improving the system's learning abilities, and attenuating its learning disabilities. And since social learning proceeds faster when the process is decentralized, delayered and participative, and operating through a network of units that are sensitive to local circumstances, this sort of evaluation often leads to calls for organizational redesign.[8]

THE NEW COSMOLOGY

The required new appreciative process must be designed to escape the limitations imposed by the focus on programs, on instrumental rationality and on strict financial imperatives alone, and to focus instead on issue domains as the unit of analysis, on ecological rationality,[9] and organization learning and redesign – in the search for guideposts for required actions.

This does not mean that short-run financial considerations of all sorts must be irresponsibly sideswiped. Rather, sudden savage financial cuts become only a subset of levers among many, and resolving financial problems is no longer framed as an issue tractable only by mechanical short-term cuts, but defined more wisely and in a longer run perspective as maybe tractable by governance repairs. Indeed, this is often the only reasonable way to proceed.

The new cosmology entails a new way of defining the problems: (1) by dealing directly with *issue domains* (not *programs*) to provide a broader platform (in time and space) for reframing, restructuring and retooling the portfolios; (2) by focusing first on issue domains where the federal government and the provinces are substantially involved in *de facto* composite jurisdictions, for these areas are those most likely to suffer from coordination failures; (3) by reducing waste through doing the governing work more effectively (recognizing the diversity of circumstances and premises).

Our main objective in this paper is to illustrate how such an approach might work. This will be done in three phases. First, we briefly raise a few general questions about the new dimensions of interest that need to be taken into account, as well as about the general coherence of the approach. Second, we examine two cases to show how one might be able to conduct such an analysis, and what general results one might expect, even on the basis of a very provisional query. Third, we draw, again very briefly, some lessons learned from these case studies about the promises and difficulties of a true governance review.

A FRAMEWORK

Outline of the Inquiry and Nature of the Issue Domains

This is not meant to be a template mechanically used in approaching issue domains with a view to proceeding with a governance review. As will become

Table 1
Basic questions for a fundamental governance review approach

Stage	Tasks
I	• Identification of the relevant issue domains
	• Empirical evidence of dysfunction at the issue domain level, & identification of the sources of the dysfunction
II	• Strategic focus of intervention
	• Major sources of leverage
	• Stages of intervention
III	• Short-term impact, long-term impact, and feedback expected
	• Risk exposure, and fail-safe mechanisms

obvious in the two examples we analyze in the next section (mental health, and the problems created by the Mohawk cross-border interface zone), there is much that must remain idiosyncratic in any governance approach to issue domains. Yet, some basic questions would appear to be fundamentally important in most cases when using this approach (as set out in the table above).

First, relevant issue domains are socio-technical systems that are most often the locus of overlapping jurisdictions. The interactions within the issue domain can be expected to be more densely integrated within the domain than the interactions with other segments of the social system. Moreover, to be fruitful, the inquiry must be guided by observable empirical evidence of dysfunction, along with some sense of its sources, and the extent to which different actors can be identified as potentially responsible for part of the dysfunction.

Second, it must be possible to identify a useful focus (or a small number of foci) of intervention for promoting more effective coordination and social learning, and the sort of tools that are likely to be of use.

Third, one must be able to map out the required stages of intervention, the likely impact of such action in the short and long run, the nature of the risk exposure, and the failsafe mechanisms likely to be necessary if one is to avoid disastrous derailing.

The Clark, *et al* study of higher education in Ontario[10] would qualify as an interesting and well-carried out study of an issue domain. It deals with (1) overlapping jurisdictions, and a loosely integrated socio-technical system that gives clear signs of dysfunction, and the sources of dysfunction are unearthed; (2) foci for intervention, levers, and stages of intervention are identified; and (3) expected short-term and long term impacts are gauged. The only elements that would appear to be absent from this otherwise impressive study are an evaluation of risk exposure if the proposed changes were initiated, and some suggestions of fail-safe mechanisms to mitigate the risks of failure.

Self-organizing Networks as a Way to Map Issue Domains

To help fix ideas, an issue domain could be defined operationally as a *de facto* self-organizing network.[11] To use the language of Walter J. M. Kickert et al, in most significant situations "public policy is made and implemented in networks of interdependent actors ... [i]n a network situation a single central authority, a hierarchical ordering and a single organizational goal do not exist" (2, 11). The consequence is that improving governance of these networks means "improving the conditions under which actors interact" (10).

In situations in which government decides to try to nudge the networks that provide the structure and performance of an issue domain in certain directions, steering efforts may take many forms. Two of the main ones are *negotiating* (with the government trying to act as a mediating agent of change) or *building new relations* (with the government taking on the job of bridge building and enriching the communication infrastructure in order to facilitate or enable more effective mediation and/or negotiation in the future).[12]

There are obviously many other ways for government to *instantiate* its *nudging function*.[13] We limit ourselves to these two avenues in making this preliminary case for the workability of a true governance review because they appear to be available and promising.

TWO CASES

The two cases sketched below are not fully developed blueprints of how to conduct a governance review, but simply an attempt to establish that the approach is both plausible and promising in the case of two particularly thorny problem areas.

The mental health portfolio and the Mohawk cross-border interface zone are used as illustrations because they create challenges that have not been adequately dealt with to date and promise immense financial benefits from governance re-arrangements in the medium term. Moreover, they offer a good illustration of each of the two main routes identified in the last section.

The Mental Health Initiative

The World Health Organization (WHO) has defined mental health as: "a state of well-being in which the individual realizes his or her own abilities, can cope with the normal stresses of life, can work productively and fruitfully, and is able to make a contribution to his or her community."[14]

In their 2001 report, "The Global Burden of Disease Study", the WHO, the World Bank and Harvard University estimated that 10.5% of the total burden of disease worldwide can be accounted for by mental illness, potentially increasing to almost 15% in 2020. The WHO also noted "the economic burden of mental illness is wide-ranging, long-lasting and huge – but remains largely underestimated."[15]

ISSUE DOMAIN, DYSFUNCTION, AND SOURCES OF DYSFUNCTION

Epidemiological information suggests that 3% of the population in Canada will experience a serious mental illness and another 17% will experience mild to moderate mental illness.[16] Virtually all Canadians will be touched directly or indirectly. It is certainly an issue domain of national interest.

In 1998, the economic burden of mental illnesses in Canada was conservatively estimated at $6.3B in direct costs (i.e., health care) and $8.1B in indirect costs (lost productivity, of which $6B is related to short-term disability).[17] In 1990, mental illness accounted for 4.9% of the overall direct and indirect cost of disease in Canada, while in terms of direct costs alone, mental illness ranked second only to cardio-vascular disease.[18]

Nearly fifty years ago, the Canadian Mental Health Association stated: "(i)n no other field, except perhaps leprosy, has there been as much confusion, misdirection and discrimination against the patient, as in mental illness."[19] The Standing Senate Committee on Social Affairs, Science and Technology (the Kirby Committee) reported hearing thousands of personal stories demonstrating the applicability of those remarks to the current situation. Moreover, the Kirby Committee reported in 2006 that "despite recent actions by several provincial governments [that] have begun to focus a long-overdue spotlight on mental health, it remains that the whole complex, pervasive problem of mental illness and addiction in Canadian society continues to be neglected."[20]

It also noted that no single level of government has the resources of all sorts necessary for dealing with the full range of mental health issues on its own; that mental health problems and substance abuse disorders are responsible for a large proportion of all diminished workplace productivity, absenteeism and disability in workplaces of all sectors (costing Canadian companies in the order of $18B a year recently); and that the proportion of workplace disability due to mental illness and substance abuse is increasing more rapidly than those relating to other illnesses.[21]

In its first report in late 2004, the Kirby Committee recognized "that the mental health and addiction system is not, in fact, a real system but rather a complex array of services delivered through federal, provincial and municipal jurisdictions and private providers, including initiatives by individuals with mental illness/addictions themselves. This system is a mix of acute care services in general hospitals, specialized services for specific disorders or populations, outpatient community clinics, community-based services providing psychosocial supports (housing, employment, education and crisis intervention) and private counseling, all of varying capacity, often operating in silos, and all-too-frequently disconnected from the health care system."[22]

The result is that, "in most jurisdictions, a highly fragmented (non) system has become increasingly difficult to navigate by both individuals with mental illness, and addiction and service providers. Compounding this fragmentation is ... [the fact] that ... data information systems are not yet adequately linked across the sectors concerned (e.g. health, housing, education, family benefits, work environment etc.)."[23]

Five issues were identified by the Kirby Committee as contributing importantly to the dysfunction of the mental health non-system: (1) *governance* (poor coordination); (2) chaotic service delivery systems; (3) insufficient research; (4) no straightforward way to exchange best practices and research syntheses across the country about the organization and the delivery of mental health prevention, treatment, rehabilitation and support service for knowledge producers and users; and (5) stigma and discrimination.

The federal government has an important direct role to play (e.g., for Status Indians, veterans, and federal public servants). Notwithstanding the jurisdictional disputes, it also has a long-standing interest (including financial) in health care as part of its responsibility for the long-term well being of Canadians through promoting productivity and economic growth.

STRATEGY IN MANY STAGES

The Kirby Committee revealed the existence and mapped a *de facto* not very well functioning self-organizing network – a forum where all interested parties could contribute to problem definition. By conducting its business in an open-ended way, the Kirby Committee succeeded in allowing the necessary common ground for public action to emerge while taking fully into account the inherent complexity, variety and flexibility required in a broad and sweeping strategy.

The Committee put forward 117 recommendations in all, directed at all levels of government, as well as at providers of mental health services and support. It made recommendations on issues falling outside federal jurisdiction, arguing that "no effective, systematic approach to the delivery of mental health and addiction services could have been made otherwise."[24]

Despite all the issues identified as the source of the mental health system dysfunction, improving governance was the central concern. The Kirby Committee also adopted a long-term view, and one that did not fall prey to the propensity to centralize in the name of supposedly necessary national (the code word for 'federal') strategies. What was felt necessary was better coordination, and, at a minimum, a facilitating or enabling function (at least in a transition period) to ensure a needed focus on mental health issues.

The Committee argued forcefully for the creation of the Canadian Mental Health Commission (CMHC), a recommendation supported by almost all the stakeholders and all provincial and territorial governments except Quebec. Even the opposition health critic in Ottawa gave support, and there was "universal enthusiasm [for its creation from] …those concerned with mental health in Canada."[25]

The subsequent creation of the commission and its funding for a ten-year transition period entailed:

i)   an independent not-for-profit organization at arm's length from governments and all existing mental health stakeholders (with a central focus on those living with mental illness and their families; building on complementing initiatives already underway; establishing cross-sectoral partnerships; emphasizing evidence-based policies and service delivery methods; calling for rigorous evaluation, assessment of its own activities, and regular reporting);

ii) a clear statement of its mission (e.g., facilitator, enabler and supporter; catalyst for reform of policies and improvements in service delivery; source of information for all, and educator of Canadians);

iii) a board that was arm's length from governments and interest groups, and well balanced advisory committees.[26]

In November 2009, the Commission released a framework strategy document entitled *Toward Recovery and Well-Being* drawing on the experience and thinking of thousands of people.[27] Since then, it has begun work at public engagement through round tables, online consultations on key topics, and other engagement initiatives with a view to translating the framework into a strategic plan aimed at completion by the end of 2012.

IMPACTS, RISKS, AND FAIL-SAFE MECHANISMS

The central question is: what can be done to deal as effectively as possible with the *cost containment* of government spending, and the *cost-effectiveness* of the efforts deployed?

The Kirby Committee tackled the question of how to deal relatively effectively and efficiently with the transition period to a more cost-effective public investment in mental health by dealing, *inter alia*, with two of the costliest items: (1) shifting those individuals currently treated as in-patients in hospitals who would do better in community-based care; and (2) bringing the percentage of those without affordable housing down to match general levels (something the Committee became convinced was essential).[28]

Their estimate of the transition cost was $2.4B over ten years, but savings as a result of the transition can be estimated from $.5B up to $2B *annually* beginning after the transition period,[29] making the benefit/cost ratio acceptable.

The transition strategy is not without risks. The first is that the actual transition costs may rise uncontrollably, governments being pressed to increase expenditures. The second is that the mega-community might not (or will not) shake off its sense of 'entitlement', and might also apply immense pressure for even greater government investment in this issue domain. These pressures are likely to be strong in a context where health care *in toto* is already taking quite a share of public spending.

In its recent economic survey of Canada, the OECD warned that "(i)n the longer run the soundness of Canada's finances will likely be largely determined by the decisions taken regarding the health care system ... [which] offers high-quality services to all residents ... at relatively high cost. ... With health care already accounting for around half of total provincial primary spending, meeting the fiscal and demographic challenges will require that the growth of public spending be reduced from an annual rate of about 8% seen over the last decade, toward the trend rate of growth of nominal income in coming years (estimated to be less than 4% per year), the only alternative being to squeeze other public spending or to raise taxes or user charges" (italics removed).[30]

This should act as a serious forewarning and encourage the country to tackle the governance of health care as a priority, and as well, given the existing culture of entitlements, to put in place strict measures of cost containment both for the transition period and in the steady state that will follow. There needs to be a publicly-announced strict ceiling (i) on the state share of health costs (and perhaps of the federal portion of that share), (ii) on the total costs of the transition phase in the refurbishment of the mental health regime, and (iii) on mental health costs as a proportion of health care costs in steady state (e.g. the 6.1% share of total government spending on health care of $91.4B that was estimated by the Institute for Health Economics to have been in place in 2003–04).[31]

With respect to pressure for greater government investment in mental health after the transition period, the up to $2B of anticipated annual savings (accruing to provinces/territories) ought to be clearly identified in the appropriate fiscal frameworks to show citizens that, indeed, savings have been possible, rather than simply allowing them to disappear unaccounted for in an ever expanding health care expenditure vortex.

The Mohawk Cross-Border Interface Zone

What we call the Mohawk cross-border interface zone connotes a complex nexus of places and peoples: geography (governments at three levels in two countries), First Nations (FN) – especially the Mohawk Nation (MN), the Haudenosaunee (the Six Nations Iroquois Confederacy (SNC), of which the Mohawk Nation is a member), and the groups involved directly or indirectly with them.

The Mohawk Nation itself connotes several communities in four geographic areas of Ontario, Quebec, and upstate New York.[32] Of these, the main areas of interest for the purposes of this case center on the Six Nations of the Grand River (which is home to members of all six Iroquois nations and is comprised of two reserves) to the west, the Kahnawake to the east, as well as the Bay of Quinte (Tyendinaga) east of Belleville, and the Akwesasne /St Regis in the middle, spanning the Canada-United States (as well as Ontario-Quebec) border. In particular, the 14 mile stretch of the St Lawrence River poses particularly difficult challenges in terms of government enforcement of border security and oversight of the tobacco trade. Indeed, the tobacco issue may serve as a most useful exemplar of the problems posed in and by this zone.

ISSUE DOMAIN, DYSFUNCTION, AND SOURCES OF DYSFUNCTION

As the main cause of preventable illness, disability and death in Canada, tobacco and tobacco products are highly controlled by governments (e.g. federal control of the manufacture, sale, labeling and promotion, and varying provincial regulation of sale and promotion of the industry). It is currently estimated that nearly 18% of people 15 and older in Canada smoke (at least two or three times higher for Aboriginal People). The tobacco industry is also an important source of federal/provincial tax revenue (almost $7B (split 40:60 between orders of government) in 2007–2008.[33] The industry in Canada still involves 100+ licensed growers and tens of thousands of small convenience stores, gas stations, etc., who sell these products, some of which get as much as 40% of their sales from them.

Unfortunately however, despite having what the World Health Organization asserts is one of the best regulatory regimes for tobacco control,[34] recent data show that, while smoking has declined only slightly in Canada between 2002 and 2008, the estimated percentage of contraband sales appears to have grown from 10% to 31% during the same time period.[35]

As of July 1, 2010, the price of a carton of cigarettes (including taxes) was between $70 and $106 (depending on the provincial/territorial tax rate), while the same quantity of illegal cigarettes could be bought for as little as $6.[36]

In 2008 it was estimated that the cost in lost government revenues was $1.6B.[37] Moreover, contraband has been linked to drug trafficking and terrorism involving (directly or indirectly) groups such as the Hells Angels, the Russian mafia and Hezbollah.[38] Despite the seemingly dramatic increase in contraband and its costs for the State, a Health Canada survey has pointed out that: "part of the public doesn't believe it is illegal to buy these cigarettes."[39]

The Cornwall, Ontario area has been called "ground zero" of the contraband trade. The RCMP has reported that the border security problem on the St Lawrence River in the Cornwall-Akwesasne/St Regis area "has traditionally been used to smuggle contraband to and from Canada due to its geographic and political complexity … from Canada into the US [mainly] marijuana, ecstasy and illegal migrants while weapons, cocaine and contraband cigarettes are moved from the US into Canada. This area continues to be exploited by organized crime groups from large centres such as Montreal, Ottawa, and Toronto."[40] Not unreasonably, however, cracking down on tobacco smuggling is a lower priority for the FN policing at Akwesasne and St Regis than drugs, money laundering, and human trafficking.

The Fraser Institute recently noted that, fed by unlawful manufacture of cigarettes in the United States on aboriginal territories that border Canada (primarily at Askwesasne), tobacco products designated for sale on FN reserves that are diverted to the black market are among the primary sources of contraband tobacco.[41]

The FN argue that much of this activity is not really illegal, because "(s)ome tobacco routes [e.g., within the Mohawk Nation territory] have existed for centuries ... [so that] selling tax-exempt cigarettes [on reserves to all customers, First Nations and not] is not perceived as a criminal activity, but rather as a form of economic development ...[and in fact] their [FN] community is being unfairly criminalized by law enforcement and government."[42]

Importantly, the aboriginal tobacco industry of late 2010 appears to have become a force unto itself.[43] There are said to be nearly 200 'smoke shacks' in the communities of the Mohawk Nation and several clandestine factories. This underscores reports that "[a] growing number of plants ... are firmly ensconced on some Canadian reserves where risky, international smuggling is not necessary to get the finished goods to market. That includes the Canadian side of Akwesasne and Tyendinaga ... the RCMP say."[44]

Criminal activity is not confined to reserves; it is reported that contraband cigarettes can be bought under the counter from urban retailers and (through dealers) in coffee shops and schoolyards.[45] The geographic and political complexities related to the tobacco industry in the Mohawk zone create a major challenge.

STRATEGY IN MANY STAGES

In the Mohawk zone case (as opposed to the mental health case), what is involved is not simply initiating negotiations (with government behaving as a party like the others and acting as an agent of change), but rather government having to take on the job of enriching the communication infrastructure in order to make possible effective mediation and negotiation.

The central issue is access by the Mohawk Nation to revenue generation in a particularly complex and challenging context. On the one hand, FN have a stake in reducing on-reserve criminal activity and in controlling the use of tobacco products by their members, while on the other hand they see the dominium in this issue domain as intimately connected to their sovereignty and their right to govern themselves, as well as being one of the very few sources of economic activity and revenue in parts of their territory.

As Jerry Montour, Chief Executive of Grand River Enterprises, testified to the Standing Committee on Public Safety and National Security,[46] "the only opportunities that present good employment on our First Nation territories right now are tobacco-related."

It is clear that, in some Mohawk communities, legal activities generate significant annual revenue (e.g., Six Nations of the Grand River, through the fourth-largest licensed cigarette manufacturer in Canada – Grand River Enterprise – has ploughed an estimated $1M back into economic development for the reserve, and sent $500M to government) and Kahnawake's Morris Mohawk Gaming Group brings in a large (unknown) amount of annual revenue, and may or may not plough a portion back into the community. Nevertheless, young people are said to be able to "earn $2000 a week acting as a runner [for illicit tobacco]... [while being] untouchable, because they are under eighteen."[47]

This suggests that any possibility of effective mediation and negotiation with these First Nations needs to be rooted in first establishing *a basis for partnership* with Mohawk governments, something that, in testimony to the Standing Committee on Public Safety and National Security, Mr. Mike Mitchell, former Grand Chief of the Mohawk Council of Akwesasne, described as "something [that] is going to be enacted that will, in a safe way, guarantee the safety of your people and ours ... (and) our ability to create our own laws and allow us to apply them."[48]

What seems to be required is a two-stage strategy following the lead of the successful approach used between the government of Quebec and the Mohawk at Kahnawake in mid 2009 to deal, *inter alia*, with "tobacco, petroleum and alcohol products", as well as "fiscal matters related to consumer goods and services" (presumably including internet gaming).[49]

The genesis of such a document would pose a daunting task: governments involved would necessarily include the government of New York State (and possibly the federal government of the US) as well as those of Canada, Ontario and Quebec, while the Mohawk Nation's interests would require, at a minimum, representatives from the Mohawk Nation Council of Chiefs (MNCC) or the Haudenosaunee Grand Council of Chiefs (HGCC) – part of their historic (on-going) governance regime.

The first stage might include the establishment of a small 'wise persons' group who would act as enabler, facilitator and supporter of the development of a covenant of the most general sort (as exemplified by the Quebec document provided as an appendix to this paper). The aim would be to create, cooperatively, a statement of mutual respect and understanding, including symbolic measures, and an expression of willingness to develop financial and fiscal arrangements providing for long-term economic stability, as well as a framework agreement to establish the protocol to arrive at sectoral arrangements that include fiscal matters related to tobacco and tobacco products.

The second stage would involve the negotiation *per se*. A number of principles would likely shape the intentions of the Canadian and US governments in subsequent negotiations: (i) providing practical sovereignty with respect to tobacco control (by transferring significant authority and decision-making to the MNCC/HGC with respect to tobacco control on MN territory); (ii) investing significant government resources in efforts aimed at enabling, inciting and supporting good governance for the MN in the area of tobacco control; (iii) foreseeing significant revenue sharing of proceeds from improved tobacco control accruing to Mohawk nations and others living in Mohawk territory, and governments; and (iv) not penalizing the MN unduly (financially) for the revenue earned with any new arrangement in basic areas currently funded by Canadian governments, such as health and education.

The financial costs of this approach have been estimated at federal expenditure of about $19M over 3 years for the operation of the new governance mechanism, and an expenditure of $1M in year 4 for the evaluation of results. The outcome is estimated to be a reduction of fiscal leakage by 40% (a combination of higher prices and better control), yielding an estimated minimum of $1B annually. Of this, $500M would be sent to governments and the remainder would be kept by the HGC/MNCC to be distributed as it sees fit, with agreed appropriate accountability.[50] The government expenditures could be recovered by the end of year 2.

IMPACTS, RISKS, AND FAIL-SAFE MECHANISMS

This issue domain remains troublesome for reasons of its own: "[t]he easy availability of cheap contraband tobacco ... undermines the two primary objectives of federal and provincial excise taxes on tobacco: reducing smoking prevalence and generating government revenue."[51] The question again is how to deal as effectively as possible with the *cost containment* (in this case, of government losses, and pleas for government funding flowing from its inability to enforce its own laws), as well as the *cost-effectiveness* of continuing to rely primarily on the coercive power of government when "the underlying problem ... [is to] somehow reconcile Aboriginal territorial autonomy and treaty rights with Canadian law."[52]

At the same time, there seems to be willingness on the part of key elements of the Mohawk Nation leadership to accept Canadian sovereignty and, by extension, the need to begin to tackle difficulties on MN territory caused by external lawless drivers (i.e. the heads of organized crime).

There are, however, those who do not agree, and herein lies the main risk. The Mohawk Warrior Society poses the highest risks. Its members are responsible for the national defence and security in the territory of Kahnawake, but their Facebook site now states that they "defend the rights and interests of all native peoples of Canada, in solidarity with liberation and decolonization movements around the world."[53] Its members are described as having emerged in the early 1970's as highly idealistic as well as aiming at safeguarding traditional values and upholding native claims to sovereignty. By 1996, however, the Mackenzie Institute noted that they had "come a long way from the inspired militants of 1973 ... the true legacy of the Mohawk Warriors' Society [is the Manitoba Warriors and the Indian Posse of Manitoba]: armed teenage drug dealers who believe that they need respect neither Canadian laws, the traditional authorities of the First Nations, nor the peaceful intentions of their own people." [54] It would not be surprising if this has become the view of at least some members of the Warrior Society itself.

The fail-safe mechanism lies in the conditions of control that the Mohawk Nation uses to circumscribe activities related to its own police. There is some hope that this approach might offer sufficient reassurance about a diminished threat to the national defence of the Mohawk Nation that such control would be reasonably effective, both in terms of cross-border traffic in contraband tobacco, as well as in reducing the prevalence of smoking tobacco products emanating from it.

LESSONS LEARNED

Our intent is not to derive a protocol for conducting governance review from these two cases. Rather, it is to draw attention to some of the promises and difficulties of a true governance review.

On the positive side, it is clear that the shift of focus from short-term cost cutting to the streamlining of the governance regime (with a view to reducing costs permanently in the medium and longer run) is bound to free the evaluation process of some of its least desirable fixtures in the case of issue domains that are ready for negotiation while it is likely to make some progress possible in issue domains where some preliminary work on the governance front would appear absolutely necessary before one can proceed to any form of meaningful negotiation – domains where attempts at proceeding before having built the required bridging capital may be not only entirely useless but quite toxic.

Broadening the perspectives to take into account a longer time horizon and a broader systemic view (issue domain rather than program) modifies the evaluation necessary to arrive at wise decisions with the whole system – something that is crucial for the governance of issue domains comprised of self-organized networks that must be nudged along (catalyzing the underpinning social learning), rather than through edicts.

The shift from instrumental to ecological rationality imparts a revolutionary twist to the evaluation process: this broader perspective contributes to freeing the approach from myopia, tunnel vision, and the tyranny of what Edmund Husserl called "misguided rationalism."[55] This shift – from a perspective on policy that is mired in target-shooting fantasies (that grossly overestimate our agency in dealing with always evolving, ill-structured problems) toward a perspective that emphasizes intelligence, innovation and experimentalism – should allow policy to escape from unhelpful strictures.

Finally, the governance perspective forces attention on the need to emphasize the process of organizational redesign that is necessary if a more effective, efficient and economical mode is to be found. This is done not by focusing exclusively on process, but by focusing on the way to intervene subtly to ensure that the self-organized network will improve its learning abilities and attenuate its learning disabilities through efforts to make it more delayered, participative, and sensitive to local circumstances.[56] This seemingly indirect and roundabout way of proceeding, far from being ineffective, is likely to generate more substantial and sustainable financial savings in the longer run.

However, dealing with issue domains in parallel without imposing a simplistic cost-cutting template will not necessarily be easy. The cumulative impact of myopia, tunnel-vision, and instrumental rationality (together with the presumption that the Jacobine State is the sole avenue for the emergence of any meaningful expression of the public interest) has generated a phenomenal dynamic conservatism.[57] This means that, even though we know that our present ways are ineffective, the emotional cost of scrapping much of our unhelpful accumulated intellectual capital is very high.

There is still an immense resistance to accepting the challenges of small g governance. Governance is fundamentally subversive: it reveals the pathologies of existing governing arrangements that have been built on corporatist interests, and does not serve the citizenry well. Only the pending crisis in the governing of health care may bring our democracies to their senses. For, as the OECD reminded Canada recently, the current ways of governing our health care regime can only lead to its implosion.

CONCLUSIONS

The case for a true governance review is strong, and the powers of dynamic conservatism and ineptitude are not infinite. Our two illustrations have shown the merit of tackling issue domains in the way we suggest. The fact that there also seems to be no readily available alternative approach that appears to be technically feasible, socially acceptable, implementable, and not too politically destabilizing – and that there is no hope that these problems will simply fix themselves – would appear to strengthen the case for a true governance review.

Our cases show that a more participative and focused approach to issue domains is likely to generate reforms at the governance level that promise more than short term financial savings. The 'round-about' nature of this approach does not ignore the need to be more cost effective and cost containing, but it suggests that these objectives may be secured more intelligently by taking a longer-term perspective.

The major hurdles to action on this front are not ignorance about what needs to be done but mental prisons that prevent action from being taken.

NOTES

1 Ruth Hubbard and Gilles Paquet, 2010. *The Black Hole of Public Administration.* Ottawa: The University of Ottawa Press.
2 Ibid. 25.
3 Gilles Paquet, Robert Shepherd, 1996. "The Program Review Process: A Deconstruction," in Gene Swimmer (ed) *How Ottawa Spends, 1996–97: Life Under the Knife.* Ottawa: Carleton University Press, 39–72.
4 Gilles Paquet, 1999. "Auditing in a Learning Environment," Optimum 29 (1): 37–44.
5 Thomas L. Becker, 1991. *Quantum Politics.* New York: Praeger.
6 Gilles Paquet, 1999. *Governance through Social Learning.* Ottawa: The University of Ottawa Press.
7 Charles F. Sabel, 2001. A Quiet Revolution of Democratic Governance: Towards Democratic Experimentalism" in *Governance in the 21st Century.* Paris: OECD, 121–148.
8 Gilles Paquet, 1999. *Governance Through Social Learning.* Ottawa: University of Ottawa Press.
9 Hubbard and Paquet, *The Black Hole*, 461; Gerd Gigerenzer 2001, "The Adaptive Toolbox" in G. Gigerenzer & R. Selten (eds) *Bounded Rationality: The Adaptive Toolbox.* Cambridge: The MIT Press, 37–50.
10 Ian D. Clark et al., 2009. *Academic Transformation: The Forces Reshaping Higher Education in Ontario.* Montreal & Kingston: McGill-Queen's University Press.
11 Walter J. M. Kickert et al (eds), 1997. *Managing Complex Networks: Strategies for the Public Sector.* London: Sage Publications.
12 Walter J. M. Kickert and Joop F. M. Koppenjan, 1997. "Public Management and Network Management: An Overview," in *Managing Complex Networks: Strategies by the Public Sector.* Walter J. M. Kickert et al (eds). London: Sage Publications London, 35–61.
13 Richard H. Thaler, Cass R. Sunstein, 2008. Nudge. New Haven: Yale University Press.
14 World Health Organization, November 2001. "Mental Health: strengthening mental health promotion." Fact Sheet No. 229. http://www.who.int/mediacentre/factsheets/fs220/en/, quoted in the Final Report of the Standing Senate Committee on Social Affairs, Science and Technology, "Out of the Shadows at Last: Transforming Mental Health, Mental Illness and Addiction Services in Canada," Ottawa, the Senate, 2006; Kirby Report, 2006: 412.
15 World Health Organization, the World Bank, and Harvard University (November 2001) "The Global Burden of Disease Study" and the World Health Organization, (2001). "Mental Health: New Understanding, New Hope," are both quoted in the Interim Report of the Standing Senate Committee on Social Affairs, Science And Technology, "Mental Health, Mental Illness and Addiction: Overview of Policies and programs in Canada." Ottawa, the Senate, 2004; Kirby Report, 2004: 102
16 Kirby Report, 2006, 50.

17 Kirby Report, 2004, 101.

18 Ibid.

19 Quoted in Kirby Report, 2006, xvii.

20 Kirby Report, 2006, 435.

21 Kirby Report, 2006, §16.2.1, 435–436.

22 Kirby Report, 2004, 153.

23 Ibid.

24 Kirby Report, 2006, 431.

25 Kirby Report, 2006, 432.

26 Kirby Report, 2006, 437–442.

27 Mental Health Commission of Canada, 2009 Toward Recovery and Well-being: A Framework for a Mental Health Strategy for Canada available at http://www.mental healthcommission.ca/SiteCollectionDocuments/boarddocs/15507_MHCC_EN_ final.pdf. Accessed October 5, 2010.

28 The Committee pointed out that "(s)omewhere between 30% and 40% of homeless people have mental health problems" (: 118) and heard from witnesses that "housing is protection from illness ... from the vagaries of mental illness, from the voices, from the fears ... [and that] supported housing ... is ... cost-effective ... [and] works" (: 119–120), Kirby Report, 2006: § 5.6.1, 118–123.

29 The Institute of Health Economics and the Alberta Health Services Report "How Much Should be Spend on Mental Health?" (September 2008) provides a rough estimate (which they say is consistent with the Kirby Report) and assumes that service cost in the hospital (old) and community (new) modes of care are the same. Overall savings would be $.5B annually after a 5 year transition. The source of the funds for the new (community) care however would not necessarily be part of publicly funded health care costs. As a result, the savings could be estimated to be up to 20% (the size of the shift of the treated population) of the base cost of the Report's $10B in the last year of the transition (including population growth): §5.5 pp 44–47. http://www.ihe.ca/documents/ Spending%20on%20Mental%20Health%20Final.pdf accessed October 5, 2010.

30 OECD, 2010, 9. In fact, a recent OECD Report points out that there is ample scope for efficiency savings and quality improvements (OECD 2010: 10). OECD "OECD Economic Surveys: Canada, September 2010: overview" (Economic and Development Review Committee of the OECD). http://www.oecd.org/dataoecd/ 23/38/45950025.pdf.

31 The Institute of Health Economics and the Alberta Health Services Report "How Much Should be Spend on Mental Health?" (September 2008) notes that public spending on mental health in 2003–2004 was 6.1% while the European benchmark for a minimum optimal allocation is 5%: 25.

32 Included are 6 Canadian FN reserves under the Indian Act (Kanesatake, Kahnawake, Akwesasne, Six Nations of Grand River (two reserves), Tyendinaga, and Wahta Mohawk) and 3 in the US (Ganienkeh, Kanatsiohareke, and St. Regis – which borders Akwesasne)).

33 $6.969B excluding sales taxes according to public accounts or budgets as reported by
    Physicians for a Smoke-Free Canada in December 2008 http://www.smoke-free.ca/
    factsheets/pdf/totaltax.pdf accessed 17/9/2010.

34 (WHO 2005) "Regulation of Tobacco Products: Canada Report," WHO Study Group
    on Tobacco Regulation, Geneva Switzerland http://www.escholarship.org/uc/
    item/4zd2n223?display=all

35 (Smoke-Free 2010) "Estimating the volume of contraband sales of tobacco in Canada
    – updated April 2010," research paper of Physicians for a Smoke-Free Canada
    Ottawa, Canada http://www.smoke-free.ca/pdf_1/2010/Estimating%20the%20
    volume%20of%20Contraband%20Sales%20of%20Tobacco%20in%20Canada-2009.
    pdf accessed 17/9/2010.

36 National Post Editorial Board: "An economic cancer," September 17, 2010.

37 National Post "Ottawa Need U.S. help to fight illegal tobacco," John Ivison, May,
    2008.

38 National Post Editorial Board: "An economic cancer," September 17, 2010).

39 François Damphousse, Director Quebec Office of the Non-smokers' Rights
    Association May 14, 2008 testimony to the Standing Committee on Public Safety and
    National Security.

40 RCMP 2007 "Federal Tobacco Control Strategy (FTCS): The Illicit Tobacco Market in
    Canada January – December 2006." 2010. http://www.rcmp-grc.gc.ca/pubs/
    tobac-tabac/ftcs-sflt-eng.pdf accessed 18/9/2010.

41 Natchum Gabler, and Diane Katz, "Contraband Tobacco in Canada: Tax Policies and
    Black Market Incentives," Studies in Risk and Regulation, Fraser Institute. http://
    www.fraserinstitute.org/uploadedFiles/fraser-ca/Content/research-news/
    research/publications/contraband-tobacco-in-canada(1).pdf.

42 J. Sweeting, et al. 2009. "Anti-Contraband Policy Measures: Evidence for Better
    Practice – Summary Report." Toronto, ON: The Ontario Tobacco Research Unit,
    Special Report Series. June. 65 p (35–36) (http://www.otru.org/pdf/special/s
    pecial_anti_contraband_measures_summary.pdf accessed 19/9/2010.

43 National Post "Native-made cigarettes bring wealth and disapproval to reserves,"
    Tom Blackwell September 17, 2010.

44 Ibid.

45 National Post Editorial Board, "An economic cancer," September 17, 2010.

46 Testimony to the Standing Committee on Public Safety and National Security,
    May 12, 2008.

47 Michel Gadbois, SVP Canadian Convenience Store Association, testifying to the
    Standing Committee on Public Safety and National Security, May 14, 2008.

48 Testimony to the Standing Committee on Public Safety and National Security, June 4,
    2008.

49 "Statement of understanding and mutual respect" signed June 10, 2009 and
    "Framework Agreement between Québec and the Mohawks of Kahnawake" signed
    July 16, 2009 http://www.autochtones.gouv.qc.ca/relations_autochtones/ententes/
    mohawks/ententes_mohawks_en.htm accessed 18/9/2010.

50   The independent public policy think tank, The Frontier Centre for Public Policy publishes a voluntary "Aboriginal Governance Index" annually that provides a very good example of what is possible and might stimulate useful ideas.

51   Gabler and Katz, "Contraband Tobacco," 1.

52   Gabler and Katz, Ibid., 37.

53   See for example, http://www.facebook.com/pages/Mohawk-Warrior-Society/35272274775#!/pages/Mohawk-Warrior-Society/35272274775?v=info accessed September 20, 2010.

54   "The Long Fall of the Mohawk Warriors" http://www.mackenzieinstitute.com/1996/1996_06_Military_Mohawks.html accessed 20 September 2010.

55   Gilles Paquet, 2009. *Crippling Epistemologies and Governance Failures*. Ottawa: The University of Ottawa Press, Ch. 1.

56   Gilles Paquet, 2008. *Gouvernance: mode d'emploi*. Montréal: Liber.

57   Donald A. Schön, 1971. Beyond the Stable State. New York: Norton.

Statement of understanding and mutual respect

Kahnawake and Québec, recognizing the importance of cooperative endeavours and wishing to maintain a constructive relationship on the basis of their respective principles and concepts found in the Two Row Wampum and in Government Policies on Aboriginal matters and in particular in the National Assembly Resolution of March 20th, 1985, reaffirm their commitment to the Statement of Understanding and Mutual Respect which they have signed on the 15th day of October 1998. They therefore renew their agreement to the following declaration of reciprocal political commitment.

Kahnawake and Québec, as represented by the undersigned, favor the route of discussion and negotiation for concluding and signing agreements that will be negotiated in various fields of jurisdiction.

With a strong sense of their respective culture, language, custom, laws and traditions, Kahnawake and Québec agree to negotiate with mutual respect for their national identities and each other's history and territorial occupation.

Kahnawake and Québec further agree to participate as partners in various Kahnawake economic development ventures. Québec also agrees to develop financial and fiscal arrangements that would provide for Kahnawake's long term economic stability.

To accelerate the negotiation process and bring it to a rapid conclusion, Québec and Kahnawake each have already appointed negotiators and concluded a framework agreement with a view to the rapid conclusion of sectoral agreements in the various fields of mutual interest.

To insure continued understanding and mutual respect, Kahnawake and Québec recognize the importance of regular communications between their respective representatives, including at the highest level, and commit to meet on a regular basis and whenever necessary.

Nothing in this declaration prevents Kahnawake from continuing to exercise its prerogatives to conclude agreements with any other government, in the application of its jurisdiction through its legal institutions, and in accordance with its priorities.

Signed on the _____10_____ day of _____June_____ 2009.

Michael Ahrihrhon Delisle Jr.
Grand Chief
Mohawk Council of Kahnawake

Jean Charest
Premier Ministre
Gouvernement du Québec

Pierre Corbeil
Ministre responsable
des Affaires autochtones
Gouvernement du Québec

Déclaration de compréhension et de respect mutuel

Conscients de l'importance d'une coopération active, les Mohawks de Kahnawake et le Québec, désirant maintenir entre eux une relation constructive basée sur leurs principes et concepts respectifs contenus dans la doctrine du Two Row Wampum et dans les orientations du gouvernement concernant les affaires autochtones et notamment dans la résolution adoptée par l'Assemblée nationale le 20 mars 1985, renouvellent leur adhésion à la Déclaration de compréhension et de respect mutuel qu'ils ont signée le 15 octobre 1998. En conséquence, ils réaffirment leur adhésion à la déclaration suivante d'engagement politique réciproque.

Les Mohawks de Kahnawake et le Québec par leurs représentants soussignés, privilégient la discussion et la négociation pour les conduire à la conclusion et à la signature d'ententes négociées dans différents domaines d'intérêt commun.

Fiers de leur culture, de leur langue, de leurs coutumes, règles et traditions, les Mohawks de Kahnawake et le Québec entendent négocier dans le respect mutuel de leur identité nationale de même que de leur histoire et de leur occupation du territoire.

Les Mohawks de Kahnawake et le Québec désirent également participer à titre de partenaires dans des projets de développement économique à Kahnawake. De plus, le Québec accepte de mettre en place des arrangements financiers et fiscaux propres à contribuer à la stabilité économique à long terme de Kahnawake.

Afin d'accélérer le processus de négociation et le faire aboutir rapidement, le Québec et Kahnawake ont déjà nommé des négociateurs et signé une entente-cadre en vue de la conclusion rapide d'ententes sectorielles dans les différents domaines d'intérêt commun.

Afin d'assurer le maintien sur une base continue de la compréhension et du respect mutuel, le Québec et Kahnawake reconnaissent l'importance de communications régulières entre leurs représentants respectifs, y inclut au plus haut niveau, et s'engagent à se rencontrer régulièrement et à chaque fois que le besoin s'en fera sentir.

Rien dans la présente déclaration n'empêche les Mohawks de Kahnawake de continuer à pouvoir conclure des ententes avec tout autre gouvernement, suivant ses propres priorités, dans l'exercice de ses compétences et par l'entremise de ses institutions légales.

Signée le ____10e____ jour de ____juin____ 2009.

Michael Ahrihrhon Delisle Jr.
Grand Chef
Conseil mohawk de Kahnawake

Jean Charest
Premier Ministre
Gouvernement du Québec

Pierre Corbeil
Ministre responsable
des Affaires autochtones
Gouvernement du Québec

4 Controlling Federal Compensation Costs: Towards a Fairer and More Sustainable System

JAMES LAHEY

INTRODUCTION

For all but a few specialists, employee compensation in the federal public service is a black box. Even active participants in negotiations are often unfamiliar with all the moving parts. This chapter shines light on trends in federal public service compensation over the past twenty years, describes how this compensation is "normally" determined, and assesses measures to control these expenditures. The chapter ends by suggesting changes to how federal compensation is managed that could better sustain the confidence and understanding of public servants and Canadians generally.

The argument underlying the analysis is this:

- The existing system tends to fluctuate between rapid increases and arbitrary constraints, inflating costs in "good" times and alienating employees in "bad."
- This system "works" in that the federal public service has a stable employee base and, broadly speaking, serves Canadians well.
- However, the system is likely more expensive than necessary and would benefit from greater comparability with the private sector, increased transparency, and an expanded scope for negotiations that fosters realistic tradeoffs.

Getting compensation in the public service "right" is critical. People, or more precisely their capacities and engagement, determine the success of modern knowledge-based organizations. To attract and motivate its fair share of talent as experienced leaders retire, the federal public service needs to offer

Figure 1
Changes in total federal public service employment 1990–2010

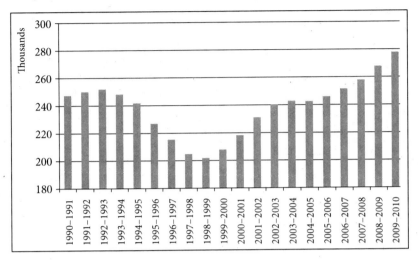

compensation that compares reasonably with the private sector. Times of restraint invite economy measures that can save money in the short run, but may destabilize employee commitment, and therefore results. Understanding better how the system works, or could work, in the longer term can help balance fairness to taxpayers and employees.

A REMARKABLE TWENTY YEARS: 1990 TO 2010[1]

The federal public service is often seen as relatively impervious to change. However, the last twenty years have brought large and rapid adjustments, as economic circumstances, attitudes toward the role of the state, and political choices by successive governments have evolved. Employment in the public service fell sharply, and then grew to surpass historic highs. Salary and total compensation costs expanded even faster as average salaries grew. These changes coincided with a shift from less toward more skilled positions, an aging of the workforce, and generational change in the leadership.

Employment

The total employee population was on something of a roller coaster ride. As Figure 1 illustrates, from a stable total of about 250,000 employees in the early 1990s, the federal public service[2] shrank during "Program Review" to nearly 200,000 in 1998–99, and then grew by nearly 40% to a total of more than 278,000 in 2009–10.

Figure 2
Changes in estimated annualized federal public service payroll, 1990–2010 ($ billions)

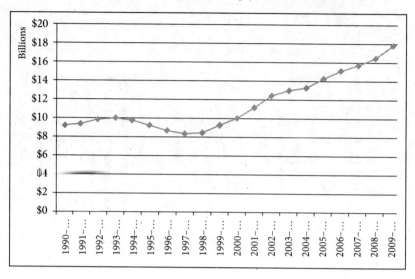

Salary Costs

The estimated total payroll[3] for these employees reached $10 billion in 1993–94, then declined to $8.4 billion in 1997–98, and finally rose throughout the subsequent years to $17.9 billion in 2009–10. Figure 2 sets out the year-by-year track. Total payroll costs grew by at least 4.6% in all but one year between 1999–2000 and 2009–10.

The average salary advanced slowly from $37,300 in 1990–91 to $40,800 in 1997–98, and then grew rapidly to $64,400 in 2009–10. Figure 3 provides the annual averages in current dollars. Using 1991–92 as the reference point, average salaries after inflation declined about 1% by 1997–98. From there, the average real purchasing power increased by about 22% over the full twenty years.

Total Compensation Costs

From a taxpayer's viewpoint, it is important to consider *all* compensation costs. Unfortunately, it was not possible to obtain figures on total compensation expenditures relating to the "federal public service" as referenced so far. However, figures from the *Public Accounts of Canada* between 2000–01 and 2009–10 are instructive. These cover not only the "federal public service," but also the Canadian Forces, members of the Royal Canadian Mounted Police, and Ministers' exempt staff.

Figure 3
Changes in estimated annualized average federal public service salary, 1990–2010 ($ thousands)

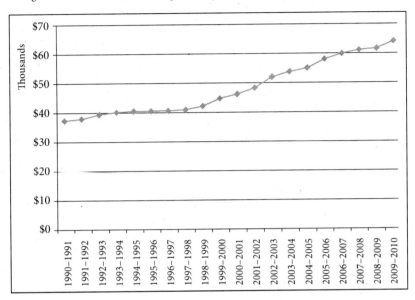

Table A
Components of total compensation for the federal public service, Canadian Forces, RCMP members and ministers' exempt staff, 2001–02 to 2009–10 ($ millions)

	2001–02	2002–03	2003–04	2004–05	2005–06	2006–07	2007–08	2008–09	2009–10
Straight Time Pay	16,517	18,073	18,991	19,623	20,931	22,064	23,040	24,758	26,065
Retro Pay	486	131	131	467	190	227	45	398	328
Overtime	488	464	442	480	527	586	655	705	730
Allowances and Premiums	842	989	1,077	1,085	1,159	1,282	1,433	1,575	1,696
Pensions	3,103	3,488	3,658	3,707	3,912	3,875	4,155	4,393	4,869
Employer Contribution for Disability Insurance	166	199	253	261	283	308	331	346	460
Health and Dental	970	1,098	1,042	1,261	1,252	1,367	1,582	1,683	1,912
Severance Pay	207	230	272	321	387	435	436	475	464
Employment Insurance	341	390	355	346	377	321	319	330	360
Workers' Compensation	96	96	102	107	117	129	130	146	151
Other/unknown / terminated objects	-67	-57	36	42	51	43	54	70	78
Total Personnel Costs	23,150	25,102	26,360	27,700	29,186	30,636	32,180	34,879	37,114

Table A lays out annual expenditures on the main components of total compensation from 2001–02 to 2009–10 for this larger universe of federal employees. Total personnel costs grew by 60% from $23.2 billion to $37.1 billion. The corresponding salary costs grew by an almost identical 58% from $16.5 to $26.1 billion. Applying the *Public Accounts* ratio of total salaries to total personnel costs (37.1/26.1 = 142%) to the average 2009–10 salary of $64,400, we can estimate total per capita compensation in the "federal public service" at about $92,000.

Employer pension contributions for current service are the second largest compensation component after salaries, and grew at almost the same rate. In 2009–10, these costs amounted to 18.7% of total salaries. The share of overall pension contributions provided by the employer in that year was 66%, with the remainder paid by employees. This compares with an employer share of 72% in 2001–02, and 51% as recently as 1991–92.[4]

The other main components of total compensation increased at different rates. For example, employer contributions for disability insurance grew by 177%. Health and dental plans doubled in cost. Allowances and premiums also doubled, while overtime costs increased more slowly (50%).

Underlying Changes in the Workforce

Behind these changes in federal public service employment and salaries over the past two decades has been an important shift in the makeup of the workforce: a simultaneous growth in "higher end" jobs, and a decline in less skilled positions.

Between 1995–96 and 2006–07[5], the ten fastest growing classification groups were Computer Systems (+102%), Information Services (+101%), Economists and Social Scientists (+98%), Biologists (+98%), Law (+95%), Physical Sciences (+83%), Administrative Services (+80%), Executives (+51%), Commerce Officers (+48%), and Financial Management (+46%). Overall, these groups increased from 19% to 31% of the public service.

Conversely, those groups that shrank were generally of the less skilled type: Secretaries (-90%), Electronics (-57%), Data Processing (-43%), General Labour (-39%), General Services (-39%), Ships Crew (-20%), and Clerical and Regulatory (-16%). These groups in total declined from about a third of the public service (34%) to a fifth (21%).

Such factors as the emergence of the "knowledge society," increased reliance on computing and on-line services, as well as more frequent litigation and the challenges of managing growing complexity and scrutiny, made such shifts inevitable. This transformation could only increase the average salary. The impact was likely in the range of 6 to 8%, when we compare the cost of the "restructured" public service with what a public service with the "old" composition would have cost.[6] This constitutes about one-third of the real increase in average salaries in this period.

Three other forces increasing average real salaries deserve note:

- *Collective bargaining outcomes above inflation* – Collective agreements concluded after collective bargaining resumed in 1997–98 frequently included economic adjustments that exceeded the actual inflation encountered during the agreements. Also, it was not uncommon for settlements to include terms that restructured salary scales upwards, for example, by adding an increment within a pay band. During the period of most rapid real increase (from 1997–98 to 2002–03), these factors contributed about 8% to raising the average real salary.[7]
- *Pay equity settlements* – The settlements of complaints under the *Canadian Human Rights Act* relating to "equal pay for work of equal value" raised substantially the salaries of female-dominated classification groups (e.g. the Clerical and Regulatory group). Although concentrated in a few groups, these settlements increased overall average salaries by at least 2%.[8]
- *Shifts in the distribution of jobs by level within a classification group* – This phenomenon, often referred to as "reclassification," increases average salaries by raising job classifications within a particular group. Such changes are largely offset when incumbents at or near the top of a pay band leave and their successors start at the bottom. Between 1990 and 2003, the net impact on average salary was small, totaling about 1.5%.[9]

The impact of three other trends is difficult to specify, but each likely contributed upward pressure:

- *An aging workforce* – Older workers generally earn more than those with more limited workforce experience. Despite extensive new hiring, the federal public service in 2010 was much older than in 1990. As of March 2008, about 120,000 out of 225,000 permanent employees had been appointed in the nine years following 1999.[10] This renewal of staff was driven both by replacing retirees or others leaving the public service, and by the increase in positions.

    Nevertheless, as Figure 4 shows, the share of the public service aged between 50 and 59 years nearly doubled from 15.3% in 1990[11] to 27.8% in 2010. The portion between 20 and 39 conversely fell from 51.5% to 36.7%.
- *Concentration in the National Capital Region* – Since the end of the 1990s, there has been a steady increase in federal public servants working in the National Capital Region (NCR). In 1993, the ratio was one-third inside to two-thirds outside the NCR. In 2000, the ratio was still 35.5% to 64.5%. By 2010, the NCR portion of the public service had grown to 40.6%. We find almost the same number of public servants (about 168,000) outside Ottawa-Gatineau in both 1990 and 2010, while the number working at headquarters rose from about 84,000 to over 110,000. Anecdotally, positions outside the

Figure 4
Distribution of federal public servants by age band in 1990, 1999 and 2010

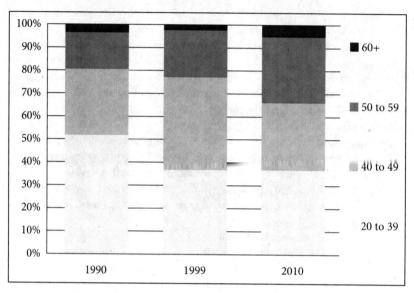

NCR tend to carry lower classifications than those at headquarters. Thus a structural shift towards the NCR could be expected to push average salaries upward.

· *Greater female participation* – During the two decades under review, the gender balance of the public service reversed. In 1990, men constituted 54.4% and women 45.6%. By 2010, women outnumbered men 55.2% to 44.8%. Most of the growth in female participation has been in officer as opposed to support positions. For example, in the Law classification group, women increased from 38% in 1990 to 52% in 2005. What this means for average compensation remains unclear, however, beyond the impact of pay equity settlements already noted.

Some Points of Comparison

It is important to compare these figures to broader indicators of employment and compensation in the Canadian economy. On employment levels, the federal public service has declined as a share of the Canadian total between 1990–91 and 2009–10, from about 1.8% to 1.65%. However, this latter proportion has increased from 1.52% in 2005–2006.

On salaries and total compensation, it is difficult to make meaningful comparisons. The Canadian Federation of Independent Business (CFIB) publishes an analysis every five years as new census data becomes available. The CFIB's

December 2008 publication *Wage Watch*, based on the 2006 Census, asserts that on average federal employees enjoyed a premium of 17.3% on salaries and over 40% when benefits are included.

However, comparisons based on broad sources such as the Census or the Labour Force Survey likely overstate the situation. The job mix within the federal public service does not align with that of the overall economy. Both top-paying and low-paying jobs are essentially missing by comparison. For example, according to 2001 Census data, 59% of federal employees' salaries fell in the range between $40,000 and $80,000, versus only 35% in the Canadian private sector.

While job titles offer a reasonable basis for reporting census data, they provide little guidance in comparing across organizations. For example, such terms as "economist" or "manager" can refer to vastly different requirements. A study completed by the author in 2006 for the Treasury Board Secretariat concluded that, as comparisons "were tailored more and more rigorously to track the actual characteristics of particular jobs and occupations in the federal public service, the purported salary premiums shrank in significance."[12]

In the absence of more detailed comparisons, it is reasonable to judge that on average federal public service wages likely do enjoy a modest premium versus the overall Canadian labour market, perhaps in the order of half of that claimed by the CFIB study, i.e. around 8% or 9%. In terms of total compensation, the federal public service pension is of course an advantage compared with most private employers. Combined with other benefits, again something in the order of half of the premium reported by the CFIB seems probable, i.e. around 15% to 20%.

The overall picture hides important nuances, however. First, the largest "premium" applies to those female-dominated classification groups that have benefited from pay equity settlements. Since pay equity policies intend to counter gender bias in the labour market, such a "premium" should come as no surprise. Second, except at the lowest level, executive total compensation lags the private sector, with the gap wider the higher the position. Third, because the federal public service pays "national rates" for nearly all its employees, compensation no doubt surpasses local rates in some labour markets, but may lag in others.

Whatever a rigorous comparison of salaries and total compensation might show, it is instructive to examine relative rates of change. Figure 5 compares real average salary growth between 1991–92 and 2009–10 in the federal public service with three indicators of salary change in the broader economy: average weekly earnings, average hourly earnings (only available from 1997–98) and average major wage settlements in the private sector.[13]

The federal public service average salary declined in real terms through much of the 1990s, and only caught up to the cumulative increase in key indicators of wage increases in the broader economy at the end of the decade. The

Figure 5
Comparison of real average salary growth in the federal public service with indicators of real wage increases in the broader economy from 1991–92 to 2009–10 (1991–92 = 100)

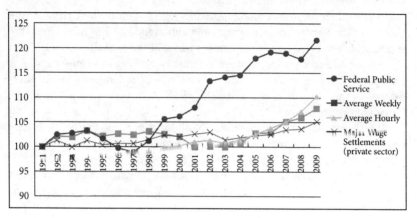

first years of the 2000s witnessed much faster increases in the federal public service than in the broader economy. Later rates of increase have been similar for all these indicators.

The net result over two decades is that the cumulative real increase of the average salary in the federal public service has been at least twice that of the average weekly and hourly wages in the Canadian economy, and major wage settlements for unionized employees in the private sector. This finding must be qualified by acknowledging that the federal public service data includes the effect of a marked alteration in the mix of jobs. Similar changes have been occurring in the whole economy, but probably not to the same degree. Thus this comparison may overstate somewhat the relative increase in the federal public service.

A Few Thoughts on the Last Two Decades

Not unlike the Canadian labour market as a whole, the federal public service has been remade since 1990. The trends towards greater professionalization and an older workforce are common to many large employers. Rapid population shifts have also not been unknown elsewhere. Still, the scope of change in the federal public service is striking and little appreciated.

Whatever future research may reveal about how salary and total compensation levels in the federal public service compare with the broader Canadian economy, the scale of growth in the eleven years from 1998–99 to 2009–10 has been remarkable. Forty per cent more employees, more than a doubling of the total salary mass (+110%), and a 52% increase in the average salary invite questions about the rationale for these increases.

The impact of movement towards the knowledge-intensive workers has been documented above. On employee population growth, the 2000s have certainly brought increased demands in such areas as security, health protection, national defense, litigation, and internal controls. On the other hand, compared with the early 1990s, the federal government has transferred responsibilities to provinces or the private sector in such fields as labour market training, air navigation, airport administration, printing and building maintenance. It is clear from such sources as the *Annual Reports* of the Public Service Commission that most departments and agencies have been active during recent years in new appointments to the public service.[14] Whether such widespread growth is necessary and appropriate is a matter of judgment.

Rapid growth can actually work against effectiveness. Large numbers of new employees joining over the course of a few years are difficult to assimilate, especially when experienced leaders are retiring at historically high levels. The combination of elevated rates of retirement and expansive new hiring has encouraged "churn," i.e. rapid movement from one position to another, and not uncommonly, accelerated progress through the ranks.[15] As the total population stabilizes in the next few years in response to the re-emergence of federal deficits, such churn can be expected to diminish.

HOW COMPENSATION SPENDING IS NORMALLY DETERMINED

Broadly speaking, changes to employment levels and salaries drive total compensation. But how are these matters decided? On occasion, the Government has used legislation to impose compensation controls for a specified period. But in "normal" times, the main components shaping compensation spending are: budgetary allocations for salaries, transfers from non-salary to salary budgets, collective bargaining, salary determination directly by the Treasury Board, benefits negotiations, and policy decisions regarding the pension plan. The first two components largely shape employment levels, and the rest the cost of those employees.

Budgetary Allocations for Salaries

Every year, Parliament approves Main and Supplementary Estimates for government expenditures. These include allocations for personnel costs, principally salaries. Most of the increases and decreases in the level of employment in the public service result directly from the level of funding made available by the Government. This amount is the product of a myriad of micro-allocations ultimately approved by the Treasury Board Ministers. These decisions mainly implement Cabinet decisions to introduce or revise federal policies and programs. They also respond to Treasury Board Secretariat recommendations regarding the cost of maintaining existing programs.

Transfers from Non-Salary to Salary Budgets

Since the 1980s, senior managers have had authority to shift money between salary and non-salary spending in order to optimize how programs are delivered. For such transfers, $1.20 of non-salary funds is needed to convert to $1.00 of salaries. This is aimed at capturing the benefits costs that are paid centrally by the Treasury Board on behalf of all departments. Such transfers can be substantial. For example, during the period between 1997–98 and 2002–03, there was an estimated net increase of about $1.2 billion in this area, assisting departments both to cover salary increases not fully funded by the Treasury Board, and to hire additional staff.[16]

Collective Bargaining

Since most (over 90% in March 2010) federal public servants are union members, in normal circumstances negotiated collective agreements determine the level of salaries and terms of employment such as leave and allowances. Separate contracts are negotiated with seventeen distinct unions for twenty-seven bargaining units in the main departments and agencies for which the Treasury Board is the employer. These covered about 206,000 employees in 2009–10. Separate employers (principally the Canada Revenue Agency) with about 65,000 employees negotiate separate contracts for their bargaining units.

The Public Service Alliance of Canada (PSAC) represents about 127,000 workers (more than 60%) in the core public administration. The Professional Institute of the Public Service of Canada (PIPSC) represents nearly 38,000 (about 18%). The fifteen other unions range in size from the Canadian Association of Professional Employees (CAPE) with about 14,000 members down to three unions representing fewer than 100 workers each.

Collective bargaining in the federal public service is governed by the *Public Service Labour Relations Act (PSLRA)*. Disputes may be resolved either through conciliation with the possibility of a strike if certain conditions are met, or through arbitration. The current PSLRA came into force in 2005. It contains various changes from the previous Act regarding the acquisition of the right to strike that have not yet been tested in practice. These include, for example, the need to negotiate or obtain a Public Service Labour Relations Board (PSLRB) decision on an essential services agreement, and the need to obtain a strike mandate through a secret ballot not more than sixty days before a strike begins.

More salient than the complexities of labour law, however, is how the collective bargaining process has played out when it has been allowed to function without legislative intervention. During the twenty years under review, collective bargaining was in force or unrestricted only about half the time, from 1997 until 2008, covering four rounds of bargaining. In both 2001 and

2004 there was intermittent strike action, mainly by PSAC members, prior to settlements being agreed.

Broadly speaking, the employer's approach seems to have been to offer salary increases aimed at matching expected inflation, and to add elements to encourage union members to ratify the tentative agreements. Inducements included such items as reducing the number of pay zones for workers with regional pay rates, adding increments within a pay band, increasing leave entitlements, or adding allowances (for example for groups experiencing high labour demand). These offers did result in ratified agreements; however, their overall cost contributed to average salary increases exceeding actual inflation levels. In an era of low inflation, "selling a settlement" appears to have needed sweeteners to convince union negotiators to send an offer for ratification. The 2010 settlement with three PSAC bargaining units, which eliminates future severance pay accumulation, may represent a shift in this approach.

Salary Determination Directly by the Treasury Board

The Treasury Board determines salaries for non-unionized public servants. For the first level of executives (EX 1), the policy is to match total compensation in the federal public service to their peers in the private and broader public sectors (including pay based on performance, but not long-term incentives such as stock options). For higher levels of executives and deputy ministers, there is a fixed increment of 12% or 15% between levels. Executives and deputy ministers also participate in a performance pay plan that allows most of them to earn additional amounts based on their delivery against objectives. A small proportion of executives can also obtain a bonus for exceptional performance.

For other non-unionized workers, salary levels are usually set in line with what has been agreed for their unionized colleagues in the same classification group. Some senior non-executive managers excluded from union membership are also eligible for performance pay.

Benefits Negotiations

Benefits such as the health and dental plans and the disability plan covering federal public servants are negotiated with the unions collectively in a forum known as the National Joint Council. This body, co-chaired by a senior Treasury Board official and a union leader, also offers a venue to try to resolve grievances before they go to the PSLRB for adjudication, and for informal conversations on people issues.

In practice, substantive changes to benefit plans have been limited in recent years. Attention has focused more on their governance and administration, especially the health care plan. However, the costs of these plans have been growing at or faster than the rate of salaries, largely as a result of employee aging and rising drug costs. By separating negotiation on these benefits from collective bargaining on wages, there is little possibility of considering potential tradeoffs across the various areas of compensation spending.

Policy Decisions Regarding the Pension Plan

The federal public service pension plan is established and governed by statute and not directly the subject of collective bargaining. In practice, the Treasury Board President has set up a union-management Pension Advisory Committee that permits union representatives to advise on the design and financing of the plan. Nevertheless, the Treasury Board decides in the end on the terms of the pension plan and submits legislation to Parliament as required to implement policy changes.

Employee contributions covered about 34% of the cost of current service entitlements in 2009–10. The aim is to reach a 40% employee contribution share by 2013. No substantive changes in employee entitlements have been introduced for over a decade.

How the Pieces Come Together (or Not)

Cumulatively these processes and policies shape the compensation paid to federal public servants in "normal" times. Two observations suggest themselves. First, the pieces have not been consciously managed as a system. Each process or policy has its own participants, rationale and traditions. These certainly overlap, especially on the union side, but decisions about the pieces are usually taken without much reference to their impact on the whole federal investment in employee compensation.

Second, the principal roles of departmental line managers are in seeking funding for new or amended programs or policies, and in designing their organizations, including the mix of classification groups and levels. For most such leaders, including many deputy ministers, the other aspects of the compensation puzzle are mysterious, decided by others. Unlike in the private sector, there is thus little opportunity or incentive for operational managers to seek ways to align compensation with work design in the service of augmenting productivity.

MEASURES AVAILABLE TO CONTROL (OR REDUCE) COMPENSATION COSTS

In times of financial difficulty, budget making necessarily seeks savings or reduced spending growth everywhere, especially in areas deemed discretionary. At the federal level, personnel costs were a modest 16.5% of expenditures in 2009–10.[17] Nevertheless, $37.1 billion is a large amount. Symbolically, it is desirable for the federal government to be seen to "tighten its own belt." Thus finance ministers, media commentators and citizens always look for diminished personnel spending as part of any campaign to reduce deficits.

There are at least five ways to control spending on compensation: reducing hiring; laying off existing staff; constraining the growth of salaries or spending on benefits; reducing salaries or benefits; or increasing the employee share of the cost of benefits.

Reducing Hiring

This is the simplest option for controlling costs, particularly after several years of rapid growth in the employee population. Each indeterminate employee costs on average about $92,000 in total compensation, not to mention the cost of office space, computers, training, travel etc. So every 1,000 new employees not hired saves more than $100 million per year.

Simply cutting in half the recent net additions of more than 7,500 new employees annually would save something like $400 million per year. Eliminating all new hiring, including replacement of those retiring (in the range of 3% to 3.5% annually) and those leaving for other reasons (around 2%)[18] would save more than $2 billion annually. Almost two-thirds of this would be a reduction in current expenditure since departing employees would not be replaced.

There is therefore exceptional flexibility to achieve savings without layoffs. Two cautions, however. Excessive tightening of new hiring would threaten the capacity of the public service to deliver services that Canadians expect, and it would weaken internal controls as managers squeeze "overhead" to meet frontline pressures. Further, twisting the tap too tight, especially beyond a few years, could leave the public service with a new "missing generation" such as resulted from the freezes of the mid-1990s.

Intended hiring reductions can be implemented arbitrarily through freezes on hiring, or phased in through restrictions on operating budgets. Freezes are seemingly decisive. However, they seldom last because the wrong people leave and many simply must be replaced. As exceptions multiply the freeze collapses in confusion. Less dramatic but more effective is the option of constraining operating budgets, the policy that the Conservative government sensibly chose in its 2010 Budget. This approach can seem slow initially to deliver, as managers scramble to cover personnel costs through internal reallocations. But sustaining operating budget freezes or reductions over a period of years is certain to succeed, and with the least possible disruption of crucial activities.[19]

Laying Off Existing Staff

Clearly the federal government is a long way from needing to lay off existing staff. However, this was done in the mid-1990s when rapid deficit reduction was seen as imperative and staff departures were slow. In five years, employment declined by at least 40,000. This happened with surprisingly little rancour, in part with the aid of temporary incentive programs.[20] The "Early Retirement Incentive" (ERI) permitted eligible employees declared surplus to retire early without normal reductions to their pension. The "Early Departure Incentive" (EDI) provided cash based on salary, age and years of service to permanent employees declared surplus from departments with large reduction targets. These programs allowed unaffected employees wanting to leave to substitute for affected employees who preferred to stay.

In 2000, the Treasury Board Secretariat estimated the cost of these departure incentive programs at $4.2 billion, with an annual net saving in personnel costs of $3 billion as of 1999.[21] These figures capture the problem with departure incentives. To work they must be generous, but as such they are costly and their impact perhaps fleeting. The cost per departure was more than $100,000. On the other hand, the savings dissipated rapidly, with the population returning by 2004–05 to its level prior to Program Review.[22]

The impact on employees and the public service was also acute. While the incentives dampened potential strife, the process of deciding what areas and which individuals to declare surplus was destabilizing. Employees felt at risk and devalued, distracting them from their work. Often the strongest employees opted to leave. The loss of valued colleagues and the need to pick up much of their work left those remaining feeling like victims. Trust was frayed as everyone struggled to work through the reductions. So substantial staff reductions are possible, but costly. Of course, targeted reductions where work is eliminated through processes such as Strategic and Operational Reviews remain a practical option.[23]

Constraining the Growth of Salaries or Benefits

Spending on salaries and benefits is driven principally by collective agreements in "normal" times. On at least five occasions affecting sixteen years since 1967, the federal government has intervened through legislation to control compensation growth.[24] Since the 2007 Supreme Court of Canada decision regarding legislative interference with collective bargaining in the health sector in British Columbia, the legitimate scope for such interventions has become doubtful.[25] Thus the most recent *Expenditure Restraint Act, 2009* built on an existing settlement with the Public Service Alliance of Canada and permitted collective bargaining on some points, albeit within fixed economic increases and a prohibition on altering pay scales or allowances.

With uncertainty affecting the option of legislating compensation, collective bargaining is the primary vehicle for achieving affordable personnel costs. The 2010 Treasury Board settlement with three of five PSAC bargaining groups is thus intriguing. Terms included salary increases, as well as an end to accumulating severance pay, although laid off employees will enjoy improved severance. Existing entitlements to severance could be paid out immediately, or on leaving the public service.[26] This is a creative example of reducing employer costs in the long run, while providing employees with raises in line with expected inflation, and the possibility of a lump sum pay out of severance. If other unions cannot agree on terms that the government considers compatible with eliminating the federal deficit, however, the stage will be set for legislated controls, and a showdown in the Supreme Court on the constitutionality of such action.

Reducing spending on most benefits would entail collective bargaining with the unions jointly. Without severe limitations on coverage, savings would be relatively small. In any case, restrictions could likely be agreed only as part of some larger settlement, as in the case of severance.

The federal pension plan is statutory, so it could be adjusted with Parliament's approval. Certain provisions could be considered for change, especially in the light of increased life expectancies. The likeliest area would be the "early retirement" provision, which allows public servants aged 55 years with at least 30 years of service to retire without penalty. Moving the minimum age up or increasing the minimum years of service would offer meaningful savings to the pension plan in the longer term.

Increasing the Employee Share of the Cost of Benefits

Employee contributions to the cost of their benefits vary from 34% for the pension plan, to 15% for disability insurance, to nothing for the health and dental plans (except for hospital coverage for private or semi-private rooms). Consideration could be given to employees paying a larger share of the costs of these programs.

The government has already launched a phased increase in employee pension contributions towards 40% of current service costs by 2013. This is responsible, but does not go far enough. The employee contribution share for major public sector pensions in Canada with benefits similar to the federal plan is generally 50%. Notable examples include the public service, municipal employees' and teachers' plans in Ontario, and the public service plans in most provinces.[27] There seems no credible reason why the federal plan would limit employee contributions to 40%. Moving to 50% at the federal level would of course be controversial (for example, it could imply instituting a form of joint governance with the unions) and would need to be phased in over several years, but it could be done.

Instituting or increasing employee contributions to the health, dental and disability plans could also be considered. Most employees would probably prefer to contribute more rather than see reduced coverage. Indeed given the choice, many employees might well prefer expanded coverage, and accept commensurate contribution increases in order to benefit from group rates.

Overview on Reducing Costs in a Time of Restraint

Reducing compensation costs is possible. Least painful is reducing hiring, first by limiting or eliminating net growth, and if necessary by not replacing some of those leaving the public service. Fortunately, this option will yield the largest and most immediate (as well as long-term) savings. Accomplishing this through constraining operating budgets, as opposed to hiring freezes, is the better way to go. Managers can trim without putting priority work at risk.

All the other options are much more difficult to implement, more controversial, and less likely to save much. Specific layoffs where work is discontinued is feasible and normal. But federal experience with large-scale layoffs in the 1990s should inspire prudent hesitation. Constraining salaries or benefits likely requires union agreement through collective bargaining, unless a pressing crisis were to emerge. With skillful negotiating this area may give positive results, but never easily. The exception might be the early retirement provision of the pension plan, since it is statutory, although savings would be long-term since existing entitlements would likely need to be "grandfathered." Increases in employee contributions, especially for the pension plan, make sense and could likely be implemented, but again the pay-off would take years. Both types of changes to the pension plan would have solid policy rationales and likely useful symbolic value.

A crucial aspect of any strategy for controlling compensation costs is dealing respectfully with employees. Clumsily applied constraints risk costing more in employee distraction or disillusion than they appear to save. Sensible approaches would avoid demeaning rhetoric designed to prepare the ground for cuts, arbitrary measures poorly explained, and peremptory changes leaving little time to adjust expectations. No one likes compensation restraint or increases to contributions, or the possibility of layoffs. But public servants' commitment to serving Canadians is strong, and reasonable measures to tackle legitimate financial pressures can be accepted if they are truly necessary and humanely applied.

TOWARDS A SUSTAINABLE SYSTEM FOR DETERMINING FAIR COMPENSATION IN THE FEDERAL PUBLIC SERVICE

The recent experience of the federal public service demonstrates a tendency for employment and compensation to alternate between relatively rapid growth and freezes, imposed restraints or even reductions. This inspires the question whether there is a way to manage employment and compensation change that can reduce such fluctuations.

Employment growth has been the most potent driver of increased compensation costs during the 2000s. Thus more attention to guiding the trajectory of employment change would be critical to dampening upward pressures. In principle, this is a task for the Ministers of the Treasury Board supported by officials of the Secretariat, as controllers of the expenditure budget. In practice, employment levels result from innumerable program-specific decisions to direct funds to personnel costs. There is certainly the option of introducing limits on positions or "full-time equivalents" from the centre. However, the simplest way to channel decisions to staff without tying managers' hands unduly is to manage operating budgets more assiduously, and to make it harder (or at least more expensive) to transfer funds from non-salary to salary budgets.

Turning to the growth in per employee compensation costs, we enter a byzantine world of local classification decisions, central collective bargaining, and Treasury Board decisions and policies. Disciplining these processes has always been difficult.

Trying to decree from the centre the distribution of positions by classification group and level is doomed. Only local managers can gauge the skills needed for the work to succeed. However, a combination of careful management of overall operating budgets and periodic audits of classification decisions can assure reasonable oversight.

The toughest area to manage sustainably and credibly is that of salary levels and benefit costs. While the federal public service bargaining environment is influenced by the Canadian economic and employment climate, it tends to persist in its own "micro-climate" of expectations that at a minimum salaries will meet inflation or a bit more, and while benefits may not be improved, at least they will always be there. It is this culture that has lead successive governments to intervene in periods of economic stress to force outcomes that could not be reached through collective bargaining.[28]

While the system will no doubt retain its essential messiness, there do appear to be at least three steps that might foster less frequent resort to arbitrary adjustments:

EMPHASIZE COMPARABILITY

For more than a century, the basic principle of federal public sector compensation has been comparability in salaries and benefits with the broader Canadian labour market[29]. Paying less is unfair to public servants; paying more is a burden on taxpayers. Other principles, such as that of "equal pay for work of equal value" can override comparability for policy reasons, but no better standard has been suggested as a general guide.

The problem is how to apply the concept. There can be much debate about how to compare public sector jobs with those outside. Joint studies between the Treasury Board and unions on such comparisons have not fared well, since in effect bargaining starts with the selection of what to compare. Such problems do not vitiate the importance of the idea, however. So the minimum is to insist on the pertinence of the principle. A potentially fruitful course for bringing this perspective into the debate would be to explore existing third-party surveys of salaries and benefits as broad indicators of where comparability may lie.[30] In some cases, federal public service salaries might have to be raised to achieve comparability; in others, increases might have to be minimal for a period to restore alignment.

Increase Transparency

Currently, there is little accessible detail regarding federal public sector compensation levels and trends. Greater public exposure and accountability for spending in this area would put downward pressure on increases when the federal coffers are overflowing. Such information, particularly if combined with usable data on private sector comparability, would assist public servants to get outside their "micro-climate" and appreciate better what salaries and benefits are reasonable in a broader labour market context. Slower increases in "good times" will make it more feasible to defend compensation levels in downturns.

Broaden the Scope of Negotiations

All forms of compensation are charges on the public purse. Nevertheless, the traditional approach of separate negotiations and policy work in silos such as collective bargaining mainly on salaries, joint negotiations on the main benefit plans, and policy on pensions, makes tradeoffs extremely difficult to discuss, let alone achieve. Ideally the Treasury Board should see itself as managing total compensation within affordable limits, and negotiate with the unions from this perspective. Adoption of the *Public Service Equitable Compensation Act (PSECA)* in 2009, which requires the employer and unions to deal with pay equity through regular collective bargaining, is a step in this direction.

The centralized character of most federal public service collective bargaining makes it extremely difficult to address the link between productivity and compensation. The details of what makes for improved productivity are specific to workplaces or processes, usually well below the level of a department. In the private sector, compensation increases often depend on improved business results. The Treasury Board should develop ways to build into its collective agreements locally negotiated components that could foster better productivity.

CONCLUSION

These measures would seek to constrain compensation from growing too quickly during budget surpluses and provide a rationale for avoiding arbitrary reductions in all but the direst of economic downturns. Such a system would be worthy of support from public servants and from taxpayers in both good times and bad. With less volatility and less reason for political leaders to indulge in populist attacks on public servants in times of deficit, Canada's public servants can continue to focus their best ideas and efforts confidently on serving Canadians with enthusiasm and pride.

NOTES

1 The Treasury Board of Canada Secretariat supplied the figures in this section. The author is responsible for how they are interpreted and displayed. Kaveh Afshar created the figures and assisted with the analysis.

2 The term "federal public service" includes employees of departments and agencies for which the Treasury Board is the employer, plus "separate employers" such as the Canada Revenue Agency. Excluded are the Canadian Forces, members of the Royal Canadian Mounted Police, Crown corporations and Ministers' exempt staff. The employment totals are from the federal pay system, averaging the number of employees on the last day of each month.

3 Total and average salaries are estimates based on multiplying salary rates for each classification group and level by the applicable populations. Actual expenditure on salaries are less reliable since they include fluctuating amounts such as back pay.

4 Based on a study by the author for the Treasury Board of Canada Secretariat completed in 2006, *Expenditure Review of Federal Public Sector Compensation Policy and Comparability,* which can be accessed on the Treasury Board website by clicking on the "Reports and Publications" tab on the home page, then on "Other Reports" at the bottom of the second screen, and finally on the report title in the items listed for 2007. Volume Two: Compensation Snapshot and Historical Perspective, 1990 to 2003.

5 These years were selected to avoid comparability problems. After 2006–07, classification reforms in the Canada Revenue Agency and the creation of the Border Services classification group make comparisons for some key groups impossible.

6 This estimate is based on work by the Treasury Board of Canada Secretariat.

7 Lahey, *Expenditure Review,* Overview, p 18.

8 Ibid, Overview, p. 19.

9 Ibid, Volume One: the Analytical Report and Recommendations, p. 76.

10 Figures prepared by the Public Service Agency, 2008.

11 All percentages refer to March data.

12 Lahey, *Expenditure Review*, Overview p.28.

13 The federal public service figures are those cited earlier. The average weekly and hourly wages are from Statistics Canada, and the private sector wage settlements data is compiled by the Labour Program of Human Resources and Skills Development Canada and reported in their website *Major Wage Settlements.*

14 For example, Table 44 on page 154 of the 2009–10 Public Service Commission *Annual Report.*

15 See the October 2008 study by the Public Service Commission on *Mobility of Public Servants*, which documents rapid movement within the public service in certain groups. On accelerating advances in levels see the example on the Economist (ES) group cited in Lahey, *Expenditure Review*, Volume One, p. 77.

16 Lahey, *Expenditure Review*, Volume Two, pp. 87–89.

17 *Public Accounts of Canada 2009–10*, Volume II, Table 3, page 1–21.

18 Public Service Commission, *Mobility of Public Servants*, Figure 3 – "Overall public service growth versus separations." This chart excludes separate employers as well as temporary and casual employees of the core public administration. Nevertheless, such a large portion of the public service (about three-quarters) is a reasonable indicator of the whole institution.

19 Making it harder to transfer money from non-salary to salary budgets can accelerate the process. At a minimum it would make sense to raise the conversion cost from the current $1.20 of non-salary spending for $1.00 of salaries to something like $1.30. This appears closer to the true extra cost of centrally funded benefits. See Lahey, *Expenditure Review*, Volume One, pp. 239–240 and recommendation 6.2.

20 Jocelyne Bourgon, *Program Review: The Government of Canada's Experience with Eliminating the Deficit, 1994–1999, A* Canadian *Case Study*, The Centre for International Governance Innovation, 2009, p. 22.

21 Auditor General of Canada, *2001 December Report*, Chapter 12 Follow-up on Recommendations in Previous Reports, paragraph 12.97.

22 It could be argued that in the absence of the Program Review reductions, the federal public service would simply have added the increases of the last ten years to the previous population. In this scenario, the investments in Program Review staff reductions were "worth it."

23 Strategic Review is a Treasury Board sponsored process for reconsidering the existing programs and expenditures of departments on a five-year cycle, leading to cuts or reallocations in the order of 5%. The 2011 budget tabled in March 2011 proposes reviewing all departments and agencies in one year, looking for cuts of up to 10% to be announced in the 2012 budget.

24 These occasions were: 1975–1978 with the *Anti-Inflation Act*; 1983–1985 with the *Public Service Compensation Restraint Act*; 1991–1993 with the *Public Sector Compensation Act*; 1993–1997 with various *Budget Implementation Acts* implementing Program Review reductions; and 2006–2011 with the *Expenditure Restraint Act*.

25 This decision was *Health Services and Support – Facilities Subsector Bargaining Association v. British Columbia* 2007 SCC 27 [2007] 2 S.C.R. 391. The case affirms a constitutional obligation to bargain in good faith. This has spawned additional challenges to legislative restraint on collective bargaining. Further decisions by the Supreme Court will be needed to clarify under what circumstances legislation imposing labour contract terms may be acceptable under the *Charter of Rights and Freedoms*.

26 Kathryn May, "PSAC, Treasury Board reach a deal: Wages to rise 5.3% over next 3 years," *Ottawa Citizen*, October 5, 2010.

27 Lahey, *Expenditure Review,* Volume One, p. 167. The Saskatchewan public service has a defined contribution plan.

28 The psac agreement ratified in December 2010, which cuts back on severance entitlements, is an exception to the norm. Whether it is an aberration remains to be seen.

29 See a brief history of "comparability" in regard to federal public sector compensation in Lahey, *Expenditure Review,* Volume One, Chapter 2, pp. 15–40.

30 Private compensation consulting firms such as Mercer maintain benchmark databases that include details on salaries and other compensation for many types of work. Examples include: it, human resources, finance, administration, legal, etc. Such data compares salaries for entry, experienced and senior staff, showing typical salary progressions.

5 Regulatory Agency Budget Cuts: Public Interest Support through a Better Approach

DEREK IRELAND, ERIC MILLIGAN,
KERNAGHAN WEBB, AND WEI XIE

INTRODUCTION

Over the next five years or so, the Government of Canada, Canadian provincial, territorial and municipal governments, and other OECD country governments will be under significant fiscal pressure to reduce their regulatory and other budgets in order to control government spending and decrease government deficits and debt.[1] Additional motivation will be provided by the perceived need to reduce the regulatory burdens and compliance costs of industry and other regulatees in order to promote economic recovery, efficiency, national competitiveness and higher tax revenues in the future.

The main argument of this chapter is that, compared with the approaches employed in the past, improved information and methods, combined with recent advances in regulatory economics and related literatures, are now available that, if adopted, would allow governments to better target their regulatory budget reduction efforts. The first section of the chapter reviews past approaches and the second explores recent advances in the literature. The third section presents the preliminary design of a comprehensive, dynamic systems and risk-based analytical framework. The framework is designed to help regulators, line departments and central agencies to assess the extent to which and how quickly reduced budgets for specific regulatory regimes and instruments might erode the motivation and incentives of regulatees to comply with regulatory requirements.

The conclusions in the final section of the chapter provide possible extensions to the framework, including additional examples to illustrate how the analytical framework can be used to indicate why similar budget reductions can lead to very different compliance outcomes depending on the system dynamics of a specific regulatory regime.

To be clear, this chapter does not address whether the behavior previously mandated by a regulatory regime could be sustained on a "voluntary" basis in the absence of regulatory provisions. The provisions would not be repealed. Rather, the question is whether satisfactory compliance levels with existing regulatory requirements could be sustained for the period in which regulatory agency budgetary cutbacks are applied, so as to ensure continued management of regulatory risks and achievement of the public policy objectives sought through regulatory intervention.

METHODS USED IN THE PAST TO CONTROL AND REDUCE REGULATORY BUDGETS

Governments and their central agencies and line departments have used various methods to cut regulatory agency budgets during periods of fiscal stress and/or regulatory reform. Governments as well as departments with multiple regulatory responsibilities have frozen all regulatory budgets or reduced them all by the same arbitrary amount, say 10 or 20 percent. This approach appears to be broadly consistent with current federal government policy as described in the budget of March 2010, offers the perceived advantages of simplicity and equity, and is consistent with the limited information available to many federal regulators regarding the causal links between regulatory budgets, the compliance levels of regulatees, and private and public regulatory costs, outcomes and benefits.

A second approach is to focus reductions on regulatory regimes and budgets that are least popular with the current government and its business supporters and political base.

A third approach is to hold a program review type "tournament" where the winners arguably are the regulatory agencies and their senior managers that are best able to articulate their cases, and use their bureaucratic, political, business and other non-government connections to maintain and even increase their current budgets. These "tournaments" can be either government wide as with Program Review in the mid-1990s, or internal to departments. The latter approach is reportedly now taking place under Strategic Review, where large departments have the responsibility to decide which regulatory agency, program and other budgets to cut based on internal departmental criteria which likely vary across departments.

The remainder of this chapter argues for an alternative or fourth approach by advancing an analytical framework that would promote a more nuanced and effective fact-based method to regulatory agency budget reductions that would result in less reduction in compliance levels and less cost and risk to the public interest. Our focus is primarily on ensuring that public interest concerns continue to prevail even though an era of overall fiscal austerity is now underway.

KEY INSIGHTS FROM THE LITERATURE

The argument for, and development of, the analytical framework uses on a selective basis the expanding regulatory economics literature, which takes account of recent advances in a large number of related economics and other disciplines. Based on the concepts of benefit-cost analysis and law and economics, the regulatory economics literature contends that company compliance with formal laws and regulations requires strong penalties and enforcement capabilities and a high probability of being caught and penalized. Otherwise, non-compliance simply becomes a small low-risk cost of doing business that rarely is incurred by the regulatee.

However, the pioneering work of George Stigler on regulatory outcomes and capture questions whether strong penalties, budgets and enforcement capacities necessarily result in high regulatory compliance and benefits.[2] In addition, recent advances in the institutional and political economy literatures have found that, at the small community level, compliance with informal rules that are community developed, enforced and "owned" by members of the community often (but not always) have better compliance performance than formal regulatory regimes that are enforced by the state and other third parties.

This research on small community self-regulation originally emphasized natural resource communities, but has been extended to other relatively small communities and groups such as oligopoly industries with a smaller number of suppliers, supply chains, innovation systems, and multi-company business groups, networks, and communities.[3]

The literature on information asymmetries and failures indicates that industries and markets, where manufacturers, retailers and other vendors and service providers have a significant information advantage over their business customers and final consumers, often do not generate competitive and efficient outcomes that are satisfactory to customers, consumers, and the total economy and society, even when there are a large number of sellers.[4] Many of these markets supply so-called "experience and credence" goods, whereby, compared with "search" goods, it is much more difficult for business customers and final consumers to protect themselves from non-complying producers and vendors.

In addition, regulators and other government agencies are at an information disadvantage compared with regulatees when attempting to enforce the rules against non-complying companies. Therefore, contrary to the predictions of Chicago School economists, more information, a larger number of suppliers, and more product and vendor choice for consumers in these markets do not necessarily result in competitive, efficient and fair markets, more satisfied business customers and final consumers, and greater compliance with the formal and informal rules of the marketplace.

The application of behavioural economics to regulatory regimes provides a number of insights that in many ways extend the findings from information economics. Behavioral economics research on industries in transition from regulation to more competitive market structures indicates that deregulation, privatization and regulatory reforms in e.g. passenger air and other transport, electricity and other energy sectors, water and other utilities, telecommunications and financial services have often fallen far short of the expectations and predictions of their business, government and academic supporters on such indicators as competition, innovation, business customer and final consumer satisfaction, and compliance with the remaining formal and informal rules.

Unsatisfactory deregulation outcomes are particularly found in industries where overdependence on market incentives and outcomes in the early years operate in combination with information asymmetries and failures and such behavioral biases as: (i) information and product choice overload, (ii) framing effects where consumer decisions are influenced by how information is presented to them in advertising and other mechanisms, (iii) endowment, status quo and sunk costs effects, and loss and risk aversion, which lead to high perceived and actual switching costs of business customers and final consumers, the entry deterrence strategies of incumbents, and consumer and producer inertia, [5] and (iv) over-confident consumers and other supply chain participants.[6]

The second insight, found as well in the institutional and regulatory literatures, is socially and culturally influenced "endogenous" preferences, obligations, and decisions.[7] In contrast to the first insight, endogenous preferences can result in greater compliance with formal and informal rules because of the expectations of business customers and consumers, investments in reputation and corporate social responsibility by regulated companies and industries, and the emergence of habits, routines and a "compliance culture" within an industry that favours compliance over non-compliance.[8]

The third insight involves the concept of small "nudges," whereby in some circumstances regulators, working perhaps with compliant regulatees and other affected parties, can identify and employ framing effects, default options and other "behavioral biases" in a positive manner to replace costly and intrusive command and control regulation.[9]

The conflicting insights from these literatures are also important to the chapter's analytical framework. The industrial organization and regulatory economics literatures on market power and regulatory capture contend that highly concentrated industries with few suppliers are able to force lower quality non-complying products on their business customers and final consumers and are able to use their super-competitive profits to lobby politicians and regulators for highly permissive regulation and for regulatory forebearance and "shirking."[10]

However, some oligopolistic and other industries that supply highly differentiated products are driven by the profit motive to comply with formal regulations as well as the voluntary standards of the industry, because compliance results in formidable barriers to entry and sunk costs for potential entrants. Stable oligopolistic industries and markets with few suppliers and very little entry, exit and churning are also easier to regulate by government, and are easier to self-regulate by industry. Suppliers know and monitor each other and report non-complying conduct to the government regulator or their industry association in order to level the playing field and maintain their competitive advantage.

One of the questions raised by these economic literatures are why some oligopolies and other industries have a culture that favours fair competition and regulatory compliance; while others with similar market structures have a culture that privileges anticompetitive conduct, rent seeking and non-compliance with the formal and informal rules of the market. Advances in these literatures that apply non-cooperative and cooperative game theory have explored this question with some success.[11]

This research employs the concepts of institutional inertia, stasis and path dependence to illustrate that each industry and regulatory regime have a distinct history and culture that are shaped by the many transactions and other interactions over an extended period between: (i) competitors, suppliers, business customers, final consumers and other participants in the affected supply chain; and (ii) the regulator, regulatees and other supply chain participants who e.g. complain to the regulator about the non-compliant behaviour of regulatees.

Applying the theory of dynamic repeated games in laboratory experiments and field research indicates that in many but not all circumstances the shared information, learning, expectations and values emerging from these interactions can result in a competitive game and pro-compliance culture that: (i) promotes compliance with the formal rules, even when regulatory penalties, enforcement capacities and budgets are comparatively modest; as well as (ii) compliance with informal rules that are developed through these interactions and that "fill in the gaps" in the formal rules and regulations.[12] On the other hand, interactions within other industries with broadly similar characteristics can result in a business culture and informal rules of business conduct that encourage non-compliance with the formal rules that can be particularly detrimental to regulatory outcomes and the public interest when regulatory budgets and the risks of being investigated and penalized are substantially reduced.

AN ANALYTICAL FRAMEWORK FOR ASSESSING
THE DYNAMICS OF COMPLIANCE RISK

Drawing on the literatures reviewed in the previous section, it is possible to construct a framework that would allow government officials to make more informed judgements about the likely consequences of reductions in regulatory agency budgets on compliance levels. These judgments would be based to some degree on regulator experience, knowledge of the industry and speculation about future events and outcomes. However, this situation would be no different than the assessments that regulators and other officials make when proposing and implementing new regulatory requirements.

As stressed at the outset, the fact that regulations will continue in force as mandatory behavioural prescriptions is critically important to this analysis. However, a complex interplay of economic and social factors shapes the context for regulatee decision making and the actual decisions they make. These non-regulatory causal influences and mechanisms interact with perceptions of existing regulations and together influence compliance risk.

The classical deterrence model, which remains the major influence on the design of regulatory compliance regimes, assumes that regulatees are rational risk calculators whose decisions to comply or not to comply are based on their assessment of the likelihood of detection, the likelihood of sanction, and the severity of sanction. But this view is incomplete. Regulatees, like the rest of us, are also social and political actors. As social actors, they tend to follow the group they belong to. As political actors, they are "ordinarily inclined to comply with the law, partly because of a belief in the rule of law, partly as a matter of long-term interest."[13]

In some cases, reduced regulatory budgets may not translate into significantly increased non-compliance because the continued existence of the legal requirements, coupled with the power of the non-regulatory causal influences, will ensure sufficient "momentum" to sustain compliance levels for the full period that regulatory agency expenditure restraint is applied. In other cases, the array of non-regulatory influences on compliance will be relatively weak and the activities of regulators will be critical to managing compliance risk. Governments that can learn to distinguish between these two sets of circumstances will be better able to find the appropriate balance between the transitory fiscal imperatives that prompt the periodic bouts of regulatory budget restraint with the continuing economic and social policy goals that underlie the extensive array of public interest regulatory requirements.

This chapter proposes that governments approach this task by applying an analytical framework that categorizes non-regulatory causal influences on compliance into six broad categories: social norms, market characteristics, the nature of the regulated good, the sunk costs of compliance, the international regulatory landscape, and the opportunities for co-regulation.

The Power of Social Norms

"Corporate actors are ... also often concerned to do what is right, to be faithful to their identity as a law abiding citizen, and to sustain a self-concept of social responsibility."[14]

Social norms can be extremely powerful influences on behaviour, far more powerful than the law itself. Social norms and the law often work together in a self-reinforcing "system." In some cases, the law or regulation may simply reflect the prevailing social norm (e.g., prohibitions against murder), while in other cases social norms may change to accord with the behavioral constraints specified in the law or regulation. The prevalence of drunk driving has fallen considerably over the last two decades, partly due to tougher laws, increased penalties, aggressive enforcement, but also due to changes in the social acceptability of driving when impaired.

On the other hand, if the law and social norms are not congruent (e.g., traditional aboriginal hunting and fishing practices vs. wildlife regulatory regimes or limits on the duration of shifts for truck drivers vs. industry practice), then budgetary cutbacks that translate into reduced compliance monitoring and enforcement activity are more likely to result in increased compliance risk.

Social norms that reinforce regulatory requirements can be shaped by firms and industry associations in a manner that promotes high standards of conduct and corporate social responsibility. Complying with an industry's social norms reduces uncertainty, stress, and information and transactions costs, and provides a sense of belonging to a community and subjective well-being to companies and their managers and employees. If regulatees operate in markets in which social norms, codes of conduct or forms of self-regulation are working well, temporary reductions in the "regulatory footprint" resulting from budget cutbacks may have only marginal impacts on regulatory compliance and outcomes.

It is important to exercise caution, however, when weighing the potential impact of social norms on regulated activity. The perceived legitimacy of the regulation can be a critical factor that influences its congruence with social norms. If the regulated population and other affected parties including final consumers have not accepted the legitimacy of the "problem" that the regulations are intended to address, or if they consider the regulatory requirements to be ineffective, poorly designed or too onerous, sustained levels of compliance and enforcement activity are likely to be necessary to ensure acceptable compliance rates.

> "Business managers have their own strongly held views regarding proper public policy and business conduct. Sometimes, they violate rules and regulations from principled disagreement, because they find them arbitrary and/or unreasonable."[15]

Finally, even the strongest social norms do not ensure 100% compliance; (but of course, making a law or a command and control regulation does not ensure complete compliance either!) Some percentage of the regulated population, ranging up to 20% in some regimes, will be "amoral calculators," who have calculated the risks and simply will not comply. Regulatory programs that have adopted risk-based targeting strategies for compliance monitoring and enforcement have already focused much of their resources on these types of actors. Reduced regulatory agency budgets and enforcement activity will have little impact on a population in which noncompliance is already endemic.

The greater concern about regulatory agency cutbacks leading to an increase in compliance risk arises from the possibility that cutbacks will trigger a diffusion process that is similar to the network dynamics of an epidemic. The consequence may be a dramatic increase in the number of formerly compliant regulatees who detect the change in enforcement activity, become concerned about losing market share to non-compliant competitors, and (perhaps reluctantly) decide that they need to "level the playing field" by becoming non-compliant themselves.

Market Structure

When the regulated conduct takes place within the context of a functioning market,[16] the characteristics of that market and the goods or services provided in that market may also influence the extent to which changes in the intensity and reach of compliance and enforcement activities influence compliance risk. A variety of inter-related market attributes will be relevant including: the degree of supplier concentration and market competition and "contestability"; the extent to which suppliers or purchasers (either collectively or individually) can exercise market power; the availability of reasonably close product substitutes; the prevalence of information asymmetries; the structure of affected supply chains; and the extent of time delays in the flow of information that influences the decisions of regulatees and their suppliers, business customers and final consumers. These issues are addressed in the following sub-sections.

The risk of eroding compliance may be lessened in relatively stable markets characterized by low rates of entry and exit, relatively few suppliers, and competition based more on reputation for product quality and safety and good service rather than low prices. In this situation, if the industry is largely compliant with the regulatory requirements when the budget reductions are implemented, this method of doing business is likely "embedded" within the industry's history and culture even when the products are experience or credence goods. Any short-term advantages from "cheating" could be massively offset by long-term harm to reputation and competitive positioning. Suppliers may not be willing to take that risk.

By contrast, if the market is highly competitive based on low cost and price, with a large number of suppliers, high entry, exit and churning rates and little attachment to the industry, cutbacks in regulatory oversight can pose a far greater risk to erosion of compliance levels. This is particularly true when the goods and services are sold to vulnerable consumers who are less able to protect their own interests. Compliance risks may be further increased if the market is characterized by information asymmetries that make it difficult for even better informed and more demanding customers to make sound purchasing decisions.

Product Characteristics

The likelihood of being able to sustain acceptable levels of compliance through periods of reduced regulatory budgets is also influenced by the nature of the goods and services offered in a regulated marketplace. As was noted above, in some industries where products are differentiated and competition is based largely on the reputation of suppliers, there is less risk that reduced budgets and enforcement activity will erode compliance.

In other industries, where products are highly differentiated experience or credence goods, the compliance risk dynamics can be more problematic. Pervasive information asymmetries, arising from the nature of the products, become important indicators of compliance risk.

Particular caution should be exercised when the regulated products are high-value goods and services that are purchased infrequently and where other factors, such as social norms, market structure and the context for the transaction, that might otherwise help to sustain compliance levels, are much weaker. These factors help to explain why governments closely regulate pharmaceuticals, other health care products and funeral services, and why governments are under pressure to better regulate mortgage agents and providers and financial advisers after the American sub-prime mortgage fiasco and global financial crisis of 2007–2008.

In sum, the effects of regulatory agency budgetary cutbacks on regulatory compliance and outcomes depend not only on market structure, the extent of competition and product characteristics. Market stability and churning, industry history and culture, and how regulatees have competed in the past and are expected to compete in the future are also important to regulatory risk, compliance and outcomes after regulatory agency budgets are reduced.

Sunk Costs of Compliance

Regulated firms not only produce goods and services. They also "produce" regulatory compliance by spending on compliance costs. Although compliance cost burdens may be reduced over time through regulatory innovations and technological improvements, regulatees will still consider the sunk costs of their past investments in compliance. These costs include investments in both hard and soft assets for: (i) equipment, materials, technology, training, and relationships with suppliers needed to ensure compliance; and (ii) building a reputation with business customers, final consumers and regulatory authorities for fair competition and regulatory compliance.

Many firms establish long-term relationships with their suppliers, business customers and final consumers by providing high quality and safe goods and services and by investing in long-term marketing and product promotion activities. They also have incentives to build constructive relationships with their employees, through investments that better ensure compliance with worker health and safety regulations, employment standards, and privacy safeguards.

These investments secure valuable tangible and intangible assets. Protecting the value of these assets may induce regulatees to comply with regulations despite a perceived lower risk of detection and sanction. However, given the depreciation of capital goods as well as intangible assets through time, the existence of sunk costs cannot be relied upon to motivate compliance indefinitely.

The Global Regulatory Landscape

Over the past two decades, increasing market globalization and freer international trade and investment have changed the Canadian regulatory landscape. This presents new challenges as well as opportunities.

On the one hand, increased imports from less developed countries, whose regulatory regimes are typically characterized by weak enforcement and compliance, have placed increased demands on Canadian regulators. On the other hand, Canada may be able to "free-ride" on the stronger regulatory enforcement and compliance programs of our major trading partners. The United States and European Union have high product safety standards and major retail chains have a strong incentive to abide by them. When economies of scale and scope are important, Canadian manufacturers that participate in global supply chains have strong incentives to comply with these regulatory standards regardless of whether similarly high standards are enforced in Canada. In this situation, it may be possible for Canadian regulators to reduce compliance and enforcement budgets with little negative effect on the public interest.

Capitalizing on Co-Regulation

Another way in which governments can reduce regulatory agency budgets while minimizing the adverse impacts on the public interest is by optimizing the opportunities for private sector, civil society, community, and consumer involvement in regulatory design and implementation. This is referred to here as "co-regulation," although as demonstrated below, co-regulation can take place in a variety of ways.[17] The case study examples of co-regulation provided in this sub-section also illuminate the importance of some of the other issues and causal factors described in this chapter.

One example comes from the competition law context. This approach pertains to potential discrepancies between the price charged for products at the cash register, and the listed price (referred to as "double-pricing"). The

Competition Bureau has endorsed a "scanner price accuracy code" whereby participating merchants[18] agree to provide a product to customers at no cost up to a maximum of $10, when the customer is overcharged as a result of scanner price inaccuracies that are brought to the attention of the merchant.[19]

This approach involves a private regulatory instrument (the code), which was developed with the involvement of the Consumers' Association of Canada. The code's effectiveness depends on customers bringing incidents of non-compliance to the attention of participating merchants, and on the active involvement of private sector industry associations, individual retailers, a consumers association, and individual consumers in its development and implementation.[20]

The code reduces the need for the Competition Bureau to expend enforcement resources on the prohibition against double pricing found in the Competition Act. The motivation for industry associations to spearhead the development of the scanner price accuracy code came from their desire to establish a national approach to scanner price accuracy issues, avoid enforcement actions, and be seen by consumers as proactively addressing double pricing problems. Another motivation for private sector action is that the comparatively small pain of refunding a customer creates a method for the merchant to become aware of a mis-pricing problem through a systematic approach that allows management to track and address problematic activity.

This is an instance of "regulated self-regulation" in the sense that the private regulatory activity is overseen and approved by the regulatory authority. The Competition Bureau retains the authority to bring an enforcement action on scanner price accuracy whenever warranted. This is a good illustration of a low cost but effective "nudge" as described in the behavioral economics literature.

A second example where regulators are tapping into private sector energies revolves around the private actions provision in section 36 of the Competition Act. Pursuant to this provision, it is possible for one business to bring an action directly against another business to address an issue of alleged non-compliance with the terms of the Competition Act. Both Telus Communications and Rogers Communications have brought section 36 actions against competitors concerning alleged instances of misleading advertising relating to whether particular telecommunications services were or were not the "most reliable," the "largest" or the "fastest."[21]

When industry players bring actions directly against each other, this reduces the need for Competition Bureau officials to undertake expensive investigative activity and bring enforcement actions – while the Bureau retains a residual capability to bring enforcement actions when appropriate. In effect, the costs associated with addressing alleged instances of non-compliance are largely borne by the industry itself, without drawing on limited enforcement resources funded by the taxpayer.

Another example of co-regulation comes from the fisheries management context.[22] Historically, fisheries were viewed as a common pool resource, and were regulated through top-down command and control government allocation approaches whereby the fishers had no long term stake in the fishery. This led to classic "tragedy of the commons" situations as witnessed by the collapse of the East Coast cod fishery, which resulted from a "free-for-all" where everyone fished to their maximum authorized capability because no fishers had an incentive to behave otherwise.

In 1995, the Department of Fisheries and Oceans (DFO) began to introduce "community-based management systems" for the inshore East Coast fishery. Under this system, each community of fishers is allocated a quota, and a governing structure for each community is put in place. Community Management Boards are created to implement decision-making such as: development of a community harvest plan, controlling the activities of member fishers, and development and implementation of penalty provisions for violations and trip limits. Elected members normally are the fishers, but in some cases non-fishing representatives are also members. These boards provide input into in-season management and develop, implement and monitor controls on the activities of the community fleet, including dockside monitoring of catches.

All this takes place within an overarching government regulatory framework. While studies suggest that problems still remain, they also conclude that the participatory management approach has had a positive impact on conservation, has reduced community conflict, and has received wide industry acceptance in comparison with the previous top-down allocation process. The latter process created an adversarial system with little positive dialogue between government and industry and little cooperation among regulatees.

A final example of co-regulation comes from the mining sector, where mining companies are developing impact and benefits agreements (IBAS) with local communities (often indigenous). Under these agreements, companies commit to profit sharing, hiring and training persons from the local community, supporting local development, using local contractors, and involving community members in monitoring of environmental and social progress. The IBAS are private agreements between the participating companies and communities.[23]

However, during the government's environmental impact assessment and related regulatory approval processes that precede authorization of any mining development, the appropriate regulators look for indications that communities are "on side" with the proposed development. Companies that can indicate that impact and benefit agreements are in place with local communities, with communities standing beside them to support such statements, are more likely to be favourably received at the regulatory approval stage. Following the approval stage, government regulators retain the authority to bring enforcement actions should incidents of non-compliance arise.

From the standpoint of a dynamic systems and risk-based analytical framework, what these various examples of co-regulation suggest is that there is potential for regulators that are facing budgetary cutbacks to harness private sector, civil society, consumer and citizen energies and capabilities in support of continued achievement of regulatory objectives. The challenge is to identify those circumstances where there are tangible, ongoing incentives for the private sector and civil society to participate on an equal footing. This requires the creation of the appropriate regulatory/administrative structure to promote and support co-regulation; while maintaining a residual but still credible monitoring and enforcement capability to address non-compliant behaviour and ensure that co-regulatory approaches do not stray from their public policy objectives.

Implications for Public Goods and Common Pool Resources

This chapter largely focuses on regulatory regimes, compliance levels and outcomes that are mediated and strongly influenced by transactions involving private parties in markets. Much regulation, of course, is aimed at controlling the production and use of public goods (e.g., privacy, public safety) and common pool resources (water, air, fisheries).

These goods are often not directly subject to market discipline; and thus the likelihood of compliance with applicable regulatory requirements will not be heavily influenced by factors such as market structure or product characteristics. They may, however, be influenced by social norms and obligations, sunk compliance costs, and information asymmetries between regulatees, the regulator, and other affected parties.

Reducing regulatory agency budgets in domains such as environmental protection or regulation of common property resources is, therefore, more likely to produce outcomes harmful to the public interest. After the budget of the Ontario Ministry of Environment was cut by 43 percent between 1995 and 1998, Ontario reportedly became the most polluted province in Canada; and evidence of the deterioration in the province's environmental condition has been described as widespread. In the case of the Walkerton tragedy, an inquiry concluded that "the provincial government's budget reductions led to the discontinuation of government laboratory testing services for municipalities in 1996."[24]

Public safety regulation is another area in which caution should be exercised. After budgetary reductions resulted in reduced monitoring of the safety regulation for explosives, an increased incidence of non-compliance was found, which then prompted greater reliance on costly enforcement action by regulatory authorities. More research is needed to fully appreciate the differences between private goods, public goods, merit goods and common pool resources and to develop the implications of these differences for the analytical framework described in this chapter.

Finally, and perhaps most significantly, cutbacks often have effects on the productive capacity of regulatory programs that last far longer than the duration of the expenditure restraints. Although reductions in O&M budgets will clearly affect a program's capacity to carry out ongoing operations in the short-term, the more significant impacts are long-lasting reductions in the strategic resources of the program. These include: (i) human resources including the inability to hire replacements for departing experienced employees, (ii) overall reduction in the experience and competencies of staff, (iii) inability to maintain ongoing training and skills development, (iv) atrophy of critical intelligence networks in both the regulated community and among beneficiaries, (v) rust-out and obsolescence of equipment, and (vi) erosion of networks with regulatory authorities in other jurisdictions. All these strategic resources can eventually be rebuilt, but the time required to restore these capabilities may exceed the time needed for a powerful downward spiral in regulatory compliance to take hold.

CONCLUSIONS AND FUTURE POSSIBILITIES

Several conclusions emerge from this analytical effort to review past approaches and advocate a better approach to dealing with likely regulatory agency budget cuts in the coming period of austerity.

The chapter provides regulators, departments and central agencies with a checklist of key issues and causal factors to be considered when reductions in regulatory agency budgets cannot be avoided. Regulatory budget cutbacks are less likely to result in serious reductions in compliance and performance when: products and transactions are less complex; industries are more stable and mature; corporate reputation for product quality and social responsibility is important to competitive advantage; well governed global supply chains and large retailers and other business customers with buyer power discipline company behaviour; larger trading partners have the regulatory resources and will to maintain high compliance levels during a period of fiscal restraint; and competitive markets and co-regulation provide voice and exit opportunities to consumers and other stakeholders.

In contrast, the risks for compliance and performance are higher for markets and industries with the opposite characteristics such as: social norms and a business history and culture that favour non-compliance; substantial instability, entry, exit and "churning"; large imports from emerging market economies; significant information asymmetries, switching costs, and buyer inertia; and, public and merit goods and common pool resources that are less subject to market discipline.

The conceptual analytical framework is best illustrated and tested through exploring the compliance and related effects of previous regulatory budget cutbacks. We have not had the space and time to provide detailed case studies.

Furthermore, regulators and central agencies are reluctant to share information on major budget reductions that had adverse effects on compliance and performance; or on reverse situations when regulatory cutbacks had minimal effects on compliance for fear that their agencies will be targeted in the next round of fiscal restraint.

Nonetheless, the chapter illustrates why and how similar regulatory agency budget cutbacks can have different consequences for compliance and performance depending on the characteristics of the regulatory regime. At one extreme, deregulation, combined with minimal regulatory budgets and political will to enforce the remaining rules, largely explain the meltdown in the American subprime mortgage market of 2007–08, which led to the global financial crisis and recession.[25]

Similar forces help to explain the major problems faced by competition and consumer protection regulators over the past two decades in combatting the dramatic growth in telephone marketing, Internet and related consumer scams and frauds. Both situations are consistent with what could be called "Gresham's law of regulation," whereby non-compliant behaviour forces out compliant behaviour, to the point where the continuing existence of entire industries and markets are placed at risk.

At the other extreme, competition authorities in many countries are now addressing anticompetitive mergers, cartels, abuses of dominance, and other anticompetitive conduct and arrangements, despite limited budgets in comparison with the large number of transactions that take place each day in the modern economy.

Reasonable levels of compliance with competition rules despite limited regulatory agency budgets can be explained by several factors. These include: social norms that on balance favour competition; complaints to competition authorities from competitors, suppliers, business customers, final consumers and civil society groups; and the significant monetary costs and losses in reputation that result from defending and losing a competition law case. Moreover, voluntary compliance with competition rules is in the self-interest of legal and economic advisers, whose reputations and high salaries and fees are based on their ability to keep their companies and clients out of trouble with the competition authorities.

Other regulatory regimes with similar characteristics are achieving reasonable compliance rates with comparatively small budgets as a consequence of social norms, market and product characteristics, reputation effects, a favourable compliance culture, and/or regulatee self-interest. These regimes could include intellectual property rights, corporate governance, product safety, and, at least in Canada, the conventional products of federally regulated financial intermediaries. Markets and industries with these and other characteristics may be able to accommodate budgetary cutbacks with limited decreases in compliance and performance.

There are some additional issues in the literature that cannot be fully captured in the conceptual cause-and-effect framework described earlier but are important to the chapter's overall argument.

A regulatory agency experiencing a major budgetary cutback can introduce regulatory efficiency measures. Agency overheads could be reduced. The agency could launch a major business and public education program in order to increase voluntary compliance and public awareness of the negative consequences for them and the Canadian economy and society of non-compliance.

The agency could hold discussions with other Canadian regulators with similar mandates in order to reduce overlap and duplication and implement joint enforcement strategies; or could establish and strengthen agreements of mutual cooperation, support and recognition with foreign regulators that are enforcing the same or similar regulations. The regulatory agency could better target its more limited resources on the goods, services, activities, transactions, companies and industries that are more problematic for regulatory compliance and performance.

A regulator experiencing serious cutbacks could request approval to significantly increase the penalties for violations and the number of people and entities subject to penalties. The latter could go beyond the offending companies to include their managers and senior officials, industry associations and their officials, and legal and economic advisors who e.g. are advising their companies, members and clients that they can now "break the law with impunity."

To have the desired effect, increased penalties could be supported by a leniency and whistle blower program; some kind of "criminal conspiracy" type provision to be applied to the above individuals and entities; and a public information program which emphasizes why serious penalties are needed to protect the public from serious harm and thus increase "moral outrage" when regulations are violated.[26]

Finally and less advisedly, the affected regulators could be less than fully transparent regarding the cutbacks in regulatory budgets and enforcement capacities, through for example capitalizing on their information advantages by providing only generic information so that a specific regulatee would not know whether its activities are directly affected; and/or through strategic communications initiatives that would publicize the outcomes from the enforcement cases that are undertaken. Communications strategies along these lines should be carefully designed to minimize the downside risks. Regulatees may learn from their agency contacts that enforcement activities have been curtailed, or could learn for themselves based e.g. on fewer inspections that they now have a safer environment for non-compliance. The result in either case would be a reduction in credibility and trust between the regulator and regulated companies that could further undermine future compliance.

These additional issues further illustrate the complex relationships between regulators and regulatees that need to be addressed in future research in order to turn the conceptual framework described in this chapter into an actual analytical framework and simulation model.

NOTES

1 This chapter addresses the budgets allocated by governments to their regulatory activities and entities. Throughout the chapter, the terms regulatory agencies and regulators are used interchangeably to encompass stand-alone independent boards and commissions such as the Canadian Radio and Television Commission (CRTC) and the Nuclear Safety Commission, as well as other regulatory agencies and units that are either within or at least have some ties to a ministry or department such as the Canadian Competition Bureau and the National Parole Board.

2 G. Stigler, "The Theory of Economic Regulation," *The Bell Journal of Economics and Management Science*, 2(1): 3–21 Spring, 1971.

3 E. Ostrom and J. Walker, eds., *Trust and Reciprocity: Interdisciplinary Lessons from Experimental Research.* New York: Russell Sage Foundation, 2003.

4 J. Stiglitz, "Information and the Change in the Paradigm in Economics," Columbia Business School New York, Prize Lecture, December 8, 2001.

5 C. Wilson and C. Waddams-Price "Do Consumers Switch to the Best Supplier?" ESRC Centre for Competition Policy, School of Economics and School of Management, University of East Anglia, March 2007.

6 The sunk cost effect is particularly important to the analytical framework described in the next section. Sunk costs are the expenditures and investments of consumers and producers that cannot be recovered when there are major changes in e.g. technologies, policies, and regulations; or when a producer exits a market or a householder relocates from a depressed to a more prosperous area where house prices are much higher.

Based on the premise that "bygones are bygones," conventional microeconomics presume that sunk costs will have no effect on the decisions of producers, consumers and other market participants. However, industrial organization and behavioural economics demonstrate: (i) how incumbents use sunk cost investments to discourage entry, (ii) why producers stay with a product, technology or production process much longer than they should to avoid the financial and psychological costs of making the necessary changes, and (iii) why consumers remain loyal to a product, service provider and/or vendor when better alternatives are available.

7 S. Bowles, "Endogenous Preferences: The Cultural Consequences of Markets and Other Economic Institutions," *Journal of Economic Literature* 36: 75–111, March 1998.

8 W. Harrington, "Enforcement Leverage When Penalties Are Restricted," *Journal of Public Economics* 37: 29–53, 1988.

9 R. Thaler and C. Sunstein, *Nudge: Improving Decisions about Health, Wealth and Happiness.* New Haven and London: Yale University Press 2008.

10 S. L. Harris, "The Global Financial Meltdown and Financial Regulation: Shirking and Learning – Canada in an International Context," in G. Bruce Doern and Christopher Stoney, editors, *How Ottawa Spends 2010–2011: Recession, Realignment and the New Deficit Era.* Montreal and Kingston: McGill-Queen's University Press 2010, 68–86.

11 R. Richter, "The New Institutional Economics – Its Start, Its Meaning, Its Prospects," *European Business Organization Law Review* 6: 161–200, 2005.

12 The theory of dynamic repeated games encompasses continual interactions and exchanges among the players, bounded rationality especially about future outcomes and conduct, in particular imperfect foresight about future payoffs, bounded self-interest and no end in sight for the "repeated game."

13 R. Kagan and J. Scholz, "The Criminology of the Corporation and Regulatory Enforcement Styles," in *Enforcing Regulation*, K. Hawkins and J. M. Thomas editors. Boston: Kluwer-Nijhoff, 1984.

14 I. Ayres and J. Braithwaite, *Responsive Regulation: Transcending the Deregulation Debate.* Oxford: Oxford University Press, 1992.

15 F Corneliussen, "Justifying Non-Compliance: A Case Study of a Norwegian Biotech Firm," CARR Discussion Paper No. 20 2004.

16 The regulated conduct would need to relate to either the attributes of the good or service (e.g., quality, safety) or to the manner in which the market transactions are carried out (e.g., representations, documentation, etc.).

17 For a recent discussion of the meaning of co-regulation and related terms, see L. Senden, "Soft Law, Self-Regulation and Co-Regulation in European Law: Where Do They Meet?" *Electronic Journal Of Comparative Law* 9 ((1) January 2005, http://www.ejcl.org/91/art91-3.html.

18 The participating merchants are signatory companies who are members of the Canadian Council of Grocery Distributors, Canadian Federation of Independent Grocers, Canadian Association of Chain Drug Stores, and Retail Council of Canada, with 8000 retail outlets across Canada.

19 Competition Bureau, Code of Practice: Scanner Price Accuracy Code (2002), accessible at: http://www.competitionbureau.gc.ca/eic/site/cb-bc.nsf/vwapj/ct02381e.pdf/$FILE/ct02381e.pdf.

20 K. Webb, "The Voluntary Codes Phenomenon," in K. Webb, editor, *Voluntary Codes: Private Governance, the Public Interest, and Innovation.* Ottawa: Carleton Research Unit for Innovation, Science, and Innovation, 2004.

21 See A. Ackhurst and S. Mclean, "Canada: A Year of Significant Change: From "Per Se" to "Made in Canada," February 18, 2010, accessible at: http://www.mondaq.com/canada/article.asp?articleid=94068.

22 E. Peacock and C. Annand, "Community Management in the Inshore Groundfish Fishery on the Canadian Scotian Shelf," in R. Townsend, Ross Shotton, H. Uchida, editors. *Case Studies in Fisheries Self-Governance*, FAO Fisheries Technical Paper. No. 504, 2008.

23 IBAs are essentially private contracts that are entered into voluntarily, legally binding, project-specific, and often not described in existing legislation.

24 Environmental Commissioner of Ontario, *Open Doors: Annual Report* Toronto 1998; and D. O'Connor, *The Walkerton Inquiry.* Toronto: Ministry of the Attorney General May 2002.

25 D. Ireland and K. Webb "The Canadian Escape from the Subprime Crisis? Comparing the U.S. and Canadian Approaches," in G. Bruce Doern and Christopher Stoney, editors, How *Ottawa Spends 2010–2011: Recession Realignment and the New Deficit Era.* Montreal and Kingston: McGill-Queen's University Press, 2010, 87–108.

26 J. Darley, "Morality in the Law: The Psychological Foundations of Citizens' Desires to Punish Transgression," *Annual Review of Law and Social Science* 5 1 22, 2009.

PART TWO

Selected Issue and Departmental Realms

6 Harper Energy and Climate Change Policy: Failing to Address the Key Challenges

DOUGLAS MACDONALD

INTRODUCTION

The Stephen Harper government faces three challenges when making policy in the inter-related and overlapping fields of energy and environment. The first, which has faced all governments in Canada and elsewhere since environmental issues came on the policy agenda in the 1960s, is the inherently conflicting policy objectives in each. Because it is so important to economic development, the dominant energy-policy goal of all governments is security and reliability of supply at the lowest possible price and also with reasonable price stability. Reducing the environmental impacts of energy, however, contradicts that goal because doing so increases energy costs. Eliminating coal-fired electricity production and increasing supply from new renewables, for instance, are currently driving up electricity prices in Ontario, causing political problems for the McGuinty government. Carbon sequestration, if successful, will increase the cost of deriving energy from oil (how much will depend upon the extent to which the cost of sequestration is socialized through government subsidy, rather than paid by energy producers).

The second challenge, more specific to climate change, is the very different economic interests of fossil-fuel producing provinces such as Alberta and Saskatchewan, compared to hydro-electric provinces such as Manitoba and Quebec. For the carbon provinces, climate change policy is a major threat: for the hydro provinces it is a challenge, but also an economic opportunity, in terms of green economic growth and possible electricity exports. During the past twenty years, these conflicting interests, based in physical realities of geography and amplified by culture and politics, has been primarily responsible for the failure of the federal and provincial governments to collectively develop and implement effective national climate-change policy.

Thirdly, it is extremely difficult for any federal government to develop autonomous energy and environment policy, due to the deep integration of the Canadian and American economies. Canadian business leaders have consistently argued that, for competitiveness reasons, Canadian climate-change policies cannot be more stringent than American, leading to the wrenching debate over Kyoto Protocol ratification. More recently, concern has arisen that American federal climate change policy, coming from Congress or the Environmental Protection Agency, will impose border adjustment taxes, making Canadian exports less competitive. Another concern is American legislation based on carbon intensity of fuels which will have the effect of closing the US market to tar-sands oil unless some kind of exception is made by the Americans on energy security grounds. The Harper government must juggle environment-economy and carbon-hydro conflicts all within a very narrow margin of manoeuvre, without completely abandoning policy sovereignty.

These three difficulties have been compounded by the way in which governmental jurisdiction respecting energy and environment has recently become fragmented. The Canadian system of federal-provincial intergovernmental relations used to develop national climate-change policy suffered a near death blow with Kyoto ratification by the Chretien government in the face of determined provincial resistance; limped along under the Martin government as Canada's greenhouse gas (GHG) emissions increased significantly rather than reduced; and uttered its final death rattle with the election of the Harper government in January, 2006.

Today, there is no institutional mechanism in place for co-ordinating federal-provincial climate policy, nor for addressing interprovincial issues related to electricity, such as Newfoundland's objections in spring, 2010 to the proposed sale of New Brunswick Hydro to Hydro-Québec. To the extent any such mechanisms exist, they run along north-south cross-border lines, in bodies such as the Western Climate Initiative (WCI) made up of a number of US states and the Canadian provinces of British Columbia, Manitoba, Ontario and Quebec. An even weaker degree of co-ordination exists between the two federal governments in the form of the Canada-US Clean Energy Dialogue.

No institutional mechanisms link subnational cross-border policy co-ordination with corresponding cross-border efforts at the federal level. As a result, the Stephen Harper government is facing the three policy challenges set out above while operating in a field in which the provinces are both highly motivated and have undeniable constitutional and political power and without benefit of established, formal processes or governing bodies which can be used to achieve the two essential tasks of policy co-ordination. Those are, first, developing coherent, national federal-provincial policy and, second, ensuring it is to at least some degree aligned with policy south of the border, while maintaining policy sovereignty.

The first purpose of this chapter is to provide critical analysis of the way in which the Harper government is currently operating in this daunting policy context. This is done by first providing a chronological review of the relevant policy decisions it has made during the past year, with discussion of both the way in which jurisdictional fragmentation has influenced the decision itself and the likelihood that implementation will result in effective policy. Secondly, summary analysis is provided of the ways in which the federal government is or is not addressing the three basic challenges outlined above. The third objective is to provide suggestions for how the Harper government might better navigate through these rocky waters, something which is done in the concluding section of the chapter.

The argument advanced is that the Harper government is failing to address all three of these challenges. It is ignoring the environmental implications of energy development; is making no effort to address the problem of differing provincial interests with respect to climate change mitigation; and has abandoned, with one exception, climate change policy sovereignty. The federal government must change the trajectory of environment-energy policy by engaging with the provinces as equal partners. As set out below, it must work with them to develop a national energy policy which addresses these three basic challenges and thus contributes to Canadian unity and autonomy.

HARPER POLICY DECISIONS AND NON-DECISIONS

To a large extent, recent federal policy making has largely involved the implementation of previously announced policy. These lines of policy activity are reviewed, before discussing the new policy initiatives of the past year: internationally, alignment with the "Copenhagen Accord"; new regulations governing fuel efficiency of motor vehicles; the decision, if possible, to sell Atomic Energy of Canada Limited (AECL); announcement of plans to regulate coal-fired electricity-generation plants; and, in the category of non-decisions, failure to speak publicly on the Quebec-New Brunswick-Newfoundland electricity dispute or to respond to industry requests for the development of a national energy policy.

To briefly recapitulate, the Harper government announced in 2006, shortly after taking office, that Canada would not attempt to achieve the Kyoto goal of reducing greenhouse gas (GHG) emissions to 6% below 1990 levels. It introduced the Clean Air Act which addressed both toxic air pollutants and GHGs, relaxing planned industrial regulation for the latter, but then in the spring of 2007, in the face of public opposition, replaced the Act with non-legislative climate policy which was effectively a return to previous Liberal policy. There was no return, however, to previous governments' attempts to develop co-ordinated federal-provincial policy. Asked about the implication of BC's new plans for both a carbon tax and trading system, developed as part of the WCI, for his own government's policy, federal Environment Minister Jim Prentice said simply provinces were free to act on their own.

Co-ordination with the US, on the other hand, was a priority. In November, 2008, immediately after the election of Barack Obama who has promised federal climate-change legislation, the Harper government proposed publicly and with as much fanfare as possible, a Canada-US climate-change treaty which would both harmonize policy and ensure continued access to the US market. The new President, however, was not interested, forcing the Canadian government to settle for the Clean Energy Dialogue (periodic discussion by government officials) during President Obama's visit to Ottawa in February, 2009. Despite the lack of any treaty talks, the new federal government policy of alignment included explicit statements that the federal government would not regulate GHG emissions from the oil and gas sector until the US did.

In terms of spending, the 2009 budget switched energy research and development funding from renewables to carbon sequestration, the approach preferred by Alberta and Western Canadian energy interests. In November, 2009, a meeting of federal and provincial environment ministers was convened, for the first time since 2002, not to develop co-ordinated national policy but instead to brief the provinces on plans for the fifteenth Conference of Parties to the United Nations Framework Convention on Climate Change, to be held in Copenhagen in December. At that meeting, the federal government's inaction on the climate file was attacked not only by environmentalists, but also by the Ontario and Quebec governments.

Thus during the 2006–09 period, the major lines of the Harper government energy and environment policy were made clear. These included support for fossil-fuel extraction and export through such things as development of carbon sequestration technology; completion of the harmonization of federal policy with that developed in Washington; a similar following of the US policy lead at the international level; and no attempt at all to influence provincial policy or to develop co-ordinated federal-provincial policy. It was on this basis that policy decisions were made in 2010 and early 2011.

In terms of climate-change foreign policy, the federal government followed the US lead in January, 2010, when it changed its policy objective from a reduction of total Canadian greenhouse gas emissions of 20% below 2006 levels by 2020 to 17% below 2005 levels. This was done in order to ensure complete harmonization with the Obama administration position (which in turn was based on legislation earlier adopted by the House of Representatives – since by November, 2010, there has been no corresponding Senate legislation and thus there is doubt as to whether the US really has a current reduction target, a doubt greatly reinforced by the Republican Party victory in the mid-term 2010 US elections).

Minister Prentice had earlier stated: "It is absolutely counter-productive and utterly pointless for Canada and Canadian businesses to strike out on their own, to set and pursue targets that will ultimately create barriers to trade and put us at a competitive disadvantage."[1] In that same speech, the Minister underlined Canadian support for the agreement reached at Copenhagen amongst the US, China, India, Brazil and South Africa for voluntary, non-binding targets, acceptance of international monitoring of progress and an unspecified total of international financing to assist mitigation in developing nations (the agreement was not formally adopted by the Conference of Parties but instead "noted").

Minister Prentice made it clear why his government supported the Copenhagen agreement in preference to the Kyoto Protocol. First, because it included the US (unlike Kyoto), it provided a "reinforced framework"[2] for its policy of aligning Canadian federal policy with American and, secondly, unlike Kyoto it included all major emitters, including China and India. The Harper government, unlike Liberal governments before it, had never accepted the principle of "common but differentiated responsibility" adopted by the United Nations Framework Convention on Climate regime, which largely exempted southern developing states from requirements to reduce emissions, given historic responsibility for the problem of the north. In this regard, support for the Copenhagen Accord over the Kyoto Protocol was consistent with Harper government policy from the beginning. The desire to see the US included in any international treaty to which Canada was a party was consistent not only with Harper government policy, but also that of its Martin and Chretien government forerunners. The imperatives flowing from economic integration have molded all Canadian climate policy with the single exception of Kyoto ratification.

Domestically, the most significant energy and environment policy initiative was imposition of new motor-vehicle fuel-efficiency standards, developed in co-ordination with similar standards imposed by the Environmental Protection Agency (EPA) in the US and announced on the same day by both governments. In a news release dated April 1, 2010, Environment Canada stated it was taking this step to "further harmonize our climate change action with the Obama administration."[3] The new standards are expected to reduce relevant motor-vehicle GHG emissions by 25% by 2016. The policy development process nicely illustrates the interconnected nature of both Canada-US and also subnational-national policy making in both countries.

The original impetus came from California and a number of north-eastern US states, in the face of opposition from the G.W. Bush administration. The Obama administration, on the other hand, moved to adopt the California standards, which were eventually incorporated into the new, 2010 standards.[4] Before the Canadian federal government announcement, however, Quebec in January, 2010 had enacted legislation imposing the California standards in that province. Environment Minister Jim Prentice in a speech on February 1, 2010 in Calgary condemned the Quebec government action, saying "one of the most glaring examples of the folly of attempting to do it alone ... [is] the new and unique vehicle regulations in the province of Quebec."[5] The Quebec Environment Minister, Line Beauchamp, then replied that Quebec was not acting alone: "She argued that Quebec was part of a group that includes 15 American states representing 40 per cent of the North American auto market that have adopted what's known as the 'California standard' to reduce greenhouse gas emissions on new vehicles."[6] On April 1, 2010, the same day the Canadian and US governments announced their harmonized standards, the Quebec Ministry of Environment issued a news release hailing this as a "victory for Québec and federated states" in influencing national policy and saying Quebec would co-operate.[7]

As can be seen, the basic policy dynamic in this instance was as follows: initial action at the US subnational level, in California, followed by other US states; subsequent action at the Canadian subnational level, as Quebec decided to follow their lead; harmonization by the US federal government with the California standard; harmonization by the Canadian federal government with the US federal government. This illustrates the themes set out above. First, we see a loss of policy sovereignty, in that at both jurisdictional levels, Canadian governments are policy takers, not initiators. Secondly, within Canada federal and provincial policy is being co-ordinated more or less by happenstance, accompanied by public bickering, because there are no institutional mechanisms being used to develop co-ordinated national policy. As discussed below, this absence of a means to co-ordinate will ultimately undercut the effectiveness of policy because, by definition, subnational jurisdictions like the US coal states and Canadian carbon provinces are a major source of the problem and yet are under no compulsion to participate in climate change policy-making.

Adding further confusion to this dynamic, some three months after announcing the co-ordinated motor-vehicle standards, Environment Minister Jim Prentice announced a new policy initiative which was explicitly, he said, *not* aligned with similar US federal government action. On June 23, 2010, he announced that the government would regulate coal-fired electricity generation plants, in the form of requiring a transition to low emitting sources as existing plants reach the end of their economic life by 2020.[8] Prior to this announcement, in a speech delivered June 15, 2010, the Minister had explained that policy co-ordination was needed in transportation because "we [in Canada and the US] drive the same cars and trucks."[9] He went on to say, however: "Our countries are different and, in areas such as electricity, where Canadian circumstances and American circumstances are not the same, we will not hesitate to pursue a policy direction that reflects our differing circumstances."[10] In April of 2010, however, the Minister had said that he would continue to co-ordinate oil and gas industry regulation with that of the US because it is a "trade-exposed" sector which competes internationally and he was concerned about loss of jobs and investment if Canadian policy differed from American.[11]

Although we need to read it into the Minister's remarks, since he provided no explicit explanation of why some climate policy is aligned and some not, it seems that the nature of the industrial sector is the determining criterion. An additional complementary factor may well be the preferences of the industrial sector itself. Because it sells into an integrated North American market, the auto industry has for many years advocated policy harmonization. The oil and gas industry has consistently taken the same position, most notably as it publicly battled to prevent Kyoto ratification, arguing that divergence from US policy would cause economic harm.

The electricity industry, by contrast has not objected to Canadian unilateral action. The Canadian Electricity Association reacted to the Minister's June 23 announcement by saying: "The industry welcomes the prospect of improved predictability in government decision-making now that the policy framework is established, and looks forward to working with the government in developing these regulations." The industry had earlier advanced a policy proposal very similar to this, in that it would have guaranteed no requirement to reduce emissions until generation plants had reached the end of their economic life.

In this case, it may be that integration with the US market lead the industrial sector to invite, rather than attempt to block, Canadian unilateral action. The export of electricity to the US market is an attractive option for the Canadian industry, and a strategy which has been pursued in particular by Hydro-Québec and the Quebec government. As the US moves to put a price on carbon, as it is likely to do, despite the current failings of the Obama administration, electricity produced without fossil fuel sources will become increasingly attractive. This strategy is suggested by a news media report that at a meeting with electricity industry executives in April, 2010, Minister Prentice "made it clear the government intends to highlight Canada's relative advantage in clean electricity compared to US reliance on coal."[12] The other factor possibly explaining the industry's welcoming acceptance of the June 23 announcement is that it gives regulatory certainty, coupled, as noted, with a guarantee that plants will be allowed to continue to operate until reaching the point at which they would need to be replaced in any case.

What is less clear about this policy initiative is the role of the provinces and in particular their silence after the Minister's announcement – the dog that did not bark. Traditionally, the provinces and in particular the larger ones (BC, Alberta, Ontario and Quebec) have been jealous of any direct federal regulation, using federal law, within their borders. This federal-provincial friction led to provincial litigation in the case of federal environmental assessment and has been settled by agreements, most notably the 1998 Harmonization Accord, in others. In this case, not only is the federal government declaring its intent to regulate within provincial borders but it is regulating *provincially-owned utilities*.

During the earlier acid rain policy process, the Ontario Ministry of Environment severely reprimanded their Environment Canada counterparts simply because they wanted to *talk* to Ontario Hydro, let alone subject it to federal regulation.[13] In the face of those objections, federal officials dropped their plans to communicate directly with the Ontario utility. Today, however, we see the federal government announcing plans to regulate its successor, Ontario Power Generation, with no subsequent complaint from Ontario. That can only be explained by the fact that Ontario, and the other provinces, had previously been consulted and given their consent. That in turn suggests there is at least some current degree of federal-provincial policy co-ordination, even though it is not taking place in the public eye.

By contrast, a lack of federal-provincial co-ordination, public or private, was clearly seen in 2010 with respect to federal nuclear policy. With adoption of the budget legislation by the House of Commons and, after some delay, the Senate on July 14, 2010, the federal government was given power to sell Atomic Energy of Canada Limited. Such a move is in keeping with the ideology of the Harper government and also a pragmatic response to the way in which AECL, plagued by such things as the failure of its isotope productions and ongoing deficits, has required large federal subsidies.

Sale prospects were diminished, however, by the decisions of both Ontario and New Brunswick, in 2009 and 2010 respectively, to decline to purchase AECL reactors. Ontario, faced with declining electricity demand after the recession has temporarily shelved the decision on which reactor to buy, while New Brunswick selected French Aereva in preference to AECL. Since the federal and provincial governments are unable to reach agreement on plans whereby AECL could sell its product at the very least within its own country, presumably with federal subsidy, the federal government privatization policy is undercut.

A similar lack of coordination, was displayed in the case of the proposed sale of New Brunswick Hydro to Hydro-Québec in the spring of 2010. Newfoundland, worried that Quebec would use its New Brunswick ownership to block transmission of Newfoundland electricity to the US market (and smarting for many years from Quebec refusal to renegotiate Churchill Falls rates), complained very publicly about the proposed sale. At the end of the day, however, the affair was settled not through any form of intergovernmental agreement, but instead because of powerful objections by New Brunswick voters. As in the case of Quebec motor-vehicle emission regulations, we see Canadian provinces strongly influenced by events south of the border, but without any institutional mechanisms, either federal-provincial or Canada-US, which can be used to co-ordinate policy.

Another instance of a failure to coordinate was provided during the past year by the cold shoulder given by the federal government to a proposal developed by energy industry firms, academics and environmentalists for a process to develop a national energy strategy. Such a strategy is needed, analysts like Jeffrey Simpson argue, to allow the federal and provincial governments to work together to address issues such as the Quebec-New Brunswick-Newfoundland imbroglio or the possibility of improving east-west electricity transmission, to say nothing of the fundamental need discussed below, of a coherent national climate change policy.[14] The Harper government, however, has given no public acknowledgement that it recognizes any such need or any encouragement to the authors of the proposed national strategy.

Late in 2010, Minister Prentice resigned to take a job in the private sector. John Baird acted as temporary Environment Minister and then in January, 2011, former television news anchor Peter Kent was appointed to the position. The new Minister's first major public statement said nothing about his plans to protect the environment, but instead offered a defence of the western oil sands as "ethical" because other oil-producing nations, such as Saudi Arabia, are less democratic and less concerned with human rights than is Canada. The US, the Minister said, should choose Canadian oil-sands oil over other sources for that reason.[15] Prime Minister Harper made the same claim immediately afterward.[16] There was no indication a change of minister would lead to any change of policy, only a change of policy discourse.

ADDRESSING THE THREE POLICY CHALLENGES

What can we see, in the events chronicled above, of the way in which the Harper government has addressed the three challenges documented at the beginning of the chapter? In terms of the first, it is now recognized that the inherent conflict between energy policy (intended to contribute to economic development) and environmental policy (intended to reduce impacts of energy use) can be significantly reconciled by adopting a policy of green energy development which both provides economic opportunities and assists the transition away from fossil fuel sources. For some time now, China has been investing significantly in development of green energy technology. Such a policy is also being implemented in Germany and other European countries, as well as at the European Union level, and within Canada by provinces such as Ontario and BC. In the former, the McGuinty government after it came to power successfully used public subsidy to attract motor-vehicle investment in the province and now is in the process of using the same policy instrument to attract green energy investment. The Ontario Premier has stated there is a need to supplement the traditional source of Ontario jobs and wealth creation, the motor-vehicle industry, and that he now sees green energy as a new driver for Ontario economic growth.

No such policy, however, is being put in place by the federal government. Funding for energy research and development, as noted, was shifted from renewable technologies to carbon sequestration and no climate-related funding was provided in the 2010 budget. Environmentalists have repeatedly pointed to the discrepancy between the US, in which green energy plays a significant role in federal stimulus spending, and Canada in which it does not. The 2008 election was fought in part on exactly this policy option, in the form of then Liberal Leader Stéphane Dion's proposal for ecological tax shifting to assist the transition to a new, green economy. Having publicly condemned such an initiative during the campaign, the Harper government has not mentioned it since. Instead, with the singular exception of coal-fired electricity generation discussed above, federal energy and environment policy now consists only of a pledge to follow the lead of whatever happens in Washington. After the failure of the effort by Senators Kerry, Graham and Lieberman to garner support for Senate climate legislation comparable to that passed by the House of Representatives – an effort which failed in part due to both incompetence and lack of engagement by the Obama White House[17] – it is clear that President Obama has neither the interest nor the political capital necessary to enact climate change legislation during his first term. His administration is taking some actions however in that, effective January 1, 2011, the Environmental Protection Agency (EPA) has implemented standards for greenhouse gas emissions from new electricity-generating plants and oil refineries and plans to announce regulations for existing plants, to come into effect in 2012.[18] The final policy result is uncertain, however, since these regulatory efforts will almost certainly be the subject of extensive litigation.

The Harper government has shown no interest in a policy thrust which sees climate change action as an economic opportunity. Instead it has hitched its wagon to carbon sequestration and to the US star, whose velocity and direction are unknown.

The nature of the second challenge, differing provincial economic incentives respecting greenhouse gas mitigation, has recently been illustrated by two studies. In 2007, the National Round Table on the Environment and the Economy published a proposal for a set of policies, using either a carbon tax or a cap and trade system, which would lead to significant reduction in greenhouse gas emissions. Significantly, the model for a reduction of 20% by 2020 shows: Alberta responsible for 36% of total Canadian emissions in that year, but 48% of total reductions; Saskatchewan responsible for 6% of the total emissions but 10% of the reduction; Ontario responsible for 27% of emissions but only 20% of reductions; and Quebec responsible for 11% of emissions but only 7% of reductions. The two carbon provinces, as they fear, are being asked on the evidence from this study to shoulder a larger burden than others in this policy prescription.

In 2009, the Pembina Institute and Suzuki Foundation released a set of recommendations for policy intended to reduce emissions by 25% below 1990s levels by 2020, accompanied by modeling of their economic impacts. In this model, Alberta GDP falls 12.1% below business as usual by 2020;

Saskatchewan's falls 7.5%; Ontario is not affected and Quebec falls 1.3%. The report states: "The urgent need to address the enormous GHG emissions from the coal-fired electricity and petroleum sectors in Alberta and Saskatchewan accounts for the reductions in the projected rates of growth in these provinces."[19] The message intended by the environmentalists in this study was that Canada could achieve a significant goal without doing major damage to its economy over the 10 year projected period. The press headlines, however, focused upon the outraged reactions of the two carbon provinces.

Climate change is the intractable policy problem it is for Canada not primarily because of the total cost of action, but instead due to the deep national unity implications of allocating that cost. There are many ways to reduce emissions, including fuel-switching, building insulation and changes in transportation. Ideally, the policy maker would select amongst those options using only the criteria of effectiveness and efficiency. That cannot be done, however, because of the political implications of the choice. While some options, such as buildings, are distributed relatively evenly on a per capita basis throughout the country others, such as fossil fuel extraction, are geographically concentrated.

As the NRTEE and Pembina figures show, this means effective policy will cause some regions and provinces to bear higher costs than others. Canada is a decentralized, often precarious federated state in which the provinces own the resources, and in which those high-cost regions are able to speak with a loud and effective voice. As has been pointed out by many analysts, action to reduce emissions by lead provinces such as British Columbia are at present being undercut by emissions growth in others such as Alberta. Differing economic incentives coupled with the nature of Canadian federalism have, however, meant that to date the political problem of cost allocation has not been addressed.

Currently, the Harper government is doing nothing to address this problem and, if anything, is making it worse. In 2009, Saskatchewan announced it has adopted the same objective as the government of Canada (as noted above, now changed slightly to align with the US international commitment) and had signed an agreement in principle with Ottawa to negotiate an "equivalency agreement" (a mechanism under the Canadian Environmental Protection Act whereby, provided provincial standards are "equivalent" to federal, federal law is not applied in the province).[20] In April, 2010, BC and Ottawa signed a similar agreement.[21] This means the federal government is not only willing to ignore unilateral provincial action but also to legitimize and codify it through bilateral federal-provincial agreements – the exact opposite of an effort to cajole, threaten and subsidize provinces to act as part of a national program intended to achieve one single broad objective.

While the Harper government has not acted to meet either of the first two challenges, it most certainly has taken policy action to address the implications of Canadian reliance upon the US economy. As noted, immediately after the election of President Obama the federal government proposed a Canada-US climate treaty which, had it been successful, would have potentially provided a secure institutional basis for alignment of policy, thereby avoiding both the perceived problem of loss of Canadian competitiveness due to more stringent regulation or the reverse, loss of export access due to what the US might perceive as inadequate climate standards. The proposal for a treaty and subsequent statements that the federal policy would fully align its policy with US federal policy (except, as noted, for coal-fired electricity generation) was not as significant a departure from previous policy as it might seem. Essentially, the Chretien and Martin administrations also did little on climate change because the US federal government was doing little. In November, 2008, however, with the election of an activist President who had committed to bringing in a national US program, doing nothing was no longer an option – hence the treaty proposal, which in fact was simply another step in a consistent policy of alignment followed by the Chretien, Bush and Harper governments.[22]

Two years later, in 2011, the situation is very different since the original assumption underlying the Canadian offer of a treaty, that the Obama administration would take policy action and US states would necessarily fall into line, no longer holds. It is unclear what policy action, if any, will be taken at the federal level in the US in the form of EPA regulation but in the absence of new law, US states are likely to continue to act unilaterally. Subnational initiatives, such as the Western Climate Initiative seem to be faltering (a number of US states have withdrawn).

Even if they continue in some form, as is likely, the important thing about these Canada-US subnational bodies is that by definition they can never become anything more than coalitions of the willing. The US coal states and Canadian oil provinces show no likelihood of joining, which significantly limits their ability to contribute to effective policy in either country. Thus at the present time *some* Canadian policy – motor vehicle standards at the federal level, cap-and-trade planning in BC, Manitoba and Ontario – is aligned with American policy, while *other* policy – coal-fired electricity at the federal level, industrial GHG emissions in Alberta and Saskatchewan – is not. More significantly, it is not at all clear what total US policy, the unco-ordinated sum of federal and state actions, Canada should align with. Here too, accordingly, because of changed circumstances in Washington – essentially, President Obama's decision not to engage with the issue and also now Republican control of the House of Representatives- the Harper government is failing to meet the challenge posed by economic integration.

A NATIONAL ENERGY POLICY?

What could the federal government do to more successfully meet the three core challenges of energy and environment policy? The answer is to display active leadership in working with the provinces to develop and implement a new, green, pan-Canadian energy and environment policy encompassing fossil fuels, nuclear, electricity and GHG emission mitigation by means of both renewable energy sources and building and transportation initiatives. Since the objective would be to obtain economic benefit from moving toward green energy it would address the first challenge; including the provinces as full partners, as discussed below, would address the second; and, thirdly, it would be aligned with US policy, but from a position of policy leadership, rather than lost sovereignty.

Roger Gibbins has argued that despite the enormous barriers to such an effort, such as widely divergent provincial interests, not to mention the political memories of the interventionist 1980 federal Liberal National Energy Program (NEP), it would be possible since it would follow in the Canadian tradition of national, intergovernmental projects in areas such as health, social assistance and immigration.[23] Such a national policy would provide a number of benefits, including: (1) bringing clarity and predictability to the sum of federal and provincial regulatory policies, an objective of the energy industry leaders currently pressing for such an initiative; (2) gaining the economic and job-creation benefits attendant upon framing the climate-change issue as an economic opportunity, rather than cost; (3) improving the effectiveness of climate-change policy by addressing the undercutting effects of Alberta and Saskatchewan policy, something in line with both demands of environmentalists and Canadian public opinion; and, (4) regaining policy sovereignty relative to the US, while moving in the direction US policy is certain to take in future, rather than staying mired in the current Canada-US state of disjointed confusion. Beyond these policy specific benefits, such an effort would, as a modern-day incarnation of John A. Macdonald's national railway, contribute to building and unifying the nation. As Professor Gibbins says: "There is simply too much at stake, and too much experience to suggest that while success may be elusive, it is not impossible."[24]

Such a policy cannot be created by any federal government acting alone, given the legal and political power of highly motivated provinces, and so must be done with full participation by both levels of government. This immediately raises the question of how the federal government, having decided to lead such an initiative, should proceed. Is success more likely achieved by building upon the existing institutional framework, primarily the Canada-US subnational bodies, to create new institutional mechanisms, or should it fall back on the institutional system used to develop climate policy up to 2002, co-ordinated by the Canadian Council of Energy Ministers and Council of Energy Ministers?

Neither of these options is appealing. The first does not include the two key carbon provinces, is entangled with US states and has not been in place long enough to provide a solid institutional base. The second was marked by failure, unable to overcome the veto power inherent in its consensual, lowest-common-denominator process. Instead, as suggested by Roger Gibbins, the answer lies in the established system of intergovernmental relations which has been successfully used during the past century to establish the national programs which stitch this country together.

To do this, several things are needed which were not present in previous federal-provincial climate change processes. The first is negotiation of the national GHG reduction target at home, with full participation by the provinces, rather than in the fora of the Kyoto regime in which the provinces play the role of, at best, advisors to the federal government and, at worst, spectators. Canada has been unable to develop a national program, and by default fallen back on unilateral action by each jurisdiction in some cases co-ordinated with US action, because many provinces never accepted the national goal.[25] In November, 1997, the federal-provincial system generated agreement on one goal, stabilization at 1990s levels, but the Chretien government then brushed that aside and instructed its diplomats to accept a three percent reduction below 1990 levels (the final goal negotiated at Kyoto in December of that year was a 6% reduction).

Not surprisingly, provinces then felt no obligation to achieve a goal imposed upon them unilaterally by the federal government. This time, the goal must be established through a federal-provincial negotiating process in which the federal government has previously given a commitment to take the outcome into the international arena, without alteration. All provinces now have their own targets, which would provide the opening position for negotiation. A committed federal government could then work to induce provinces to commit to targets which would add up to national action significantly more ambitious than at present.

The federal government would also have to depart from previous practice in another manner – the thorny issue of allocation of the cost of the total reduction amongst sources and provinces would have to be explicitly negotiated. During the previous process, this was the issue continually on the minds of all involved – what will this mean for economic prospects in my province? – but it was never explicitly discussed by ministers.[26] The basic stumbling block, that per capita and per GDP emissions are much higher in Alberta and Saskatchewan, which means achieving effective policy imposes much higher costs upon those two than others, can no longer be ignored.[27] Different provinces will have to reduce by different amounts (something required in any case by the efficiency criterion, which demands that cuts be made at the lowest possible per tonne of reduction cost) and, in addition, side-payment compensation must be part of the negotiations.

Recently Saskatchewan Premier Brad Wall has publicly objected to any form of national program which will result in revenue transfers from his province to the rest of Canada resulting from cap-and-trade sale of permits or carbon taxation. Snodden and Wigley have suggested that this cost allocation problem be addressed by federal government policy action putting a price on emissions, whether through cap and trade or a carbon tax, accompanied by a guarantee that all resulting revenues will be returned to each province.[28] This proposal at least addresses the essential issue of cost allocation, but suffers one fatal flaw – it is dependent upon federal law, something which will never be accepted by the western carbon provinces. Alberta in 2002 enacted its own climate legislation with the explicitly stated objective of putting a legal stumbling block in the way of federal law. The Saskatchewan equivalency agreement would preclude federal regulation. Instead, any national program will have to be a co-ordinated system of federal and provincial law and policy. The provinces own the resources and have always been the ones to regulate pollution – at the end of the day, Canadian national climate change policy, like acid rain and almost all other environmental policy, must rest upon the basis of co-ordinated provincial law. The argument that provinces might then renege through failure to effectively implement their law is valid, but can be addressed by monitoring, publicity and negotiation.

Roger Gibbins correctly points out, first, that any major federal-provincial program requires federal leadership and, secondly, that at present the provinces are doing more on climate policy than is their federal counterpart. Accordingly, the necessary first step in the creation of a national energy and environment policy is "to bring the federal government to the table."[29] He suggests that might be done through policy dialogue amongst non-state actors to develop a blueprint for a national program. This strategy is showing some results, since there are indications the Council of Environment Ministers will discuss a national energy policy at its 2011 annual meeting.

That undoubtedly would be helpful but, given the weak role in cabinet played by energy and environment ministers, something else is needed as well. The electoral incentives facing the federal parties must be changed sufficiently so that federal leadership, in full partnership with the provinces and couched in terms of environmental need, economic opportunity and national aspiration, resonates with voters. The federal government, of whichever party, must be shown the *political* benefits in a minority government Parliament, above and beyond the policy value, of such a national vision. To do that, a way must be found, through willingness to discuss their very real needs and fears and address them through compensation, to bring the western carbon provinces to the table as well. Only once they have shown signs they might play will a federal government sit down to deal the first hand.

CONCLUSIONS

In summary, the federal government cannot continue to ignore the provinces as it develops environment-energy policy. Given their constitutional and political powers, they must be accepted as full partners in the process of developing a new, coherent national (federal-provincial) energy policy which balances both economic and environmental implications. Canadian climate change targets must be set through federal-provincial negotiation, not in Washington or by the international regime. The cost of the total Canadian emission reduction thus agreed upon must be allocated amongst sectors and provinces using the established procedures of intergovernmental relations and equitable cost sharing. If that can be done (admittedly a tall challenge), the federal government will then be in a strong position to negotiate both with our American partner and the other members of the international climate-change regime.

NOTES

1 Speaking Points for The Honourable Jim Prentice, PC, QC, MP, Minister of the Environment to the Members of the University of Calgary School of Public Policy and the School of Business, Calgary, Alberta, February 1, 2010.
2 Ibid.
3 Environment Canada, News Release, April 1, 2010: "Canada and the United States Announce Standards for Regulating GHG Emissions from New Vehicles."
4 Greg Keenan, Steven Chase, and Nathan Vanderklippe, "Canada, U.S. team up to restrict auto emissions," *Globe and Mail*, April 1, 2010.
5 Speaking Points, Prentice, February 1, 2010.
6 Rhéal Séguin, "Ottawa Accused of Caving in to Auto Industry," *Globe and Mail*, Feb. 3, 2010.
7 Québec Ministry of Sustainable Development, Environment and Parks, News Release: "A Victory for Québec and Federated States," April 1, 2010.
8 Environment Canada, News Release, "Government of Canada to Regulate Emissions from Electricity Sector," June 23, 2010; Shawn McCarthy, "Ottawa Tells Energy Firms to Start Powering Down Coal-Fired Plants," *Globe and Mail*, April 25, 2010.
9 Speaking Notes for The Honourable Jim Prentice, PC, QC, MP, Minister of the Environment at the Canadian Energy Forum, Ottawa, ON, June 15, 2010.
10 Ibid.
11 Shawn McCarthy and Gloria Galloway, "Ottawa Stalls on Oil and Gas Emissions Rules," *The Globe and Mail, Report on Business*, April 16, 2001.
12 Shawn McCarthy, "Ottawa Tells Energy Firms to Start Powering Down Coal-Fired Plants."
13 Douglas Macdonald, *Policy Communities and Allocation of Internalized Cost: Negotiation of the Ontario Acid Rain Program, 1982–1985.* PhD dissertation, York University, 1997.
14 Jeffrey Simpson, "Canada Suffers for its Energy Incoherence," *Globe and Mail*, April 19, 2010.

15 Steven Chase, "Peter Kent's Plan to Clean Up the Oil Sands' Dirty Reputation," *The Globe and Mail*, January 7, 2011.

16 Steven Chase, "'Dirty'? 'Ethical'? The Oil-Sands Fight Renews," *Globe and Mail*, January 8, 2011.

17 Ryan Lizza, "The Political Scene: As the World Burns," *The New Yorker*, October 11, 2010.

18 Shawn McCarthy, "Greenhouse Gases: New U.S. Emission Rules to Put Spotlight on Ottawa," *Globe and Mail*, January 3, 2011.

19 The Pembina Institute and David Suzuki Foundation, *Climate Leadership and Economic Prosperity*, 2009, 4.

20 Government of Saskatchewan News Release, "Saskatchewan Takes Real Action to Reduce Greenhouse Gas Emissions." 2009.

21 Environment Canada News Release, "Canada and British Columbia Sign Agreement to Address Climate Change," April 6, 2010.

22 This argument is made in Douglas Macdonald and Debora L. VanNijnatten, "Canadian Climate Policy and the North American Influence," in Monica Gattinger and Geoffrey Hale, eds, *Borders and Bridges: Canada's Policy Relations in North America*. Don Mills: Oxford University Press, 2010.

23 Roger Gibbins, "Creating a Canadian Energy Framework: If You Build it, They Will Come," *Policy Options*, 31, no. 5, May, 2010, 61–63.

24 Ibid.

25 This point was made repeatedly in confidential interviews with climate officials from four Canadian provinces.

26 Confidential interviews.

27 As shown by the Pembina and NRTEE studies cited above and Amalia Yiannaka, Hartley Furtan and Richard Gray, "Implementing the Kyoto Accord in Canada: Abatement Costs and Policy Enforcement Mechanisms." *Canadian Journal of Agricultural Economics* 49, 1, 2005, 105–126.

28 Tracy Snodden and Randall Wigle, *Clearing the Air on Federal and Provincial Climate Change Policy in Canada*, IRPP Choices, 15, no. 11, December, 2009.

29 Gibbins, "Creating a Canadian Energy Framework," 62.

7 Time to Get Serious about the Strategic Environmental Assessment of Federal Government Policies and Plans

FRANÇOIS BREGHA

INTRODUCTION

The integration of environmental considerations into the design and implementation of public policies, programs and plans so that they are more environmentally sustainable is commonly referred to as Strategic Environmental Assessment (SEA). SEA is a decision-making tool that has its roots in the recognition that strategies that anticipate and prevent adverse environmental impacts are usually more effective and cheaper than strategies that try to correct these same impacts after the fact. In its landmark report making the case for a new development paradigm founded on sustainability, the World Commission on Environment and Development (the "Brundtland Commission") argued strongly for environmental factors to be given the same weight and considered at the same time as social and economic factors in decision-making[1].

The case for systematically integrating environmental factors into decision-making has become even more compelling in the quarter century since the Brundtland Commission issued its report as the following Canadian examples illustrate:

· The collapse of the northern cod fishery, largely as a result of over-fishing, resulted in the loss of tens of thousands of jobs and has cost some $2 billion in income support and retraining.[2]
· The Ontario Medical Association (OMA) estimates that air pollution is a contributing factor in almost 9,500 premature deaths per year in Ontario.[3]
· The failure until recently to regulate effectively the long-term environmental effects of industrial and military activity under federal jurisdiction has

saddled Canadian taxpayers with a financial liability associated with site clean-up estimated at over $3 billion (excluding the costs of decommissioning nuclear facilities).[4]
- The consumption of fossil fuels is contributing to climate change, leading to coastal erosion, more widespread insect infestations (e.g., by 2028, the Mountain Pine Beetle in British Columbia is expected to cut timber supplies by one third and cost 20,000 jobs[5]), more frequent extreme weather events and the accelerated melting of the Arctic ice cap.[6]

Policies that encourage urban sprawl, thus ingraining high energy and financial costs for transportation and other services; or support the draining of wetlands, thereby raising the risk of flooding during extreme weather events; or promote consumption, thus creating more wastes (e.g., the accelerated tax write-off of computer equipment); or subsidize specific crops, leading to the cultivation of marginal land and increased soil erosion, all provide additional instances of the unintended costs that can result from ignoring environmental factors in policy and program design.

But if the federal government recognized the need to conduct "environmental impact assessments for all proposals coming before the Cabinet for decision"[7] as early as 1990, why is it still doing such a poor job at it twenty years later? Is it because the tool it chose, strategic environmental assessment, is inadequate to do the job as designed? Or is it because political will is lacking, notwithstanding public assurances to the contrary? This analysis argues that SEA has been both inadequately designed and has suffered from political indifference. This chapter starts by defining strategic environmental assessment and explaining what makes it different from *project* environmental assessment and other instruments to integrate environmental considerations into decision-making; then examines the federal government's experience in SEA implementation, highlighting the results of various audits and one government-wide evaluation; and finally proposes additional measures to strengthen the process.

WHAT IS STRATEGIC ENVIRONMENTAL ASSESSMENT?

As the Commissioner of the Environment and Sustainable Development (CESD) explains, "the purpose of strategic environmental assessment is to help us avoid making environmentally costly mistakes before a particular course of action is decided".[8] The International Study of the Effectiveness of Environmental Assessment[9] defines SEA as a "systematic, proactive process for evaluating the environmental consequences of policy, plan or program proposals in order to ensure that they are fully included and addressed at the earliest appropriate stage of decision-making on a par with economic and social considerations."

Several attributes in this definition are worth underlining:

- *Systematic*: the analysis of environmental considerations should be rigorous;
- *Earliest appropriate stage*: the opportunity to influence policy and minimize environmental costs declines as the policy takes shape and various parties develop stakes in the initiative;
- *On a par with economic and social considerations*: to the extent possible, the analysis of environmental factors should be integrated with economic and social analysis.

Within these attributes, SEA remains a flexible tool that can take varying forms[10] depending on the needs of the institution and the nature of the assessment: a procurement policy, a regulatory proposal or a regional development program, to name three examples, may all have environmental implications that should be considered but the SEA process to do so should be customized to reflect their inherent differences. In Canada, the term "SEA" is thus generic and encompasses both the fluidity and variability of policy development as well as the greater predictability of a planning process.[11] This flexibility is both a strength and a weakness: while it has made it easier for federal departments to implement SEA, the absence of commonly-agreed methodologies has also led to wide variations in the quality of the SEAs conducted.

In all cases, SEA represents an explicit acknowledgment that economic development authorities[12] share a responsibility for environmental protection with environmental and resource conservation agencies and therefore need to consider the environmental implications of their policies just as they already consider other relevant matters (e.g., financial costs; administrative feasibility; effectiveness) in their policy formulation process.

Notwithstanding its name, SEA should also be used to *inform* policy, plan or program formulation and not be limited to just an *evaluation* of a proposal's environmental impacts after it has been developed. By introducing new analytical criteria, including science and evidence-based analysis early in the decision-making process, SEA can shed a broader light on the range of options available to meet a given policy objective and provide a fuller understanding of their implications. At its core, therefore, SEA is about sound decision-making, that is, providing ministers and senior managers with the relevant environmental information they need to make informed decisions.

By addressing the environmental implications of policies, programs and plans early in the decision-making process, the Canadian government argues that SEA can:[13]

1 optimize positive environmental effects and minimize or mitigate negative environmental effects;

2 consider potential cumulative environmental effects;
3 implement the Federal Sustainable Development Strategy;
4 save time and money by drawing attention to potential liabilities for environmental clean-up and other unforeseen concerns;
5 streamline project-level environmental assessment by eliminating the need to address some issues at the project stage;
6 promote accountability and credibility among the general public and stakeholders;
7 contribute to broader governmental policy commitments and obligations.

SEA, therefore, is not simply project environmental assessment carried to another level. Rather, SEA focuses on other considerations than project assessments, such as cumulative and long term effects and the coherence of planned development policies with national environmental objectives. As Figure 2 shows, project assessment and SEA share similarities but they also have different focal points and triggering mechanisms. In addition, project assessment has a statutory base while SEA rarely does.[14]

SEA, of course, is not the only instrument that governments have to integrate environmental considerations in their policies, plans and programs. Beside regulations and "green" taxes or subsidies, these include:

· Setting government-wide environmental policy goals to guide all policy-making;
· Formulating sustainable development (CESD) strategies;
· Setting new government-wide decision-making process requirements (e.g., Ontario Environmental Bill of Rights, the Manitoba and Quebec *Sustainable Development Acts*);
· Creating advisory and monitoring institutions (e.g., Commissioner of the Environment and Sustainable Development, National Round Table on the Environment and the Economy);
· Incorporating environmental considerations into procurement policies and the operations of government facilities.

While all these instruments have their place, none can substitute fully for the routine role that SEA should play in integrating environmental considerations in the design of government policies, plans and programs.

Finally, it is important to note that the implementation of an SEA process does not necessarily imply that environmental considerations will always prevail. Decision-makers will always retain the prerogative to trade off environmental values in favour of economic, ideological or social ones if they choose. The systematic consideration of environmental factors, however, implies that these trade-offs should be explicit and transparent, and that decision-makers should be accountable for them.

Figure 2
Comparison of SEA and project EA

	Strategic environmental assessment	Project environmental assessment
Application	Policies, programs and plans	Physical projects
Legal status	Not legislated	Legislated
Stage of decision-making	As early as possible in policy development process. Can frame subsequent project EAs	Usually conducted after a project design is well-advanced
Scope of analysis	Can be broad both in time and space. Can consider cumulative, synergistic and indirect effects	Geographically specific. Focus tends to be on direct physical effects of the project
Consideration of alternatives	Can address whether an initiative should go forward, plus where and what type of projects should be implemented	Focus is primarily on how to design a project to reduce adverse environmental effects
Procedures	Procedures must be adapted to decision-making process within ministry	Standard, government-wide, procedures
Mode of application	Self-assessment	Self-assessment with third-party assessment for selected projects
Trigger	Ministerial or Cabinet decision	Decision involving federal land, funding or regulations.

SEA PRACTICE IN THE FEDERAL GOVERNMENT

While the Canadian government was one of the world's first to mandate SEA in 1990, little progress was made in the first decade of implementation, leading the CESD to issue a critical report of federal practice in 1998.[15] The government responded by issuing a more detailed directive in 1999 (the *Cabinet Directive on the Environmental Assessment of Policy, Plan and Program Proposals*) which it updated in 2004 (once more in response to a critical CESD audit) and again in 2010. The Directive focuses federal SEA to decisions that meet two conditions:

1 Proposals submitted to an individual Minister or Cabinet for decision; and
2 Proposals that raise important environmental issues.

The federal SEA process can be characterized as follows:

· It is *not legislated* but it is not completely voluntary either, as the Cabinet Directive stipulates when SEAs are to be conducted.

- It is *selective*. While ideally, SEA would be applied to all policy decisions, resource and time constraints dictate a narrower application.
- It is a *self-assessment process*. Departments are responsible for conducting their own assessments. Privy Council and Treasury Board officials are supposed to ensure that SEAs are conducted where appropriate but do not control for content as they seldom have the needed sectoral expertise.
- Because of its association with Cabinet documents, SEA is also largely *secretive*. Although the Directive requires that departments issue a Public Statement for their detailed SEAs,[16] the large majority of SEAs conducted are preliminary scans only and therefore escape this requirement.
- The process is *flexible*. Within the Cabinet Directive broad guidelines, individual departments have customised SEA processes to meet their specific needs.

This last characteristic deserves to be underlined. There is no recognized methodology to value the environment, no common structured approach with agreed standards and practices as there are for project-level environmental assessment, let alone financial (*viz.*, the guidelines for financial accounting known as Generally Accepted Accounting Principles) or economic analysis (*viz.*, Treasury Board's cost-benefit analysis guide). As a result, there is no profession dedicated to advancing environmental valuation or other techniques that would support SEA. The contrast between economic or financial analysis on the one hand and environmental analysis on the other is striking; the fact that it is allowed to endure speaks to an implicit double standard in policy analysis.

An evaluation of SEA practice across the federal government conducted in 2009 concluded that the process as a whole remained largely ineffective.[17] The Cabinet Directive is not being implemented consistently across or even within departments, or comprehensively (i.e., SEA is not applied to all major government decisions and not all of the suggested considerations are taken into account). Where the Directive is applied, it is typically done too late in the policy, plan and program development process (sometimes even after Cabinet approval) to influence it; the bureaucracy and politicians often perceive SEA as a process imposition rather than as a helpful methodology to develop more environmentally-appropriate proposals;[18] it seldom includes an adequate analysis of all environmental implications, of alternatives to implementing the proposal, of cumulative effects, or of public concerns. As a result, only a quarter of SEA coordinators and managers surveyed as part of the evaluation believed that SEA leads to substantive changes in policy, plan and program proposals.[19]

There are exceptions to these generalizations: a few departments and agencies have made a serious commitment to SEA and developed internal management systems and various tools to promote good practice; departments with a natural resource or economic development mandate generally do a better job of implementing SEA than departments with a social mandate where the relevance of environmental factors is less obvious and where less capacity to conduct environmental analysis exists; departments have greater success integrating environmental considerations into plans than into policies and programs because the process for developing plans is usually predictable and driven from the bottom while the process for developing policies is often politicized, open-ended and unpredictable.

The main reasons for the uneven progress twenty years after the first Cabinet Directive on SEA was issued include:

- *Inability to conceptualize the relevance and applicability of SEA to policy-making*
  Most policy analysts do not have the training or experience to identify more than the most obvious environmental implications of policy, plan or program proposals. Fewer still have been trained to develop an initiative to maximize environmental sustainability objectives. Most of them may only conduct a single SEA during their career and have little incentive therefore to take the training to become skilled at it. As a result, many analysts struggle to see the relevance or value of SEA to their work because they do not have the tools and information to link the socio-economic drivers associated to their proposals to their environmental effects.
- *Lack of effective government-wide oversight and quality control*
  A self-assessment process cannot perform effectively without appropriate accountability measures and quality control. The Directive, however, does not identify a mechanism for ensuring compliance.[20] A large majority of interviewees contacted during the evaluation believed that this was a major barrier to the Directive's successful implementation. The existing approach to managing the government's SEA portfolio does not include penalties for non-compliance, incentives for doing SEA well, or opportunities for scrutiny from non-government stakeholders that might force the adoption of better practices. Furthermore, success stories or lessons learned are not widely publicized or promoted across the federal government.

The majority of departmental officials interviewed as part of the evaluation argued strongly that the Privy Council Office (PCO) should hold departments accountable for completing SEAs for Memoranda to Cabinet,[21] even though the Cabinet Directive gave it no role in the SEA process until 2010 and the latest Directive acknowledges its importance only in passing. As the secretariat to cabinet, PCO is responsible for managing the agendas of cabinet committees and deciding when a proposal is ready for consideration by ministers. In doing so, PCO acts as a gatekeeper, ensuring that all relevant departments are consulted, setting a strict format for cabinet submissions and stipulating what issues must be addressed. As part of its effort to control government spending, for example, PCO recently re-wrote the guidelines for preparing Memoranda to Cabinet to require an explicit attestation by senior departmental managers of the accuracy of the financial information presented.

PCO officials, however, believe that it is ministers themselves who are accountable for implementing the Directive and that their Office should only play a challenge function in ensuring that the Directive is respected, a role they have played inconsistently in the past. PCO analysts have heavy workloads, work in relative isolation from each other, tend to move frequently and few have received SEA training. These factors make it difficult for PCO to ensure that departments live up to the Directive's intent.

- *Pressures of the policy development process*
  The inherent nature of the policy process, often characterized by high political stakes, confidentiality, short timelines, and controlling the message discourages an open and comprehensive analysis of policy options, including their environmental implications. It is worth noting in this regard that Canada is one of the few countries applying SEA to policy (most restrict SEAS to programs and plans).
- *Lack of senior management support*
  Departmental analysts and SEA coordinators noted that the success of their SEA processes is correlated to the level of engagement by senior management in their respective organizations. This support is lacking in some departments.
- *Insufficient methodological guidance and limited opportunities to enhance capacity*
  The majority of government officials interviewed during the evaluation argued for improved training and guidance on how to do an SEA as opposed to what process to follow. Aside from the generic training courses provided by CEAA that focus principally on process, there are few training opportunities to improve SEA capacity and enhance analysts' technical skills in the majority of social and economic-based departments.

The government has played down methodological challenges by arguing that SEAS "do not necessarily require specialist information and skills, or a substantial commitment of resources and time."[22] While meant to reassure, this message also trivializes SEA by giving the impression that it only requires a simple analysis that anyone can conduct. This may be true for routine SEAS, but one of the reasons why federal practice has been largely ineffective is that specialist information and skills are unavailable or not mobilized when needed.

These evaluation findings are largely consistent with the four CESD audits conducted in 1998, 2000, 2004 and 2008[23] (*viz.*, insufficient senior management commitment in individual departments, insufficient central agency over-sight, incomplete guidance, limited integration into decision-making, inad-equate training, unclear accountability). Other studies[24] have come to similar conclusions.

In October 2010, the federal government announced several changes to improve SEA practice. The most important of these was to link the SEA pro-cess explicitly to the environmental objectives and targets in the new Federal Sustainable Development Strategy.[25] This Strategy, mandated under the 2008 *Federal Sustainable Development Act* represents the first attempt to present the environmental objectives the government is pursuing in a comprehensive manner. The Strategy also breaks new ground by more explicitly linking sus-tainable development to core government planning and reporting systems, emphasizing measurement and reporting on progress, and linking SEA to the Strategy's implementation.

The articulation of environmental goals and measurable targets is impor-tant to SEA because all considerations of environmental impact must sooner or later make a determination of how much impact is acceptable (*viz.*, how "clean" should a river be: so one can drink its water? Swim in it? Use it for in-dustrial purposes?). Such a determination requires the definition of measur-able science-based targets that can guide policy-making or program design. These benchmarks can take different forms ranging from permissible con-centration levels for selected pollutants to policy commitments to set aside a predetermined percentage of a country's surface as protected areas.

Developing such objectives is not easy, particularly for a geographically diverse federal state such as Canada, and helps explain why previous efforts have been abandoned.[26] Sweden, a smaller, more homogeneous and unitary state, took almost a decade to articulate its national environmental objectives but it found that this significant political investment had helped focus public debate on the issues of greatest importance and thus increased the efficiency of environmental policy.[27]

The other improvements to SEA the government announced in 2010 include:

- the recognition for the first time that central agencies such as PCO have a role in ensuring that departments fully consider the SEA directive in their cabinet documents;
- greater transparency, through more prescriptive reporting requirements; and
- encouraging the use of SEA analyses as an input into program evaluation.

The Federal Sustainable Development Strategy's claim that it will place environ-mental issues "firmly on the same playing field as the country's economic and social priorities",[28] however, appears exaggerated, since the Strategy includes no new commitments to action (except in the area of the government's own operations) and no additional financial resources. Nevertheless, the compilation of these objectives and targets in a single document, along with a mandated progress reporting system, should provide analysts conducting SEAs with clearer benchmarks against which to design or assess their policy options.

In summary, the current federal SEA practice, based on distributed responsibilities and self-assessment, does not receive sufficient oversight and support from central agencies in order to be effective. As well, there are few consequences to departments for inadequately implementing SEA (other than the occasional public embarrassment from a poor performance audit). As a result, there is insufficient overall accountability for implementation of the process at the government-wide level. The absence of an explicit definition of roles and responsibilities for such oversight in the Guidelines represents a major impediment to the Directive's effectiveness. Finally, central agencies have not played the same challenge function on the quality of SEAs as they have on the other matters that must be incorporated in memoranda to cabinet and Treasury Board submissions before they go to ministers.

MAKING THE PROCESS MORE EFFECTIVE

The continued deterioration in environmental conditions (as documented in *Canada's Performance Reports* and elsewhere,[29] e.g., loss of biodiversity, worsening ground-level ozone), supports the case that the federal government will need to improve the integration of environmental considerations into the design of its policies, plans and programs in order to promote more environmentally-sustainable forms of development. Some of these improvements can be inferred from the analysis above. If the government truly wanted to protect the environment, it would:

· redraft the Cabinet Directive to better articulate roles and responsibilities, make deputy ministers accountable for SEA implementation and designate a central agency to monitor compliance;
· provide greater clarity around key methodological challenges and provide more rigorous training;
· create a stronger community of practice and establish a clearinghouse for information; and
· institute quality assurance processes within departments and articulate clearer management outcomes for the Directive's implementation.

While such process improvements are clearly needed, they are unlikely to be sufficient in and of themselves in yielding an effective SEA process. Some observers have also recommended that at least part of the process be legislated in order to create more certainty about rules and expectations and to allow for independent enforceability.[30] Even legislation, however, is unlikely to be enough without also addressing four additional supportive factors. These are: a re-conceptualisation of SEA's purpose; an improved environmental information base; greater transparency; and a more supportive political environment.

A Re-Conceptualised SEA

SEA has to inform policy, program and plan *design* rather than just mitigate the environmental effects of a proposal already developed and it has to become more than an exercise in process compliance. This often requires re-thinking how a strategic objective should be met. For example:

- Is increasing the supply of energy, water or cars the economically- and environmentally-optimal way to meet the needs of Canadians or should greater efforts be made to increase efficiency of use?
- How should the precautionary principle[31] inform government decisions?
- What value should be given to the ecological services provided by nature (e.g., pollination of crops, water filtration and storage in wetlands, forest carbon sinks) when analyzing the costs and benefits of natural resource development policies or programs?

Answers to these questions have profound implications for the environmental (and social and economic) implications of policy or program choices. When such questions are not asked, or are answered implicitly in favour of undifferentiated economic growth, the contribution SEA can make to policy analysis is reduced. As stated above, the application of SEA does not presume an overriding societal goal of environmental sustainability but it can shed light on the trade-offs being made between environmental protection and short term economic growth, and between present and future generations. SEA's greatest value lies in the structured examination of alternatives – alternative objectives to meet a given goal, or alternative policy or program designs.

The misuse of SEA at the federal level is best demonstrated by the current exaggerated focus on process compliance and insufficient attention to desired environmental outcomes. As a result of criticisms from the CESD and others that their approach to SEA was ineffective, federal departments have raised internal awareness, assigned roles and responsibilities for triggering, conducting and signing off their SEAs, and designed forms and tracking systems to manage the process. Compliance has gone up (the proper forms are being filled out) but effectiveness has not (most SEAs have not altered the essence of the proposed policy, program or plan).

Instead of being perceived as an externally-imposed obligation to be met through a report or a checklist, SEA should be seen as a series of risk-reducing targeted interventions through which analysts inject relevant environmental considerations at each stage of policy, plan or program development.[32] These interventions should include the identification of measurable environmental outcomes in critical areas whose achievement could be monitored as part of the overall plan or program performance framework. Focusing SEA on critical issues, and tying it more closely to program performance parameters, would bring it into the mainstream of program management practice and would therefore make it more influential.

Re-framing the SEA process does not have to imply a return to first principles for every government decision: it still makes sense to tailor the level of effort to the anticipated environmental effects, as the Cabinet Directive now suggests, but it would require adhering more closely to the Directive's spirit and less to its form.

An Improved Information Base

Policy-making, program design and planning, all rely on sound information to reach outcomes that are effective, efficient and fair. Not surprisingly, information collection, analysis and dissemination are core government responsibilities. But while Statistics Canada enjoys a deserved reputation for excellence for economic and social statistics, Canada has no equivalent for environmental statistics. Most environmental and natural resource information is collected at the provincial/territorial level and is often difficult to aggregate to provide a national picture. The same is true at the federal level where environmental information is collected by different agencies to meet their own program needs and cannot always be adapted to different uses.

In a quarter century of environmental reporting, Environment Canada has published:

- Three *State of the Environment* reports, the last one in 1996;
- A series of National Environmental Indicators bulletins;
- One *Tracking Key Environmental Issues* report (2001);
- One *Environmental Signals* report (2003); and
- Four reports on the Canadian Environmental Sustainability Indicators (CESI) initiative focusing on a handful of environmental indicators.

In addition, Statistics Canada reports on *Human Activity and the Environment* annually since 2002 and other departments continue to report on their respective sectors (e.g. fisheries, mining, agriculture).

The first four initiatives listed above have all been discontinued. The lack of sustained funding (CESI received funding for only two years in the 2010 budget) has stemmed in part from an inability to develop a clientele for such information, leading to the proverbial chicken and egg question: what comes first, the demand for more timely and targeted environmental information or a product that is policy-relevant?

In 2001, the Task Force on a Canadian Information System for the Environment concluded that Canada lacked both a strategic approach to environmental information and key environmental information.[33] Ten years later, the situation has not improved significantly: Canada has no national network of water quality monitoring sites (an issue for the achievement of the water quality goal in the Federal Sustainable Development Strategy) nor a monitoring system capable of tracking the effectiveness of measures to reduce greenhouse gas emissions (an issue for the achievement of the climate change target in the Strategy).[34]

Tracking progress against the targets in the Federal Sustainable Development Strategy will help make environmental indicators more policy-relevant and may spur the formulation of metrics and information systems to support the new departmental reporting requirements. Nevertheless, a significant investment in environmental information is likely to be required both to make existing data more useful and to fill in existing gaps. SEA will be handicapped as long as environmental statistics continue to lag so far behind economic and social statistics.

Greater Transparency

The arguments in favour of greater transparency in the SEA process are both general and specific. At a general level, a strong democracy depends on well-informed citizens and interest groups having access to comprehensive and reliable information about their government's activities. Transparency therefore can promote public trust and confer more legitimacy on public policy decisions. The specific reasons to increase the transparency of the SEA process are to inform the public debate, increase accountability, and especially to improve its quality. SEAs are often done in a hurry, late in the decision-making process, conducted for reasons of compliance rather than to improve the proposal at hand, and led by individuals who usually have little environmental training. All these factors significantly impinge on the quality and effectiveness of the SEAs being prepared.

In addition, the environment is an under-represented value in government decision-making because it is relatively new. Economic interests have more representatives around the cabinet table than the environment and more powerful advocates outside.[35] Greater transparency, therefore, would help reduce the risk of systemic bias against the environment in decision-making.

There are practical limits, of course, to increasing the transparency of an SEA process that is applied primarily to cabinet decisions. The Cabinet Directive addresses this constraint by mandating since 2004 the release of a public statement on environment effects after departments conduct a detailed SEA (i.e., excluding most SEAs which are only preliminary scans) and cabinet has made a decision on the proposal. Compliance with this aspect of the Directive has been low: in 2008, the CESD has reported that most of the departments he examined do not issue such public statements systematically and, when they do, do not provide enough information to show how they considered environmental considerations in their analysis.[36]

While improving compliance with the Directive would clearly be a step in the right direction, the government also has other techniques at its disposal to increase the transparency of its decision-making process, including a greater use of white or green papers and multi-stakeholder consultation processes, both of which it has used extensively in the past (though not recently). Such engagement methods not only can enhance the legitimacy of the decision that is ultimately made, they often also improve its quality by introducing additional considerations to the process.

At the time of writing, it was unclear whether the measures proposed in the revised Guidelines to the Cabinet Directive (i.e., more systematic reporting of SEA practice in annual departmental performance reports) would significantly increase the transparency of the SEA process. The fact that ministers retain the right under the Cabinet Directive to discount SEAs makes greater process transparency particularly important in promoting accountability.

A More Supportive Political Environment

Civil servants and politicians do not operate in a vacuum: in a democracy, they most often reflect prevailing societal and economic values. In Canada, the electorate has not demonstrated strongly enough that it wants more environmentally-sustainable policies – and is willing to punish politically those who fail to deliver. There are many reasons for the relatively low political salience of environmental issues in Canada:

- Canada's large landmass, abundant resources and relatively small population have engendered a more complacent attitude to environmental protection than is the case in many European countries whose ecological limits are much more evident.
- Societal values, encouraging increasing material consumption as the key to a satisfying life, are deeply-ingrained and continuously-reinforced by commercial advertising. As consumption accounts for almost two thirds of Canada's GDP, policy-makers often strive to boost consumption to make the economy grow.
- Canada has produced few political or corporate leaders who have articulated a compelling environmental vision for the country which could motivate voters.
- Canadian environmental lobby groups have always been less well-funded than their industrial counterparts. In recent years, the ability of many of them to mount public campaigns has eroded.

- The capacity of the media to do investigative stories and hold the government to account on environmental matters has also declined: newspapers have reduced their environmental (and other) coverage because of dropping revenues and other media have not filled the void fully.
- Canada has relatively few policy institutes focusing on environmental issues that could raise public awareness as well as provide alternative prescriptions to government policy.
- The jurisdictional division of responsibilities among the municipal, provincial/territorial and federal levels over environmental matters is confusing to most Canadians who do not know whom to hold accountable for losses in environmental quality.

The introduction of SEA explicitly challenges the undifferentiated economic growth paradigm which has dominated government policy-making since the 1950s.[37] Greater environmental protection (e.g., a carbon tax), some argue, will be expensive, reduce competitiveness and cost jobs. Canada, the argument continues, is a small country and should not burden itself with constraints that its major trading partners have not assumed.[38] As a result of this perspective, the current political context militates in favour of decisions that support economic growth when trade-offs have to be made, particularly where the pursuit of long term environmental benefits (e.g., slowing down climate change) implies short term economic costs (e.g., higher energy prices).

Public officials will deliver, within their abilities and the mandate of their departments, policies developed on the basis of available information and agreed processes to meet government objectives. They will have difficulty justifying investing scarce resources in more comprehensive analytical approaches if there is no political demand for them and no rewards for deploying them.

These factors will not be easy to reverse and suggest that Canadians are unlikely to demand that the federal government improve its SEA process soon, notwithstanding mounting scientific evidence of environmental degradation. On the other hand, exogenous events, such as an environmental crisis or decisions made by our major trading partners have been known to shift domestic public opinion, sometimes very rapidly.

CONCLUSIONS

In recent years, adherence to the process requirements of the Cabinet Directive, although not universal or complete, has been growing across the government: awareness of the Directive's requirements has increased, more departments have institutionalized SEA processes and SEAs are being done more systematically. But this increased activity has had little demonstrable impact in contributing to the federal government's environmental protection efforts, or precluded the pursuit of environmentally destructive policies.

While successive governments have acknowledged the importance of sustainable development, fighting climate change and considering environmental factors in decision-making, they have also:

· provided tax write-offs (now expired) to accelerate the development of the Alberta oil sands;
· repeatedly invested in the automobile industry, whose products are one of the chief causes of greenhouse gas emissions;
· continued to encourage population and undifferentiated economic growth, both of which are likely to lead to greater material throughput and increased production of wastes, making environmental sustainability harder to achieve.[39]

These initiatives are all legitimate and can be defended, but each raises major environmental issues. An effective SEA process would have highlighted the environmental implications of these decisions and helped identify alternatives that reduced adverse environmental effects. Instead, environmental considerations are often an after-thought in such decisions, when they figure at all. As a result, SEA has not furthered more environmentally-sustainable forms of development nor visibly increased the coherence of federal policies.

After twenty years of practice at the federal level, SEA's promise remains largely unfulfilled: the theoretical benefits listed in the Cabinet Directive, as this analysis has shown, are still just that. While this chapter has identified methodological, informational, management and political barriers which have hampered SEA's effective implementation, the absence of a consistent government commitment to environmental sustainability remains the single most important explanation for the current situation. It is too early to know what impact the improvements announced in the Federal Sustainable Development Strategy will have but they are clearly insufficient to remedy the many deficiencies identified by the CESD in his reports.

It is clear that no federal government has internalized the Brundtland Commission's message summarized at the beginning of this chapter about giving environmental factors the same weight as economic and social ones, notwithstanding numerous public affirmations to that effect. On the contrary, successive governments have made cosmetic changes to the decision-making process in the hope that these would suffice to reconcile environmental and economic imperatives and promote more sustainable forms of development. The environmental evidence shows that the changes to decision-making need to be much more profound and that SEA, among other tools, must be applied more rigorously to influence policy and program design.

As outlined at the beginning of this chapter, the costs of an ineffective SEA process can be substantial. The current inadequacies of the federal SEA process ensure that Canada will continue to pay a heavy, yet largely avoidable, environmental price for many future government decisions.

NOTES

I would like to thank Bob Gibson, Andrew Ferguson, Peter Morrison, Pierre Sadik, and Tom Shillington for their helpful comments on an earlier draft of this chapter.

1 World Commission on Environment and Development, *Our Common Future*. Oxford University Press, New York, 1987.

2 Millennium Ecosystem Assessment, *Ecosystems and Human Well-Being: Synthesis*. Island Press, Washington, DC, 2005.

3 Ontario Medical Association, "Alarming new report shows smog is responsible for 9,500 deaths in the province each year," Press release, 6 June 2008.

4 Commissioner of the Environment and Sustainable Development, chapter 3 – *Chemicals Management – Federal Contaminated Sites, March Status Report* Commissioner of the Environment and Sustainable Development, 2008.

5 Marke Andrews, "BC communities will continue to be devastated by the pine beetle," July 21, 2010, *Vancouver Sun*. The BC Ministry of Forests and Range estimates that the mountain pine beetle has now killed a cumulative total of 675 million cubic metres of timber and affected 16.3 million hectares, more than five times the size of Vancouver Island. http://www.for.gov.bc.ca/hfp/mountain_pine_beetle/ The pine beetle infestation is driven by both inappropriate forest management practices and warming weather.

6 Intergovernmental Panel on Climate Change, *Climate Change 2007*. World Meteorological Organization, United Nations Environment Program, New York, 2007. http://www.ipcc.ch/publications_and_data/publications_ipcc_fourth_assessment_report_synthesis_report.htm.

7 Government of Canada, *Canada's Green Plan*, Government of Canada, 1990, 162.

8 Commissioner of the Environment and Sustainable Development, *Report, Chapter 4 Assessing the Environmental Impacts of Policies, Plans and Programs*, Commissioner of the Environment and Sustainable Development, 2004, 4.

9 International Study on the Effectiveness of Environmental Assessment *Final Report: Environmental Assessment in a Changing World*. Canadian Environmental Assessment Agency, International Association for Impact Assessment, 1996.

10 See R. Verheem and J. Tonk "Strategic environmental assessment: one concept, multiple forms" *Impact Assessment and Project Appraisal*, 18, no. 3, September 2000: 177–182.

11 Many European countries apply SEA only to planning processes.

12 Development authorities include departments whose primary mandate is economic development, e.g., Finance, Industry, Transport and Natural Resources.

13 Canadian Environmental Assessment Agency, *Strategic Environmental Assessment: The 2010 Cabinet Directive on the Environmental Assessment of Policy, Plan and Program Proposals and Guidelines for Implementing the Directive*. Canadian Environmental Assessment Agency, 2010. http://www.ceaa.gc.ca/default. asp?lang=En&n=B3186435–1

14 Environmental assessment legislation for projects can be found everywhere in Canada and around most of the world. Where it occurs, SEA, however, is rarely

legislated although some countries have done so for plans. One can read a history of federal environmental assessment approaches in Stephen Hazell, *Canada v. The Environment: Federal Environmental Assessment 1984–1998*. Canadian Environmental Defense Fund, 1999.

15 Commissioner of the Environment and Sustainable Development, *Report, Chapter 6 Environmental Assessment – A Critical Tool for Sustainable Development*, Commissioner of the Environment and Sustainable Development, 1998.

16 The Cabinet Directive sets out two levels of analysis: a preliminary scan for most decisions and a detailed study for decisions that raise significant environmental issues.

17 The author led the team that conducted the evaluation. See Stratos Inc, *Evaluation of the Cabinet Directive on the Environmental Assessment of Policy, Plan and Program Proposals*, June 2009. Report prepared for the Canadian Environmental Assessment Agency.

18 Aura Environmental Research and Consulting Ltd., *Strategic Environmental Assessment Toolkit*, 2009. Report prepared for the Canadian Environmental Assessment Agency.

19 In 2004, the cesd noted that "generally, departments and agencies do not know how the strategic environmental assessments they have done have affected the decisions made, and in turn, what the ultimate impacts on the environment are," 22.

20 cesd, *Status Report of the Commissioner of the Environment and Sustainable Development to the House of Commons*, chapter 9 Strategic Environmental Assessment, March 2008.

21 Both the cesd and the House of Commons Standing Committee on Environment and Sustainable Development have made the same argument. See cesd, March 2008 report, 15.

22 Government of Canada, *Strategic Environmental Assessment: Guidelines for implementing the Cabinet Directive*, 6.

23 cesd, Reports to the House of Commons, 1998, 2000, 2004, 2008. In its 2004 report, the cesd concluded that "most departments have not made serious efforts to apply the directive," 28.

24 See for example Greg Wilburn, "Strategic Environmental Assessment, Sustainable Development and Good Governance." Thesis submitted in support of a Master of Arts, Royal Roads University, 2005.

25 Environment Canada, *Planning for a Sustainable Future: A Federal Sustainable Development Strategy for Canada*. Environment Canada, October 2010, 8.

26 In 2006, Environment Canada abandoned a year-long effort to develop National Environmental Objectives.

27 Bengt Rundqvist and Peter Wenster, March 2005, The Swedish System of Environmental Quality Objectives," Presentation to Environment Canada.

28 Environment Canada, *Planning for a Sustainable Future: A Federal Sustainable Development Strategy for Canada*, October 2010, 3.

29 See, for example, Commission for Environmental Cooperation (2008), *North America 2030: An Environmental Outlook;* oecd (2004), *Environmental Performance Reviews – Canada;* Environment Canada (2001), Tracking Key Environmental Issues.

30 High Benevides, Denis Kirchhoff, Robert Gibson, Meinhard Doelle, *Law and Policy Options for Strategic Environmental Assessment in Canada*, December 2008. Report to the Canadian Environmental Assessment Agency. The CESD commented in her 2004 report that the government should consider legislating SEA if improvements could not be demonstrated within several years.

31 Principle 15 of the 1992 United Nations Declaration on Environment and Development states that "where there are threats of serious or irreversible damage, lack of full scientific certainty shall not be used as a reason for postponing cost-effective measures to prevent environmental degradation."

32 Parks Canada and the Canadian International Development Agency are moving to such an approach.

33 Task Force on a Canadian Information System for the Environment, *Final Report* Ministry of Public Works and Government Services, Ottawa, October 2001.

34 CESD, *Comments on the Draft Federal Sustainable Development Strategy*, 7 June 2010.

35 Andrew Mayeda and Mark Kennedy: "Industry, oil execs get most access to PM: records," *Postmedia News*, October 2, 2010. In the two years since July 2008, records kept by the Office of the Commissioner of Lobbying show that Prime Minister Harper met industry representatives more than 50 times but only once with an environmental organization.

36 CESD, Status Report to the House of Commons, chapter 9, Strategic Environmental Assessment, March 2008.

37 Peter Victor, *Managing Without Growth*. Edward Elgar, Northhampton, 2008.

38 This is the argument that the Harper government has invoked for waiting for US policy before regulating greenhouse gas emissions more aggressively.

39 Peter Victor, *Managing Without Growth*, traces the influence of economic growth on public policy since the 1950s.

8 Science and Technology in Canada: Innovation Gaps and Productivity Traps

DAVID CASTLE AND PETER W.B. PHILLIPS

INTRODUCTION

Public investment in science and technology (s&t) has increased at an unprecedented rate during the past decades throughout the industrialized world and has become synonymous with wealth creation and competitiveness. Canada has generally invested in s&t at rates that are in the region of the Organization for Economic Cooperation and Development (oecd) averages, but has not been at the forefront of science and technology research and development (r&d). Nevertheless, the investments are considerable, which naturally raises the question of value-for-money and comparisons with other countries raise questions of competitiveness. Have Canadians been the beneficiaries of public s&t investment because valuable new products and services are reaching markets? Have Canadians become more prosperous as technology is licensed abroad, and have public investments increased productivity and created trade surpluses?

A review of the data suggests the answers to both questions is no. Beginning with a review of federal s&t expenditures, it is apparent that spending has in recent years plateaued. Very modest increases across spending categories support positive announcements about improved funding, but reflect projections rather than firm commitments and are not inflation-adjusted. Stagnant s&t funding has been linked to an innovation gap between Canadian and oecd countries, and while other factors such as scarce venture capital or risk aversion partly explain low innovation, reduced investments obviously will not stimulate innovation. Linked to the declining rates of innovation is the growing gap in productivity between Canada and other oecd nations. A sluggish economy, low rates of innovation, and an artificially high dollar are among the factors that could lead Canada into a productivity trap.

As the Harper Conservative minority government continues to ring-fence its spending by narrowing its interpretation of federal responsibility, s&t funding increases cannot be anticipated. A difficult situation emerges in which provinces may be compelled to fill the gap to remain competitive, but would do so unevenly because of the significant inequalities in fiscal and R&D capacity. At the same time, the federal government is launching a comprehensive R&D spending review, which may further entrench federal spending and limit transfers to provinces. When these events are considered in light of the innovation gap and potential productivity trap, the trajectory does not look good for Canadian prosperity.

Rather than addressing innovation and productivity problems directly, the government continues a pattern of economic sooth-saying by diverting attention to the relative stability of the Canadian financial sector following the global financial crises. The reality is that the financial sector's relative health is a definite boon to Canadians who have not had to endure collapsing property markets or bank bailouts, but it is not an economic cure for declining innovation and productivity. In the worst-case scenario, Canada is sleepwalking its way to a lost decade, from which it could take a generation to recover.

BUDGET 2010–2011: SCIENCE AND TECHNOLOGY SPENDING

Budget 2010: Leading the Way on Jobs and Growth[1] was the second federal budget of the Harper Conservative minority government dedicated to *Canada's Economic Action Plan*. The context of the budget was the global financial crises of 2008. By 2009, there were signs that liquidity was being restored to markets, largely as a result of government-backed bank bailouts in the United States and Europe. Compared with Iceland, where capital was lost because gross domestic product (GDP) was insufficient to cover bank losses, or Ireland where bank bailouts required massive European Union loans, Canada appeared to have been unscathed by the chaos.

This is true at least in the financial sector, but Canada's major trading partners, the United States and the European Union, slumped, with the result that there has been less demand for Canadian goods, particularly as the US dollar and the Euro dropped relative to the Canadian dollar. Meanwhile, Canada was already committed to two stimulus budgets in 2009 and 2010, in which the tiresome slogan of 'shovel-ready' projects became the proxy for government make-work projects of the Hoover variety, involving large spending on infrastructure strategically located around the country. As the global finance sector has stabilized and begun to recover, the focus in most countries is fiscal recovery, moving from record deficits brought on by public money used to bail out private banks to more sustainable operations. Again, Canada did not rack up similar deficits, but that has not prevented a climate of austerity; economic and political constraints yielded a budget of restraint for the 2010–2011 fiscal year, and as Chapter 1 shows, for 2011–2012 and beyond.

The 2010 Budget statement had two clear, underlying principles that motivated it. The first was that, where possible, budget lines for core areas should remain roughly the same or show slight increases, perhaps out of political expediency to claim that the first year of the Economic Action Plan was working. s&t expenditure by government department or agency increased on average by 4%, although this increase is mostly attributable to increases to the Canadian Foundation for Innovation (cfi) and the National Research Council (nrc). Drawing on examples exclusively related to science and technology spending, the three granting councils received modest increases to their base budgets: $3m for Social Sciences and Humanities Research Council (sshrc); $13m for Natural Sciences and Engineering Research Council (nserc) and $16m for the Canadian Institutes of Health Research (cihr). Another $18m was made available to support the indirect costs and programs related to research, such as those associated with technology transfer. The budget for Genome Canada, which had run the course of its 2006 multi-year commitment, was $75m, and reflects Genome Canada's 2009 request to Industry Canada to launch a new competition, nullifying the angst that dominated the public debate about science and technology in the post 2009 budget period.[2]

Three new Networks of Centres of Excellence were announced (NeurodevNet ($19.6m); grand nce ($23.5m); Carbon Management Canada ($25m)), as were several multi-year commitments. In the two-year category, Atomic Energy of Canada received $300m, the National Research Council clusters initiative received $135m; Next Generation Renewable Power Initiative received $100m; Medical Isotopes, $48m; and the new Post-Doctoral Fellowship Program, a five-year commitment, $40m. In the five-year category, the Canadian Space Agency received $397m and triumf, the Vancouver-based particle and nuclear physics laboratory, received $222m. Furthermore, all of the appropriate regional buttons were pushed: the Arctic Research Station received $18m; Atlantic Canada Opportunities Agency, $19m; Canadian Economic Development for Quebec Regions, $14.6m; and Western Economic Diversification, $14.7m.

The second guiding principle appears to be that the Conservative government was continuing the approach it had described in the 2007 science and technology strategy, *Mobilizing Science and Technology to Canada's Advantage*.[3] The s&t strategy is ostensibly a science and technology innovation strategy, but closer examination of the document and the Government's implementation of the strategy reveals that it is at root a commercialization strategy. Its focus was to move away from heavy investment in higher-education-led basic research, characteristic of the budgets of Finance Minister Paul Martin;

Table 1
Expenditure by department or agency

Department or Agency	Year 2009/10	Year 2010/11	% Difference 2010/11 v. 2009/10
	$M		
Agriculture and Agri-Food Canada	425	420	-1.2
Atomic Energy of Canada Limited	476	435	-8.6
Canada Foundation for Innovation	395	488	23.5
Canadian Institutes of Health Research	300	933	-0.3
Canadian International Development Agency	453	409	-9.7
Canadian Space Agency	356	391	9.8
Environment Canada	748	742	-0.8
Fisheries and Oceans Canada	287	286	-0.3
Health Canada	550	555	0.9
Industry Canada	847	884	4.4
National Defence	426	441	3.5
National Research Council Canada	718	767	6.8
Natural Resources Canada	599	772	28.9
Natural Sciences and Engineering Research Council of Canada	1058	1087	2.7
Social Sciences and Humanities Research Council of Canada	692	683	-1.3
Statistics Canada	713	790	10.8
Other	1562	1549	-0.8
Average change			4.0

Adapted from *Federal Scientific Activities 2010–2011*. Ottawa: Statistics Canada, 2010.

during the years of Chrétien Liberal majority government Canada climbed in the OECD from 15th to 5th in gross expenditure on research and development (GERD).

Instead, the focus has shifted towards a no-frills, spend-where-it-counts approach to the commercialization of research. Already in this vein the Network of Centres of Excellence program creating Centres of Excellence for Commercialization and Research (CECR) had been introduced. In Budget 2010 three significant initiatives extended this approach. First, the College and Community Innovation Program ($15m) was established to assist colleges to "make important contributions to advancing Canada's innovation capacity by working with businesses and playing a key role in translating knowledge into practical applications that open new markets and create high-value jobs" because the "applied research and training capacity at colleges and polytechnics is a tremendous resource for building a more knowledge-driven economy."[4] Second, the already mentioned National Research Council Canada Regional Innovation Clusters Program was set up to try to seed eleven regional innovation clusters across all ten provinces in targeted sectors to "support the development of dynamic Canadian firms, generate jobs and transform local economies."[5] Third, the Small and Medium-sized Enterprise Innovation Commercialization Program acts as a risk mitigation plan for SMEs. Federal departments and agencies "will adopt and demonstrate the use of innovative prototype products and technologies developed by small and medium-sized businesses,"[6] thereby providing the opportunity to prove new products and services while gaining early clients through early adoption.

Another relatively unnoticed but potentially important initiative is the announcement that the Canadian Foundation for Innovation (CFI) – which had invested by April 2010 more than $4.3 billion in 6,784 research infrastructure projects in Canadian universities, colleges, research hospitals and non-profit research institutions – will provide operating funding for 'major science initiatives' funded by CFI. The Federal Budget 2009 provided CFI with $600 million in new funding, which included a new $185 million program designed to provide up to 40% of the operating costs at major science initiatives (MSI) over the 5 year period from 2012–13 to 2016–17.

In the past year, CFI has determined that an MSI may be eligible for operating costs if it meets six criteria. First, the facility must have received a one-time contribution of at least $25M in capital funding from the CFI, host specific and substantial equipment, and have significant human and operational resource needs beyond what is usually present in Canadian research institutions. Second, the facility must compare with the best in the world and provide an environment to conduct leading-edge research. Third, the MSI should be a purpose-built national facility created to offer a unique capability to all Canadian researchers, in a non-standard discipline or research area and otherwise not available elsewhere in Canada. Fourth, the MSI must have a formal governance structure, including a Board of Directors that is responsible for such matters as long-term strategic and multi-year business planning and risk management at both strategic and operational levels. Fifth, one or more eligible institutions must own the facility. Sixth, the facility must be operating and accessible to a broad range of researchers from across Canada through an established merit-based access policy. CFI is currently working with other federal agencies to determine which MSI meet these criteria and how the funding might flow.

A Statistics Canada analysis of the budget for science and technology begins by noting the modest increases throughout the budget.[7] The $11.7B allocated to S&T for 2010/2011 is a rise above the $11.3B in 2009/2010, but it is a forecast whereas the year previous' commitments reflect actual expenditures. By

Table 2
Extramural expenditure by sector

| | Year | | % Difference |
	2009/10	2010/11	2010/11 v. 2009/10
		$M	
Business enterprises	1,019	1,105	8.4
Higher education	3,078	3,169	3.0
Canadian non-profit institutions	485	454	-6.4
Provincial and municipal governments	486	481	-1.0
Foreign performers	581	560	-3.6
Other performers	54	53	-1.9
Total research and development	4,610	4,729	2.6
Business enterprises	831	906	9.0
Higher education	2,772	· 2,848	2.7
Canadian non-profit institutions	311	273	-12.2
Provincial and municipal governments	453	444	-2.0
Foreign performers	206	220	6.8
Other performers	37	39	5.4
Total related scientific activities	1,094	1,093	-0.1
Business enterprises	188	199	5.9
Higher education	306	321	4.9
Canadian non-profit institutions	175	182	4.0
Provincial and municipal governments	33	37	12.1
Foreign performers	376	341	-9.3
Other performers	16	13	-18.8
Overall average			0.6

Adapted from *Federal Scientific Activities 2010–2011*. Ottawa: Statistics Canada, 2010.

late 2011, it may be possible to look back and see a larger rise, parity or lower expenditures. The latter is a distinct possibility because of the budget's proposed R&D spending review, discussed in the final section of this chapter.

If, however, the projection bears out, the expenditure would be consistent with the incremental rises in current or 2002 constant dollars.[8] The $11.7B figure can be disaggregated into $5.9B for spending within federal departments and agencies, and $5.8B is allocated to higher education, and the private for- and non-profit sectors. Viewed another way, the projected expenditures consist of $7.4B on direct R&D activities and $4.3B on related scientific activities (RSA) that directly support R&D but that also support federal regulatory responsibilities. Again, there are modest rises (see Table 2) by sector, although the non-profit sector was quite substantially reduced.

Figure 1
Year-to-year percent differences in extramural S&T expenditures

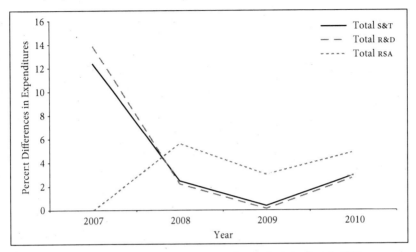

Adapted from *Federal Scientific Activities 2010–2011*. Ottawa: Statistics Canada, 2010.

Federal budgets give analysts and commentators an opportunity to study who has gone up and who has gone down, and provide ample opportunity for speculation about the relationship between year-to-year changes to budget lines and the priorities of the government (see Figure 1).

With respect to S&T projections for 2010/2011, there are few major changes in the direction and scope of support. For example, the latest release of data from the OECD shows that Canada's absolute and relative position is not improving. Canada as a whole expended US$25 billion on R&D in 2008, equal to about US$755 per capita or 1.84% of our current GDP. The average for the OECD was about US$789 per capita or 2.33% of GDP (table 2). This measure ranged from a high of about 3.6% in Sweden to a low of about 0.5% in Mexico. The US expended US$1,309 per capita or about 2.77% of its current GDP on R&D.

These aggregate numbers mask some important features of our relative performance in science and technology related R&D. Canada has about 20% more researchers per capita than the OECD average (but about 20% fewer than the US) and publishes approximately 4.5% of all basic research in academic journals,[10] yet at the same time the cost of each scientific publication is above OECD average.[11] Conventional wisdom says if there is a strong science and technology R&D base acting as an "ideas pump" into the economy, resulting wealth and prosperity described by Prime Minister Harper should be in evidence. The difficulty is that it is not occurring. Productivity is lagging both expectations and the key comparison countries.

Table 3
S&T Indicators – Canada US and OECD[9]

Expenditure Type	Country		
	Canada	US	OECD
Gross expenditure on R&D, US$ billion PPP, 2008	$25.0	$398.2	$935.7
$ per capita, 2008	$755	$1309	$789
% GDP, 2008	1.84	2.77	2.33
% GDP, average 1981–2007	1.68	2.62	2.16
% financed by			
– industry	48	67	65
– government	33	27	28
% performed by			
– industry	54	73	70
– higher education	35	13	17
– government	10	11	11
FTE researchers, 000, 2008	143	1,494	4,128
– per million	4.3	4.9	3.5

SCIENCE AND TECHNOLOGY INNOVATION AND PRODUCTIVITY

The fundamental challenge is that all of our investments and efforts are not translating into higher productivity, which is the foundation for a rising standard of living. The OECD data for 2009 shows that the average Canadian works about 8% longer than an American citizen, harder than the OECD average (almost 13% more than the average OECD person), and more than all of our key comparator countries. Despite this extra effort, we generate GDP per capita about 19% below the US average and barely equal to the average of the OECD countries. Mark Carney, Governor of The Bank of Canada, recently remarked that Canada has "lost competitiveness over a number of years. This is a product of the level of the currency. It is also a product of a relatively poor productivity performance vis-à-vis the US, but also compared to other countries that export into the United States as well."[12]

Perhaps most frustrating of all, Canada's efforts since 2000 to increase productivity have not changed the trends. The term 'productivity' is frequently avoided in political discourse because of its uncomfortable association with job losses – enhancing 'prosperity' is the new positive veneer – but the reality cannot be ignored. Canada's problem has not gone away and the trends are disturbing. Over the last 25 years, multi-factor productivity has risen a mere

Table 4
OECD Productivity Data

	GDP per head of population, USD	GDP per head cf. US (US=100)	GDP per hour worked, USD	Gap in labour utilisation with respect to US	Hours worked per head of population	Gap in GDP per hour worked cf US
Australia	39337	84	47	3%	837	-18%
Canada	37945	81	43.3	6%	876	-25%
France	33679	72	54.5	-23%	618	-5%
Germany	36452	78	53.3	-15%	684	-7%
Japan	32421	70	38.2	3%	848	-33%
UK	36538	78	47.6	-4%	768	-17%
US	46581	100	57.4	–	812	–
OECD	33697	72	43.4	-3%	777	-24%
G7	39409	85	50.6	-4%	779	-12%

(Data extracted from OECD on 13 Jan 2011 from OECD.Stat)

Table 5
Multi-Factor Productivity in Canada and Key Comparator Countries, 1985–2009)

	1985–2009	1985–1990	1990–1995	1995–2000	2000–2005	2005–2009
Australia	0.9	-0.2	1.5	1.5	0.9	0.2
Canada	0.3	-0.6	0.5	1.6	0.5	-0.7
France	1.1	2.5	1.1	1.4	0.8	-0.5
Germany	0.9	..	1.4	1.3	0.7	0
Japan	1.6	3.3	0.8	0.8	1.5	1.5
United Kingdom	1.3	0.9	1.4	1.5	1.2	1.2
United States	1.1	0.7	0.7	1.5	1.7	0.7

(Data extracted on 13 Jan 2011 from OECD.Stat)

0.3% per year in Canada (compared with rises range from 0.9% per year in Australia to 1.6% in Japan and 1.1% in the US), and in the past four years all of the productivity gains of the earlier part of the decade were wiped out.

The problem is not with federal spending, but with the uptake and use of federal support and the ability of federal support to generate corresponding private sector investments in R&D and commercialization.

Regarding the consequences of lagging innovation and productivity, Kevin Lynch, former Clerk of the Privy Council and Secretary to the Cabinet from 2006–2009 and now Vice-Chair of the BMO Financial Group, sees gloom ahead. Writing in *The Globe and Mail*, Lynch acknowledges the public supports for innovation in Canada, the enviable financial situation which includes "lower debt as a proportion of the economy, low and stable inflation, and a very sound banking system," and the significant public-sector investments in higher education and research particularly during the 1990s.[13] He argues Canada has two Achilles' heels that affect rates of innovation; one is the shortfall of venture capital; the other is weakness in information and communication technologies (ICTs).

Lynch makes four recommendations. First, that a "Productivity and Innovation Council" be established to benchmark and then stimulate innovation with the target of making Canadian innovation stand in the top quartile and adding $5,000 *per capita* GDP within a decade. Second, he recommends that whatever is blocking venture capital be remedied – another expert panel would be delegated to fix the problem. Third he recommends the government identifies the best science and mobilizes it quickly, and fourth, that Canada seek to brand itself.

Lynch's proposed remedies are less incisive than his analysis – branding and addressing intellectual property are old chestnuts and may just be epiphenomena to the real problem – and reports of expert panels are populating dusty shelves in various departments and governments in Ottawa. Globe and Mail columnist Jeffrey Simpson, announcing the Council of Canadians 2009 report, *Innovation and Business Strategy: Why Canada Falls Short*,[14] remarked that "[s]mall countries such as Sweden, Finland, Denmark and South Korea focus on these issues with an intensity that reflects the urgency they deserve. In Canada, we write reports."[15] But on the subject of productivity Simpson and Lynch agree, almost word for word. Simpson: "Productivity is a word editors dislike, television disdains, politicians fear, and from which the general public recoils. It's the great Canadian bore..."[16] Lynch: "There are few issues that evoke a blank stare more than productivity. Upon hearing the word, people either react with lack of interest or recoil in fear that what is coming is a lecture on working harder."[17] The regrettable picture they jointly paint is a of a country blessed with natural resources, an educated population and next to no strife, and yet innovation lags and it is now visibly affecting productivity.

Lynch rightly points out that the 'old' excuse in the 1990s for low productivity was national debt and deficits, problematic pension plans, high corporate tax, and high-risk premiums from stocks and bonds. These problems are to a major extent remedied, yet "business-sector productivity growth was actually worse in the decade that just ended."[18] Lynch thinks that Canada is about to become mired in a productivity trap where falling productivity is accompanied by declining American and European demand for Canadian goods and services, a climbing Canadian dollar, an aging population and flat or declining labour productivity.

Compounding the problem for Canada is that raising the pace must happen in a race where competitors are moving more quickly; "[w]e seem to be standing still" entrepreneur Terry Matthews says to David Crane in his

Research Money article on innovation.[19] Crane's point is that there is less slack in the system to work with when countries like South Korea, with its many innovative brands, large labour pool and strong labour productivity, begin to compete directly with Canada. Similarly, economies like India and to a greater extent China have recently doubled their R&D intensity and have GDP growth in the double digits. For Canada these impressive increases are ominous black clouds in light of the total size of the economies and spell heavy weather for countries with small populations and productivity declines, like Canada. The trends need to be reversed to maintain Canadians' enviable standard of living.

CORRECTIVE ACTIONS

Canada's predicament is one of shrinking expenditure on science and technology, weak levels of innovation, and declining productivity, all in a context of global financial instability with highly competitive emerging economies on the rise. The 2010–2011 budget is a conservative budget of a Conservative government committed to a two-year plan of stimulus spending without being exposed to the worst hardship of the global financial crises. In this respect the minority government budget 'minds the shop' without launching significant new initiatives across the board. In the case of science and technology spending in particular, various groups criticized the budget for spending too little on higher education and research support when there is ample evidence that innovation and productivity could use a boost.

The Coalition for Action on Innovation in Canada (CAIC), a predominantly private-sector organization co-chaired by John Manley and Paul Lucas, has led a private sector initiative to boost innovation and address weak productivity in Canada. In October 2009, CAIC convened a national roundtable to address threats to Canadian prosperity arising from global competition, aging demographics, and weak productivity. In October 2010, CAIC (of which Castle is a member) released a ten-point plan to stimulate productivity and innovation.[20] The ten point plan includes: 1) reform of R&D tax support; 2) expansion of the pool of risk capital; 3) bolstering the intellectual property regime; 4) strengthening ties between business and academe; 5) calls on private sector expertise to guide public expenditures; 6) accelerating the adoption of innovative products and services; 7) the launch of a national 'learning and innovation' initiative; 8) recruiting and retaining international academic leaders; 9) nurturing and strengthening innovation clusters; and 10) promoting continued advocacy for innovation.

The CAIC action plan was released prior to the announcement of the terms of reference for the comprehensive federal R&D spending review panel, and was intended to give voice to a non-government perspective on the direction and tenor of the review. The plausibility of the approach relates to the broad nature of the original description of the spending review, which said that the government, "in close consultation with business leaders from all sectors and our provincial partners, will conduct a comprehensive review of all federal support for R&D to improve its contribution to innovation and to economic opportunities for business. This review will inform future decisions regarding federal support for R&D. The Government is currently developing the terms of reference for the review."[21]

Outside of government circles, the proposed spending review is considered to be among the more important announcements in the budget. *Research Money* convened an on-line panel shortly after the release of *Budget 2010* of five experts to discuss the impact of the budget on science and technology spending. Even before the release of the terms of reference, the comprehensive R&D spending review was regarded as an important and necessary undertaking. David Wolfe, who coordinates the Innovation Systems Research Network at the University of Toronto, said the review "needs to start with a better understanding of size and industrial composition and then proceed to a more realistic assessment of what needs to be done."[22] Tom Brzustowski, RBC Financial Group Professor of Commercialization in Innovation at the University of Ottawa, indicated the way forward: "Start from first principles and do a root cause analysis to develop a modern strategy rather than an incremental, line-by-line review of what we have today."[23] Brzustowski emphasized that so long as spending on science and technology R&D is only treated as a line-item expense, and not explicitly linked to wealth creation, innovation, productivity and prosperity will suffer.

The terms of reference for the comprehensive R&D spending review announced in Budget 2010 were finally released in December 2010. The Government announced that a six-member expert panel (with two private sector members and four drawn from the academic community) is tasked with providing recommendations on maximizing the effect of federal programs that contribute to innovation and create economic opportunities for business. The panel was asked to review three types of federal R&D initiatives: (1) tax incentive programs such as the Scientific Research and Experimental Development (SR&ED) program; (2) programs that support business R&D generally (e.g., Industrial Research Assistance Program) or sector-specifically (e.g., Strategic Aerospace and Defence Initiative); and (3) programs that support business-focused R&D through federal granting councils and other departments and agencies, including research at universities and colleges (e.g., Centres of Excellence for Commercialization and Research). The panel is expected to build on the evidence presented in *Innovation and Business Strategy: Why Canada Falls Short*, a 2009 report by the Council of Canadian Academies[24] and STIC's *State of the Nation* report from 2008.[25] The panel is mandated to report back in one year to the Minister of State (Science and Technology) with concrete recommendations.

Meanwhile, others in and outside government are honing their arguments. Some sectors have realized recently that the 2007 strategic statement on

Mobilizing Science and Technology to Canada's Advantage – which targets investment in Canada's entrepreneurial, knowledge and people advantages in environmental science and technologies, natural resources and energy, health and related sciences and technologies and information and communications technologies – has resulted in their activities being excluded from consideration. The effect of being excluded is that existing and new S&T programs are not open to the other sectors (such as Canada's highly competitive, science-driven and export-leading agri-food sector), including the renewed National Centres of Excellence. Moreover, the Canada Excellence Research Chairs program has explicitly rejected any proposals to invest in other than the four targeted areas. As a result, these groups are mobilizing resources and seeking to engage with the federal R&D review, with various parliamentary committees and with various other partners in Ottawa to reverse this highly focused strategy.

WORRYING TRENDS

Federal science and technology funding in Canada has leveled off in recent years, and the federal budget for the 2010–2011 fiscal year is no exception. As the government prepares for the comprehensive R&D review, projected expenditures suggest rises, but actual expenditures might be lower. Although this might be characterized as stagnation, it is probably worse. Even though Canada is experiencing relatively low levels of inflation, and inflation is well-controlled, the rate at which the cost of doing advanced S&T research increases is generally higher than the rate of inflation. This is as true of R&D activities as it is of the science undertaken for regulatory and monitoring activities. These related scientific activities (RSA) include "scientific data collection, information services, special services and studies and education support, as well as administration of extramural RSA activities, all of which support R&D activities" and "which complement and extend R&D by contributing to the generation, dissemination and application of scientific and technological knowledge."[26] RSA expenditures comprise an important part of federal spending from the perspective of provinces that are the direct beneficiaries of RSA expenditures in higher education institutions and businesses carrying out extramural federal activities. Provinces are indirect beneficiaries of RSA expenditures where federal intramural expenditures support provincial R&D activities, for example, in regulatory science.

Extramural RSA expended by higher education institutions, for example, benefit provinces directly since higher education is provincially controlled yet the S&T purse strings are to a major extent federally controlled. During the 2006–2010, one observes steady increases in RSA from $127M in 2006/07 to $192 in 2010/11, which looks encouraging on the face of it (see Figure 2). During the same period, however, there is considerable volatility in the percent change from year to year, which would present a challenge to provinces

Figure 2
Higher education related scientific activities

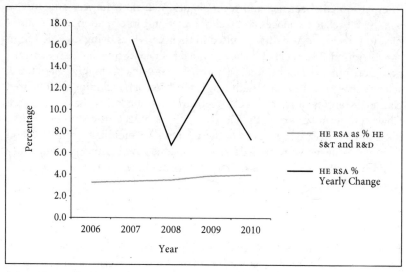

Adapted from *Federal Scientific Activities 2010–2011*. Ottawa: Statistics Canada, 2010.

and their higher education institutions attempting to plan for the sustainability of labs and personnel. The most significant figures emerge only when the RSA is considered as a proportion of higher education expenditure on S&T and R&D combined – there has been no increase to speak of in five years.

The issue of extramural RSA and the provinces illustrates the broader issue about the provinces' ability to adapt to stagnant federal funding for S&T. The federal government has, with health as with higher education, signalled to provinces that, where provincial jurisdiction applies, the federal government can be expected to observe constitutional arrangements. Provinces wishing to increase S&T and R&D therefore face the challenge alone and do so with varying results. National gross domestic expenditures on research and development (GERD) peaked in 2001 at 2.09%, held steady until 2006, but thereafter dropped to an average of 1.92 from 2007–09 (and as low as 1.87% in 2008).[27] By province in 2008, the last year for which there is reported expenditure data, the range was 0.81 for Saskatchewan to 2.61 for Quebec, and only Ontario and Quebec were above the national average of 1.87, which translates to *per capita* expenditure of $1080 and $1023 respectively.[28] Overall provincial contributions to GERD have been fairly constant (see Figure 3) with relatively minor rises and falls in the period. By performing sector, Ontario tends to do better than other provinces (64%) because the province includes the lion's share of the federal labs and because of the concentration of Canada's industrial GERD.[29] Alberta and Saskatchewan maintain relatively high levels of provincial

Figure 3
Percentage of Provincial GERD Contribution

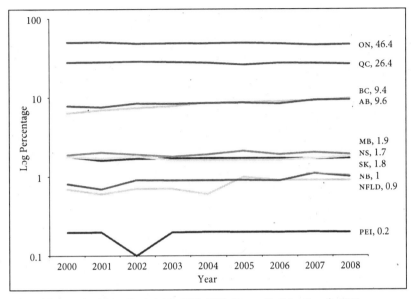

Adapted from *Federal Scientific Activities 2010–2011*. Ottawa: Statistics Canada, 2010.

funding to their total GERD, above 10% compared to the rest below 6%, and in Quebec, Ontario and Alberta the private sector contribution hovers around 50%.[30]

These figures indicate that the during a period in which there is widespread concern about the implications for innovation and productivity of stagnant federal s&t funding, the provinces have not increased their expenditures, and there is significant variation – in some cases more than double *per capita* expenditure – between provinces in their capacity for GERD expenditures. There have been symbolic gestures, such as Alberta's changing nomenclature around innovation and ingenuity, and Ontario's appointment of a provincial science advisor, which harkens back to the defunct office of the National Science Advisor. But when Ontario, a province historically viewed as national economic bedrock becomes the recipient of fiscal equalization payments,[31] expectations of gap filling by provinces become suspect.

CONCLUSIONS

The OECD recently released its innovation strategy, *Getting a Head Start on Tomorrow* in which it describes a 'mobilising vision' that will help "governments improve economic performance, address societal challenges and enhance welfare, through innovation" through "policy coherence and effective co-ordination" and "horizontal as well as vertical co-ordination of policies."[32] The OECD argues for five pillars in this strategy: 1) empowering people to innovate; 2) unleashing innovation; 3) creating and applying knowledge; 4) addressing global and social challenges through innovation; and 5) improving the governance and measurement of innovation. In light of the stagnant S&T spending in Canada, the innovation gap and the looming productivity trap, it is clear that Canada is not fully succeeding by the lights of the OECD strategy.

In many ways Canada has already gone through a lost decade, the term used to describe Japan's slump in the 1980s, and it faces another. While public investments in S&T have increased to some extent, more could have been invested and more could have been achieved. The impressive gains in scientific knowledge and technological know-how are not being translated into socio-economic benefit in Canada by innovators, and innovation is not translating into productivity gains. There is a rising level of angst in the public sector and elsewhere that Canada has not got the right strategy for realizing the benefits of a knowledge-intensive economy. One sign is that while the OECD is encouraging governments to work on developing strategically coordinated policy frameworks, Canada has become increasingly focused on tactical manoeuvres like the Centres of Excellence for Commercialization and Research – alarmingly close to the disregarded tactic of picking or replicating winners. How many Research in Motion's can Canada create and sustain, one might ask, and would it not be better to think of something new? While the government is trying to put a positive spin on its policy and the economy, there are unambiguous signs that change is in the wind. The 2010 budget held the course but the recently announced R&D review, the rumblings from excluded regions and sectors, the pontificating by public intellectuals, the engagement of leading industrialists such as Terry Matthews and the proactive agenda of groups like the CAIC all suggest that while the strategy now is steady-as-she-goes, we are likely to revisit the underlying assumptions of our policy and some change will emerge.

NOTES

1 Government of Canada, *Budget 2010: Leading the Way on Jobs and Growth*. Ottawa: Public Works and Government Services Canada, 2010.
2 P.W.B. Phillips, and D. Castle. 2010. "Science and technology spending and innovation," in *How Ottawa Spends 2010–2011: Recession, Realignment and the New Deficit Era*, edited by C. Bruce Doern and Chris Stoney. Montreal: McGill-Queen's University Press, 2010.
3 Government of Canada, *Mobilizing Science and Technology to Canada's Advantage*. Ottawa: Public Works and Government Services Canada, 2007.

4 Government of Canada, *Budget 2010: Leading the Way on Jobs and Growth*.
5 Ibid.
6 Ibid.
7 Statistics Canada, *Federal Scientific Activities 2010–2011*. Ottawa: Statistics Canada, 2010.
8 Ibid, Table 1–1.
9 Organization for Economic Cooperation and Development (OECD), *Main Science and Technology Indicators 2010–11*. OECD: Paris 2010. Available at http://www.oecd.org/dataoecd/9/44/41850733.pdf.
10 D. King, "The scientific impact of nations." *Nature* 430, 2004, 311–16.
11 L. Leydesdorff and C. Wagner, "Macro-level indicators of the relations between research funding and research output." *Journal of Informetrics* 3, 353–62, 2009
12 Quoted in P. Vierra, "Low Productivity Holding Us Back," *National Post*, January 20, 2011.
13 Kevin Lynch, "Canada's productivity trap." *Globe and Mail*, January 29, 2010.
14 Council of Canadians, *Innovation and Business Strategy: Why Canada Falls Short*. Ottawa: Council of Canadians, 2009.
15 Jeffrey Simpson, "Needed urgently: more creativity from the business class," *Globe and Mail*, May 25, 2009.
16 Ibid.
17 Kevin Lynch, "Canada has everything going for it – except innovation," *Globe and Mail*, July 21, 2010.
18 Ibid.
19 David Crane, "Canada needs to take innovation seriously." *Research Money* 24 (2): 8, 2010.
20 Coalition for Action on Innovation in Canada, *An Action Plan for Prosperity*. Ottawa: CAIC, 2010.
21 Government of Canada, Budget 2010: *Leading the Way on Jobs and Growth*, 78.
22 Research Money, "Expert panel argues for a solid research base, greater coherency in S&T investments," *Research Money* 24 (4): 3, 2010.
23 Ibid.
24 Council of Canadians, *Innovation and Business Strategy: Why Canada Falls Short*.
25 Science Technology and Innovation Council, *State of the Nation 2008*. Ottawa: STIC, 2009.
26 Statistics Canada, *Federal Scientific Activities 2010–2011*.
27 See Table 1 of Statistics Canada. *Gross Domestic Expenditures on Research and Development in Canada (GERD), and the Provinces*. Ottawa: Statistics Canada, 2010.
28 Ibid., Table 2.
29 Ibid., Table 4.1.
30 Ibid., Table 4.2.
31 David Crane, "Canada needs to take innovation seriously," *Research Money* 24 (2): 8.
32 Organization for Economic Cooperation and Development (OECD), *OECD Innovation Strategy: Getting a Head Start on Tomorrow*. Paris: OECD, 2010.

9 Health Care Spending and the Politics of Drift

VANDNA BHATIA

INTRODUCTION

Health care spending has once again begun to ring alarm bells for politicians and commentators around the country, after the relative calm of the past six years. The signs are numerous, ranging from an enigmatic silence on the issue from official Ottawa to the anxious hand-wringing exhibited by bankers, newspaper columnists and physicians' organizations and the more pragmatic assessments of provincial leaders. Long the harbinger of intergovernmental tensions, health care spending is set to engulf the federal-provincial agenda in the next few years as negotiations are ramped up on a replacement agreement for the *10-Year Plan to Strengthen Health Care* which expires in 2013–2014.

So what's at stake in these negotiations? Likely more than any particular government is either willing or able to undertake. First and most obvious is the issue of costs. In the decade between 2000 and 2009 healthcare spending outpaced inflation and population growth, rising from 9.1% of GDP to 11.9%.[1] As a component of provincial budgets, healthcare accounts for about 40% of provincial program spending (when debt servicing charges are excluded). For much of the decade, these increases were driven by consumption and fuelled by economic growth and rising, predictable transfers from the federal government.

Following the recent recession, federal and provincial governments are in the midst of sizeable budgetary deficits and dealing with the prospect of significant retrenchment in spending over the next few years. This has apparently triggered the most recent alarm about healthcare spending with fears that it will crowd out other program areas, such as education, if it is not contained. Although there appears to be consensus on the need to rein in spending in the short term, the broader long-term questions – how much can and should governments spend on health care – have yet to be addressed.

Of course, the issue of healthcare spending in Canada cannot be divorced from a discussion of federal-provincial relations. The issue of program transfers from Ottawa to the provinces looms large for all governments since a significant portion of the growth in health expenditures has been paid for with substantial cash infusions from Ottawa following the Martin Liberals' *10-Year Plan*. The *Plan* guaranteed an annual 6% increase in cash transfers for health care up to and including the 2013–14 fiscal year. The Harper Conservatives continued with the plan when elected in 2006 in part because it restored a semblance of intergovernmental peace after decades of acrimonious relations on the health file.

Given its current fiscal position and somewhat optimistic deficit-slaying deadline, it seems rather unlikely that the Harper government will be willing to commit to another such period of largesse in the short to medium term. Apart from – or perhaps because of – the fiscal issues, intergovernmental relations on health care have long been characterized by jurisdictional disputes about the federal role. The 'open federalism' promoted by the Harper government pledges a return to classical federalism in which the federal spending power is circumscribed and jurisdictional roles are respected. This vision may be central to the federal position on transfers but provincial governments are far from united around it – in health or any other policy sector. Nor have Canadians shown any sign of desiring a federal withdrawal from the health-care scene. The coming negotiations are bound to reopen these old debates and will test the political will of the federal government in persevering with its vision of a more decentralized federation.

This latter issue raises the final factor that is at stake. In six years of governing, the Harper government – when not championing wedge issues that appeal to its base – has repeatedly traded its conservative, grass-roots ideals for pragmatic politics to appease the electorate, and sometimes the opposition, to stay in office. On the health file, the government's talking points about its commitment to Medicare have not changed and it seems clear that pragmatism will outweigh ideology when it comes to negotiating health transfers. Given the perils of tinkering with such a popular program even in their new majority government status, the Conservatives' discourse of lean government and open federalism will undoubtedly be tempered by short-term political calculation.

However, while health transfers to the provinces may be front and centre on the political agenda over the next few years, the real action (or in this instance, inaction) will likely be a continuation or acceleration of policy drift on the Canada Health Act. Passive federal enforcement of the conditions, rather than a reopening of the Act itself, is the least visible and least contentious way for the Harper government to pursue both its lean government and open federalism agendas. Before turning to each of these issues, the next section of this chapter presents a brief overview of recent policy and spending trends.

Less than a decade ago, the country was consumed by the issue of health care. Discussion of the sustainability of Medicare had "become the national pastime."[2] After lurching from crisis to crisis in the media and faced with a crisis of confidence among Canadians, governments launched investigations, commissions and task forces to examine what was ailing Medicare and how it could be fixed – preferably for a generation. There was the Royal Commission on Health Services led by former Saskatchewan premier Roy Romanow and the Senate committee investigation led by Michael Kirby; five provinces issued reports between 2000 and 2002, including Alberta's Mazankowski Report, Saskatchewan's Fyke Commission and Québec's Clair Commission.

Many of the recommendations emanating from these reports focused on improving the quality and efficiency of services rather than a major overhaul of the system. They included advice about improving access to and organization of primary care and homecare; better health human resources coordination and planning; and integration of information systems to improve planning, organization and delivery of care.[3] In 2000, 2003 and again in 2004, high profile First Ministers' Meetings (FMM) resulted in much talk of visions and reform targets. They ended with provincial governments walking away with fat cheques from Ottawa to recoup their losses from the reductions to transfer payments made in previous decades. Despite the talk, research and considerable volume of ideas put forward in the early 2000s, there is scant evidence that much has changed in Canadian Medicare.

Of all these events and non-events, the *10-Year Plan* remains the most salient policy and spending decision of the federal government in the past decade. The *Plan* is the outcome of the September 2004 FMM in which the federal government committed to increasing health transfers by about $41 billion over 10 years. The increase would occur through a 6% annual escalator to the Canada Health Transfer (CHT), with some smaller amounts dedicated to problem areas such as wait time reductions, primary care reform, more comprehensive homecare and pharmacare programs, health human resource planning and performance reporting.[4] When the Harper government took office in 2006, it continued with the *10-Year Plan* and as one of its five governing priorities announced a new Wait Times Guarantee (WTG), although no new funds were allocated to implement it. Apart from the 2006 WTG and annual assurances of stability in the CHT, the Harper government has been virtually silent on Medicare throughout its tenure.

Aside from the money transferred and spent, there is little to show in the way of progress on any of the issues identified in the *10-Year Plan*, including the WTG. In its 5–year report the Health Council of Canada, created to monitor progress, concluded that the Plan "had laudable, much-needed, and ambitious goals. But has the accord had the broad national impact that government leaders intended? In short, the answer is no."[5] The Council pointed to the lack of intergovernmental progress in homecare coverage, the failure to develop a national catastrophic pharmacare program, little in the way of primary care reform and no comprehensive electronic health records. It criticized governments for failing to produce comparable data, their inconsistency of reporting, minimal information sharing and the lack of transparency on all of these issues.[6]

The Office of the Auditor General of Canada (OAGC) echoed some of this criticism, focusing on poor reporting of health indicators by provinces and the nation-wide lack of progress on electronic health records.[7,8] On the issue of wait times, the Wait Time Alliance concluded that "despite some improvement in wait time grades, long waits for care continue to be an issue and much of the wait time picture remains clouded in mystery."[9] The general conclusion seems to be that although the intergovernmental agreements of 2000, 2003 and 2004 bought time, they failed, in the words of Commissioner Romanow, to "buy change."

Provincially there is a little more progress toward making substantive changes in keeping with the volumes of recommendations produced nearly a decade ago. This past year, faced with a mounting deficit and the newly-acquired status of a 'have-not' province, the government of Ontario successfully imposed a draconian reduction in the price of generic drugs. As one of the largest single purchasers of prescription drugs in the world, the government wielded its purchasing power to slash the price of generic drugs to 25% of their brand-name equivalents and eliminate pharmacy rebates from manufacturers. The estimated savings are expected to be $535 million per year – about 14% of provincial drug expenditures. These prices will also be phased in for private sector insurance plans by 2014. The Ontario government took on and triumphed over pharmacists and pharmacies in a very public battle in which these groups threatened boycotts and predicted dire consequences for their patients. In other areas, the government also introduced 'pay-for-performance' legislation linking a portion of hospital CEO salaries to the attainment of quality improvement indicators, and pledged to move to patient-based payment for hospitals beginning April 2011, similar to the program announced in British Columbia.[10]

The British Columbia government announced a new 'patient-focused funding' initiative to pay hospitals on a per-case basis for up to 20% of their funding, beginning in 2010. The approach is intended to use financial incentives for hospitals to reduce their costs-per-case and reward them for creating efficiencies such as reducing lengths of stay, moving to more out-patient services and reducing waiting times in some services.[11] The new funding formula introduces market mechanisms into the public system and forces hospitals to compete with one another to attract patients. According the Health Minister, "That means not funding a facility just because it exists, but funding a facility because it's doing a good job of delivering services of very high quality."[12]

Finally, Québec introduced the most controversial of provincial initiatives on the health care front in this past year. The proposals follow on the recommendations of the 2008 Report of the Task Force on the Funding of the Health System, appointed by the Québec government in 2007. One is a new health premium for all residents which, when fully phased in, will amount to $200 per taxpayer and raise about $1 billion in provincial revenue. The money will be distributed to health care organizations that meet specific performance criteria – a form of market competition within the public system.[13] The second was a $25 'deductible' – essentially a user fee – payable by patients for each medical visit, and collected annually through the tax system, capped at 1–2% of personal income.

Together, the premiums and deductibles were expected to generate about $1.3 billion in revenues over four years. Both were received unfavourably by Quebeckers, but the second generated more widespread reaction, both within and outside Québec. Many groups, including physicians and other providers, argued against the deductibles as they would violate the Canada Health Act, deter necessary care and not reduce costs in the long-term. An estimated 72% of Quebeckers opposed the deductibles and the government began to backtrack on the plan within weeks of announcing it.[14] By September 2010, acknowledging that "the culture here in Québec is not ready for it," the government dropped the idea entirely.[15] However, what was most "extraordinary [was] that [the proposal] should have raised so little protest out of Ottawa, from either side of the House."[16] The tepid response from both the government and the opposition parties was charged with meaning which had less to do with health policy than with federalism, an issue to which we will return shortly.

Although the issue of parallel private financing to universal health care remains at the margins of the broader debate about Medicare in Canada, it nevertheless embodies a number of elements that will be central to the upcoming intergovernmental negotiations on health transfers. First, it raises the issue of costs – how and what can or should be paid for and by whom. Second, it challenges the principles of the Canada Health Act, and in so doing underscores Ottawa's role in a constitutionally-defined provincial jurisdiction. And finally, private financing represents an ideological perspective that many argue undermines the principles of universality and social solidarity at the very heart of Medicare.

THE SUSTAINABILITY OF HEALTH CARE COSTS IN CANADA

The key factor pushing health care back on the political agenda is costs and the sustainability of continuing increases in health expenditures into the foreseeable future. Toronto Dominion (TD) bank economists warn that "every year, government spending on health care increases more than revenues. As a

Table 1
Average Annual Growth Rates in Constant 1997 Dollars, Canada[23]

	1990–1994	1995–1999	1990–1999	2000–2004	2005–2009	2000–2009	1990–2009
Total Health Expenditures	2.2	3.0	2.6	5.1	3.7	4.4	3.5
Per Capita Health Expenditures	0.9	2.1	1.5	4.0	2.6	3.3	2.4

result the amount available for other government spending decreases. If current trends prevail, health care expenditures [in Ontario] would make up 80 per cent of total program spending by 2030, up from 46 per cent today… This is not feasible."[17]

The federal Parliamentary Budget Officer drew similar conclusions in his Fiscal Sustainability Report, focusing in particular on the fiscal impact of changing demographics on health spending,[18] as did the OECD's report on Canada's fiscal outlook.[19] Other prominent Canadians have also weighed in, including former Bank of Canada governor David Dodge,[20] former Prime Minister Brian Mulroney, and even the current federal finance minister Jim Flaherty: "The provinces are going to have to…figure out ways of providing health-care services without rampant growth. Because it's not about reducing spending on health care – it's about controlling the rate of growth so that health care doesn't run away from the level of real GDP growth in the provinces."[21]

The magnitude of increases in health expenditures depends very much on the figures one uses. Rhetoric aside, over the past two decades, total health expenditures rose from 9.0% of GDP to 11.9% by 2009, which amounts to an average annual increase of 2.4% above inflation and population growth. The fastest growth occurred during the 2000–2004 period, largely the product of significant reinvestments in health care made by provincial and federal governments following the recession of the 1990s (see Table 1). The Health Accords of 2000 and 2003 and the 10-Year Plan in 2004 placed health transfers on more predictable and stable footing. In 2009, the federal government cash transfers to the provinces amounted to $25.4 billion and are expected to total $30.3 billion when the 2004 agreement expires in 2014.[22]

The largest category of health expenditures is for hospitals which comprise 29% of the total, followed by drugs at 16% and physicians at 14%.[24] Public sector expenditures account for 70% of the total $182 billion spent on health care in Canada in 2009, with the remaining 30% accounted for by private spending. Of all categories of expenditures, spending on drugs is by far the fastest growing category in both the public and private sectors.

Beyond inflation and population growth, there are two main cost drivers in the health care system: population aging and increases in utilization or intensity. Population aging is the most often cited factor but actually contributes only in a small way to overall increases in health expenditures – between 0.8 to 1.0% – accounting for less than half of the inflation- and population-adjusted growth in the previous two decades.[25] To illustrate, in the 1998–2008 period the proportion of the population over 65 in Canada rose by about 10% but the share of health expenditures for this age group remained stable at about 44% of the total. So in fact, overall spending on the elderly has actually fallen slightly relative to the younger population. This trend is likely to continue because although the population continues to age rapidly, seniors are living more years in good health. The final few years of life are the most resource intensive, so healthy seniors are essentially delaying the steep costs associated with dying until a later age.[26] Nevertheless, as the rate of population aging increases, growth in health spending attributed to aging will rise steadily to 1.3% in the next 20 years, and then drop precipitously beyond 2030.[27]

The more significant and sustained cost driver is the increase in the age-adjusted utilization or intensity of services, particularly in the last 10 years. This is the product of numerous factors, including technological advancements such as less invasive joint replacement, utilization of new drug therapies, and increased use of diagnostic imaging. In other words, Canadians of all ages are simply using more health care services and products.

These expenditure trends suggest that there are no silver bullets to bringing health spending under control in the upcoming negotiations. To the extent that increasing demand for and consumption of health care is the primary cost driver, there are three ways governments can address the issues. First, governments simply can reduce spending and indirectly reduce demand by limiting access to services – something for which neither government nor the public appear to have any appetite, particularly after the experiences of the mid-1990s. Moreover this is a politically explosive approach if the decision is taken unilaterally by the federal government, as history amply demonstrates.

Second, governments can find efficiency improvements in the system to improve health status and the delivery and organization of services to keep health spending on an even keel. This is essentially what many of the reports earlier in the decade recommended, and was among the declared objectives of the Health Accords and 10-Year Plan. However the record of the provinces in taking action on these recommendations, despite significant federal reinvestment, has been spotty at best. This fact may embolden the federal government to take a more aggressive stance against future CHT increases.

Finally, governments can meet demands by raising additional revenues. This has been proven to be a moderately successful provincial strategy in recent years. Ontario introduced health premiums as a new revenue stream in 2004, as did Québec earlier this year. British Columbia raised its existing premiums by 6% in 2009,[28] and Alberta raised its own premiums a number of times before they were abolished in 2009. However, the net revenue impact of health premiums has been off-set by other tax reductions which have slowed the rate at which overall government revenues have increased.[29]

For provincial governments, raising taxes or premiums to pay for health care is less politically risky than cutting health care spending. However, given the precarious and seemingly perpetual minority status of the federal Conservatives, the political benefits of this approach for the federal government are far less clear-cut. Instead, the Harper government is more likely to favour vacating additional tax room in lieu of transfers or federal tax increases, leaving it up to the provinces to determine which tack to take in managing their health expenditures. This approach is also consistent with the Conservative government's broader vision of federalism and intergovernmental relations, to which we now turn.

FEDERAL-PROVINCIAL RELATIONS

The shifting tenor of intergovernmental relations in Canadian federalism is highly influenced by the exercise of the federal spending power.[30] That power has both an instrumental purpose – that is, to promote a particular policy agenda – as well as a symbolic one in defining the nature of the Canadian federation and national identity.[31] Throughout the 1980s and 1990s, unilateral federal cuts to program transfers undermined the legitimacy of the federal spending power as an instrumental tool and were central to the antipathy and competitiveness that typified intergovernmental relations throughout much of that period. The reductions left the provinces scrambling to cut health care costs and dealing with the political fallout associated with closing hospitals, longer wait times and across-the-board service reductions. At the same time these tensions were refracted through the lens of constitutional politics, entangling health policy with issues of national unity and encumbering Medicare with the future of Canadian federalism writ large. Stepping back from the brink after the razor-thin victory of federalist forces in the 1995 Québec referendum, the Chrétien government pledged a more flexible federation and a renegotiation of intergovernmental fiscal relations.

One of the outcomes of that pledge was the 1999 Social Union Framework Agreement (SUFA) which was an attempt to clarify intergovernmental relations on social policy issues, particularly those of exclusive provincial jurisdiction, and circumscribe the federal spending power. However the agreement legitimized the federal spending power even as it sought to limit it, and this was the primary reason Québec refused to endorse it. Nevertheless, following SUFA the federal government has taken a far less activist and interventionist role in health policy while at the same time increasing transfers to the provinces. It also appears to have accepted that asymmetrical federalism is the path to peace with Québec.

The last decade reflects the tempering of the pan-Canadian nationalism of the past through a somewhat more circumspect exercise of the federal spending power. The Harper government's promise of 'open federalism' appears to be an incremental progression on this decade-long path rather than a major departure from the status quo. However, it is likely that the relative peace of recent years is in part the product of the loosening of federal purse strings. Whether this balancing of the symbolic and instrumental functions of the federal spending power is sustainable through the inevitable period of retrenchment remains to be seen.

The years after SUFA witnessed a strengthening of interprovincial collaboration on health resulting in a united front against Ottawa to successfully demand more money for their treasuries. The *10-Year Plan* was the apogee of that success. Following on the heels of SUFA, the three health accords contained little in the way of national standards or outright conditions in exchange for federal dollars. Instead, "the federal Liberal government sought to use negotiations over existing intergovernmental transfers as a mechanism… to define priorities and directions for change and to have provinces commit to a reporting process with comparable indicators of progress."[32]

Rather than imposing program directives, the federal government attempted to use information – in the form of published national indicators and targets – to coordinate and influence the reform paths provincial governments might take. However, the targets and measures were vague and the program objectives ambiguous enough to leave governments with plenty of wiggle room. As already discussed, there is little evidence that the commitments made in these agreements have been substantively met. The accords also established a strong precedent for the flexible federalism that provinces had been demanding with SUFA. The *10-Year Plan* carved out a side-deal for Québec, recognizing and endorsing "asymmetrical federalism, that is, flexible federalism that notably allows for the existence of specific agreements and arrangements adapted to Québec's specificity."[33]

Scratching the surface of this apparent intergovernmental harmony however reveals that federalism issues are far from settled. Since the *10-Year Plan* was agreed to and despite significant infusions of cash, the lackluster efforts of governments to share information, let alone to take coordinated action on some high-priority items, reveal deeper divisions between them on the direction health policy should take. More importantly, in contrast with their collective demands for more money from Ottawa, provincial differences on the broader question of intergovernmental transfers, including equalization, seem irreconcilable.

The federal reinvestments in program transfers have alleviated much of the vertical fiscal imbalance that united the provinces against Ottawa in the past. While they will undoubtedly argue in unison for more money and against any reductions in future transfer negotiations, the closing of the fiscal gap makes these arguments less compelling than in the past, leaving few if any issues around which they can present a united front. For example, a key concern is the commitment the federal government has made to move to equal per capita cash transfers under the CHT, similar to the changes made in 2007 for the Canada Social Transfer. These adjustments to the CHT were deferred until the end of the *10-Year Plan*.

Ontario has been particularly vocal in pushing for a new formula, arguing that "[a]ll Canadians deserve to be treated fairly. Ontarians, however, are not being treated like Canadians living in other provinces... Ontarians ought to have the same level of per-person health care funding now provided to Canadians elsewhere in the country."[34] In its newly acquired status as a have-not province, Ontario has already benefited from the changes to equalization and the related redistributive impact of program cash transfers. The promised transition to per capita cash transfers will further benefit Ontario, along with Alberta, and will correspondingly decrease the cash transferred to other provinces.[35]

Given the stormy response Ottawa received to its equalization changes in 2007, changes in the CHT are likely to prove equally thorny. Already Québec has declared that the recent and proposed changes to the CHT were made unilaterally and that Ottawa has "reneged on its commitments" to return fiscal balance within the federation. It notes that the changes to both equalization and program transfers disproportionately benefit Ontario and that the past decade of increases in transfers has mainly benefited Ontario, British Columbia and Alberta.[36]

Apart from the technical changes in the CHT and equalization formulas, there are broader issues about the role of the federal government in the federation. Much of the discontent with federalism evinced by the provinces leading up to the SUFA had to do with Ottawa's 'disspending' power – namely, its unilateral withdrawal from social program spending under the mid-1990s Program Review federal deficit cuts.[37] There was less consensus on the illegitimacy of the spending power itself, particularly among the 'have-not' provinces that clearly stood – and still stand – to gain from federal inflows of cash.[38]

Even Québec, as evidenced in its position on per capita funding under the CHT, has not been averse to receiving federal cash despite its demands for federal withdrawal. "In short ... at the policy level, provincial stances toward the federal spending power are heavily influenced by their economic and financial interests."[39] There is greater provincial unity on the symbolic role of the federal spending power, particularly in health care. With the exception of Québec most provinces, regardless of the party in power and their relative wealth, have endorsed a pan-Canadian identity in which a strong federal government is pivotal.

So, while they may contest the nuts and bolts of fiscal transfers, no provinces apart from Québec have called for a complete federal withdrawal. Even the Harper government, its open federalism rhetoric notwithstanding, has endorsed a federal role in a range of social programs that fall into provincial jurisdiction. It has identified health care and post-secondary education as shared federal-provincial priorities; it sanctioned the 2004 health accord and introduced the Wait Times Guarantee; and it has pledged its support of the Canada Health Act.

All of this leads to the observation that the majority Harper government is unlikely to move substantively in the direction advocated by its prodigal Québec son, and recently reappointed Harper cabinet minister, Maxime Bernier. Undoubtedly warming the cockles of the Prime Minister's heart, Bernier insists that Ottawa should "end all federal intrusion into areas of provincial jurisdiction. Instead of sending money to the provinces, Ottawa would cut its taxes and let them use the fiscal room that has been vacated. Such a transfer of tax points to the provinces would allow them to fully assume their responsibilities, without federal control." In a speech that uncannily echoes the ideas of Stephen Harper, as both former president of the National Citizen Coalition and Reform Party member, Bernier goes on to argue that "ending the federal spending power, eliminating the federal programs that violate the division of powers, and transferring tax points to the provinces would be the right thing to do..."[40]

However, apart from providing political fodder about the Tories' hidden agenda to the opposition ("If you look at their objective of doing away with the spending power, and if you look at what Mr. Bernier has said and what Mr. Flaherty has said, the objective and the intent become very, very clear")[41] and perhaps raising a trial balloon to dampen expectations when the actual negotiations do begin,[42] the political realities of governing will trump this vision. As attractive as it might be for garnering federal votes from Québec, the NDP's newly dominant presence in that province renders moot any such overtures from the federalist parties in the foreseeable future. And, as long as there are voters to be wooed in the have-not provinces, particularly the Maritimes, a radical decentralization of social program spending will bleed votes from any party that proposes it.

Finally, the power of the symbolic, nationalizing values associated with the federal role in health and social programs should not be underestimated. In a nation divided by region, language and wealth, these very programs have been the hallmarks of state building and have become firmly enshrined in the public imagination. It is no mere happenstance that Medicare remains one of the defining values of being Canadian[43] or that Tommy Douglas was voted the Greatest Canadian.[44]

THE CANADA HEALTH ACT: THE PRAGMATIC POLITICS OF DRIFT

The preceding discussion leads to the conclusion that the most plausible course of action for the federal government in negotiating the next agreement on the CHT will be one that balances the need to curb its own expenditures with a minimally politically feasible policy presence in Medicare. On the surface, this implies a negotiated agreement with the provinces that provides some certainty in federal transfers for the next five year period, even if the increases to those transfers are minimal.

However, any escalator on the CHT that is less than the current 6% will tax provincial fiscal capacity to maintain current health spending levels and so it must come with a 'give'. This may take the form of a combination of tax point transfers and the implementation of the per capita CHT formula. While this would benefit the western provinces and Ontario, it will leave Québec and the Atlantic provinces, who would see a net reduction in their cash transfers, less than satisfied. Of these, it is Québec that will pose the most serious challenge to reaching an intergovernmental compromise. One way around this conundrum is to appease Québec's demands for greater autonomy which, apart from the unlikely prospect of complete federal-provincial disentanglement, might be achieved through changes to the Canada Health Act. Modifying – but not abandoning – the publicly popular Act by making it more 'flexible' would likely find favour in most provincial capitals and be in keeping with the Harper government's own open federalism agenda. Essentially, of course, such flexibility includes a legitimized role for greater private financing within the Act.

Recent events in Québec suggest that this route to intergovernmental agreement is not unlikely. The Act has long been a thorn in the side of Québec politicians, who have argued the Act represents federal intrusion into provincial jurisdiction and "is inspired by a centralizing concept of federalism which no longer has any place." Furthermore, the Québec government contends the Act "has had the effect of impeding any evolution of the health care systems in Canadian provinces."[45]

In its 2008 report, the province's Task Force on the Funding of the Health System (the Castonguay Report) recommended, among other things, that a more "flexible framework" be adapted within the Canada Health Act that would facilitate the creation of a parallel private insurance system and allow utilization-based annual deductibles for the public system. This push toward more private financing in the health care system is most prevalent in Québec, although similar arguments have been made by the governments of British Columbia and Alberta in the not-to-distant past.[46] The Québec government's position may in part be a reflection of the fact that the principles embodied by the Canada Health Act find less resonance among residents of that province than any other,[47] and that Quebeckers themselves have much weaker ties to symbols of Canadian nationhood – like Medicare – than residents of other provinces.[48]

Québec also leads all provinces in terms of the number of privately practicing physicians and privately funded clinics providing services that appear to contravene the Canada Health Act, with British Columbia following a close second, with the numbers continuing to grow.[49] And, although the dilemma it faced following the Supreme Court of Canada's decision in *Chaoulli* appears to have been at least temporarily resolved – essentially "the government opened up the market to the private sector then immediately gutted that market"[50] – the Castonguay report recommendations and the recent government proposal to introduce a utilization-based deductible suggest that the issue of private financing is far from settled.

There are indications that this debate has a foothold outside of Québec as well. Recent calls for an 'adult conversation' on health care include the option of private financing along with other reforms.[51] Proponents of this approach see a sympathetic ally in the Harper government, unlike previous Liberal administrations under Chrétien and Martin that portrayed themselves as Medicare's most ardent defenders.

While the Tories have not overtly sided with any of these advocates, neither have they openly challenged them. Moreover, a number of cases similar to the *Chaoulli* challenge are wending their way through courts around the country, and are likely to bring the issue to the forefront once again. And, although the deductible proposal was dropped in Québec in light of public opposition, Canadians are "giving increasing consideration to private provision of health care services, not so much as a replacement for the public system, but as a potential solution to the problem of sustaining the public system."[52] The public seemed to hardly be fazed by the highly publicized decision of the Premier of Newfoundland and Labrador to travel to Florida for elective heart surgery in early 2010, with 40% saying they too would be willing to pay to receive services more quickly. Support for this was highest among Quebeckers.[53]

In addition to this discursive shift, there is plenty of evidence that the Canada Health Act is outdated and ineffective. Successive federal administrations have failed to modernize the legislation to recognize and accommodate advances in medical technology and demands for services it does not cover. As a result, passive privatization is already taking place as a large and growing proportion of health care services and spending fall outside of the Act's parameters. Although provincial governments offer a patchwork of coverage for some of these services, there is no coherence across the country and a significant proportion are financed privately. Even when pressed to take action outside the Act itself, such as on a national catastrophic drug plan or homecare, federal and provincial governments have simply pushed the issues off their agendas once the glare of public scrutiny has waned.

Finally, the Canada Health Act has been allowed to become toothless as active federal enforcement of its conditions has in effect ceased, despite repeated admonishments from the OAGC and threatened legal action by its advocates.[54] The nominal penalties that have been recently applied under the terms of the Act are based on the self-reported violations of individual provinces. The terse, two-line response of the federal government to Québec's proposed deductibles is instructive: "The Canada Health Act is the law of the land. We expect the provinces and territories to abide by the Act."[55]

In this context, revising the Canada Health Act seems entirely compelling and logical, and far less controversial than the wholesale withdrawal of the federal presence from the health sector. By trading off tax point transfers and a watered-down Canada Health Act for small or no transfer increases, the federal government can meet its main objectives in negotiating a deal with the provinces that will also maintain intergovernmental harmony. Even the opposition Liberal Party – long the self-proclaimed defender of Medicare – appears on-side. Its leader has suggested that "we need to give the provinces room to experiment, within the framework established by the Canada Health Act..."[56] As one political commentator notes: "This is a sign of things to come. With the cost of health care nearing 50 per cent of provincial budgets, no federal government has any intention of withholding federal transfers in retaliation, from Québec or any other province. The Canada Health Act is a dead letter."[57]

CONCLUSIONS

Notwithstanding its endorsement of the *10-Year Plan*, the Harper government has demonstrated a profound indifference to Medicare, and has repeatedly asserted that health care is a provincial jurisdiction. Short of promoting a complete federal withdrawal, it has declared its commitment to a publicly funded system but also advocated "a flexible and sustainable system that allows for innovation and reform" within the Canada Health Act.[58]

Apart from similar anodyne statements, there has been an impenetrable federal silence on the issue for the past few years. In the meantime, health care expenditures continue to rise, exceeding inflation and population growth. Fuelled by a robust 6% annual increase in the cash portion of the CHT, health spending is currently averaging about 40% of provincial program expenditures. The sustainability of this level of and growth in spending is increasingly being called into question as the effects of the recent recession reverberate through government coffers. With the imminent expiry in 2014 of the *10-Year Plan*, the negotiation of new targets for the CHT has become the focal point of debate about the future of the health care system in Canada.

Even as Ottawa quietly seeks input into future health transfer negotiations with the provinces, the temporal and fiscal imperatives impelled by its ambitious deficit-slaying targets have laid the ground rules: federal health care spending will be ring-fenced in the coming austerity program. There will be no health care cuts but there will be little or no new money either. For provinces faced with equally, if not more, ruthless budgetary dilemmas the negotiations, such as they are, promise to be less than satisfying.

As a result, it is unlikely that provincial leaders will accede to the federal position without a fight. Instead, the premiers will use the CHT negotiations to leverage their own objectives. Inevitably, whenever the First Ministers talk about health care, the subtext of that discussion is federalism. The previous decade of health policy talk was focused on restoring the vertical fiscal imbalance in the federation, and this has largely been achieved through federal reinvestments into program transfers. In the absence of new money, the upcoming negotiations will be an opportunity for the federal government to pursue selectively its open federalism agenda and for (some) provincial governments to reclaim a little more policy autonomy. A plausible basis for consensus is a watered-down – more flexible – Canada Health Act. This may take the form of an actual amendment to the Act to modify the principles and/or the enforcement requirements, or it may simply be an implicit agreement to continue to allow the Act to drift and ultimately become irrelevant and obsolete.

NOTES

1 Canadian Institute for Health Information, *National Health Expenditure Trends, 1975 to 2009*. Ottawa, CIHI, 2010.

2 Canadian Medical Association, "Editorial: Time for a New Canada Health Act?" *Canadian Medical Association Journal*, 163, 6 (2000): 689.

3 Catherine Fooks and Steven Lewis, *Romanow and Beyond: A Primer on Health Reform Issues in Canada*. CPRN Discussion Paper No. H/05 Health Network, November 2002.

4 Gerard W. Boychuk, "How Ottawa Gambles: Rolling the Dice in Health Care Reform." In Bruce Doern, ed. *How Ottawa Spends, 2005–2006: Managing the Minority*. Montreal: McGill-Queen's University Press, 2005, 41–58.

5 Health Council of Canada, *Rekindling Reform: Health Care Renewal in Canada, 2003–2008*. Toronto: 2008.

6 Health Council of Canada, *Health Care Renewal in Canada: Measuring Up?* (Toronto: 2007).

7 Office of the Auditor General of Canada, *Report of the Auditor General of Canada to the House of Commons: Chapter 8 Reporting on Health Indicators – Health Canada*. Ottawa: OAGC, December 2008.

8 Office of the Auditor General of Canada, *Electronic Health Records: An Overview of Federal and Provincial Audit Reports*. Ottawa: OAGC, April 2010.

9 Waiting Time Alliance (WTA), *No Time For Complacency. Report Card on Wait Times in Canada* (June 2010). Accessed: http://www.waittimealliance.ca/media/2010reportcard/ WTA2010–reportcard_e.pdf.

10 Ontario, *News Release: Patient-Based Payment for Hospitals* (Toronto, Ministry of Health and Long Term Care: May 3, 2010) Accessed: http://news.ontario.ca/mohltc/en/2010/05/patient-based-payment-for-hospitals.html.

11 British Columbia, *News Release: B.C. Launches Patient-Focused Funding Province-Wide* (Victoria: Ministry of Health Services, April 12, 2010) Accessed: http://www2.news.gov.bc.ca/ news_releases_2009–2013/2010HSERV0020–000403.htm.

12 Kevin Falcon, as quoted in Rod Mickelborough, "B.C. pioneers new formula for funding hospitals." *The Globe and Mail*, April 13, 2010, A7.

13 Antonia Maioni, "Health Care Funding: Needs and Reality." *Policy Options*, May 2010, 69–72.

14 CBC, "Quebecers against fee for MD visits: poll." CBC online, May 10, 2010. Accessed: http://www.cbc.ca/health/story/2010/05/10/mtl-doctors-visit-fee-poll.html.

15 Ingrid Peritz, "*Québec* drops $25 *user-fee* plan for doctors' visits," *The Globe and Mail* September 23, 2010, A9.

16 Andrew Coyne, "It's like putting a puzzle together," *Macleans. ca* (April 9, 2010). Accessed: http.//www2.macleans.ca/2010/04/09/it%e2%80%99s-like-putting-a-puzzle-together/.

17 Toronto Dominion (TD) Economics, *Charting a Path To Sustainable Health Care in Ontario*, (Toronto: May 27, 2010): 2.

18 Parliamentary Budget Officer, *Fiscal Sustainability Report*. Ottawa: Office of the Parliamentary Budget Officer. February 10, 2010.

19 Organization for Economic Cooperation and Development, OECD *Economic Surveys: Canada*. September 2010. Accessed: http://www.oecd.org/eco/surveys/Canada.

20 John Geddes, "The health care time bomb," *Macleans.ca* (April 12, 2010). Accessed: http://www2.macleans.ca/2010/04/12/the-health-care-time-bomb/

21 Flaherty, as cited in Christine Dobby, "Curb health costs: Flaherty," *Telegraph-Journal*. St. John: July 16, 2010: A1.

22 Canada, Department of Finance, *Fiscal Reference Tables*. Ottawa: Public Works and Government Services Canada, October 2010.

23 Canadian Institute for Health Information, *National Health Expenditure Trends, 1975 to 2009*.

24 Ibid.

25 TD Economics; Marc Lee, *How Sustainable Is Medicare?* Ottawa: Canadian Centre for Policy Alternatives, September 2007.

26 Lee, *How Sustainable Is Medicare?*; Organization for Economic Cooperation and Development, "Projecting OECD Health and Long-Term Care Expenditures: What Are the Main Drivers?" OECD *Economics Department Working Paper* No. 477 (2006)

27 Parliamentary Budget Officer, *Fiscal Sustainability Report*.

28 Wendy Steuck, "B.C. to increase health premiums," *The Globe and Mail*. September 2, 2009: A6.

29 F. Béland, "Arithmetic failure and the myth of the unsustainability of universal health insurance." *Canadian Medical Association Journal* 177, no. 1 (2007): 54–57. Also, according to OECD data, tax revenue as a percentage of GDP in Canada dropped by 3.7% between 1990 and 2008. Organization for Economic Cooperation and Development, *Revenue Statistics 1965–2008* (2009). Accessed: http://www.oecd.org/ctp/taxdatabase.

30 James Bickerton, "Deconstructing the New Federalism," *Canadian Political Science Review* 4, no. 2–3 (2010): 56–72.

31 Harvey Lazar, "The Spending Power and the Harper Government," *Queen's Law Journal*, 34 (2008): 125–140.

32 Keith Banting, in Hamish Telford, Peter Graefe and Keith Banting. "Defining the Federal Government's Role in Social Policy: The Spending Power and Other Instruments." IRPP *Policy Matters* 9, no.3 (2008): 108–120.

33 Canadian Intergovernmental Conference Secretariat, *Asymmetrical Federalism That Respects Québec's Jurisdiction – News Release* (September 16, 2004). Accessed: http://www.scics.gc.ca/ cinfo04/800042012_e.pdf

34 Ontario Ministry of Finance, *Ontario Economic Outlook and Fiscal Review* (Toronto: Government of Ontario, 2008): 35. Accessed: http://www.fin.gov.on.ca/en/budget/fallstatement/2008/08fs-annex3.html

35 S.M. Fard, *The Canada Health Transfer*, Library of Parliament Discussion Paper (Ottawa: PRB 08–52B)

36 Finances Québec, *2009–2010 Budget, Section G: Update on Federal Transfers*. Accessed: http://www.budget.finances.gouv.qc.ca/budget/2009–2010/en/documents/pdf/BudgetPlan.pdf

37 Peter Graefe, in Hamish Telford, Peter Graefe and Keith Banting, editors. "Defining the Federal Government's Role in Social Policy: The Spending Power and Other Instruments." IRPP *Policy Matters* 9, no. 3 (2008): 54–107.

38 Bill Curry, "Alberta, Québec unite to challenge Ottawa," *The Globe and Mail*. June 16, 2010: A10.

39 Lazar, "The Spending Power and the Harper Government," para. 6

40 Maxime Bernier, "Restoring Our Federal Union." Speech to the Albany Club by the MP for Beauce. Toronto: October 13, 2010.

41 Ujjal Dosanjh, as quoted in Heather Scoffield, "Opposition suspicious of Tory plans for national conversation on health reform," *The Globe and Mail*. October 18, 2010: Accessed: http://www.theglobeandmail.com/news/national/opposition-suspicious-of-tory-plans-for-national-conversation-on-health-care-reform/article1762578/

42 Keith Beardsley, "Is Maxime Bernier the hidden agenda?" *National Post Online* (October 13, 2010). Accessed: http://fullcomment.nationalpost.com/2010/10/13/keith-beardsley-is-maxime-bernier-the-hidden-agenda/.

43 Stuart Soroka, *Canadian Perceptions of the Health Care System*. Toronto: Health Council of Canada, February 2007.

44 CBC News Archive, *And the Greatest Canadian of All Time Is...*, November 29, 2004. Accessed: http://archives.cbc.ca/politics/parties_leaders/clips/11120/.

45 Québec, Task Force on the Funding of the Health System, *Getting Our Money's Worth*. Québec: Gouvernement du Québec, February 2008: 254, 255.

46 Lisa Gregoire, "Alberta's hybrid public-private 'third way.'" *Canadian Medical Association Journal* 174, no. 8 (2006): 1076; Andrea Ventimiglia, "BC to reform health care." *Canadian Medical Association Journal* 174, no. 8 (2006): 1077.

47 Soroka, *Canadian Perceptions of the Health Care System.*

48 Angus Reid Public Opinion, *News Release: Canadians Truly Proud of Flag, Hockey, Armed Forces and Health Care System.* (June 30, 2010). Accessed: http://www.angus-reid.com/polls/43116/canadians-truly-proud-of-flag-hockey-armed-forces-and-health-care-system/.

49 J.G. Smith, "A snapshot of private health care in Canada," *Health Frontiers* 2, no.4 (2006). Accessed: http://www.cimca.ca/newsletter/issue02_04.html; and A. Shimo, "The rise of private care in Canada," *Macleans.ca* (April 25, 2006). Accessed: http://www.macleans.ca/article.jsp? content=20060501_125881_125881.

50 Colleen Flood, in André Picard, "Canada, it's time to get our Health Act together," *The Globe and Mail.* November 8, 2010: A8.

51 Organization for Economic Cooperation and Development, OECD *Economic Surveys: Canada;* Brian Mulroney, "Productivity: Canada's weakest link." *Policy Options,* December-January (2011):6–10; Rod Mickelburgh,"The outspoken surgeon medicare advocates love to hate," *The Globe and Mail.* November 6, 2010: A16.

52 Soroka, *Canadian Perceptions of the Health Care System.*

53 Angus Reid Public Opinion, *News Release Most Canadians Are Not Upset with Danny Williams Over Trip to U.S. Hospital.* (Feb 17, 2010). Accessed: http://www.visioncritical.com /wp-content/uploads/2010/02/2010.02.17_HealthCare_CAN.pdf.

54 Vandna Bhatia, "Social rights, civil rights and health reform in Canada," *Governance* 23, no.1 (2010): 37–58. Ann Silversides, "Canada Health Act breaches are being ignored, pro-medicare groups charge," *Canadian Medical Association Journal* 179, no.11 (2008): 1112–3.

55 David Johnson, "Feds mum on fee to visit MD," *Montreal Gazette.* April 1, 2010: A1.

56 Michael Ignatieff, "Speech to Mirabel Chamber of Commerce" (April 8, 2010). Accessed: http://www.liberal.ca/newsroom/speeches/remarks-to-the-mirabel-chamber-of-commerce-and-industry/.

57 Coyne, "It's like putting a puzzle together."

58 Carly Weeks, "Calls grow to limit doctors' slice of health-care pie," *The Globe and Mail.* October 29, 2010: A1.

10 Industry Canada as Economic Regulator: Globalive and the Lessons of Political Licensing

RICHARD SCHULTZ

"Power alone is never sufficient to produce legitimate authority.
Hudson Janisch[1]

INTRODUCTION

Although the overwhelming focus for students of telecommunications regulation in Canada has long been the Canadian Radio-television and Telecommunications Commission (CRTC), the December 2009 announcement by Industry Minister, Tony Clement, that the Government of Canada was reversing the CRTC's decision on the grounds that the new entrant into the cellular telephone market, Globalive, was ineligible to operate as a telecommunications carrier, forcefully reminded us that there are two telecom economic regulators in Canada, not one.[2] The original decision by the CRTC was based on the conclusion that Globalive was not controlled in fact by Canadians and therefore did not meet the requirements set out in section 16 of the Telecommunications Act and is not currently eligible to operate as a telecommunications common carrier. In announcing the reversal, the Industry Minister went to great pains to argue that the Government's action did not constitute a change in Canadian policy regarding foreign ownership of Canadian telecommunications firms, but was a determination that applied only to Globalive.

Almost all of the subsequent public debate over the Cabinet action concentrated on the foreign ownership issue and on the benefits that would flow from enhancing competition, issues raised by Cabinet in its reversal.[3] The premise of this chapter, however, is that the Cabinet's reversal of the CRTC decision raises more fundamental issues than Canada's foreign ownership rules and whether Cabinet exceeded its authority, an issue currently before the courts.[4] The more important issues arise from the increasing importance of the role of Industry

Canada as an economic regulator, as the decision-maker in the allocation of spectrum, and more specifically the procedures and processes that are, or should be, employed by Industry Canada as an economic regulator.[5]

The central argument in this chapter is that Industry Canada, as demonstrated by the Globalive decision, employs procedures that lack transparency, do not ensure impartial treatment of those subject to the procedures and are not clearly free of political interference. Moreover, I argue that Industry Canada, in its role as economic regulator for spectrum management, is in conflict with Canada's commitments made when Canada signed the Basic Telecommunications Agreement under General Agreement on Trade in Services in 1997 wherein binding commitments were made to adhere to telecommunications regulatory practices set out in the World Trade Organization (WTO) Regulation Reference Paper, a paper for which Canada was one of the primary advocates.[6]

The chapter consists of four parts. The first section sets out the powers that Industry Canada may exercise in spectrum regulation pursuant to its statutory authority under the Radiocommunication Act. As this is important to the subsequent discussion, this section also provides a summary analysis of how these powers evolved and the nature of their original purpose compared to the role they have come to play. The second section provides an analysis of the primary factors that led Industry Canada, and its predecessor department responsible for telecommunications (the former Department of Communications) to assert its role as an economic regulator in this sector. The third section provides an analysis of the sequence of events and the processes employed that led the Cabinet to overturn the CRTC decision that Globalive was ineligible to operate. The final section compares the procedures employed by Industry Canada to those employed by the CRTC in the exercise of their respective regulatory functions as well as those procedures that are supposed to govern Cabinet political appeals. This section will also analyze the commitments Canada has made to the WTO and demonstrate that our current domestic procedures for spectrum regulation are in conflict with our international trade commitments. Conclusions then follow that address possible ameliorative actions to reconcile the problems identified.

INDUSTRY CANADA AS ECONOMIC REGULATOR

The statutory authority establishing the role of Industry Canada, and its Minister, is found in the Radiocommunications Act.[7] For our purposes, the central powers that establish the department as an economic regulator are in clause 5 as follows:

(1) Subject to any regulations made under section 6, the Minister may, taking into account all matters that the Minister considers relevant for

ensuring the orderly establishment or modification of radio stations
and the orderly development and efficient operation of radiocommunication in Canada,
(a) issue
(i) radio licences in respect of radio apparatus,
(i.1) spectrum licences in respect of the utilization of specified radio
frequencies within a defined geographic area, ... (and)
(e) plan the allocation and use of the spectrum. ...

It was under these provisions that Industry Canada had originally granted
Globalive, as well as several other applicants, a spectrum license to provide a
new advanced wireless telecommunications service in Canada. This was to
give effect to its announced policy of seeking to enhance competition in this
sector by setting aside some portions of spectrum that new entrants could bid
for in its auction of particular radio frequencies. As part of this process, applicants had to establish to Industry Canada's satisfaction that they were "qualified" to participate in the auction, that is, they met the foreign ownership and
control requirements in the *Telecommunications Act*.[8]

Those requirements are that wireless carriers must be "Canadian-owned
and controlled." Industry Canada did not employ a public process to establish
how firms met those requirements nor did it provide evidence that they did in
fact meet them. It simply announced, as in the case of Globalive, that the firm
met the requirements.[9] Subsequent developments in this process, including
the CRTC's decision and the Cabinet review, are analyzed in more detail in the
third section of the chapter below.

Although Industry Canada now emphasizes that its spectrum management and authorization (licensing) powers enable the department to pursue
economic policy-making objectives such as promoting competition in the
wireless sector, it is important to note that this has not been the traditional purpose of such powers. Indeed the legislated purpose of those powers,
namely "ensuring the orderly establishment or modification of radio stations
and the orderly development and efficient operation of radiocommunication in Canada" not only dates from 1989 amendments to the former *Radio
Act*, which also renamed the *RadioAct* the *Radiocommunication Act*, but was
not initially conceived in such ambitious terms. According to a study com-
missioned in 1987 by the former Department of Communications, the then
responsible department, still on Industry Canada's website, spectrum management was considered to have a relatively narrow, primarily technical purpose, not a broad-gauged planning function.

In this regard, Professor David Townsend asserts that "...controlling the
levels and sources of interference to and from radio devices is, and has always been, the most important and prominent feature of spectrum management for the federal government."[10] To support his claim, Townsend points
to Sections 4(b)(i) and (ii) of the 1985 *Radio Act* which state, in part that

"The Minister may issue licences in respect of radio stations ... and technical construction and operating certificates ... for such terms and subject to such conditions as he considers appropriate for ensuring the orderly development and operation of radiocommunication in Canada."

The significance of the role of Industry Canada as economic regulator is underscored by the economic importance of the wireless sector that grows in significance each year. For example, in 2009, wireless revenues of $16.9 billion constituted 41% of the telecommunications services market, compared to 23% in 2002.[11] In 2009 wireless connections exceeded wireline local and access connections (including residential and business connections), 23.8 million connections versus 18.7 million connections in comparison.[12] Wireless services represent the next frontier in telecommunications, with the continuing launching of newer and faster networks, and a burgeoning array of services and applications, including mobile broadband access and mobile broadcasting services. The economic importance of this sector cannot be overstated.

Additional support for narrowly construing the spectrum management function of the Minister is found in Section 4 of the existing *Radiocommunication Act* which permits the Minister to delegate "any power, duty or function" he is granted to "... any person authorized by the Minister to do so, and if so exercised or performed, shall be deemed to have been exercised or performed by the Minister." It is highly unlikely and irregular for broad-based policy-making tools, including economic regulatory oversight, as opposed to technical certification, to be delegated to departmental officials without some form of political scrutiny and supervision. The next section addresses the issue of these powers have taken on their broader contemporary role.

FROM TECHNICAL SPECTRUM CERTIFICATION
TO ECONOMIC POLICY MAKING

To move from technical regulation to control radio interference as the primary regulatory objective to employing the same powers to influence both the overall structure of economic competition in the telecommunications sector and the specific firms permitted entry (not to mention overriding, even if only for a specific firm, a fundamental component of legislated telecommunications policy) is a profound policy shift. The question of why and how this shift occurred needs to be addressed because it goes to the heart of why the Globalive decision is so problematic.

The answer to this question is straightforward. The transformation from technical spectrum regulation to planning spectrum management, through economic regulation, was undertaken to satisfy the long-thwarted policy making ambitions of departmental officials, first dating from the former Department of Communications and subsequently thereafter to officials in Industry Canada to whom responsibility for telecommunications policy issues had been transferred in 1993.

The Department of Communications was created in 1969 when spectrum management was transferred to it from the Department of Transport. The new department envisaged its role as the architect of a transformation in Canadian communications, including telecommunications, policy. At its creation, its new minister, The Honourable Eric Kierans, immediately emphasized the department's planning role and its ambition to "evolve a national communications plan and a national communications policy to integrate and rationalize all systems of communications whether those of today such as telephones, microwave relays, telex, TWX, telegraph and the Post Office, or those of tomorrow: communications satellites; sophisticated information retrieval systems linking computers which exchange and store information of all kinds, waveguides, lasers, and so on up to the "wired city" of tomorrow."[13] Unfortunately, the Department of Communications almost immediately, and then for several decades following, was stymied in fulfilling its grand ambitions. Initially, the opposition came from provincial governments not prepared to surrender jurisdiction to the federal government or to embrace the policy objectives that government wished to pursue.[14]

An even more formidable challenger was the CRTC, which gained jurisdiction over telecommunications regulation from the Canadian Transport Commission in 1976 when its name was changed from the Canadian Radio and Television Commission to the Canadian Radio-television and Telecommunications Commission. The Department of Communications initially presumed that it would be able to control the CRTC not only through existing political appeal mechanisms which permitted the government, on the advice of the Minister of Communications, to vary or veto CRTC decisions but also through a proposed power in new telecommunications legislation to issue policy directives to the agency prior to its receipt of individual applications. Unfortunately, despite several attempts in the 1970s and 1980s, the Department was unsuccessful in obtaining new legislation that would make it the primary policy architect that it aspired to be.

More significantly, the CRTC aggressively pursued and satisfied its own policy objectives for the telecommunications sector. Over a 15 year period from 1977 to 1992, in a series of controversial decisions, the CRTC was able to fundamentally and irrevocably transform the traditional monopoly industry structure into a vibrant competitive structure such that, for instance, the traditional monopolists lost significant portions of their market share to new entrants both in the terminal equipment (telephone-sets etc.) and long distance markets. The local telephone monopoly market was also opened to competition.[15] Throughout this period the Department of Communications and subsequently Industry Canada, was relegated to the status of frustrated spectator.

Departmental frustration was obvious in the early 1990s when the Government made another, this time ultimately successful, attempt to enact new telecommunications legislation. Even on this occasion, a fundamental departmental objective was stymied. In the 1992 version of what became the *Telecommunications Act*, passed in 1993, the department again sought to re-capture policy primacy, most notably by means of one of its legislative propos-als which was to enable the Minister to take control of the wireline industry entry and exit through a licensing power based on the Radiocomm model – and simultaneously reducing the Commission to an advisory role, as explained below. The language of this proposal was remarkably similar to that which had been included in the *Radiocommunication Act* as amended in 1989. The Minister was to be empowered to grant licences "taking into account all matters the Minister considers relevant." The strength of the opposition to this propos-al from industry, academic and other parties convinced the Senate Committee on Transportation and Communications, with a Conservative majority, which had been sent the legislation for pre-study, to recommend that the provision be removed, a recommendation the Minister and the Government accepted. A case can be made that this rather ham-fisted attempt by the department to gain policy control was a major contributing factor to the Government's deci-sion taken months later to abolish the Department of Communications and transfer its telecommunications mandate to Industry Canada.

The Department of Communications did have one major policy success in this period, a success that is germane to the Globalive case, namely the origi-nal licensing of cellular telephone services for Canada in the 1980s. The over-riding objective of the Department with respect to licensing cellular service was that it, and it alone, would be the sole decision-maker both for the actual licensing and especially for the policy decisions that would shape the specific licences to be granted.

The process began in 1982 when the Department issued a statement entitled "Cellular Mobile Radio Policy and Call for Licence Applications."[16] The basis for the ministerial licensing would be the traditional licensing powers under the then *Radio Act*. Originally the Department intended to follow the American Federal Communications Commission model of dual licensing by region, by granting dual licenses for 23 Census Metropolitan Areas (CMA) throughout Canada. One set of licences would be granted to the incumbent telephone com-panies in these areas, the other to a new competitor. Seven new companies ap-plied for the other licences, two for all areas and the other five for less than the 23 CMAs. The Department quickly came to appreciate that it faced fundamental obstacles in its approach both from the CRTC which would have to grant per-mission for the new entrants to interconnect their cellular systems with those of the incumbent telephone companies, and more importantly from a number of provinces which indicated that they were opposed to competition and prom-ised to refuse such interconnection to the companies then under their jurisdic-tion or in three cases owned by the provincial governments.[17]

A committee of Department of Communications officials undertook the review of applications. There was to be no public hearing but applicants were given an opportunity to meet individually with the committee to discuss general matters subject to the injunction that the meeting was not an opportunity to lobby departmental officials. Although the meetings were to be confidential, some of the applicants complained about information being leaked to other applicants about their applications. Moreover, some participants concluded that contrary to the no-lobbying injunction, lobbying was indeed going on. As a lawyer for one of the applicants recounted: "… we knew full well that everybody was lobbying like crazy, not only with the then Minister of Communications but also virtually every other member of Cabinet to get some kind of angle on the licensing process."[18]

In September 1983, the department issued a new call for applications but this time under a new set of criteria. Now in addition to the incumbent telephone companies being granted a cellular licence for their territory there would be only one licensee for "an integrated national system." In addition applicants were encouraged to form alliances with equipment manufacturers so as to promote Canadian manufacturing and technology. The new criteria appeared to have been influenced by one of the original applicants who had applied for a licence for all of Canada. Subsequently, however, a new company, Cantel (now part of Rogers Communications Inc.), was given the licence but no reasons were given to explain why this application was superior to the others. The process was widely regarded as questionable, if not illegitimate, by a number of participants and observers save, of course, for the successful applicant. As Romaniuk and Janisch stated shortly after the licence had been granted: "From a procedural point of view, the absence of public hearings and lack of any adequate opportunity to comment on rival applications, combined with extensive *ex parte* contacts, must render the final decision somewhat questionable. As well the substantive limits adopted, inasmuch as they bore no discernible relationship to the *Radio Act* are equally questionable."[19] For those in the telecommunications sector with long institutional memories, the Globalive licensing process was depressingly "déjà vu all over again."

LICENSING GLOBALIVE

In November and December 2007, Industry Canada publicly announced the licensing framework for the issuance of Spectrum licences in the Advanced Wireless Services ("aws") band.[20] The aws band is used to deliver a wide range of wireless telecommunications services.

As described by the Department, aws comprise "a wide range of applications, such as cellular telephony, data, multimedia, Internet Protocol (ip)-based applications and broadband Internet access using third generation (3G) cellular and other technologies."[21] Importantly, the framework set aside part of the available aws spectrum for licensing new entrants to the wireless market with the purpose of "fostering greater competition in the Canadian wireless

	Chronology
November 2007	Industry Canada establishes licensing framework for AWS
May 2008	AWS spectrum auction begins
July 2008	Auction closes – Globalive successfully bids $442 million for 30 licenses
August 2008	Globalive submits its documentation on ownership to Industry Canada
December 2008	CRTC staff letter initiates CRTC review of Globalive ownership
March 2009	Industry Canada issues spectrum licenses to Globalive
September 2009	CRTC hearing on Globalive's ownership
October 2009	CRTC issues decision against Globalive
December 2009	Government issues Order-in-Council overturning CRTC decision on Globalive

telecommunications market…with a goal of lower prices, better service and more choice for consumers and business."[22] The framework also established the rules and requirements for the competitive bidding process as well as a number of other technical requirements.

While the Government's decision on the auction framework for AWS was formally based on a public consultation process that began earlier in 2007, it was also a reflection of a long protracted public relations and lobbying battle between the incumbent wireless providers and a number of prospective new entrants. The battle lines were drawn initially in a speech to the Canadian Club in Ottawa by Pierre Karl Péladeau[23], wherein he baldly stated that Canada was a third world nation in terms of wireless penetration, prices and services. In one bold statement, Quebecor – no doubt encouraged by other prospective entrants – provided voice to consumer complaints and frustration and largely defined the subsequent public policy debate on the need for additional competition in the wireless market and the concomitant rules.

The actual AWS auction was held between May and July 2008. Globalive Wireless LP was among some twenty-seven qualified bidders. It successfully bid approximately $442 million for 30 AWS spectrum licenses, covering all of the provinces except Quebec.[24] No other entrant managed to secure such a similarly broad geographic footprint. At the completion of the auction, twelve new entrants obtained licences from the part of the spectrum set aside for new entrants, but it was Globalive that emerged as the most significant new player, having secured the necessary financing along with its large number of spectrum licences. Otherwise the auction results were largely as anticipated, with the three national incumbent wireless operators obtaining most of the licences for the non-set aside spectrum. In addition, several other new entrants emerged as significant regional players, including Videotron (Quebecor) in Quebec, and Shaw (a predominantly Western-based cable operator) in its operating territories.

With the auction complete, the winning bidders, including Globalive, had to demonstrate their compliance with the Canadian ownership and control requirements under the Radiocommunications Act before spectrum licences could be issued.[25] After completing its ownership and control review and determining that the firm was Canadian-owned and controlled within the meaning of the Radiocommunication Act[26] and the associated Radiocommunication Regulations, Industry Canada issued spectrum licences to Globalive on March 13, 2009 (and received payment for those licences).

Having successfully obtained the spectrum licences necessary to enter the market, Globalive was introduced to one of the anomalies of the Canadian telecommunications regulatory environment – carriers that hold radio spectrum licenses are subject to separate ownership and control reviews by both the Minister of Industry under the Radiocommunication Act[27] and by the CRTC under the Telecommunications Act[28] on precisely the same issue. While it falls to Industry Canada to conduct a proceeding for a licence to start up a new wireless carrier business, it is the CRTC's role to ensure compliance on an ongoing basis to ensure the eligibility requirements of a telecommunications common carrier under the Telecommunications Act are met.

So it was that on 22 December 2008, CRTC staff sent a letter to Globalive, as well as to all the other successful AWS bidders not already operating as common carriers, indicating that the CRTC was prepared to review Globalive's ownership prior to the commencement of its operations, in order to ensure that it met the Canadian ownership and control requirements. As prescribed, Globalive submitted its corporate documents to the CRTC in early April 2009, but shortly thereafter a new regulatory "game" began to take shape.

On April 20, 2009, the CRTC received a letter from TELUS requesting a public proceeding to review the ownership and control of Globalive. This was followed a few days later by a similar request from Shaw Communications. Globalive opposed these requests, but following a short proceeding on the appropriateness of holding a public, rather than the usual confidential review,[29] the CRTC determined that a public hearing was required for Globalive.[30] The regulatory process that followed was comprehensive and combative. Many of Globalive's responses to written information requests (interrogatories) from the CRTC were filed in confidence, but were subjected to further challenges for disclosure by the intervening parties that had grown to include Rogers Communications, Bell Canada, Canadian Cable Systems Alliance, along with TELUS and Shaw. Of these, Bell, Rogers and TELUS were given status to appear at an oral hearing that took place on September 23–24, 2009 on the top floor of CRTC headquarters.

On October 29, 2009, the CRTC issued its decision regarding the ownership and control of Globalive.[31] Essentially, the CRTC found that Globalive was Canadian in terms of "legal control" but that there was non-Canadian "control in fact" by Orascom, its principal foreign investor. Although the CRTC acknowledged that Globalive had "made numerous significant changes to its corporate structure and documents in order to address many of the Commission's concerns" (including during the course of the two-day oral hearing), the CRTC identified additional changes it considered were necessary to be made. In this regard, the CRTC's principal concern related to the fact that Orascom had provided Globalive with the vast majority of its debt financing (approximately 99%), and concluded that even if the additional changes were made, it would not lead to a finding that Globalive met the ownership requirements. Put simply, the CRTC found that, while Globalive met the "legal" test that it was not foreign controlled, it failed a more nuanced test of "control-in-fact."[32]

Globalive's response to the CRTC's decision was predictable, and public. In a written statement, Globalive chairman Anthony Lacavera called the ruling "... a bad day for Canadian consumers" adding that, "Canadians deserve competition in wireless and this decision represents a major step backwards."[33] Globalive's public positioning suggested that an appeal to Cabinet was likely forthcoming and that its launch plans would be delayed. In addition, the timing was crucial given that the prime Christmas sales season was fast approaching, an ideal time to launch its new network. Not surprisingly, Globalive highlighted its claims of 800 newly hired staff, including some 200 jobs at a call centre in Peterborough.

The jobs issue was a key element of Globalive's public arguments, coming at a time when the Canadian economy was in the midst of a deep recession characterized by record job loss numbers. No doubt these arguments were not lost on a minority Conservative government seeking to improve its electoral standing in southwestern Ontario. As well, Globalive's public comments highlighted the fact that consumers would continue to be denied an alternative to the established service providers – a problem that the spectrum auction was meant to address.

Globalive was similarly active behind the scenes. In the lead up to the CRTC's planned decision date, Globalive retained a number of external advisors and lobbyists. It had already retained senior legal counsel from McCarthy Tetrault in the form of Hank Intven, as well as Jan Skora, a recently retired Director General from the Radiocommunication and Broadcasting Regulatory Branch of Industry Canada. Globalive added several lobbying and public relations resources, notably Earnscliffe Strategy and the CGI Group. Earnscliffe personnel working on the file included Mike Robinson and Elly Alboim, as well as Geoff Norquay, who had previously served as Director of Communications for Stephen Harper when he was the Leader of the Official Opposition. From CGI came additional strategic advice and access to the PMO through Ken Boessenkool, a close associate of Stephen Harper who played important roles in the 2004 and 2006 national Conservative election campaigns.

In the weeks preceding the CRTC's ruling, senior executives from Globalive and its external lobbyists met with senior staff in Tony Clement's office, as well as with key senior bureaucrats from the Industry Canada. Similar meetings took place in the immediate aftermath of the CRTC's decision, as well as interdepartmental meetings between Industry Canada officials and staff from the Prime Minister's Office and the Privy Council. The response from the Government of Canada was not long in coming. Within two days Minister Clement had indicated that the Government of Canada would "review" the CRTC's decision, and within a week directed the companies that had opposed Globalive at the public hearing to provide him with their written comments on the CRTC's decision in light of the Minister's announced "review."

On December 10, 2009, the Government of Canada issued Order in Council P.C. 2009–2008, which varied the CRTC's decision after reaching a different determination about whether Globalive met the "control in fact" test. In a public statement Minister Clement indicated that "In our determination, Globalive is a Canadian company that meets the Canadian ownership and control requirements."[34] The Government noted that, when assessing control in fact, the Telecommunications Act does not require a determination that a telecommunications common carrier is controlled by Canadians but rather that it not be controlled by persons that are not Canadian, and that the Governor in Council considered the same facts considered by the CRTC and came to a different conclusion than the CRTC.[35] The Order-in-Council was carefully crafted and took note that Cabinet had fulfilled all of its statutory obligations under section 12 of the Telecommunications Act which concerns itself with variation, rescission or referral of CRTC decisions by the Governor in Council. It stated that the record of the CRTC's proceeding was considered, as was the input of the relevant provincial Ministers of Communications.

It is noticeable, however, that this review was procedurally different from any other Cabinet appeal review conducted since the passage of the 1993 Telecommunications Act. Section 12(1) of the Act provides that where the CRTC has made a decision under the Telecommunications Act, the Governor-in-Council may, within one year after the issuance of the CRTC decision, order, vary or rescind the decision, or refer it back to the Commission for reconsideration of all or a portion of it. Section 12(1)states: "Within one year after a decision by the Commission, the Governor-in-Council may, on petition in writing presented to the Governor-in-Council within ninety days after the decision, or on the Governor in Council's own motion, by order, vary or rescind the decision or refer it back to the Commission for reconsideration of all or a portion of it." Prior to the passage of the 1993 Telecommunications Act, there were actually no procedural safeguards or established processes in relation to Cabinet review of a CRTC decision. The 1993 Telecommunications Act added a requirement contained in section 13 for the Minister to notify the provinces of his intention to make a recommendation to the Governor-in-Council for the purpose of any Order issued pursuant to section 12. In addition, the Telecommunications Act created a role for the CRTC as a "post office," requiring it to inform interested parties once a petition to Cabinet was received by the Privy Council Office. The convention that emerged following the passage of the 1993 Telecommunications Act is comprised of several components. First, as stated, when a petition is submitted to the Privy Council, a copy is also provided to the CRTC, who in turn provides notice of the petition to all of the participants in the proceeding associated with the decision under review. Second, Industry Canada issues a notice and a copy of the petition that is published in the Canada Gazette. The notice also invites public comment by a specified date and designates an Industry Canada official as the recipient of public comments. Third, Industry Canada publishes the petitions as well as public comments received in response to the Gazette notice on the Department's web site. These processes, along with the required provincial consultation, normally take several months and most petitions to Cabinet are ruled on shortly before the statutory time limit of one year from the date of the CRTC's decision.

In the Globalive case, no petition to Cabinet was presented to the Governor-in-Council by any party. Rather, the Governor-in-Council acted on its own motion, a power it may exercise pursuant to section 12 of the Telecommunications Act. By proceeding by that route, the need for formal notice by the CRTC or by Industry Canada was obviated. As for public comment, none is required by statute. However, as noted above, Industry Minister Clement took the additional step of calling for and receiving both written and oral submissions from the principal parties involved. As a result, the preconditions for the exercise of power to vary or rescind a CRTC were met: The CRTC had made a decision. Within the statutorily prescribed time limit, the Governor-in-Council, on its own motion, and after consulting with the provinces as required under section 13 of the Act, varied that decision.

It therefore appears that the Government of Canada satisfied the procedural requirements of the *Telecommunications Act* in varying the CRTC's decision on Globalive – though, as noted previously, the legality of the Order-in-Council is currently being challenged in the courts. Legality aside, for our purposes the greater concern is the lack of transparency associated with the initial Industry Canada decision to grant Globalive a spectrum licence and the subsequent overturning of a CRTC decision on the same issue on the basis of advice from the same officials that made the initial decision within the Industry Department.

In this case, there can be no criticism of the CRTC in relation to the transparency of its processes. The CRTC followed conventional quasi-judicial practices and a newly established public and transparent process in reviewing the Globalive file. In advance of addressing the Globalive situation, the CRTC changed its processes for reviewing complex telecommunications ownership transactions to permit greater input from interested persons. In sharp contrast, there is no public record whatsoever of the process followed by Industry Canada in reaching its conclusion that Globalive was eligible to hold the AWS licences it obtained in the AWS spectrum auction. Similarly, there is no public record of how the Department of Industry arrived at the conclusion that Globalive was eligible to participate in the AWS auction in the first place.

Unfortunately, and of great concern, the same is true for most other aspects of the policies and decisions associated with the AWS auction (and other spectrum licensing decisions). There was a public consultation process associated with the auction policy and associated rules, but that process consisted only of a notice, public comments, and brief policy determinations. There is no guarantee of procedural fairness or transparency. Did the Department officials rely on information not included in the consultation process? Was that information tested? What advice was provided to the Minister by Industry Canada officials, and more importantly, on what advice did the Minister rely in making his determinations? Finally, how can it be argued that the process and the concomitant decisions are necessarily fair and in the public interest when the same officials are involved in the process of making one decision and are subsequently responsible for advising the Minister on a conflicting decision rendered by another regulator?

UNSTRUCTURED DISCRETION
AND A PROBLEMATIC PROCESS

In the author's view, the preceding suggests there were two fundamental problems with the Globalive decision. The first is that the exercise of ministerial discretion both in granting Globalive its original spectrum licence and subsequently in overturning the CRTC's decision that the firm was ineligible to operate as a telecommunications common carrier represents unstructured discretion at its worst. It will be recalled that the Radiocommunication Act allows the Minister to take "into account all matters that the Minister considers relevant for ensuring the orderly establishment or modification of radio stations and the orderly development and efficient operation of radiocommunication in Canada...." This suggests that the Minister may take into consideration any factor he wishes. It was the fear of such unbridled discretion that provoked such widespread opposition when the previous Mulroney Conservative Government suggested that the Minister of Communications should be given a telecommunications licensing power under essentially the same terms. The Senate Committee that studied the proposed legislation was sufficiently impressed by this opposition that it urged the Government to reconsider its proposal, which it did.

The second problem, which flows from the first, is that the absence of a transparent process leaves the observer unsure of the factors that the Minister, and subsequently the Cabinet, considered in its decision-making. In the initial licensing by the Minister, although there was a consultative document issued prior to the decision-making, no one can be certain that that document had any impact on the outcome. Similarly, in the absence of articulated reasons for its decision to overturn the CRTC's finding that Globalive did not meet the Canadian ownership and control requirements set out in section 16 of the Telecommunications Act, other than the statement that the Cabinet, on the advice of the Industry Minister, had concluded that the CRTC had erred in its decision that Globalive was not Canadian-controlled "in fact," we cannot determine what considerations went into this decision.

The exercise of their discretionary powers by the Cabinet and the Industry Minister are especially troubling when compared with constraints, both substantive and procedural, that the CRTC is subject to. While one can criticize the open-ended, ambiguous, conflicting and unranked statement of policy objectives found in the Telecommunications Act, there is at least one positive aspect that flows from the statutory policy statement: it requires the CRTC to exercise its judgment in a manner that is grounded in the law. If it does not, then those subject to its decisions have recourse to the courts. Furthermore, the CRTC is subject to rigid rules of procedure that if not followed can lead to legal challenges. In its decision-making on Globalive, for example, as established above, the CRTC convened a public proceeding to review the ownership structures of those successful bidders in the departmental auction who were not already operating as telecommunications carriers.

In the case of Globalive, both Globalive and other interested parties were allowed to file evidence, make oral submissions, and address questions or "interrogatories" to the firms, all of which became part of a public record. In addition, to protect confidential commercial information, the CRTC hearing panel conducted an *in camera* session to review the applicant's ownership with its investors, senior officers, directors and financial and legal advisors. Subsequently the CRTC issued its detailed written decision, cited earlier, that, based on its review of the evidence, Globalive was controlled in fact by a non-Canadian firm and therefore did not meet "the requirements set out in section 16 of the Act and is not currently eligible to operate as a telecommunications common carrier."[36] Compared to the CRTC process, one could not imagine a less transparent, procedurally challenged process than that followed by the Industry Minister and subsequently the Cabinet.

The deficiencies of the Globalive political licensing process stand out as well from an additional perspective. Canada is not only a signatory but was an early and strong advocate for the WTO General Agreement on Trade and Services (GATS) that profoundly liberalized telecommunications markets around the world. A key component of WTO/GATS is the Reference Paper on Regulatory Principles. This paper is premised on the need for timely, transparent government processes and non-discriminatory treatment of market participants in a liberalized trade environment. Canada's commitments under WTO/GATS are set out in Canada's Schedule of Specific Commitments, the Reference Paper on Regulatory Principles, and the Annex on Telecommunications addressing access to public telecom networks by users. The principles to which Canada committed in these documents relate to access to network services, allocation of scarce resources, interconnection, licensing, universal service, and discrimination by carriers who are major suppliers.

Generally, these are matters addressed by the primary economic regulatory authority for the sector – but in Canada's particular regulatory design, it should apply no less to Industry Canada when it acts as an economic regulator than it does to the CRTC. While it may be argued that Industry Canada's role is a hybrid one, as it is simultaneously responsible for telecommunications policy, as well as the technical regulation of spectrum, it nevertheless exercises economic regulatory control in precisely the manner contemplated in the Reference Paper. Industry Canada's licensing processes decide on the allocation of a scarce resource and ultimately dictate market structure. Its policymaking and rulings on wireless roaming and tower sharing are "access" and "interconnection" issues that are not substantively dissimilar to the CRTC's regulation of support structures or its mandating of "equal access" in its framework for competition in the provision of long distance services.[37] Arguably, Canada's commitments under WTO/GATS, and specifically under the Reference Paper on Regulatory Principles, should apply equally to Industry Canada and the CRTC when those institutional players practise economic regulation. Whereas the CRTC behaviour was consistent with these commitments, that of Industry Canada and the Cabinet were arguably fundamentally in violation of them.

CONCLUSIONS

As stated at the outset of this chapter, most of the debate over the Globalive licensing has focused on either the positive effects it will have on broadening competition in the cellular sector or on the loosening of the current restrictions on foreign investment in Canadian telecommunications. The author of this chapter has long supported both objectives. The argument, however, is that the attractiveness of the policy outcome must be balanced against the decision-making process that public policy-makers employ in reaching that outcome.

In this respect we believe that the Globalive process was fundamentally flawed. Indeed, we would conclude that the fears of the author of this chapter have been realized in the Globalive case. In assessing the original ministerial licensing proposed in the 1992 version of the Telecommunications Act, I argued that, with a political licensing system, "... we will not know if the Minister and the Cabinet have been consistent, prudent, honest, or indeed lawful in its implementation of the law. We will not know if the Minister or Cabinet has been arbitrary or capricious in its decision-making. We will not know if the Minister or Cabinet has been subject to, and a participant in, manipulation by politically effective groups or individuals."[38]

Absent a court decision that overturns the Cabinet decision, the licensing of Globalive is now irreversible. That said, the larger issues of the political licensing and the role of Industry Canada as an economic regulator need to be addressed. This is particularly true because, as this chapter is being written, the Department has issued a consultative document with respect to the next round of spectrum licensing scheduled imminently.

There is a simple solution to ameliorate the problems of unstructured political decision-making and the concomitant absence of transparency and due process. Canada should consider adopting the approach common to most other members of the OECD, namely to assign spectrum licensing to an independent regulatory agency. This was in fact a recommendation of the Telecommunications Policy Review Panel in 2006 whose views were so influential when Maxime Bernier was Industry Minister. Furthermore, the CRTC has also frequently called for the transfer of this power subsequently, but of course, has not been successful to date. [39]Unlike Great Britain, the United States, Australia, most European countries and many developing nations, Canada is one of the few countries that assign spectrum licensing and management to a political authority, a governmental minister. The central benefits of an independent regulator are well understood: transparency, stability and consistency in process, freedom from political interference and publicly exercised enforcement.[40] Transferring spectrum licensing and management to the CRTC or a new agency need not, indeed should not, undermine policymaking by elected authorities. Political policy-making combined with independent regulatory licensing would be an ideal combination. The Globalive decision illustrates how far we are from that ideal regulatory world.

POSTSCRIPT

As this chapter was being prepared for publication, the Federal Court announced its decision on the Globalive application. The result was a major setback for the Government in that the Court ruled that Cabinet had exceeded its authority by not acting within the statutory mandate of the Telecommunications Act in its decision to overrule the CRTC. More specifically the Court ruled that the Cabinet had "stepped outside [the] provisions [of the Telecommunications Act] by inserting a previously unknown policy objective into section 7, namely that of ensuring access to foreign capital, technology and experience" ... and consequently "misdirected itself in law." It ruled that the Cabinet decision must be quashed but ordered its judgment stayed for 45 days. See Federal Court, Docket T-26–10, Citation: 2011 FC 130 issued February 2, 2011. The preceding citation is from para 50. For public commentary, see Steven Chase, "Telecom ruling puts a leash on Tory cabinet authority" *Globe and Mail*, Feb. 4, 2011, and Richard Brennan "Court rejects ruling that allowed Wind Mobile to begin operating" *Toronto Star* February 4,

2011. The decision was appealed to the Federal Court of Appeal, which heard the appeal in late May 2011 but, as of writing, no decision has been announced. If the Government loses, it is highly likely it will seek leave to appeal to the Supreme Court of Canada.

NOTES

The author would like to thank Hudson Janisch, Michael Ryan, Ted Woodhouse, and Stephen Schmidt for their advice on particular sections and especially Alan Hamilton for his incredibly thorough editorial and substantive review of the chapter. In particular, he would like to acknowledge the very important intellectual contribution made by Ian Scott who both inspired the chapter and guided its writing. He represents a professor's highest ambition: the student who becomes the teacher.

1 Hudson Janisch, "Kneeling at the Chancellor's Foot: Due Process at the Department of Communications." Paper presented to the Law Society of Upper Canada Conference on Communications Law and Administration, Toronto, April 1987.

2 Order-in-Council P.C. 2009–2008, issued on December 10, 2009; Review of Globalive Wireless Management Corp. under the Canadian ownership and control regime CRTC Telecom Decision CRTC 2009–678, Ottawa, 29 October 2009, and Telecom Decision CRTC 2009–678-1 (Erratum), Ottawa, 4 November 2009.

3 See, for example, *The Globe and Mail*, "A pirouette that is good for Consumers," Dec. 12, 2009, and "Road Map with real influence," December 29, 2009.

4 Public Mobile Inc. (Applicant) and (Respondents) Attorney General of Canada, Globalive Wireless management Corp., Bell Canada, Rogers Communications Inc., Shaw Communications Inc., and TELUS Communications Company, Application under S. 18 and S. 18.1 of the Federal Court Act, Court File No. T-26-10. The Applicant, Public Mobile, wants the court to declare that Governor in General's decision of December 10, 2009 to overturn the CRTC's original decision denying Globalive a licence and to declare that Globalive was not controlled by non-Canadians and therefore eligible for a telecommunications license was made either without jurisdiction or beyond the jurisdiction of the Governor in General, and thus contrary to the law. See the Postscript below for the most recent development in this case.

5 The issues and concerns raised in this chapter continue to be significant as can be demonstrated by the March 2011 announcement from Industry Canada of the procedures and process that will govern the next spectrum auction. See Industry Canada Notice No. DGSO-001-11 – Decisions on Revisions to the Framework for Spectrum Auctions in Canada available at http://www.ic.gc.ca/eic/site/smt-gst.nsf/eng/sf09998.html.

6 Fourth Protocol to the General Agreement on Trade in Services, Agreement on Basic Telecommunications, Reference Paper which can be accessed at http://www.wto.org/english/docs_e/legal_e/legal_e.htm.

7 *Radiocommunication Act* (R.S., 1985, c. R-2).

8 Section 6(1)(b) of the *Radiocommunication Act* states that the Governor in Council may make regulations prescribing the eligibility of persons to whom radio authorizations may be issued, including ownership and control eligibility criteria. Sections 9 and 10 of the Radiocommunication Regulations outline eligibility criteria, effectively cross-referencing the ownership and control requirements of the Telecommunications Act and the associated Canadian Telecommunications Common Carrier Ownership and Control Regulations.

9 The results were announced in the following press release: 15 Companies Bid Almost $4.3 Billion for Licences for New Wireless Services OTTAWA, July 21, 2008 available at http://www.ic.gc.ca/eic/site/ic1.nsf/eng/04175.html.

10 "Canadian Municipalities and the Regulation of Radio Antennae and their Support Structures" Study was performed pursuant to Research Contract 36100-7-0027 between the Department of Communications for Canada and the University of New Brunswick (U.N.B.). Principal Investigator was Professor David Townsend of the U.N.B. Faculty of Law. Available at http://www.ic.gc.ca/eic/site/smt-gst.nsf/eng/sf09377.html. No pagination is provided.

11 CRTC Communications Monitoring Report, July 2010, Figure 5.1.3, 114.

12 CRTC Communications Monitoring Report, July 2010, Table 5.1.8, 117.

13 Canada, *House of Commons Debates*, February 27, 1969, 66.

14 See Robert J. Buchan *et al., Telecommunications Regulation and the* Constitution Montreal: the Institute for Research on Public Policy, 1982 and Richard Schultz and Alan Alexandroff, *Economic Regulation and the Federal System*, Toronto: University of Toronto Press, 1985, 90–93.

15 The irony here is that officials from Industry Canada joined an unofficial coalition which was not successful to oppose its own minister's pro-competition policy objectives. See Richard Schultz, "Telecommunications: What a Difference a Minister Can Make" in Alan Maslove (ed.) *How Ottawa Spends 2008–2009*, (Montreal: McGill-Queen's University Press, 2008).

16 DOC Notice No. DGTN-006-82/DGTR-017-82. In this section I draw on Robert Glendenning, "The Licensing of Wireless Technologies in Canada: An Examination of the Use of Ministerial Licensing in Canada" unpublished MA Thesis, McGill University April 9, 1999.

17 It is important to note that complete federal jurisdiction over telecommunications only occurred in 1989 as a result of the Supreme Court of Canada decision in Alberta Government Telephones v. Canada (Canadian Radio-television and Telecommunications Commission) 2 S.C.R. 225.

18 Glendenning, op. cit. p. 34.

19 Bohdan S. Romaniuk and Hudson N. Janisch, "Competition in Telecommunications: Who Polices the Transition?" *Ottawa Law Review*, 1986, Vole 18, 626–627.

20 Speaking Points, The Honourable Jim Prentice, PC, QC, MP, Minister of Industry, Official Auction Announcement, Toronto, Ontario November 28, 2007 available at http://www.ic.gc.ca/eic/site/ic1.nsf/eng/01528.html.

21 Notice No. DGTP-002-07 – Consultation on a Framework to Auction Spectrum in the 2 GHz Range including Advanced Wireless Services (February 16, 2007).

22 P.C. 2009–2008 cited in footnote 1.
23 Notes for an address by Pierre Karl Péladeau, President and Chief Executive Officer, Quebecor Inc.: Canadian Club of Canada, April 17, 2007.
24 At that time, Globalive Wireless LP was owned by Globalive Wireless Management Corp. (Globalive). Globalive's beneficial owners were: Globalive Canada Holdings Corp.; Globalive Communications Holdings Ontario Inc., controlled by Anthony Lacavera; Weather Investments S.p.A. including Orascom, controlled by Naguib Sawiris; and Mojo Investments Corp., controlled by Michael O'Connor.
25 Successful bidders were to submit ownership and control documentation to Industry Canada for review within 10 business days of the cessation of bidding. Globalive submitted its documentation to Industry Canada on 8 August 2008.
26 Which has the same legal requirements for determining Canadian ownership and control as the *Telecommunications Act*.
27 Radiocommunication Regulations, SOR/96–484, section 10.
28 Section 16.
29 More specifically, in Canadian Ownership and Control Review Policy, Telecom Regulatory Policy CRTC 2009–428, as amended by Telecom Regulatory Policy CRTC 2009–428–1, the CRTC established a new framework consisting of a four-type review framework for ownership and control reviews under the *Telecommunications Act*. The CRTC determined that in cases where the review involves complex or novel governance structures or financing arrangements, a public, multi-party process with an oral hearing phase might be required, which was subsequently the process used in the Globalive review (type 4 review).
30 See Proceeding to consider the Compliance of Globalive with the Ownership and Control Regime, Telecom Notice of Consultation CRTC 2009–429, initiating a public, multi-party review, including an oral hearing phase, of Globalive's ownership and control.
31 Telecom Decision CRTC 2009–678.
32 CRTC Telecom Decision CRTC 2009–678 (as amended), para. 95–119).
33 Globalive News Release, October 31, 2009.
34 Government of Canada Varies CRTC Decision on Globalive OTTAWA, December 11, 2009, available from http://www.ic.gc.ca/eic/site/ic1.nsf/eng/05211.html.
35 In this context, "Canadian" is defined in the *Telecommunications Act*. A corporation is Canadian-owned and controlled if (a) not less than eighty per cent of the members of the board of directors of the corporation are individual Canadians; (b) Canadians beneficially own, directly or indirectly, in the aggregate and otherwise than by way of security only, not less than eighty per cent of the corporation's voting shares issued and outstanding; and (c) the corporation is not otherwise controlled by persons that are not Canadians (section 16.(1)(3) of the *Telecommunications Act*).
36 CRTC Telecom Decision CRTC 2009–678, para 119.
37 Both roaming and tower sharing have been mandated by Industry Canada. Wireless roaming arrangements are established through legal agreements between carriers. Roaming occurs when a subscriber of one wireless service provider uses the facilities

of another wireless service provider. This second provider has no direct pre-existing financial or service agreement with this subscriber. Tower sharing involves the use of a competing operator's tower or other support structure for mounting antennas and other electronics (e.g., transmitter/receivers transceivers, digital signal processors, control electronics).

38 Richard Schultz, "The 'New' Canadian Telecommunications Legislation," Centre for the Study of Regulated Industries, McGill University April 28, 1992, 27.

39 See the report of the Telecommunications Policy Review Panel available at http://www.ic.ca/eic/site/tprp-gecrt.nsf/eng/rx00059.html#T7. The relevant pages are 5–22 to 5–27. See page 5–22 in particular regarding the OECD observation that spectrum is typically managed by the regulator, and the key benefits of an independent regulator. Recommendation 5–10 on page 5–26 is to transfer the licensing power from Industry Canada to the CRTC.

40 Ibid., at 5–27.

11 Use It or Lose It? The Conservatives' Northern Strategy

FRANCES ABELE[1]

INTRODUCTION

… when Canada tried to impress the world's finance ministers and media with its Arctic identity by holding a summit in Iqaluit, a remote and somewhat inaccessible town of 7,000 just below the Arctic Circle in Nunavut, it didn't completely work. "It looked like the Canadians had just arrived there – they didn't seem to know the place any better than we did," one European official told me. (Douglas Saunders, "We See Our Arctic as a Colony" http://www.theglobeandmail.com/news/opinions/we-see-our-arctic-as-a-colony/article1466684/)

Iqaluit may be reached by non-stop jet from Ottawa in about three hours, making it hardly "somewhat inaccessible," except in the mental maps of most southern Canadians. Reflecting its history as a mid-twentieth century air-base, then a regional centre and later a government town, Iqaluit is an atypical Nunavut community.[2] It is also quite unlike the other territorial capitals, in size, history and social character. The choice of Iqaluit for the international meeting of finance ministers had of course little to do showing them what Canada's north is really like. The locale was chosen to make a domestic political point (it is in Minister of Health Leona Aglukkaq's riding) and an international one (the North is Canadian). For the rest, it merely illustrated one of the persistent features of Canadian political life: the North is at once a resonant national symbol but a relatively invisible part of the country.

This chapter assesses the Conservatives' vision for northern Canada as expressed in Throne and other speeches, their northern policy statements (the Northern Strategy and the Statement on Northern Foreign Policy) and selected social, economic, environmental and political measures. These are measured against the very large northern challenges that concern all Canadians. I conclude that, while there have been some important steps in the right direction related to infrastructure, knowledge about the North and foreign policy, two deeply important policy challenges have been virtually ignored. These are the need for: first, measures to sustain social and political development and democratization in northern institutions, and second, implementation of an effective Canadian response to global warming. Furthermore, a close analysis of the Conservatives' use of political rhetoric and the concrete measures that they have taken reveals a pronounced shift from the path followed by previous (Liberal) governments. In areas of exclusive federal jurisdiction, the Conservative government has been willing to spend – or at least to make large spending commitments. To a degree not seen since the 1950s, the Conservative government claims the North as a territory to be developed in the national interest, defining that interest, and consequently federal policy, almost entirely in terms of defense and economic development. With this stance, the federal power is poised to override – or at best ignore – the process of political and social development that reflects the purposes of notherners themselves, and of other Canadians who support them, in building the basis of a just society in the territorial North. Northern community and regional interests risk being superseded by federal purposes in national defence and economic development. At the same time, the dynamic system of intergovernmental relationships and practices built up over the last three decades by northern Aboriginal and public governments and previous federal governments is being largely ignored. Indeed, the delicate balancing and negotiation that has enabled so much cooperation and progress towards new governing arrangements which feature a more equitable role for Aboriginal people is being replaced by a much less resilient "command and control" approach.

THE CONSERVATIVE VISION

Can the Prime Minister be counted among those Canadians who "[don't] seem to know the place any better than we did"? His comments on Canada's northern interests might lead one to believe that this is the case: "Canada has a choice when it comes to defending our sovereignty in the Arctic; either we use it or we lose it. And make no mistake, this government intends to use it. Because Canada's Arctic is central to our identity as a northern nation. It is part of our history and it represents the tremendous potential of our future." The Prime Minister's repetition[3] of the "use it or lose it" phrase suggests that Canadians have not heretofore been "using" the North, at least not in the terms that would reinforce sovereignty. This ignores the "use" – the long-term habitation– of the Northlands by Canadian Inuit, Dene, Cree and other Aboriginal peoples, as well as the shorter term residency of thousands of others who have made the North their home. The prime ministerial slogan also apparently contradicts the spirit of the 1985 statement of the then Progressive Conservative government, which affirmed Canada's full northern boundaries with reference to Inuit occupation from time immemorial.[4]

Yet Stephen Harper's governments have been remarkably attentive to the territorial North. The Prime Minister followed the example of Paul Martin and others before him in making his first official visit a northern one. Since then, there have been at least two Prime Ministerial trips a year.[5] The Harper government broke new ground in appointing Leona Aglukkaq Minister of Health; she is the first Inuk Cabinet minister. In the five years that it has been in power, the government has established a northern regional development agency, lent firm support to the Mackenzie Gas Project, launched a process to revise the regulatory process governing northern development, signed an agreement-in-principle to devolve more powers to the Northwest Territories government, made steady progress in defining northern national parks and park reserves, announced a number of military expenditures, refurbished northern research establishments, and announced the construction of a new "world class" northern research station at Cambridge Bay. A full Northern Strategy policy statement has been released and, in line with this, a Statement on Northern Foreign Policy. Interest has been sustained: the North received substantial attention in the 2007, 2008 and 2010 Throne Speeches, as well as significant commitments of new funding since the election of 2006.

There is no mention of the North in the first brief Throne Speech, read after the election of the Conservative government in 2006. This is not surprising. There are just three federal seats in the Northern territories and as usual northern issues hardly surfaced during the 2006 election campaign. The October 16, 2007 Speech from the Throne, on the other hand, devotes substantial space to the North and, in retrospect, can be seen to provide a fair reading of the Harper government's overall approach to the region. There is substance in this Speech, but also a rhetorical nod to the North's enduring symbolic value in southern Canada. The section entitled Strengthening Canada's Sovereignty and Place in the World invokes the spirit of D'Arcy McGee: "The Arctic is an essential part of Canada's history. One of our Fathers of Confederation, D'Arcy McGee, spoke of Canada as a northern nation, bounded by the blue rim of the ocean. Canadians see in our North an expression of our deepest aspirations: our sense of exploration, the beauty and the bounty of our land, and our limitless potential."[6] Concretely, the 2007 Throne Speech committed the government to "an integrated northern strategy focused on strengthening Canada's sovereignty, protecting our environmental heritage, promoting economic and social development, and improving and devolving governance, so that northerners have greater control over their destinies." It promised action to improve housing for northern First Nations and Inuit. A "world-class arctic research station" was announced, to focus on environmental science and resource development. There was a commitment to complete comprehensive mapping of the Arctic seabed, to provide "new arctic patrol ships and expanded aerial surveillance," and to expand the Rangers, a northern resident militia. The Speech returns to a lyrical northern theme in conclusion, comparing Canada to "the North Star ... A guide to other nations; through difficult times, Canada has shone as an example of what a people joined in common purpose can achieve. Yet Canada's greatest strength lies in its energy and determination to move forward and build a better future."

The pivotal 2007 Speech from the Throne thus expresses the Conservative government's vision of and for the North. The North is seen not merely as one of the regions of Canada; rather, it is claimed as an internationally recognized symbol of Canadian identity. This perspective is probably not so far from how many Canadians who do not live in the North see it, when they think of the North at all. The imagery is certainly in line with the perspective of other Canadian leaders, from D'Arcy McGee through John A. Macdonald and John G. Diefenbaker.[7] The 2008 and 2010 Speeches continue in this vein, with remarkable consistency considering that the Conservatives had governed through two minority governments, a global financial crisis and recession, and considerable Parliamentary tumult.[8]

TWO NORTHERN STRATEGIES:
LIBERAL INTERGOVERNMENTALISM,
CONSERVATIVE UNILATERALISM

The Conservative government's Northern Strategy, announced in 2008, identifies four "integrated priorities": exercising Arctic sovereignty, protecting our environmental heritage, promoting social and economic development, and improving and devolving northern governance. Under these headings are reported some very large commitments, as well as the usual miscellany of small steps and aspirations. The priorities are indeed "integrated" in the sense that many of the positive measures taken by the government serve more than one priority area. For example, almost all of the initiatives (regardless of the "priority" under which they are reported) support Canada's northern sovereignty, since all demonstrate a commitment to the region, and there is an economic development aspect to most of the military and other new construction that has been announced.[9]

The Conservative's Northern Strategy occupies some of the policy space created by work begun under the preceding Martin government. In December

Table 1

Comparison of the Northern Strategy Liberal Government (2004)
and Conservative Government (2008)

Priorities	
Martin Government December 2004	Harper Government 2008–
Strengthening governance, partnerships and institutions	Improving and devolving governance
Establishing strong foundations for economic development	Promoting economic and social development
Protecting the environment	Protecting our environmental heritage
Building healthy and safe communities	Promoting economic and social development
Reinforcing sovereignty, national security and circumpolar cooperation	Strengthening Canada's sovereignty
Preserving, revitalizing and promoting culture and identity	Nothing reported

2004, after a period of public discussion and intergovernmental consultation, Prime Minister Martin and the premiers of the three territories released "a framework for the first ever jointly developed Northern Strategy."[10] Table 1 compares the main elements of the two governments' approaches to the Northern Strategy.

In terms of both process and content, there is a significant difference between the two Northern Strategies. The Conservatives have shown a different conception of the federal role in the North – one in which the federal government acts unilaterally in areas of exclusive federal control, eschewing the development of intergovernmental relations with northern governments. The 2004 Northern Strategy was announced jointly by Prime Minister Martin and the three territorial premiers. It began with a vision statement, followed by a set of process-oriented principles, before reaching "proposed long-term goals and objectives" (see Table 1). The document indicated where consensus was found and acknowledged that further collaborative policy development would be required. In this respect the Martin government's approach to northern policy is a good example of his government's highly collaborative approach to intergovernmental relations, an effect of which is that the territorial governments were treated in a "province-like" way. This was in line with the trajectory of northern political development since the 1970s, which had seen territorial governments develop most of the features of provincial governments, including participation in intergovernmental fora such as Western Premiers meetings, Northern Premiers meetings, and First Minister's Conferences. At the same time, the Martin government included Aboriginal governments and organizations in

many high level discussions, the most important of these being the deliberations that led to the Kelowna Accord.[11]

In contrast, the 2008[12] Conservative Northern Strategy made no reference
to process and did not envision future high level intergovernmental discussions. The Strategy was announced by Prime Minister Harper, speaking not
for a consensus of leaders but for "the Government": "The Government supports a vision of a new North that realizes its full social and economic potential and secures its future, for the benefit of all Canadians. Our integrated
Northern Strategy supports this vision by focusing on four integrated priorities: economic and social development, governance, environmental protection, and sovereignty."[13] Behind the difference in intergovernmentalism,
there is a readily apparent difference in substance. The 2004 version of the
Northern Strategy establishes timelines for devolution of control of non-
renewable natural resources to Northwest Territories and Nunavut (spring
2005 and December 2008, respectively). The first deadline was not met before the January 2006 federal election that removed the Martin Liberals from
government, and it is impossible to know whether devolution agreements
would have been concluded by now had the Liberals remained in power. The
Conservatives' version of the Northern Strategy sets no target dates.[14] Indeed,
since the Conservatives came to power, movement in negotiations on devolution of control of non-renewable natural resources natural resources has been
slow. An agreement-in-principle between the federal government and the
Government of the Northwest Territories was reached in September 2010 and
it was signed by these parties in January 2011. The agreement-in-principle has
been repudiated by most of the Aboriginal groups; there have been protests
and threats of legal action.[15] With respect to Nunavut, progress towards transferring control of natural resource development – and a new revenue sharing
scheme – has been even slower. While a protocol to govern negotiations has
been agreed, and a federal "representative" has been in place for some time, no
federal negotiator has been appointed and the process seems to be stalled.[16]

Another notable difference in emphasis in the 2004 Liberal and 2008
Conservative versions of the Northern Strategy concerns recognition of the
inter-relatedness of political, social, cultural and economic development. The
Conservative version makes no reference to culture and identity, and there is
no separate category for social development. Under the Conservatives, 'social
development' is always mentioned in tandem with economic development,
as if the two were not only related (as they surely are) but also impossible to
discuss separately (which is not the case). An examination of the measures
taken under the Northern Strategy to date suggests that this is more than a semantic accident. There are very few measures focused on social development,
and none dealing with culture and identity. Without wanting to slice semantic
differences too finely, it is noticeable that while the Liberal Strategy speaks

of "establishing strong foundations for economic development" and "building healthy and safe communities," the Conservative Strategy refers only to "promoting economic and social development" without reference to either foundations or communities. Considering massive infrastructure deficits in the North[17] and the special conditions of the predominantly Aboriginal communities especially, this is a significant difference in emphasis and approach.

Northern *political* development receives short shrift in the Conservative strategy. This is striking, if only because the transformation of northern political life over the last forty years – and with it, the Canadian political landscape– is seen by many as one of Canada's great achievements and one that is still a work in progress.[18] Through peaceful political advocacy, Aboriginal people have left the position of political outsiders, administered and ill-understood, to become leaders in the development of a wide range of innovative new political institutions in northern Canada. Modern treaties (comprehensive claims agreements) affirm their land and other rights and provide for transfers of capital to Beneficiary[19] organizations, providing them with powerful collectively managed economic leverage. New governing institutions, including various forms of new Aboriginal governments created pursuant to modern treaties, are just finding their feet. Yet, in the Conservative Northern Strategy, northern political development receives cursory attention. The overall objective is "improving and devolving governance" (compared to the 2004 goal of "strengthening governance, partnerships and institutions"); the main action item under that heading has to do with regulatory reform, a priority for industry but not necessarily for all northerners.

When one considers the imagery of the Throne Speeches, which associates Canadian identity with the North in a way that asserts southern Canadian interests, the Prime Minister's solitary announcement of the 2008 Northern Strategy, the absence of any references to partnerships with northern governments, the absence of political leadership in addressing outstanding comprehensive claims issues and the sluggish pace of negotiations on devolution, the lines of the federal approach are apparent. The Harper Conservatives' approach harkens back to much earlier periods of federal northern policy, when the interests and wishes of northerners were dealt with as a matter of federal discretion, under exclusive federal control. The Prime Minister's vocal preoccupation with sovereignty and defence, and somewhat quieter but firm focus on northern resource development, mark a narrowing of the federal role to areas where there is exclusive federal jurisdiction (foreign policy) and very strong federal – and national – interest (non-renewable resource development). The approach of several previous governments, including that of the Martin government, was also informed by an awareness of Canada's national interest in northern resources and northern development. In contrast to the Harper Conservatives' approach, however, previous governments envisioned progress in the North as a matter of social and political as well as economic development. For all the power intrinsic to the federal role, these earlier approaches took intergovernmentalism – constructive engagement of federal, territorial and Aboriginal governments – for granted. As I argue later in the chapter, there are likely to be costs associated with the Harper government's stance, including accelerated conflict, a loss of momentum in political development, and neglect of pressing issues of social development.

CANADA'S CONTRIBUTION TO CIRCUMPOLAR STABILITY

No one doubts that the coincidence of the opening of arctic waters due to global warming and sharply rising global demand for northern resources requires a strong and effective Canadian response.[20] Canada has the second longest Arctic coastline after Russia, and an economy oriented to commodity exports. Although the Northeast Passage (connecting the Barents Sea to the Asian Pacific along the Arctic coast of Russia) is likely to be more important for shipping, no doubt the Canadian north, and particularly the Northwest Passage, will see increased shipping and tourist traffic as the permanent sea ice continues to recede.

Greenland, Alaska, Russia and the Scandinavian countries have differently shaped economies, but they are all endowed with non-renewable natural resources and threatened by climate change. Each has a large Aboriginal population and, as has been the case in Canada, has built over the last thirty years a number of institutional means to ensure greater Aboriginal self-determination. Thus Canada and its neighbours, all bordering the Arctic Ocean, share many interests. However, there are also points of friction concerning boundaries, crossboundary pollution and, more recently, competition for off-shore resources.

Circumpolar diplomacy has long been a Canadian strength and Canada has been effective in institution-building towards a stable circumpolar region. Canadian negotiators were important in the international process to establish the United Nations Convention on the Law of the Sea in the 1970s, which still provides the framework for interaction among the circumpolar nations.[21] Northern Aboriginal people and the Government of Canada played a key role in the establishment of the Arctic Council. The Arctic Council, established in 1996 by the Ottawa Declaration, is a high level forum for cooperation among the eight Arctic countries (Canada, Denmark, Finland, Iceland, Norway, Russian Federation, Sweden, and United States). Circumpolar Aboriginal peoples' organizations are members as Permanent Participants.[22] The particular focus of the Arctic Council has been sustainable development and environmental protection. It has no enforcement power. Appropriately, Canada's first Circumpolar Ambassador, appointed in 1994, was Mary Simon, a very well-respected Inuit leader who had been instrumental in the development of circumpolar international cooperation, and in the creation of the Arctic Council itself.[23]

However, for a time after the 2006 election, it appeared that Canada's well-established place in circumpolar affairs was beginning to erode. There were three Conservative Ministers of Foreign Affairs in the thirty months between February 2006 and October 2008. None of them held office long enough to develop an understanding of the complicated northern file. The first, Peter MacKay, distinguished his term by eliminating the position of Canada's Circumpolar Ambassador. The second, Maxime Bernier, appeared to be out of his depth and preoccupied with other matters; he was removed from the post after a scandal involving careless handling of documents. The third, Vancouver former Liberal David Emerson, had a strong and natural interest in the Asia Pacific and softwood lumber; he held the Foreign Affairs post only briefly during the five month run-up to the 2008 election.

Lawrence Cannon has been Minister of Foreign Affairs since October 2008 and, during this term, has made steady progress in re-establishing the importance of diplomacy in the Arctic in the context of Canadian national interests. In this effort he has been supported by expertise in the federal Department of Indian Affairs and Northern Development, as well as that of his own department, and by his colleague ministers of Indian Affairs and Northern Development[24]. In August 2010, Minister Cannon released the Statement on Northern Foreign Policy. It was described, accurately, as the "international lens of Canada's Northern Strategy." Both the goals and the imagery are interesting:[25]

> The Arctic is fundamental to Canada's national identity. It is home to many Canadians, including Aboriginal peoples, across the Yukon, the Northwest Territories and Nunavut, and the Northern parts of many Canadian provinces. The Arctic is embedded in Canadian history and culture, and in the Canadian soul. The Arctic also represents tremendous potential for Canada's future. Exercising sovereignty over Canada's North, as over the rest of Canada, is our number one Arctic foreign policy priority. Our vision for the Arctic is a stable, rules-based region with clearly defined boundaries, dynamic economic growth and trade, vibrant Northern communities, and healthy and productive ecosystems.

Canada will assume the rotating chair of the Arctic Council in 2013, and the release of the Statement on Northern Foreign Policy will have been heartening to Canada's circumpolar neighbours, who must have been dismayed at the post-Liberal turn in Canadian polar leadership.[26] This is true despite some tensions in the Statement, which once again identifies Canada with the North (this time, the Arctic is seen to be embedded in the Canadian soul) but, in the next breath, acknowledges that the North is also a homeland to Aboriginal peoples. The North has tremendous potential for Canada's future and "exercising sovereignty" is "our number one Arctic foreign policy." Yet "our vision" is for a "stable, rules-based region with clearly defined boundaries, dynamic economic growth and trade, vibrant northern communities, and healthy and productive ecosystems." These statements are not directly contradictory, but they do pull in different directions – sovereignty over the land of our "soul" in contrast to recognition of Aboriginal peoples' rights and participation in a "rules-based" region. Nor are the goals listed in the vision straightforwardly compatible; they involve trade-offs (environment against economic growth being only the most obvious). All the countries in the circumpolar basin face these choices. What they hope for is an orderly and coordinated approach to such decisions.

What specific challenges do the Conservatives face? Despite the strange Prime Ministerial anxiety over routine Russian boundary patrols in 2010,[27] there is little of concern with respect to Canada's borders. There are only two relatively minor northern boundary disputes, one with the United States in the west and another with Denmark in the east. Both are under discussion on the basis of mutual recognition of sovereignty.[28] At the moment Canada has no boundary issues with Russia and, the Cold War having ended some time ago, there is not much likelihood of a Russian invasion. All of the circumpolar countries except the United States have ratified the United Nations Convention on the Law of the Sea and it is likely that undersea resources issues will be resolved through that process. Canada will have to be attentive, but the process will be orderly and as far as it is possible to predict, will not involve forceful incursions.

Conservative commitments related to national defence and Arctic sovereignty have been substantial, although no money has yet been spent on the larger ticket items. Measures include the announced establishment of a Canadian Forces Army Training Centre in Resolute, a modest (15%) increase in the size of the Rangers, creation of a deep-water harbour at Nanisivik, and, in collaboration with the United States, mapping of the seabed in order to establish Canada's claim pursuant to the United Nations Convention on the Law of the Sea. The aging Louis St.-Laurent icebreaker is scheduled to be replaced by a somewhat larger new ship, to be named after Prime Minister John G. Diefenbaker. The 2008 federal budget indicates that the cost will be $720 million and that the ship will be built in Canada. It is estimated to require 8–10 years to build such a vessel. The icebreaker is in addition to the 2007 announcement of construction (in Canada) of 6–8 new "Arctic Patrol Ships," a good deal smaller than the proposed Diefenbaker but with icebreaking capacity. At this writing, no contracts for either the Diefenbaker or the Arctic Patrol ship construction have been let – these major expenditure commitments are pending. There has been some discussion of replacing the Aurora Long Range Patrol aircraft, but by far the most expensive measure is the controversial decision to purchase F-35 jets, which would in part be used in the service of sovereignty patrolling and to respond to incursions into Canadian airspace.[29]

Government support for northern science has long been associated with sovereignty and defence.[30] Under the Conservatives, northern research, underfunded for a couple of decades, has received welcome infusions of cash. Some of the additional funding is due to Canada's participation in the International Polar Year,[31] which has galvanized the northern research community and improved Canada's international reputation as a centre for northern research and expertise. There has been other new money as well. The construction of a high arctic science station at Cambridge Bay in Nunavut, while never a strong demand from the northern scientific community, demonstrates a commitment to northern research and is an illustration of the way in which research effort can be used to maintain a sovereignty-enhancing public presence. Under the Arctic Research Infrastructure Fund (part of the national infrastructure spending program), $85 million in additional funding paid for much needed renovations and improvements to Canada's Arctic research infrastructure during 2009–2011.[32] Finally, the academic granting councils have all earmarked substantial funds for northern research programs, an investment decision based upon studies and academic advocacy that began in the 1990s, to address a shortfall in northern research funding.

NORTHERN SOCIAL AND ECONOMIC WELL-BEING

From the perspective of the people who live in the North, the current federal vision of the North as a fundamental expression of Canadian identity is a mixed blessing. To the extent that this perspective affirms the North's importance, the attention is welcome – and under this government, there has been plenty of attention. On the other hand, this vision of the North "claims" it for southern purposes in a way that no Canadian region has been so claimed since, perhaps, the opening of the West after the National Policy of 1879.[33] It is easy to move from recognizing that the North is integral to Canadian identity to considering that its resources are meant to be used for national purposes, with the possibility of overlooking or downgrading the implications for northern residents and their own purposes.

If northerners had written the Throne Speeches, one might have found a somewhat different emphasis. The three territorial premiers occasionally comment on their shared priorities for the North, as in this 2009 statement:[34] "Maintaining healthy, sustainable communities in partnership with the federal government continues to be a priority for premiers. Continued health care funding, housing, skills and training, and the effective northern involvement in the new Canadian Economic Development Agency (CanNor) are practical examples of ways the territories can work with Canada to implement the goals of the Northern Vision and Northern Strategy." A 2010 northern opinion survey[35] found that, for northerners, "infrastructure to augment individual, economic and environmental capacity" is a priority, and they reported finding that housing, educational, road and environmental infrastructure they lived with to be "woefully" inadequate. There was urgent concern about environ-mental and disaster response capacities. Another high priority was socio-cultural identity and "preservation of traditional ways of life (language and culture)." There was "tepid" northern support for a stronger military presence and action on sovereignty-related issues, the only exception being strong sup-port for the Rangers, and interest in their professional development.

There has been scant federal attention to most of these issues. The Northern Strategy implementation reports mention extensions of existing programs of national application, in such areas as labour market development, and mod-est changes to the program that subsidizes the Northern importation of food. Substantial funds were committed for social housing, very important in a re-gion where most people cannot afford to build or buy their own homes.[36] But many large challenges have received cursory attention, if any, including: im-proving K-12 educational attainment, particularly among Aboriginal people; making post-secondary education equitably accessible to northern residents; addressing with positive measures the cataclysmically high suicide rate across the North; improving health care delivery, improving search and rescue and emergency response capabilities, and addressing the high rates of tuberculosis and other infectious diseases in many northern communities.

Education and health care are matters of provincial responsibility elsewhere in the country and, in the territorial North, they are assigned to the territorial governments. The Conservative government has been remarkably reluctant to venture into these fields. It has been reluctant even to comment on mat-ters of health and education in outlining northern priorities – despite contin-ued funding of some long-standing federal programs of national application (in suicide prevention for example) that are active in the territorial north as elsewhere in the country. This stance places the fiscally dependent territories (especially Nunavut and NWT, where resources revenues are not available) in a potentially very difficult position; lacking sufficient own-source revenues, they struggle to maintain standards of northern health care and education. Provincial jurisdiction notwithstanding, federal governments have not tra-ditionally been hesitant to spend in these areas when the national interest is at stake.[37] The current government's official pronouncements and ideological position would seem to incline it away from such actions.

A second great issue of fundamental importance to northern societies is climate change. In the North this means warming and unpredictable weather, as well as many practical difficulties in a land where everything from housing construction to harvesting depends upon permafrost, ice and snow. This is probably the most far-reaching challenge in northern policy and it directly affects the well-being of all northern communities. Inuit leader Sheila Watt-Cloutier has been an international advocate for action on climate change, work that earned her a Nobel Peace Prize nomination in 2007.[38] Film-maker Zacharias Kunuk's latest documentary, *Qapirangajuq: Inuit Knowledge and Climate Change*, describes the changes already occurring in the Arctic.

Dealing with climate change has been a focus for the circumpolar Aboriginal organizations, Inuit Circumpolar Council and the Arctic Athabaskan Council and, for many years, there has been modest but sustained federal funding for this work. Canadian Aboriginal peoples have long played a strong role in these international organizations, and they have placed a high priority on circumpolar diplomacy in the matter of environmental protection. Canadian scientists have been active in the international movement of scientists to understand and to explain the changes that are upon us as global warming brings about multifaceted and far-reaching changes, many felt first in the North.

Perhaps unsurprisingly given the Conservative government's overall treatment of climate change, this major issue for the North is never mentioned in Throne Speeches, and it receives understated treatment in actual policies. Official statements[39] recognize the reality of climate change and the warming of the Arctic, noting a range of impacts, including degrading permafrost, shorter winters, thinning sea ice, changes to wildlife migrations, changing water levels and quality, and unpredictable weather. Attention is entirely upon adaptation to these changes, rather than prevention or mitigation of the source of the problem. Despite the visibility of these dramatic effects in Canadian territory, there has been no vigorous federal response to reduce greenhouse gas emissions.

Like no other issue, climate change policy throws into relief the regional, ideological and electoral political tensions that lie behind any attempt to define "the national interest." Regional interests differ. The Conservatives' approach to the North, which insists upon its role as an expression of the Canadian "soul" and effectively claims northern development for national goals, obscures recognition of northern regional interests and distinct northern tensions. Northerners too must balance the need for economic development and attendant local employment and business opportunities with the measures that must be taken to provide sustainable livelihoods and a healthy environment for northern residents. These issues are particularly pointed in a region where most industrial development will involve resource extraction for export, but for this region as for all other Canadian regions, decisions taken in the national interest must be moderated by regional concerns.

MANAGEMENT OF THE NORTHERN ECONOMY

In Nunavut and the Northwest Territories, with the exception of lands held in common by treaty Beneficiaries, non-renewable natural resources are under federal control and revenues from development come directly to the federal purse. Both territorial governments seek more province-like access to resource development decisions and revenue. Management of natural resources and a share of resource revenue has been devolved to the Yukon territorial government.[40]

Devolution of responsibility for non-renewable resource development would be an important source of greater financial independence in the two eastern territories, and it would improve their capacity to shape their economies. But the challenges of northern development decision-making remain huge, wherever the loci of authority reside. Relative to the size of the territories, their populations are small and dispersed. The economic base is a delicate mixture of harvesting, non-renewable resource development, and public expenditures.[41] Choices are difficult and the pressures are substantial: harvesting is important to the stability and well-being of the over 100 predominantly Aboriginal communities where about half of northerners live, while northern non-renewable resource development is of urgent interest to the largest economies and the largest corporations in the world. There is no question that the North's growing populations require wage employment and business opportunities, but there are large questions about how best to ensure economically and environmentally stable and sustainable opportunities for these. Canada has developed a particular regulatory system for balancing all of these pressures, as well as other local, regional and national considerations, in making public policy choices.

The northern regulatory system is relatively new, having been created as a consequence of the sixteen modern treaties (also known as comprehensive claims agreements) negotiated by Aboriginal groups and the federal government between 1984 and 2005.[42] The treaties resolve land ownership issues for almost all of the territorial north, create new political institutions, and mandate a number of co-management bodies that manage water, wildlife and other resources. Some (impact review boards) are engaged whenever major development projects are in prospect. All of the boards have constitutional protection, since they exist pursuant to the treaties. Most have the option or the requirement to hold public hearings, an important value being citizen participation and oversight of major decisions.

There have been complaints from industry, particularly the oil and gas industry, about the "complexity" of the system, and it is true that the design was far from Cartesian. The set of institutions that exist are particularly complex in the Northwest Territories, where four comprehensive claims agreements are in force and there are areas where matters of jurisdiction and management are still unresolved. The system was created over time by negotiators working more or less independently, and it is not surprising that it has imperfections. Consideration of reform is complex, since the regime has constitutional protection (because the comprehensive claims agreements do) and because so many potentially conflicting aims and interests are at play.

The northern regulatory system has received particular attention from the Conservative government. The 2008 Throne Speech hinted loudly that the government intended to proceed with the Mackenzie Gas Project[43] (then still under regulatory review) and to "reduce regulatory and other barriers" to resource development. The 2010 Speech again mentions the Mackenzie Gas Project, noting that the Joint Review Panel[44] established to examine it had completed its report after. In the same breath, the Speech commits the government to "reform the northern regulatory regime to ensure that the region's resource potential can be developed where commercially viable while ensuring a better process for protecting our environment." These ideas were given effect in the 2007 Cabinet Directive on Streamlining Regulation and the appointment of Calgary engineer and lawyer, Neil McCrank, to study the situation. The McCrank report makes a number of recommendations to improve the regulatory process, commenting: "While no regulatory bodies escape complaints, the complexity and the lack of capacity of the regulatory systems in the North have attracted a greater degree of justified criticism than a typical regulatory body. A number of these criticisms can be addressed through process and system improvements, which are detailed below. However, some of the concerns call into question the very structure of the regulatory systems in the North, especially in the Northwest Territories."[45]

In May 2010, under the federal Northern Regulatory Improvements Initiative, a federal negotiator began discussions with the Aboriginal authorities, whose treaties, concluded or in process, are implicated in changes to the regulatory system, and with other northerners.

Northern resource development is growing in importance, for northerners and for the national economy. Exploration expenditures are substantial. Between 2005 and 2009, exploration and deposit appraisal expenditures, not including work for extension of known reserves, averaged $507 million a year –22 % of the total for Canada. The trend appears to be upward: in the territorial north, mineral exploration expenditures in 2010 were estimated at $538 million for the North (19% of the national total). The 2010 amount includes $280 million solely for Nunavut. And there have already been sufficient discoveries to support substantial development. Both the Joint Review Panel and the National Energy Board have reported on the Mackenzie Gas Project, a massive plan to develop known gas reserves in the western NWT and to transport these by pipeline to southern markets; to date there has been no announcement of a Cabinet decision on the project. Currently there are two operating mines in Yukon, as well as small-scale placer gold mining.[46] The Northwest Territories has one tungsten mine and three diamond mines in production and some in prospect, including a possible beryllium mine near Yellowknife. In Nunavut, there is one operating gold mine and several in prospect, including a uranium mine near Baker Lake and several mines on Baffin Island.

All of these projects are subject to regulatory review and all carry significant environmental and social impact, as does much resource exploration. Because of the regulatory system that is now in place, in addition to other provisions of the northern treaties, northern people and Aboriginal organizations have considerable purchase on decision-making. This fact does "slow down" decisions, but arguably, it is also a mechanism for ensuring that development decisions take local and regional, as well as national, interests into account. While some procedural improvements are probably needed – especially where multiple comprehensive claims agreements are having cumulative effects on the overall system, as in the NWT – it is important that any reforms to operations preserve the real democratic gains that are embodied in present institutions.

Further, the northern regulatory system does not exist in a vacuum, but rather is part of the new array of political institutions that are the result of Aboriginal people's organization and activism. There are many checks and balances now. For example, consider that in the run-up to climate change meetings in Cancun, where Canada once again met wide international criticism for once again failing to take action to reduce greenhouse gas emission, Environment Minister John Baird "re-announced" that Lancaster Sound would be protected from petroleum exploration and development. This announcement was made just months after his government authorized a German research vessel to conduct such activities in the Sound, an initiative was halted by legal action by the Qikiqtani Inuit Association, which has constitutionally protected rights in the area.

A second aspect of the Conservatives' northern economic development strategy is reflected in the establishment of a regional development agency for the North, on the model of the Western Diversification Fund or Atlantic Canada Opportunities Agency. The Canadian Northern Economic Development Agency (CanNor) consolidates federal programming for northern economic development, with a commitment of about $133 million annually.[47] These funds have been dispersed to a wide range of northern organizations, and used to support a range of northern-generated small ventures. They may be seen as an attempt to support development and diversification in the Northern economies.

As Table 2 indicates, most of the funds have gone to Aboriginal organizations and governments (Aboriginal and public), with not-for-profits garnering nearly one-fifth of the funds. Almost no grants were made to northern businesses. In line with pre-existing program guidelines (and certainly, northern needs), the bulk of the funding has been for infrastructure development and projects related to resource development, with northern tourism a distant second.

The range of projects funded through CanNor, and the agency's opportunity to develop strong axes of communication with northern organizations (due to its offices in the North) suggest that it could develop into an important interlocutor for northern interests in federal decision-making, supplementing the role already played by the Department of Indian Affairs and Northern Development.

NORTHERN DEMOCRACY AND POLITICAL DEVELOPMENT

This chapter has so far given scant attention to northern political development, arguably one of the most substantial Canadian achievements of the last forty years. In that period, territorial colonial administrations at varying

Table 2

CANNOR

Grants by Recipient, 2009–10

Recipient Type	Estimated Number of Recipients	Total Spending	% of Total Funding
Aboriginal Development Corporations/ Organizations	12	$8,634,770	12%
Aboriginal Businesses	2	$463,000	<1%
Aboriginal Governments and Organizations	10	$7,086,180	10%
Municipal Governments[1]	26	$11,191,825	16%
Territorial Governments	?5	₹??,0⎡1,߲ΓΓ	⏌⎯ ⎞ⵁ
Non-Profit Organizations	20	$9,861,958	14%

1 If there were multiple recipients for a project this was counted; and if a municipality received funds more than once, this was counted as a separate project.

Source: Canadian Northern Economic Development Agency. *News Releases.* Available at: http://www.cannor.gc.ca/mr/nr-eng.asp. For more detail, see Appendix B.

Table 3

Spending by the Canadian Northern Development Agency (CanNor), 2009–10

	Grants by area of endeavor		
Area of Endeavor	Estimated Number of Recipients	Total Spending	% of Total Funding
Infrastructure	43	$26,744,195	38%
Research and Knowledge	14	$5,328,265	8%
Resource Development/Extraction	12	$24,957,000	35.5%
Service Delivery/Business Development	12	$6,320,738	9%
Tourism and Culture	18	$6,239,928	9%
Other (not categorized)	2	$666,000	<1%

Source: Canadian Northern Economic Development Agency. *News Releases.* Available at: http://www.cannor.gc.ca/mr/nr-eng.asp.

stages of democratic development have been replaced by fully elected legislative assemblies. Two new territories have been created, by division of the old Northwest Territories following a plebiscite and vigorous negotiations by Aboriginal groups. Modern treaties (comprehensive claims agreements) have been negotiated by all but a small minority of northern Aboriginal groups, and they are working within and further developing a variety of new governing forms. It has been a remarkable period of constitutional innovation and popular debate. While much has been accomplished, there is much yet to be done. Completing the northern processes of political and institutional innovation and finding ways to ensure that the original agreements are given effect are still high priorities for northern peoples and northern governments.

There remain a number of outstanding irritants. Federal capacity to live up to the terms of the modern treaties has been imperfect, particularly with regard to building the institutions required to sustain new relationships with the new northern political institutions.[48] Territorial governments have been disappointed by the slow pace of negotiations concerning devolution of power over natural resource development from the federal government to the Northwest Territories and Nunavut,[49] while Aboriginal organizations in the Northwest Territories watch anxiously to see that this is done in a way that does not diminish their hard-won new institutions. And there are still outstanding issues concerning Aboriginal land rights in the parts of the North where satisfactory agreements have yet to be concluded, though these are some of the very areas in which major resource development is occurring and will increase.[50]

Each of these areas has the potential to fester into a major problem. The modern treaties embody the best hopes of a generation who laboured long to develop means of political integration of northern Aboriginal societies that were compatible with both governance in the rest of Canadian and Aboriginal governing traditions. As is the way of these things, the Aboriginal societies compromised the most. The treaties are really the framework within which new territorial governing practices and a new relationship between Aboriginal people and the Crown are being built, and they must be nourished by appropriate attention on the federal side. There are some signs that this will not happen. For example, Nunavut Tunngavik Incorporated, the Beneficiary organization in Nunavut, has found it necessary to sue the federal government for sixteen (alleged) breaches of the Nunavut Agreement, and a total of $1 billion. The case is, expensively, currently before the court.

In this context, it is striking that the only reference to northern governance in the Conservatives' Northern Strategy concerns devolution, which has moved slowly, and includes no references to institutional development on the federal side to raise federal capacity to deal with the new Aboriginal and other governments that have been established. Simple matters of implementation are a major irritant for the Beneficiary organizations, and these have not surfaced on the federal priority list at all.

CONCLUSIONS

In contrast to immediately previous governments, the Harper governments have rather firmly asserted federal interests from a perspective that associates Canadian identity with "northernness." This approach tends to read northern interests – both Aboriginal and non-Aboriginal – out of the official narrative, except as they embody national purposes. This allows the government to obscure or overlook existing northern problems and needs, and to ignore both northern voices and northern complexities. While federal policy has paid lip service to some northern priorities, the large and looming challenges of infrastructure renewal, social and cultural development and consolidation of political innovations have been largely ignored. The Harper government's abandonment of meaningful intergovernmentalism has meant that a very narrow definition of the national interest (focused on defence and non-renewable resource development) has emerged.

There is no doubt that there is an important and indissoluble *national* interest in northern development, and the federal government certainly has a duty as the primary guardian of this interest, on behalf of all Canadians. It must be remembered though that "All Canadians" includes the citizens who live in the North. The route towards advancement of Canadian interests lies through the realization of northerners' social, political and economic objectives, in this most inventive, diverse and inspiring part of the country.

NOTES

1 I am grateful to Mel Cappe, Nick Falvo, Katherine Graham, Peter Harrison, Jack Hicks, Sheena Kennedy, David C. Miller, Paul Quassa, F. Leslie Seidle, Deborah Simmons, Chris Stoney, Annis May Timpson, Richard Van Loon, Graham White and three insightful reviewers whose day jobs prevent me from thanking them publicly.

2 The city of Iqaluit is near an old fishing site on Frobisher Bay. Non-Inuit settlement dates from 1941, when the United States built an airstrip as part of the war effort. Iqaluit is more than twice the size of any other community in Nunavut, with by far the greatest proportion of non-Aboriginal people (over half) and as a transportation hub for the territory; it is served by daily jet aircraft and several airlines.

3 This statement that is quoted was made on July 9th, 2007 at the military base in Esquimalt. CBC News, Monday July 9th, 2007 http://www.cbc.ca/canada/story/2007/07/09/arctic-cda.html. Mr. Harper repeated the sentiment as recently as August 2010: "The first and highest priority of our northern strategy is the protection of our Arctic sovereignty," Harper said, speaking to reporters. "And as I have said many times before, the first principle of sovereignty is to use it or lose it." CBC News "Arctic Sovereignty a Priority: Harper" (August 23, 2010) http://www.cbc.ca/politics/story/2010/08/23/harper-north.html accessed on November 21, 2010.

4 See Frances Abele, "Conservative Northern Development Policy: A New Broom in an Old Bottleneck," in Michael J. Prince, ed. *Tracking the Tories: How Ottawa Spends 1986–1987*, Methuen 1986, pp. 149–178; and Abele, "Beyond the Blue Horizon: Northern Development Policy in the Mulroney Years," in Raymond Blake, ed. *Examining the Legacy: The Era of Prime Minister Brian Mulroney*. McGill-Queen's University Press, 2007. The prime minister's comment could even signal, to international observers, a new lack of confidence in Canadian sovereignty. If there is no problem, why mention it?

5 There have been two or three official visits a year by other Ministers of the Crown. As Governor-General, Michaël Jean visited annually.

6 Canada, Speech from the Throne, October 16, 2007.

7 A conversation with Richard Powell stimulated this line of thinking about the sequence of Conservative Canadian leaders whose imagination was caught by the resource potential of the North. See Richard Powell, "Configuring an Arctic Commons?" *Political Geography* 27 (2008) 827–832; Richard C. Powell, "Science, Sovereignty and Nation: Canada and the Legacy of the International Geophysical Year, 1957–58," *Journal of Historical Geography* 34 (2008); 618–638.

8 The latest (2010) Speech from the Throne also, and again, asserts the symbolic importance of the North to Canadian identity: "*We are a northern country.*[original emphasis] Canadians are deeply influenced by the vast expanse of our Arctic and its history and legends. Our Government established the Northern Strategy to realize the potential of Canada's North for northerners and all Canadians." In this Speech, the high arctic research station is 're-announced', and there is a terse reference to "further steps toward territorial devolution."

9 See Appendix A and Frances Abele, Thomas J. Courchene, F. Leslie Seidle and France St-Hilaire, eds. *Northern Exposure: Peoples, Powers and Prospects in Canada's North*. Montreal: Institute for Research on Public Policy, 2009, pp. 588–590.

10 Frances Abele, "Conservative Northern Development Policy: A New Broom in an Old Bottleneck," in Michael J. Prince, ed. *Tracking the Tories: How Ottawa Spends 1986–1987*, Methuen 1986, 149–178; Frances Abele and Katherine Graham, "Plus Que Ça Change: The North and Native Peoples," *How Ottawa Spends 1988–89*. Carleton University Press, 1988, 113–138.

11 The Kelowna Accord was reached in November 2005, after long discussions by representatives of peak Aboriginal organizations and federal, provincial and territorial governments and just three days before the Martin government fell. The Accord committed governments to investing $5 billion over five years to improve Aboriginal peoples' standard of living. The first Conservative budget in May 2006 stated that the Accord federal funding targets in the Accord would be respected, but this has not happened. http://www.cbc.ca/news/background/aboriginals/undoing-kelowna.html

12 The Conservatives' Northern Strategy was announced and discussed in 2008, but not published until July 2009, as Canada, *Canada's Northern Strategy: Our North, Our Heritage, Our Future*.

13 http://pm.gc.ca/eng/media.asp?id=2016.

14 Of course, it is unknown whether the Martin Government targets would have been met. In the NWT, there is a significant outstanding problem concerning the relationships among newly negotiated Aboriginal governments and organizations, and the territorial government; movement towards extending the jurisdiction and powers of the territorial government is often seen by Aboriginal governments and organizations as a threat to their own interests. Reportedly, with respect to Nunavut, federal official have concerns about proceeding too expeditiously, fearing that the eleven year old government administration may lack the capacity to manage resource production.

Another factor, surely, is the enormous resource potential available from northern resources and potential federal reluctance to cede control over the direction and pace of development.

15 Aboriginal leaders are concerned that the agreement was reached by the two govern-ments without their participation, that it is not a good financial deal for Aboriginal governments and organizations, and that it transfers too much authority to the ter-ritorial government. See http://www.cbc.ca/canada/north/story/2010/11/04/nwt-aip-roland-aboriginal-meeting.html , and, on controversies attending an earlier round of devolution, Gurston Dacks, ed. *Devolution and Constitutional Development in the Canadian North*. Ottawa: Carleton University Press, 1990.

16 The case of the Northwest Territories is complex, given the existence of four dif-ferent comprehensive land claim agreements (modern Treaties) and the fact that agreements are still outstanding for certain parts of the territory. Devolution of control over non-renewable natural resources inevitably raises challenging ques-tions of coordination and risks changing the institutional balance of power among the territorial government and Aboriginal governments and organizations. The situation in Nunavut is simpler, with only one comprehensive claim agreement; the delay there appears to be entirely on the federal side. The reasons for delay are not made explicit, though the capacity of the new government of Nunavut to manage the large responsibility is sometimes questioned. It is unclear why this represents an intractable problem, given that "devolution" in the case of territories does not mean ceding total control. In the case of both territories, the stakes are very high, as the reserves of a wide range of minerals available for exploitation are enormous. See James Feehan, "Natural Resource Devolution in the Territories: Current Status and Unresolved Issues" in Frances Abele, Tom Courchene, France St.-Hilaire and F. Leslie Seidle *Northern Exposure: Peoples, Powers and Prospects in Canada's North* Montreal: Institute for Research on Public Policy, 2009.

17 For example, in Nunavut, where none of the widely dispersed communities are con-nected by road and all are resupplied by boat, none have modern docking facilities and only one has a small craft harbour.

18 Abele et al 2009 includes a range of analyses of the new institutions.

19 'Beneficiary' refers to an individual who is entitled to the benefits and subject to the provisions of a comprehensive claim agreement, such as the Nunavut Agreement. A Beneficiary organization is an organization established pursuant to the conclusion of such an agreement. These organizations are charged with implementing the provi-sions of the agreement on behalf of all Beneficiaries. They also receive the capital transfers provided for in the agreement which compensate the signatories for ceded rights to land.

20 For differing perspectives on the Canadian situation and possible responses, see Franklyn Griffiths, "Canadian Arctic Sovereignty: Time to Take Yes for an Answer on the Northwest Passage" in Abele et al, 107–136; Rob Huebert, "Canada and the Changing International Arctic: At the Crossroads of Cooperation and Conflict" in Abele et al, 77–106; Michael Byers, *Who Owns the Arctic?* Douglas and McIntyre, 2009.

21 See several chapters in E.J. Dosman, *The Arctic in Question*. Toronto: Oxford University Press, 1976.

22 The Permanent Participants are the Aleut International Association (AIA), Arctic Athabaskan Council (AAC), Gwich'in Council International (GCI), Inuit Circumpolar Council (ICC), Saami Council, and the Russian Arctic Aboriginal Peoples of the North (RAIPON). See Franklyn Griffiths, ed. *Politics of the Northwest Passage*. Montreal and Kingston: McGill-Queen's University Press, 1987; Frances Abele and Thierry Rodon, "Inuit Diplomacy in the Global Era: The Strengths of Multilateral Internationalism," *Canadian Foreign Policy* 13:3 Spring 2007.

23 Circumpolar diplomacy was pioneered by Aboriginal peoples. The Inuit Circumpolar Conference, an alliance of Inuit from four countries, published the Arctic Policy in 1991 – an early attempt to garner support for an orderly international circumpolar regime.

24 Chuck Strahl was the longest serving Minister of Indian Affairs and Northern Development, holding the post between August 2007 and August 2010. He was preceded by Jim Prentice, and succeeded by John Duncan. It is probably fair to say that for all three, the challenging and very large Indian Affairs aspect of the Ministry consumed most of their time. The Northern Strategies of both Liberal and Conservative governments are an amalgam of bureaucratic expertise and consultations with constituencies, and the reigning political purpose.

25 The full statement appears at http://www.international.gc.ca/polar-polaire/canada_arctic_foreign_policy-_a_politique_etrangere_du_canada_pour_arctique.aspx?lang=eng. In the Statement and more so in the 2010 Speech from the Throne, northern foreign policy is presented as a series of specific measures to engage with actual issues. Defence of Canada's Arctic sovereignty is a major goal, involving mapping of northern resources and waters, increasing marine safety, reduction of pollution from shipping, and work with "other northern countries to settle boundary disagreements."

26 For background, see http://www.international.gc.ca/polar-polaire/ndfp-vnpe2.aspx?lang=en#12. It is interesting to compare the Conservative's northern vision with the "soft power" approach set out in Liberal Minister of Foreign Affairs' Lloyd Axworthy's *Northern Dimension of Canadian Foreign Policy* from 2000, an approach that emphasized the power of diplomacy and avoided nationalistic references to national soul.

27 On August 25, 2010, the Prime Minister's Office issued the following statement: *On 24 August, two CF-18 Hornet fighter aircraft were launched and visually identified 2 Russian aircraft, the TU-95 Bear, approximately 120 nautical miles north of Inuvik, Northwest Territories. At their closest point, the Russian aircraft were 30 nautical miles from Canadian soil. The CF-18s shadowed the Bear aircraft until they turned around. The two CF-18s came from 4 Wing Cold Lake, Alberta. Thanks to the rapid response of the Canadian Forces, at no time did the Russian aircraft enter sovereign Canadian airspace.* http://www.cbc.ca/politics/insidepolitics/2010/08/pmo-statement-on-cf-18s-shadowing-russian-aircraft.html.

Russian arctic border patrols (resumed in 2007 after ceasing with the end of the Cold War) do signal Russian arctic capabilities and provide a means to test those of Norad. The October 2010 patrol, which did not breach Canadian airspace, was the sixth that has occurred in the last two years. Arctic defence expert Rob Huebert suggests that the longer term Russian objective might not involve Norad or Canada, but rather entails making a point with China and the European Union, both having expressed an interest in polar resources. China has commented that these should be seen as a resource for all humanity.

The Huebert interview appears at http://www.cbc.ca/video/player.html?category=News&zone=politics&site=cbc.news.ca&clipid=1574655674. See also "Norad Downplays Russian Bomber Interception" http://www.cbc.ca/politics/story/2010/08/25/cf-18s-russians-airspace.html. Opposition critics note that the alarm over the Russian flights coincided with Commons committee discussions of F-31 purchases.

28 Both Canada and Denmark claim 1.3 sq. km, Hans Island, located in the Lincoln Sea. Negotiations are underway to resolve the issue, with a resolution expected in 2011. The Beaufort Sea boundary dispute with the United States is more serious, involving a 21,500 sq. km. triangle of sea and seabed, extending from the shore. Under the United Nations Convention on the Law of the Sea both Canada and the United States must map their territorial seabeds by 2013 in order to establish a claim. The two countries have been cooperating on mapping. In 2010, it was reported that negotiations concerning the disputed triangle were once again under way.

29 At this writing, it is not clear that the multibillion dollar purchase will proceed. http://www.reuters.com/article/idUSN1611146620100716

30 Shelagh Grant, *Sovereignty or Security? Government Policy in the Canadian North, 1936–1950.* Vancouver: UBC Press, 1987; Shelagh Grant, *Polar Imperative: A History of Arctic Sovereignty in North America.* Vancouver: Douglas and McIntyre, 2010; Michael Bravo, "Arctic Science, Nation-Building and Citizenship," in Abele et al, *Northern Exposure,* 141–168.

31 Although the title of this initiative is expressed in the singular ("Year"), the International Polar Year ran from March 2007 to March 2009, and its capstone conference, for showcasing northern research, will take place in spring 2012. Canada's contribution to IPY was $156 million, the largest initial commitment of all of the participating countries. Canadian scientists and public servants played an important role in shaping international participation in the IPY, ensuring that the human dimension of northern science was included. IPY funding fell off the table as a result of three successive federal elections, and it was approved by three successive governments – the Chretien Liberals, the Martin Liberals and the Harper Conservatives.

32 http://www.actionplan.gc.ca/initiatives/eng/index.asp?initiativeID=108&mode=3

33 For more elaboration of this point, see Frances Abele, "Northern Development: Past, Present and Future" in Frances Abele, Thomas J. Courchene, F. Leslie Seidle, France St-Hilaire, eds. *Northern Exposure: Peoples, Powers and Prospects in Canada's North.* Montreal: Institute for Research on Public Policy, 2009.

34 Northern Premiers Forum Communique, Iqaluit, September 5, 2009. http://
    www.yukonpremier.ca/pdf/northern-premiers-2009–communique.pdf; and
    see Government of the Northwest Territories News Release, *Premier Responds
    to Canada's Statement on Arctic Policy* R(16)490 - Monday, August 23, 2010
    http://www.exec.gov.nt.ca/currentnews/prDetails.asp?varPR_ID=1611;
    Northern premiers urge more visible Canadian presence in polar issues
    CanWest News Service August 4, 2007 http://www.canada.com/story_print.
    html?id=7e48ca54–b386–46d3–bd2ae8ade8318629&sponsor=,

35 Ekos Research Associates , for the Canada Centre for Global Security Studies at the
    Munk School of Global Affairs and the Walter and Duncan Gordon Foundation,
    Rethinking the Top of the World: Arctic Security Public Opinion Survey, Final Report,
    Toronto, January 2011. All quotations in this paragraph are from the Executive
    Summary.

36 See the chapter by Nick Falvo in this volume. The $300 million committed to social
    housing in northern Canada appears to be one of the few expenditure decisions re-
    flected in the 2006 Kelowna Accord that were respected by the Harper Government
    when it replaced the Martin Liberals after the 2006 election.

37 Recent examples include the Canada Student Loan Program, the Millennium
    Foundation, the Canada Research Chairs program, and many initiatives in health
    care.

38 Sheila Watt-Cloutier, "Climate Change and Human Rights" Speech Delivered
    at *Climate 2050 Technology and Policy Solutions* http://www.youtube.com/
    watch?v=GlSh4XeoLBA; Watt-Cloutier, "A Principled Path" in Abele et al, *Northern
    Exposure.* pp. 69–76.

39 The information in this paragraph is found at http://www.ainc-inac.gc.ca/enr/clc/ccs/
    index-eng.asp.

40 James Feehan, "Natural Resource Devolution in the Territories: Current Status and
    Unresolved Issues," in Abele et al, 2009.

41 Frances Abele, "Northern Development: Past, Present and Future," in Frances Abele
    et al, 2009.

42 See the list and discussion in Abele et al, *Northern Exposure*, especially p. 35 and
    pp 561–594. There are some outstanding negotiations with First Nations and Metis
    in the Northwest Territories and Yukon.

43 The Mackenzie Gas Project refers to a 1,196–kilometre natural gas pipeline system
    along the Mackenzie Valley to connect northern onshore gas fields with North
    American markets. If built it would be a massive project, estimated in 2007 to cost
    $16 billion. The 2008 Speech from the Throne states "Our Government will support
    the development of cleaner energy sources. The natural gas that lies beneath Canada's
    North represents both an untapped source of clean fuel and an unequalled avenue to
    creating economic opportunities for northern people. Our Government will reduce
    regulatory and other barriers to extend the pipeline network into the North."

44 The seven member independent panel was appointed under the Canadian
    Environmental Assessment Act to advise the federal Cabinet on the MGP. The Panel

was appointed in August 2004 and reported in December 2009. The Panel's report is public: http://www.ngps.nt.ca/report.html. To date, the federal government has not made a decision on the project.

45 The McCrank report and associated federal policy statements are available at http://www.reviewboard.ca/reference_lib/index.php?section=33

46 Placer mining in Yukon goes back to the days of the 1898 Gold Rush. It entails mining alluvial deposits, often using hydraulic pressure to separate the gold.

47 This includes the $90 million Strategic Investments in Northern Development Program; $11.8 million in annual economic development funding; and $33 (over two years) in the Community Adjustment Fund. A full list of projects funded appears in Appendix B.

48 Stephanie Irlbacher Fox and Stephen J. Mills, "Living Up to the Spirit of Modern Treaties! Implementation and Institutional Development," in Abele et al, *Northern Exposure*, 233–258; Alastair Campbell, Terry Fenge and Udloriak Hanson,"Sustainable Development in Arctic Canada: Implementing the Nunavut Land Claims Agreement" Presented to the Arctic Frontiers conference, Tromso, Norway, January 27, 2010. Auditor-General of Canada, "Inuvialuit Final Agreement" Chapter 3 in *2007 Report of the Auditor General of Canada*. http://www.oag-bvg.gc.ca/internet/English/aud_ch_oag_2007_3_e_23827.html#ch3hd5c; Terry Fenge, "Implementing Comprehensive Land Claims Agreements" *Policy Options* July-August 2008; Senate of Canada, Standing Senate Committee on Aboriginal Affairs, *Honouring the Spirit of Modern Treaties: Closing the Loopholes*, May 2008. The Senate committee concluded that "[c]urrent implementation practices…appear largely to address the interests of government and minimize costs with the least disruption to existing processes." In the Senate committee's view, "until, and unless, there is a fundamental attitudinal shift, neither the federal government nor Aboriginal signatories will achieve the shared objectives set out in these agreements."

49 In the NWT, the leaked agreement-in-principle on the devolution met with objections from six of seven Aboriginal groups, who saw insufficient protection of their interests. The Government of Nunavut has been pressing for negotiations to begin, but no federal negotiator has been appointed.

50 The Dehcho Dene of the upper Mackenzie Valley are engaged in negotiations with the federal government concerning land use and resource management. They describe their situation as follows: "The Dehcho Process is the overall self-governance, lands and resources negotiations process between the Dehcho First Nations (www.dehchofirstnations.com), the Government of Canada (www.ainc-inac.gc.ca/dehcho/) and the Government of the Northwest Territories. These are typically called "Land Claims" negotiations, but the Dehcho Process is moving away from the standard land selection model towards a new option called "Shared Stewardship."" See http://www.dehcholands.org/common_questions.htm#02. Other outstanding negotiations include those of the Akaitcho Dene,(http://akaitchotreaty8.com/) and NWT Metis. For an overview, see http://www.ainc-inac.gc.ca/ai/scr/nt/ntr/pubs/pflr-eng.asp.

12 Who Pays, When, and How? Government-Assisted Housing in the Northwest Territories and the Role of the Federal Government

NICK FALVO[1]

INTRODUCTION

Much to the surprise of many observers, the federal Conservatives have made Arctic security and sovereignty one of their policy priorities since the 2006 general election campaign. And since taking power that year, the Harper government has acted on several fronts, including committing to the construction of a $720 million icebreaker.[2] What is *not* grabbing headlines are some of the serious social challenges being faced in the North, one of which is affordable housing.

This chapter examines the housing situation in the Northwest Territories (NWT), especially as it affects low-income residents.[3] Topics discussed in this chapter include the manner in which government-assisted housing is administered in the NWT, as well as the uniqueness of government-assisted housing in the NWT. Building costs, forms of government-assisted housing, recent policies of senior levels of government, and other emerging issues in the NWT combine to create a unique public policy study.

The chapter begins by discussing the study's methodology, which includes key informant interviews. It then looks at the role of the federal government in Canada's North more generally. This is followed by a brief look at the history of forced resettlement, the principal actors in the present-day administration of government-assisted housing in the NWT, followed by a consideration of what makes government-assisted housing in the NWT unique relative to other parts of Canada. A very quick look at the make-up of the NWT's Aboriginal populations – as well as some important socioeconomic indicators – will be presented, followed by a brief overview of the different sizes of NWT communities. This will be followed by a brief consideration of the various forms of government-assisted housing in the NWT, as well as a look at the government-funded "small repairs" programs. Recent funding initiatives by senior levels of government will then be discussed, followed by a consideration of two issues of great concern to the NWT's political leaders and service providers: arrears in both public housing and home-ownership programs, and the looming problem of declining federal funding for public housing, which will have an especially acute impact on the NWT relative to the rest of Canada.

METHODOLOGY

Semi-structured in-depth interviews were undertaken with key informants beginning in August 2009. Ethics approval was received by Carleton University's Research Ethics Board and a research license was obtained from the Aurora Research Institute.

While interviews with over 40 key informant interviews had taken place for the research project at the time of this writing, only interviews from ten of them are being used for this chapter. Six of these key informants have worked for the Northwest Territories Housing Corporation ("the Housing Corporation") at some point in their careers; four still work for the Housing Corporation. The sixth works for a local housing authority (LHO), the seventh works for a Yellowknife-based NGO, the eighth was interviewed specifically for his knowledge of mortgage arrears in the Housing Corporation's home-ownership units, and the ninth is an expert on social housing throughout Canada. All but three key informants were asked both broad questions about government-assisted housing in the NWT, as well as specific questions that pertain to their respective areas of specialization. The writer was directed to the key informants largely through community partners, who are acknowledged below. Appendix 1 provides a list of references for the key informant interviews specifically cited in this chapter. Interviews have been coded in order to preserve confidentiality.

Interviews with current and former tenants did not take place, in part due to the small scale and budget of the research project, and in part so as not to duplicate work being done by one of our research partners.[4] However, the research did draw on results of the housing component of the 2009 NWT Community Survey, undertaken by the Northwest Territories Bureau of Statistics in all NWT communities between January and March, 2009.

ROLE OF THE FEDERAL GOVERNMENT IN THE NORTH

The renewed interest being shown by the current federal government in Canada's North does not stem from altruism. Rather, the Harper government's

keen interest in the area is motivated almost exclusively by geopolitical factors, most notably by the large amounts of oil and natural gas that lie beneath
the surface. And while the North's natural resources used to be seen as difficult to access due to weather, that is changing very quickly.[5] For instance,
Huebert (2009) argues that: "Annual average Arctic temperatures have increased at almost twice the rate that they have in the rest of the world over the
past few decades...Reduced sea ice is very likely to increase marine transport
and access to resources. Continued reduction of sea ice is likely to lengthen
the navigation season and increase access to the Arctic's marine resources;
reduced sea ice is likely to increase offshore oil and gas extraction projects;
and sovereignty, security and safety issues, as well as social, cultural and environmental concerns, are likely to arise as marine access increases."[6]

Furthermore, in the eyes of several other countries, parts of the North are
up for grabs in terms of access and sovereignty. For instance, while our federal government claims the Northwest Passage as "part of its historic internal
waters," the United States begs to differ, claiming as recently as 2009 that the
Northwest Passage is an international strait. Moreover, both Denmark and
Russia have shown an active interest in the North in recent years, with Russia
having gone so far as to plant a Russian flag on the sea floor of the North Pole
in a highly-publicized move in 2007.[7] While important questions remain as
to who has a legal claim and who would win a challenge over the area at the
International Court of Justice (or a similar body), it is widely believed that
the more quickly a country establishes a physical presence in the North, the
greater will be the likelihood of that country either acquiring or retaining the
legal right to profit from natural resources in the area.[8]

OVERVIEW OF GOVERNMENT-ASSISTED HOUSING
IN THE NORTHWEST TERRITORIES

Shortly after the Second World War, as the state became very active in the
delivery of social welfare programs throughout Canada, the federal government began delivering social services – most notably health and education – to
Indigenous people in Canada's North on a large scale. Housing was provided as
part of this effort. But, as Abele, Falvo and Haché (2010) have recently argued,
"it entailed a sort of money trap: people who had heretofore built and main-
tained their own shelter were ever after expected to pay cash rent. These are
the origins of a system of public housing that still exists in most of the over
100 smaller, predominantly Aboriginal communities in Canada's North."[9] In
some cases, forced resettlement of Aboriginal communities disrupted both
community and family ties. It also imposed a very different way of life upon
people who had been happy where they were. Indeed, Aboriginal households in Canada's North were effectively induced to undertake a wholesale
change of lifestyle. In a span of just a few decades, they went from hunting

and making their own shelter to being forced to be far more dependent on the state for subsistence, including living in state-sponsored houses.[10] In effect, state-funded housing was used as incentive to draw people to new communities where schools and health centres, both built and funded by the federal government, were provided.[11]

According to Webster (2006), much of the increased state role was triggered by negative media attention. In the early 1950s, as international attention began to focus on the construction of the Distant Early Warning radar line, the federal government was "embarrassed" by media reports describing "Inuit destitution and government neglect."[12]

Today, the Northwest Territories Housing Corporation (generally referred to in the NWT as "The Housing Corporation") is a territorial Crown corporation, receiving substantial funding from Canada Mortgage and Housing Corporation (CMHC).[13] The Housing Corporation serves "the entire population in the NWT ... [both] Aboriginal and non-Aboriginal, with little distinction."[14] And, unlike some other parts of Canada, the NWT has no "on-reserve housing" administered by Indian and Northern Affairs Canada (INAC).[15] According to Webster (2006), "[d]espite the existence of treaties, which provide for the option of reserve creation, there are many Indian communities in the NWT but only two reserves. One of these is the tiny Salt Plains Reserve #195 near Fort Smith, while the other is Hay River Dene Reserve #1 at Hay River. The former is a little more than a collection of cabins while the latter is a reserve in the full sense, except that the NWT's government, not federal departments, is responsible for most basic services including housing."[16]

Public housing generally refers to housing that is owned and operated by a government agency, and inhabited by low-income households who pay rent (to a housing authority) that is geared to their income. Public housing in the NWT today is administered by 23 local housing organizations (LHOs), each of which is accountable to the Housing Corporation. The relationship between each LHO and the Housing Corporation is governed by an agreement that sets out roles and responsibilities of each party. Each LHO has a board of directors, management and staff "who are responsible for the day-to-day activities associated with the delivery of the program in its community." And, in principle, the Housing Corporation monitors all LHO operations.[17]

In the case of large communities, the LHO operates as an "authority," in which case its board is appointed by the minister responsible for the Housing Corporation. In the case of small communities, the LHO operates as an "association," whose board members are elected by community members at an annual general meeting. In a few cases, a band or municipality is associated with the LHO, in which case both bodies manage housing in that community via a management agreement.[18]

The NWT also has home-ownership programs. Households who participate in these home-ownership programs generally have higher monthly incomes than is the case with public housing; a household whose only source of income is social assistance, for example, would not be eligible for a home-ownership program. Yet households eligible for the home-ownership programs still generally have to fall below the "core need" income threshold, as defined by CMHC (see below). Moreover, it is more difficult to be approved for a home-ownership program if one lives in a region of the NWT where construction costs are relative high, such as on the Arctic Coast.[19]

The NWT's home-ownership programs are administered by the Housing Corporation's five district offices. The PATH (Providing Assistance for Territorial Homeownership) program provides forgivable loans, ranging from $10,000 to $125,000, to households who wish either to build or purchase a home.[20] Eligible households must have sufficiently high monthly income such that they are paying no more than 30 percent of before-tax income on shelter. Roughly 100 households apply for PATH each year, and roughly half of all applicants are approved.[21]

The Homeownership Entry Level Program (HELP) is a rent-to-own program for first-time homebuyers. Successful applicants must be low-income and must sign a two-year lease on a new home built by the Housing Corporation. HELP participants often use this two-year period to either pay off already-accumulated arrears on public housing,[22] or to build up a credit rating. Roughly 200 households apply for HELP each year, and roughly half of them are approved to begin the program. Upon successful completion of the two-year lease, participants can graduate to home ownership and bring with them $10,000 in equity accumulated during the two-year period. Many HELP graduates also apply for PATH.[23]

UNIQUENESS OF SOCIAL HOUSING IN THE NWT

Relative to Canada as a whole, the Northwest Territories (NWT) represents a jurisdiction of extremes. On the one hand, its Gross Domestic Product on a per capita basis is double the national average, due largely to the mining industry. Moreover, the Government of the Northwest Territories (GNWT) spends roughly 25 times more per capita on housing than does a typical Canadian province. On the other hand, relative to the rest of Canada, more NWT residents live in both crowded conditions and in housing in need of major repair. Indeed, for every plus, there is a minus. And that is how the NWT's housing situation ought to be understood relative to the rest of Canada – as an enigma offering both challenge and opportunity.

It should also be noted that, in terms of paying its fair share, the NWT stands up quite favourably next to Canada's other territories and provinces. Due largely to revenues derived from resource development in the NWT, the federal government received almost $17,000 per capita in revenue from the NWT in 2004. In contrast, the next largest source of revenue among Canadian provinces and territories was Alberta at just under $8,000 per capita. (This is, admittedly, counterbalanced by the almost $17,000 per capita that is also received by the NWT each year from the federal government under Territorial Formula Financing.)

The NWT territorial government currently spends 5.1 percent of its budget on housing. By contrast, the "highest housing spending" Canadian province is Saskatchewan, which spends 1.4 percent of its budget on housing. Moreover, the average for all Canadian provinces and territories is 0.7 percent. To illustrate this dramatic difference, the NWT spends $1,672 per capita on housing, while the average for the rest of Canada is $61. Thus, on a per capita basis, the NWT spends roughly 25 times more on housing than the rest of Canada.[24]

There are significant differentials in building costs, depending on the area of the NWT. It costs roughly $150 per square foot to build housing in southern areas of the NWT such as Hay River and Fort Smith, and roughly double that amount on the Arctic Coast. There are two main reasons for the substantially higher costs along the Arctic Coast. First, these areas of the NWT have few if any contractors, meaning that contractors typically have to travel there from other areas (see Map below). Thus, both their transportation and accommodation costs must be included in the cost of building. Second, and as can also be inferred from a quick look at the map, freight transportation required to barge materials to the Arctic Coast entail additional costs.[25] See map below.[26]

The average cost of building new housing the NWT is roughly $205 per square foot. The Housing Corporation typically builds "modest" three-bedroom houses that are roughly 1,000 square feet each – both as public housing units and home-ownership units – meaning that the cost of building a housing unit in the NWT ranges from roughly $150,000 to $300,000.[27] (It should also be noted that average utility costs for households in the NWT are roughly double the Canadian average. A 2005 study has pegged the annual figure at roughly $4,300 per NWT household, compared with roughly $2,100 nationally.)[28]

The average purchase price of a home in Yellowknife is almost identical to the Canadian average, at just over $300,000.[29] Yet, renting a private apartment in one of the NWT's regional centres is relatively expensive. Average rent for a two-bedroom private unit in Yellowknife is now almost $1,500 per month, representing roughly a 50 percent increase in the past decade.[30]

According to the 2006 Census, 50.3 percent of the NWT's population is Aboriginal, with 30.8 percent being Dene, 8.7 percent Métis and 10.1 percent Inuit.[31] Looking at the NWT as a whole, there are important quality of life indicators among and between the different population groups. For example, the unemployment rate for Aboriginal people in the NWT is more than four times greater than for non-Aboriginal people in the NWT. Moreover, an Aboriginal household in the NWT is almost four times as likely to report having more than one person to a room than a non-Aboriginal household in the NWT.[32]

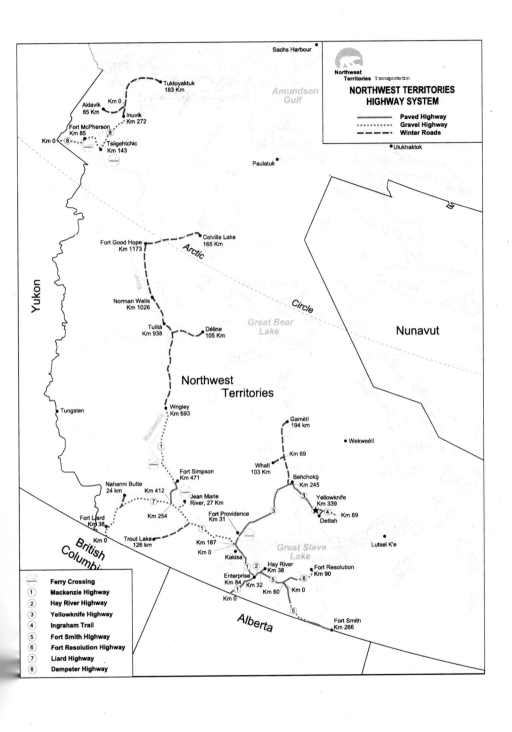

Sachs Harbour

Northwest
Territories Transportation

**NORTHWEST TERRITORIES
HIGHWAY SYSTEM**

〰〰〰 Paved Highway
········· Gravel Highway
– – – – Winter Roads

*Amundsen
Gulf*

• Ulukhaktok

Tuktoyaktuk
183 Km

Km 0

Aklavik
85 Km

Inuvik
Km 272

Fort McPherson
Km 85

Km 0 ⑧

⑧

Tsiigehtchic
Km 143

Paulatuk •

Colville Lake
165 Km

Fort Good Hope
Km 1173

Arctic

Yukon

River

Norman Wells
Km 1026

Circle

Tulità
Km 938

Déline
105 Km

*Great Bear
Lake*

Nunavut

**Northwest
Territories**

Wrigley
Km 693

Mackenzie

Gamèti
194 km

• Wekweètì

Km 69

①

Whatì
103 Km

Fort Simpson
Km 471

Behchokǫ̀
Km 245

Nahanni Butte
24 km

Km 412

⑦

Jean Marie
River, 27 Km

③

Yellowknife
Km 339

④ Km 69

• Tungsten

Km 254

Fort Providence
Km 31

③

Dettah

Fort Liard
Km 38

Km 0

Trout Lake
126 km

Km 187

Km 0

*Great Slave
Lake*

• Lutsel K'e

*British
Columbia*

Kakisa

①

①②

Hay River
Km 38

Fort Resolution
Km 90

Enterprise
Km 84

⑤

⑥

Km 32

⑤

Km 60

Km 0

Km 0

⑤

Alberta

Fort Smith
Km 266

Ferry Crossing
① Mackenzie Highway
② Hay River Highway
③ Yellowknife Highway
④ Ingraham Trail
⑤ Fort Smith Highway
⑥ Fort Resolution Highway
⑦ Liard Highway
⑧ Dempster Highway

There is also an important difference in terms of who lives where in the NWT. Aboriginal people live disproportionately in small communities, where there is a higher proportion of social housing and minimal or non-existent "market housing", as opposed to the "regional centres" (i.e. Yellowknife, Hay River, For Simpson). There is also significantly higher labour force participation in regional centres, as well as lower unemployment rates.[33]

When CMHC assesses a household's housing, they use three main benchmarks: adequacy, suitability and affordability. The adequacy standard considers whether the residents of a given household believe that it is in need of major repairs. The suitability standard refers to whether the housing unit in question has an appropriate number of rooms, as defined by the National Occupancy Standards. And the affordability standard refers to whether or not the household can afford housing at less than 30 percent of gross monthly income on housing.[34]

A simple way of thinking about housing for low-income individuals in the NWT is as follows: the housing situation is a little bit worse in the NWT's regional centres than in the rest of Canada, and a lot worse in the NWT's small communities than in the rest of Canada. According to CMHC, 2 percent of Canadian households are living in crowded conditions. The corresponding figure for Yellowknife is 3 percent, while the figure for rural NWT is 8 percent. Likewise, 8 percent of Canadian households live in housing that, according to CMHC, require major repairs; the corresponding figure for Yellowknife is 10 percent, while the figure for rural NWT is 22 percent.[35]

FORMS OF HOUSING IN THE NWT

There are a total of 14,522 housing units in the NWT. Fifty-two percent of them are privately owned[36] (i.e. owner-occupied) – a considerably smaller percentage than the Canadian average of 68 percent.[37] Just over 20 percent of all privately-owned units have been created through the NWT's various home-ownership programs.[38] As a general rule, privately-owned units in small communities have required considerably more government assistance than in the NWT's regional centres.[39] Of the remaining 48 percent of housing units in the NWT, roughly half (6,899) are private-market rental units, roughly one-third (2,249) are public housing units, and 7 percent of the total housing units in the NWT are staff housing.[40] This breakdown is illustrated in the pie chart below.

It should be noted that the cost to government of public housing is considerably higher per unit than in the case of home ownership. To create and subsidize a public housing unit in the NWT, it might cost government $2 million over a 50-year period. This includes the cost of both capital and the roughly $15,000 to $20,000 required annually by the government for operation (which includes fuel, power and water). In contrast, to support a unit in the home-ownership sector, the government pays only the capital, amounting to a total of $205,000 per unit (as per the figures provided above).[41]

Types of Housing in the NWT

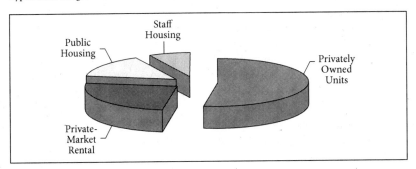

Source: Northwest Territories Bureau of Statistics. 2010. 2009 NWT Community Survey Housing Component: Overall Results Yellowknife: Northwest Territories Bureau of Statistics. January 14.

As alluded to above, there is not a single unit of "on-reserve" housing administered by INAC in the NWT.[42] And, interestingly, during annual consultations with staff from the Housing Corporation (where a community's mix of new units is determined), a handful of small communities have never opted to accept any public housing at all.[43] There are two main reasons for this. First, there is a stigma that comes with public housing – a phenomenon that occurs in all North American jurisdictions. Some communities believe that accepting public housing units encourages dependency and have therefore consciously refused to accept public housing units during annual consultations. Second, because of the increased costs associated with subsidizing public housing units versus home-ownership units, many communities have simply chosen to have more units of home-ownership units rather than fewer units of public housing units.[44]

The Housing Corporation also administers roughly half a dozen small-repairs programs in the NWT, most of which are federal programs designed by CMHC. In most cases, the recipient: a) owns and occupies a home that is in need of major repairs; b) is deemed to be in core housing need, as defined by CMHC; and c) receives assistance from one of these funds only once in their lifetime. Over 90 percent of recipients are Aboriginal persons and a disproportionate number are from small communities. Each year, CMHC provides roughly $495,000 in funding for the federal small-repairs programs being administered by the Housing Corporation, and the GNWT generally contributes approximately $150,000 on top of that. On an annual basis, between 30 and 40 NWT households typically benefit from the federal small-repairs programs, with each household receiving between $11,000 and $30,000. Funds often contribute towards a health and safety matter, such as a new heating system or sewage tank repair.[45] In addition to this, the territorial government has its own home-repair program, known as Contributing Assistance

for Repairs and Enhancement (CARE), which provides forgivable loans ranging from $10,000 and $90,000 to a relatively low-income homeowner (as defined by the aforementioned core need benchmark) to renovate and upgrade
their home.[46] Between 400 and 500 households typically apply for CARE each
year, and roughly 60 percent of applicants are approved. The vast majority
of recipients are Aboriginal persons and mostly from small communities.[47]
CARE typically provides between $4 million and $5 million per year, but provided a total of $8 million in 2009 as part of the GNWT's stimulus program.[48]
Sometimes CARE assistance is "stacked" onto a federal small-repairs program
(meaning that a recipient benefits from two programs at the same time), but
this is more the exception than the rule.[49]

There are currently roughly 400 households on the waiting list for public housing in the NWT[50] – a substantial number in light of the fact that the
NWT's total population is just over 40,000. Yet, the fact that a waiting list exists
for public housing in the NWT should come as no surprise, as the supply of
government-assisted housing in Canada has never kept up with demand, no
matter the province or territory.[51]

RECENT FUNDING ANNOUNCEMENTS

Following the dearth of federal funding for new units of social housing
across Canada throughout most of the 1990s, there have been several federal funding initiatives for social housing over the course of the past decade.
The Affordable Housing Initiative (AHI), which began in 2001, has resulted
in $10.65 million in new, one-time federal funding for social housing in the
NWT. And, according to CMHC's web site, this represents 344 units of housing
in the NWT.[52] That said, a senior official with the Housing Corporation has
stated that, in reality, the AHI was "very insignificant" for the NWT, especially
in light of the maximum amount of federal funding that could be used for
each unit. In his words, rather than actually creating new housing units with
this funding, "we absorbed this into our annual capital delivery budget."[53]

In May 2006, the federal government allocated $300 million in one-time
funding for social housing units to Canada's three northern territories. This
announcement came out of an April 2005 federal budget deal made between
then-Prime Minister Paul Martin and federal NDP leader, Jack Layton. The
agreement was a condition for NDP support for that year's federal budget.[54]
The NWT's share of this was $50 million, which was then matched dollar for
dollar by the territorial government.[55] This $100 million resulted in the cre-
ation of 450 housing units, all of which have now been built. Roughly half of
them are home ownership units, and the other half consist of public housing
units. Interestingly, even this initiative did not result in an overall increase in
the NWT's housing stock, as the new units (which were energy-efficient multiplex units) simply replaced older, detached units.[56]

The 2009 federal budget also announced a one-time commitment of $59 million for social housing in the NWT, as part of Canada's Economic Action Plan (i.e. economic stimulus). The NWT's territorial government has matched this funding, dollar for dollar. This will result in the creation of 120 new units (a mix of public housing and home ownership units). Some of the funds will be directed toward substantial repairs to existing public and home-ownership units, as well as increased energy efficiency.[57]

ARREARS

Tenants living in public housing units in the NWT pay rent that is assessed to reflect an amount that they can reasonably afford. No tenant in public housing in the NWT pays monthly rent greater than 30 percent of their gross monthly income.[58] Thus roughly three-quarters of public housing units in the NWT require rent of under $500 per month.[59]

LHOs have generally been responsible for collecting rent from tenants. A "collection rate" refers to the percentage of assessed rent owed by tenants that ends up actually being paid to their respective LHO on an annual basis. Collection rates vary from year to year and from one LHO to the next. Indeed, some LHOs in some years collect 100 percent of assessed rent, while other LHOs in some years collect none of the assessed rent.[60] While key informant interviews did not yield a clear answer as to why collection rates can be very low at times, it has been noted that LHOs with the lowest rates of collection also have the lowest-quality stock.[61] Exacerbating this already-challenging process, an administrative change was introduced in April 2006 whereby the assessment of rent on public housing units was transferred from LHOs to the Department of Education, Culture & Employment (ECE). Prior to that move, the Housing Corporation – through its LHOs – had typically collected 90 percent of assessed rent on an annual basis. But during the four-year period during which ECE handled rent assessment, an average of just 77 percent of assessed rent was collected each year.[62]

According to one key informant, under the "ECE regime," many tenants accumulated tens of thousands of dollars in rental arrears due to the above confusion. If those arrears are not repaid, those tenants will not be allowed to access NWT public housing in the future.[63] The assessment process has since been transferred back to LHOs, but not without having caused considerable disruption to tenants, landlords and the NWT's Rental Officer over the four-year period in question.[64]

When asked about the arrears situation in a February 2010 interview, a senior official with the Housing Corporation stated: "Our LHOs have histori-cally collected roughly 90 percent of assessed rent. But there are a handful of, let us say, 'challenging' communities when it comes to arrears. In two of them, the LHO board has made a decision to not pursue people in arrears in any meaningful way."[65] As indicated above, the reason for this is not clear and will be the subject of future research by the present writer.

Exacerbating the problem, according to the same official, is the fact that "many previous [GNWT] Ministers of Housing have been disinclined to put pressure on communities to pay their arrears."[66] But an even more revealing statement came from a staff member of an LHO, interviewed in August 2009, who identified the problem of rent arrears as one of a culture of non-enforcement of rental agreements by housing staff, and also of unreported earnings by renters:

> When it comes to public housing, there is a cultural divide between LHOs and the Housing Corporation. There is a notion out there that people have traditionally gotten away with paying little if any rent. Rent collection never really was a priority. This contributes to people not paying their rent. HAP [Housing Assistance Program] purchases in the early days were completely free. Eventually, government started charging for them, based on income, anywhere from 10 to 25% of real market value. There's lots of seasonal work. And the seasonal workers are not always diligent about reporting monthly income changes ... I'm an LHO. If I can collect 20% of gross income from a tenant, I'm happy with that. Indeed, lots of LHOs feel that 20–25% of income is fine and are happy with that.[67]

The above quotation reveals a rather deep-seated belief on the part of the official in charge of collecting rent that public housing tenants are charged too much in the way of rent, and that those in charge of collecting rent have rather unrealistic expectations placed upon them. Another key informant identified the problem as one of staffing, adding: "Part of the problem is simply a human resources problem. While Yellowknife or Hay River do not have a problem finding staff, it can be hard in small communities to find people to manage units. It's a thankless job."[68]

Similarly, as of January 2007, 374 of the Housing Corporation's 460 outstanding mortgages (i.e. 81 percent of them) were in arrears,[69] meaning that the owner had either not made a mortgage payment in at least six months, or had stopped making mortgage payments altogether.[70] Indeed, in its 2007 financial statements, the Housing Corporation reported that 88 percent of what it was currently owed in mortgage payments was "probably not collectible."[71] As is the case with public housing, the present writer was not able to ascertain through key informant interviews just exactly why cases of arrears are so high amongst participants in the home-ownership programs. It is hoped that future research will help shed light on this policy conundrum.

EXPIRING OPERATING AGREEMENTS

As is the case with government-assisted housing for all Canadian provinces and territories, the Government of the NWT receives substantial annual funding from CMHC. This funding not only funds mortgages – it also funds the actual operation and maintenance of the units. As per past arrangements made with CMHC, annual funding amounts from CMHC have begun to decline and will end all together in 2038.[72] If the present trajectory continues, a senior official with the Housing Corporation estimates that rent paid by tenants, combined with the current GNWT subsidy, would be able to sustain no more than half of the NWT's public housing stock.[73]

All Canadian jurisdictions face the above predicament to varying degrees. In effect, the federal government has always placed time limits on its subsidization of housing in Canada. The annual subsidy to a given unit has always had an end point. Historically, CMHC would agree to fund a unit for between 35 and 50 years.[74] And given that the federal government's involvement in funding new units of social housing began in earnest in the 1960s, those end points have already been reached on some units. Canada's northern territories are in a particularly precarious position. To be sure, more than in other jurisdictions, social housing in Canada's northern territories features high proportions of very low-income households that have been relying on relatively deep monthly rent supplements. As Pomeroy (2006) has argued, this increases the likelihood that social housing stock will be "unviable at expiry," meaning that they will be unsustainable (for a low-income tenant) without additional funding from an external source, such as the federal government.[75]

All NWT communities outside Yellowknife "have been classified as non-market communities ... [meaning that] houses can only sell for considerably less than their construction cost." Thus, whereas jurisdictions in southern Canada can deal with expiring operating agreements, at least in part, by selling off social housing units in expensive areas and using the equity "to redevelop new housing in cheaper areas," this is not as easy in NWT communities, especially outside of regional centres.[76]

One strategy the Housing Corporation has been using with the above in mind has been to sell older, detached units and then use the equity to develop more energy-efficient, multiplex housing units. Such units, while maintaining the same square footage as the older units, have energy-efficient furnaces, better insulation and better windows.[77]

CONCLUSIONS

Relative to the rest of Canada, the context of government-assisted housing in the NWT is indeed unique. Due largely to the mining industry, there is money in the NWT, and the territory is not the have-not region some would think. Moreover, notwithstanding both the high utility costs throughout the NWT and the high cost of building along the Arctic Coast specifically, the one-time capital costs of building housing in the NWT as a whole are not that much greater than in most other parts of Canada. What is uniquely challenging to the NWT vis-à-vis the rest of Canada, however, is high unemployment, especially amongst members of Aboriginal groups, and most especially in small communities. Indeed, the small communities are where housing problems – especially with respect to overcrowding and the need for major repairs – are the most acute.

While recent federal funding announcements, along with matching contributions from the GWNT, have allowed the Housing Corporation to replace old housing stock with newer units, the overall number of government-assisted units remains unchanged, which does not bode well for the 400 NWT households currently sitting on waiting lists for public housing. But, as the annual federal contributions diminish, it ought to be emphasized that this represents an opportunity to recommit. Indeed, if the federal government chooses to see its reduced annual expenditures on social housing as net savings and then invests this savings into supporting already-existing public housing in the NWT, those very units can remain viable. As Pomeroy (2006) argues:

These assets have already been paid for. It is far less expensive to invest in sustaining them than it is to replace them with new housing. That is not to say that the stock of affordable housing should also not continue to be expanded.[78]

In the post-World War II era, the federal government was embarrassed into helping NWT residents meet basic social needs, as the international spotlight highlighted the fact that Ottawa was neglecting the North. The federal government had little choice but to step up its efforts to meet social needs.[79] As the Harper government vies for a physical presence in North in an effort to make the most of geopolitical opportunity, history may repeat itself. Overcrowded housing and units in disrepair can exist when nobody is watching, but they can become glaringly obvious in the spotlight of an international race for access to oil and minerals.

APPENDIX: REFERENCES FOR KEY INFORMANT INTERVIEWS

- Informant 3 (I3)   18 August 2009   In Person
- Informant 14 (I14)   26 August 2009   In Person
- Informant 16 (I16a)   27 August 2009   In Person
- Informant 16 (I16b)   17 January 2011   Telephone
- Informant 16 (16c)   18 Jan 2011   Telephone
- Informant 21 (I21)   15 February 2009   In Person
- Informant 22 (I22)   16 February 2010   In Person
- Informant 26 (I26a)   18 February 2010   In Person
- Informant 31 (I31a)   23 February 2009   In Person
- Informant 31 (I31b)   1 October 2010   Telephone
- Informant 41 (I41)   28 September 2010   Telephone
- Informant 43 (I43)   28 December 2010   Telephone
- Informant 44 (I44)   14 January 2011   Telephone

NOTES

1 This research is part of a multi-year research project funded by the Social Sciences and Humanities Research Council of Canada. Dr. Frances Abele is Principal Investigator on the research study, and Arlene Haché is Co-Investigator.

2 Rob Huebert, 2009. "Canada and the Changing International Arctic: At the Crossroads of Cooperation and Conflict," in Frances Abele, Thomas J. Courchene, F. Leslie Seidle and France St-Hilaire (eds.) *Northern Exposure: Peoples, Powers and Prospects in Canada's North.* Montreal: Institute for Research on Public Policy, 77.

3 This research is being financially supported by the Social Economy Research Network of Northern Canada (SERNNoCa) initiative, which is funded by the Social Sciences and Humanities Research Council (SSHRC). The opinions of the authors found herein do not necessarily reflect those of SSHRC or SERNNoCa. The author wishes to thank the many key informants who gave non-attributable interviews to the writer, were very generous with their time and were thoughtful in their comments. He is extremely grateful to both Frances Abele, his northern research mentor and Principal Investigator on the research project, as well as Arlene Haché, his community mentor and Co-Investigator on the project. He also wishes to thank Julia Christensen, Bruce Doern, Gen Harrison, Stephanie Irlbacher-Fox, Leslie Pal, Steve Pomeroy and Christopher Stoney for various forms of help with this research. Finally, a special thank you to family members in Yellowknife who showed wonderful hospitality throughout the northern research. Needless to say, all errors and omissions are the sole responsibility of the author.

4 Ms. Julia Christensen (McGill University). For more on Christensen's work, see Julia Christensen, "'Everyone wants to have a place': homelessness, housing insecurity and housing challenges for single men in the Northwest Territories, Canada." In Proceedings of the International Congress on Circumpolar Health 14. Yellowknife: Institute for Circumpolar Health Research, 56–60.

5 Frances Abele, Thomas J. Courchene, F. Leslie Seidle and France St-Hilaire. "The New Northern Policy Universe" in Frances Abele, Thomas J. Courchene, F. Leslie Seidle and France St-Hilaire (eds.), *Northern Exposure: Peoples, Powers and Prospects in Canada's North.* Montreal: Institute for Research on Public Policy, 2009, 567.

6 R. Huebert. "Canada and the Changing International Arctic," 79–80.

7 F. Abele, T. J. Courchene, F. L. Seidle and F. St-Hilaire. "The New Northern Policy Universe," 565–566.

8 R. Huebert. "Canada and the Changing International Arctic," 92.

9 Frances Abele, Arlene Haché and Nick Falvo, "Homeless in the Homeland: A Growing Problem For Indigenous People in Canada's North," *Parity* 23, Issue 9 (November 2010).

10 Hal Logsdon and Debbie Seto, "Housing and Northern Lifestyles: An Historical Overview," 1992, in Rick Riewe and Jill Oakes (eds.). *Human Ecology: Issues in the*

North Edmonton: Canadian Circumpolar Institute and Faculty of Home Economics, University of Alberta, 81.

11 I3.

12 Andrew Webster, Homelessness in the Territorial North: State and Availability of the Knowledge. Report Prepared for the Housing and Homelessness Branch, Human Resources and Social Development Canada. Ottawa: MaxSys Staffing-Consulting. October 26, 2006.

13 Office of the Auditor General of Canada, *Northwest Territories Housing Corporation* February 2008, 4.

14 Webster, *Homelessness in the Territorial North*, 18.

15 Luigi Zanasi, *Discussion Paper on Expiry of Federal Funding for Social Housing: Implications for the Territorial Housing Corporations.* Whitehorse: Yukon Housing Corporation, Northwest Territories Housing Corporation and Nunavut Housing Corporation. January 17, 2007, 3.

16 A. Webster, *Homelessness in the Territorial North*, 18.

17 Office of the Auditor General of Canada, *Northwest Territories Housing Corporation: Public Housing and Homeownership Programs*, February 2008, 1–5.

18 I14.

19 I16c.

20 According to a senior official with the Housing Corporation, forgivable loans are given instead of grants because the former offer recipients more favourable tax treatment (I16c).

21 I16c. PATH participants must have not owned a house in the five years prior to application. For more on the path program, see www.nwthc.gov.nt.ca.

22 HELP participants can have up to $5,000 in public housing arrears when they begin the program (I16c).

23 Two points should be noted about both PATH and HELP. First, participants in both programs must have lived in the NWT for at least three years, including one full year in the community from which they are applying. Second, the vast majority of participants are Aboriginal persons, and mostly from small communities. For more on both programs, see www.nwthc.gov.nt.ca.

24 L. Zanasi, *Discussion Paper*, 5–6.

25 I31b.

26 Written approval for use of this map has been granted by the Department of Transportation (Government of the Northwest Territories).

27 I31b.

28 Canada Mortgage and Housing Corporation, "Chapter 7: Northern Housing," *Canadian Housing Observer 2008*. Ottawa: Canada Mortgage and Housing Corporation. 2008, 72.

29 FSC Architects & Engineers, *Creating Housing Affordability for the City of Yellowknife, Project # 2009–0150*, October, 2009, 13.

30 Canada Mortgage and Housing Corporation, *Rental Market Report: Yellowknife Highlights Housing Market Information*, Fall. Ottawa: Canada Mortgage and Housing Corporation, 2009, 3.

31 Another 0.3 percent of respondents fall under the category of "Multiple Aboriginal responses," and 0.4 percent identify as "Other Aboriginal responses." NWT Bureau of Statistics, *Population by Aboriginal Identity and Age Group: Northwest Territories, 2006 Census.* Yellowknife: NWT Bureau of Statistics.

32 Frances Abele, "Northern Development: Past, Present and Future," in Frances Abele, Thomas J. Courchene, F. Leslie Seidle and France St-Hilaire (eds.), *Northern Exposure: Peoples, Powers and Prospects in Canada's North.* Montreal: Institute for Research on Public Policy, 2009, 55.

33 F. Abele, T. J. Courchene, F. L. Seidle and F. St-Hilaire. "The New Northern Policy Universe," 571.

34 For more on this, see CMHC. 2010. *Canadian Housing Observer 2010* Ottawa, CMHC.

35 L. Zanasi, *Discussion Paper*, 4.

36 Northwest Territories Bureau of Statistics, 2010. 2009 NWT Community Survey Housing Component: Overall Results Yellowknife: Northwest Territories Bureau of Statistics. January: 14.

37 CMHC, *Canadian Housing Observer 2010*, A–11.

38 I16a.

39 I31b.

40 Northwest Territories Bureau of Statistics, 2010. *2009 NWT Community Survey Housing Component: Overall Results*, Yellowknife: Northwest Territories Bureau of Statistics. January.

41 I31b.

42 L. Zanasi. *Discussion Paper*, 3.

43 They are Colville Lake, Entreprise, Trout Lake, Kakissa Lake, Jean Marie River, Wekweet, Nahani Butte and For Liard (For Liard does, however, have 20 third-party housing units as well as some co-op housing units). None of these communities has a population of more than 200 people (I16a).

44 I26a. A community is typically presented with a certain number of "federal housing units" each year. Each such "unit" could yield for the community either one unit of public housing, or two home-ownership units. In effect, staff from the Housing Corporation would say to the community: "You have 10 federal housing units this year. What do you want your mix to look like (I26a)?"

45 I44.

46 The home must be their principal residence, and the applicant must have lived in the NWT for at least three years (including one full year in the community from which they are applying). For more on this, see: www.nwthc.gov.nt.ca.

47 I16c.

48 I31b.

49 I44.

50 L. Zanasi, *Discussion Paper*, 20.

51 For more on this general topic, see Don Drummond, Derek Burleton and Gillian Manning, *Affordable Housing in Canada: In Search of a New Paradigm.* TD Economics Special Report, June 17, 2003.

52 See "National AHI Funding Table" at http://www.cmhc-schl.gc.ca/en/inpr/afhoce/fias/fias_016.cfm.

53 I31a.

54 The deal also included $300 million in new, one-time federal funding for off-reserve Aboriginal housing, as well as $800 for social housing generally. For more on the deal, see CBC News, "PM shells out $4.6B for NDP's support," April 27, 2005.

55 Canada Mortgage and Housing Corporation, 2008, "Chapter 7: Northern Housing," 73–74. The Yukon also got $50 million of this, while $200 million went to Nunavut. The NWT was the only territory to match their share, dollar for dollar, with funding from the territorial government (I31a).

56 I31a.

57 I31a.

58 I3.

59 Northwest Territories Bureau of Statistics, 16

60 Office of the Auditor General of Canada, *Northwest Territories Housing Corporation*, 11. This is not a new development in the NWT. Indeed, in the 1980s, the Housing Corporation estimated that 70 percent of participants in the Rural and Remote Housing Program were in arrears (Robert Robson, "Housing in the Northwest Territories: The Post-War Vision" *Urban History Review / Revue d'histoire urbaine* Vol. XXIV, No. 1 (October 1995), 17.

61 I31b.

62 I31b.

63 I21a.

64 For more on this, see the Rental Officer's Annual Reports from 2006 through to 2009: http://www.justice.gov.nt.ca/RentalOffice/rentaloffice_reports.shtml

65 I31a.

66 I31a.

67 I22.

68 I3.

69 Office of the Auditor General of Canada, *Northwest Territories Housing Corporation*, 14.

70 I41.

71 Office of the Auditor General of Canada, *Northwest Territories Housing Corporation*, 14.

72 Office of the Auditor General of Canada, *Northwest Territories Housing Corporation*, 4.

73 I31a.

74 I43.

75 Steve Pomeroy, *Was Chicken Little Right? Case Studies on the Impact of Expiring Social Housing Operating Agreements*. Prepared for the Canadian Housing and Renewal Association, in association with Garry Charles, Allan Gaudreault and Paul Connelly June 2006, 2.

76 L. Zanasi, *Discussion Paper*, 14.

77   I31a.
78   Steve Pomeroy, *Was Chicken Little Right?* 48.
79   A. Webster, *Homelessness in the Territorial North,* 76.

13 The Harper Immigration Agenda: Policy and Politics in Historical Context

NEIL BRADFORD AND CAROLINE ANDREW

Canadian immigration policy is presently in a period of considerable change and uncertainty. Over the past three decades a complex set of economic, social, and cultural dynamics has challenged some of the key pillars of Canada's renowned postwar "diversity model."[1] Today, federal policy-makers face new pressures in adapting and renewing Canada's historical commitment to large-scale immigration. The challenges cut across each of the three major components of immigration policy – selection and recruitment; settlement and integration; and multicultural identity and belonging. Taking stock of the "dramatic changes in our immigration regime," many experts now voice concern about the capacity of governments to respond creatively to new conditions.[2] There is talk of "mission drift" in Canadian immigration policy, and calls for experimentation with new strategies and instruments to inform longer-term innovations that will reposition Canada for global leadership in managing unity and diversity.[3]

The aim of this chapter is two-fold: first, to offer some context for these evolving challenges, and second to interpret recent Harper government policy responses. We begin with a broad discussion of immigration as a policy field in Canada, highlighting several features that have long made it an especially complex and significant area of federal intervention. Acknowledging the full range of federal government activities in selection, settlement, and integration, Ottawa remains only one of many actors in the policy field. According to the constitution, immigration is a shared jurisdiction with federal paramountcy, but it increasingly involves provinces in leadership roles and municipal governments are becoming pro-active in the recruitment and retention of newcomers.

Tracking the evolution of federal immigration policy over the post war period, we bring into focus the major challenges of recent decades and key shifts in governance that have shaped policy design and delivery. We then explore the Harper government's efforts to place its own stamp on Canadian immigration policy. Under the active leadership of the Minister of Citizenship, Immigration and Multiculturalism, Jason Kenney, the Conservatives have clearly grasped the significance of immigration policy and their initiatives reveal both continuity and change with the approaches of their predecessors. As we will describe later, these changes are motivated both by political considerations – building an electoral base among new immigrants – and by policy considerations. Immigration thus engages both the policy and politics of the Harper administration.

The chapter also underlines the central importance of an emerging policy leadership style that has come to be known as "metagovernance."[4] Scholars of public administration have introduced the concept of metagovernance to capture how governments attempt to provide direction and maintain accountability in highly networked "societal endeavours" such as immigration.[5] The key insight of this literature is its recognition that multi-level, collaborative networks are neither wholly self-organizing nor self-governing. Rather, there is an ongoing, important 'steering' role for government, calling on new forms of leadership from both politicians and administrators. As Guy B. Peters explains, metagovernance represents "an emerging style of governing from the center that ... recognizes the need for some delegation and devolution of governing but at the same time recognizes the need for greater central direction."[6] Given the numerous players and perspectives shaping immigration policy in Canada, we conclude that metagovernance offers a useful vantage point from which to interpret contemporary federal activism.

SITUATING IMMIGRATION POLICY:
A CANADIAN FIELD UNLIKE THE OTHERS

Immigration policy is sometimes seen as a second-tier policy field in Canada and one with fairly discrete boundaries that remain fixed over time and therefore amenable to clear departmental ownership at one level of government. However, there are grounds for recasting this image. Indeed, immigration policy has always held enormous significance to Canadian national development and in recent decades has become one the most complex areas of public administration, involving not just 'joined-up government' but also collaborative governance as state and societal actors each engage the issues.

Immigration is a central theme in the construction of the Canadian story. Although not always properly recognizing the status and position of Aboriginal peoples, the Canadian narrative has basically been that of migrants who have come here and stayed here. Of course, there have been critical accounts of these immigration movements from the perspective of the settler experience, and other analyses that emphasize the racist and classist orientations of immigration policy.[7]

Yet, even these critical accounts basically reinforce the main storyline – Canada is a country built by those who came and chose to stay. Linked to this central idea has been the corresponding theme that newcomers have been welcomed. This welcome has been framed by both an economic or instrumental motivation, and a moral or intrinsic motivation. The instrumental interpretation links to an understanding of the economic benefits of immigration while the moral account highlights compassion. In fact, these two themes often co-exist in the minds of Canadian governments and citizens, and inform self-understandings of the country. The interplay is nicely captured in the conclusion of a recent comprehensive stock-taking of Canadian immigration, settlement, and integration. The editors summarize: "Canada has long been a world leader in welcoming and accepting immigrants, which in turn has contributed to Canada's growth and prosperity, as well as helping to shape our current society."[8]

Certainly, the economic argument for immigration found particularly strong expression in the early post-World War Two period. The immigration of skilled workers from Europe had a major impact on Canadian industrial and urban development as skilled immigrants found work in the expanding industrial workplaces. One of the reasons for their success was that the Canadian education system was oriented to university pathways rather than the production of skilled workers. Indeed, the capacity of post-war Canadian immigration to bring in large numbers of skilled workers enabled the Canadian education system to postpone adaptation to the technological economy. By the same token, the subsequent development of a network of community colleges, by producing a large number of Canadian born skilled workers, has had a negative impact on the employment opportunities for the more recently arrived immigrants.

Of course, the economic rationale for immigration has become ever stronger in recent years with demographic projections showing that Canadian population growth will soon depend entirely on newcomers. Canada's future economic development – its labour markets, its knowledge flows, its marketing and so forth – in the global age is increasingly tied to a continuous flow of immigrants. Moreover, the global competitiveness rationale for immigration now links to another key domestic pressure point: with an aging population, immigration also plays an important role in the workforce population growth necessary to support an increasingly large elderly population and therefore to sustain major social investments in health care and pensions that are also fundamental to the Canadian story. These social policy connections cut two ways: newcomers require timely access to a host of culturally appropriate social services, from education, housing, and health care to labour market, if they are to progress in their new country.[9]

The above discussion brings into view one facet of the significance of large-scale immigration: its interface at a macro-level with education, employment, and social policies. Attention to the ongoing needs of newcomers and their different integration pathways also underscores the dimension of complexity briefly alluded to above – the inter-governmental dynamics of immigration policy. As we will detail later, immigration policy is now on the front lines in Canadian policy experimentation with multi-level joined-up government.

In addition to these vertical relationships, there is an equally complex horizontal governance dimension.[10] Most federal settlement programming is delivered by local non-governmental organizations, and the nature of this assistance will be impacted by the particular organization providing the services and by funding terms and conditions. Settlement agencies can be ethno-specific or more 'mainstream' in their orientations, and focused on specific immigrant populations such as women or youth or more general in scope. Differences also arise in relation to the mission and mandate of the agency in question, its leadership, relations between staff and board, and within the staff. To help ensure consistency and control, the Department of Citizenship and Immigration Canada (cic) has typically relied on quite prescriptive funding models (that are themselves a source of tension among different players), but the sheer number of agencies and networks in the sector produces complex policy and program interactions.

Finally, as has been long observed in Canadian election research, immigration flows and immigration policy carry considerable political significance in Canada, specifically in terms of partisan competition and coalition formation. Foreign-born Canadian citizens vote and historically, Canada's "government party," the federal Liberals, drew wide support from the urban, immigrant dominated ridings in the post-war period. In turn, this support has been seen as related to the federal government's pro-active immigration policy in the decades from the late 1940s to the 1980s. The fact that the Liberal Party formed the government for the pivotal early post-war period (until the late 1950s) and then dominated federal politics during the late 1960s and 1970s, another period of high immigration and policy activism, solidified the link between foreign-born Canadians and that party.

However, as we mentioned earlier, this link is now being challenged by the Conservative Party who build on their own partisan multicultural legacy through Prime Minister John Diefenbaker, and who now actively court the immigrant vote. Like the economic rationale, the political significance of immigration will only grow as more newcomers become Canadian citizens. With metropolitan centres the overwhelming choice for immigrant settlement, Canada's larger city-regions become the key electoral battlegrounds among political parties.

For all of the above reasons, then, we situate immigration as a Canadian policy field that in its 'centrality and complexity' is quite unlike the others.

From a high-level symbolic perspective, immigration is central to narratives of nation-building and identity formation. At a macro-policy level, immigration impacts directions across the education, employment, and social fields. In more programmatic terms, immigration policy covers multiple, and very distinct, kinds of interventions from selection rules and regulations to information services outside the country and longer term community-based support for integration. Not only are these program elements varied, they engage multiple actors, only some of whom are federal officials, with many more coming from the settlement sector, ethnic associations and provincial and municipal governments. Finally, the political salience of immigration policy cannot be overlooked: the issues at stake speak to fundamental questions of national identity, economic and social development, and they engage a host of state and societal forces. Not surprisingly, federal parties with governing aspirations take very seriously the politics of immigration policy.

The above elaboration of the extraordinary significance of immigration policy in Canada provides essential context for the remaining sections of the chapter that offer more detailed discussions of federal policies and governance practices. We begin with the construction of Canada's postwar diversity model, the emerging challenges to its viability, and policy and governance adaptations in the 1990s and 2000s.

CONSTRUCTING AND CHALLENGING CANADA'S "DIVERSITY MODEL"

The model of Canadian diversity grew incrementally across the post-World War II years.[11] A Settlement Service was initiated in 1949 within the then Immigration Branch of the Department of Mines and Resources. In a rapid reorganization, the next year marked formation of the Department of Citizenship and Immigration, with the Settlement Service moved to the new structure. The basic framework for what has come to be known as the Canadian diversity model came into place during the 1950s and 1960s. For immigrants, the key elements included: language training, extensive use of voluntary associations and religious groups for service delivery, and broader access to income assistance and other social programmes that could assist with integration. Language training was the foundation on which other services would build. The 1959 Immigration and Citizenship section of the *Canada Year Book*, in an article on "Integration of Postwar Immigrants," set the direction for federal policy leadership in partnership with other players: "The primary step in the integration process is to learn the language ... The Citizenship Branch, under arrangements with the provincial departments of education, provides free textbooks and pays 50 p.c. of the amount expended by the provinces towards the teaching costs of language classes ... Many voluntary organizations, immigrant aid societies, and church groups also provide language instruction."[12] Indeed, the role of the voluntary or third sector in the settlement process remains a distinctive feature of the Canadian diversity model.

At the same time, in relation to the provinces, the federal government began to open access to welfare state programs of income assistance. During the 1950s and 1960s, Ottawa persuaded the provinces to extend welfare services to immigrants, leaving federal responsibility for support to refugees. It was widely assumed in these years that the job creating engine of the postwar mass production industrial economy would supply entry-level employment for newcomers, thereby limiting the pressures on both federal and provincial income security programs. Further, Ottawa introduced its 'points system' to favour skilled economic immigrants with the best prospect for rapidly achieving self-sufficiency.

In the mid-1970s, another bureaucratic reorganization occurred, this time designed to better coordinate federal economic, social, and cultural integration while also recognizing that each involves different time frames. The Department of Manpower and Immigration was assigned what was viewed at the time as the shorter term integration challenges, related to the labour market, and the Secretary of State would focus on the longer term aspects of social, cultural, and political integration. This division of policy labour set the terms for the development of the three core federal settlement policies that define the field into the present day – the Language Instruction for Newcomers to Canada (LINC), the Immigrant Settlement and Adaptation Program (ISAP) and the much smaller Host program. The largest amount of money goes to language training, largely basic level English or French, and to ISAP which funds third sector organizations for reception and orientation services, translation and interpretation services, referrals, employment assistance and counselling. The Host program operates to match individual immigrants with established Canadians who can assist in settlement and integration. The final turning point in the postwar immigration framework was the incorporation of the idea of the "two-way street" linking newcomers and their host communities.[13]

As immigration increased and became more urban in the 1970s, it was hoped that immigrants would adapt to their new environment, and equally, that the Canadian-born population and institutions would embrace diversity. In 1971, this aspiration was formally expressed through federal multicultural policy that combined recognition and accommodation of cultural diversity with support for inter-cultural exchange. Of course, much has been written about the image of the two-way street, and the extent to which the ideal of equal adaptation has been practiced by the Canadian-born population. Yet, it is certainly notable that Canadian public opinion over the post-war period – in contrast to many other OECD countries – has remained supportive of immigration and immigrants.[14]

The principles and practices associated with the Canadian diversity model established in the early post-war period, and adapted through the 1960s and 1970s as immigration increased, have been widely seen as a Canadian success story. However, the more recent past has given rise to a series of difficult challenges that calls into question traditional approaches. These challenges are rooted in the changing demographic nature of immigration to Canada; in the concentration of newcomers in particular urban centres and often high poverty neighbourhoods; and the declining economic outcomes of immigrants.

Immigration to Canada has become increasingly metropolitan and predominantly non-white. There has been a dramatic increase in visible minorities in the largest Canadian cities. Toronto and Vancouver experienced an almost threefold increase in the visible minority population between 1981 and 2001.[16] In relation to these settlement patterns, several trends are worrisome. To begin, there are declining economic outcomes for recent newcomers, especially racial minorities, despite higher levels of education than earlier immigrant cohorts.[16] Acknowledging the complexity of issues at play, several factors stand out, including changes in French and English language ability, a decline in the return on pre-Canadian education and labour market experience, the long lasting impact on immigrants who arrive in periods of recession, and the associated transformation from an industrial economy that supplied relatively high wage labour market entry points to a service economy where job growth clusters around low paid, part time work.

A related concern has been the growing spatial concentrations of immigrant poverty. This has been documented across metropolitan areas. In Toronto, the landmark study *Poverty by Postal Code* by the Greater Toronto United Way first clarified the links between recent immigrants and distressed neighbourhoods.[17] Subsequent analyses have confirmed these spatial dynamics and mapped the emergence of "three cities" in metropolitan Toronto with the third city one of concentrated poverty and recent immigrant settlement.[18] At a national level, there is now evidence of a widening income gap between richer and poorer areas in all larger metropolitan centres, with three groups – recent immigrants, Aboriginal people and lone-parent families – much more likely to live in poorer neighbourhoods.[19] While researchers agree there is not yet evidence of ethno-racial ghettos in Canadian city-regions, problems of social exclusion are evident as newcomers find themselves isolated not only from economic opportunity but also other forms of civic and social engagement crucial to the sense of belonging.[20]

At the same time, the very heavy concentration of recent immigrants in Canada's three largest metropolitan centres frames a different set of concerns about social cohesion at the national level, specifically, the uneven distribution of the benefits from immigration across an urban-rural divide.[21] There are some recent signs that immigrants are beginning to move out of the largest metropolitan areas to the second and third-tier cities but it is far from a trend. More progress in non-metropolitan immigrant settlement will require at a minimum greater investment in the capacity of smaller cities and rural communities to provide culturally appropriate services to attract and retain newcomers.

All of the above dynamics pose significant challenges to Canadian immigration policy. For example, cic's concentration on the first three years of settlement for program eligibility is increasingly out of step with the reality of much longer term, multi-faceted processes of integration. The tension is experienced most acutely on the front lines where settlement service agencies find many of their clients have been in Canada for more than three years yet continue to face daunting obstacles to integration. Understandably unwilling to turn them away, agencies must devote time and resources to private fund raising and other bridging activities that might fill the gaps. Such work involves forging holistic services across program silos customized to individual and family needs, as well as brokering new relationships among immigrant communities, mainstream organizations, and other levels of government. Compounding the challenges, the settlement agencies are not funded for networking, planning and innovation. They are funded only to deliver the existing service menu despite recognition that its offerings impose obstacles to building coherent pathways for immigrant integration.

Not surprisingly, recent reviews and evaluations of immigration policy report evidence of policy failure.[22] This is true in the economic and labour market realm, and it also appears the case in wider social, cultural, and political dimensions of integration. The political representation at federal, provincial and municipal levels in the large Canadian cities dramatically underrepresents visible minorities, Aboriginal people, youth and women. As one recent study summarized: "There is an archetype of the Canadian elected official – white, middle-class, middle-aged, Christian, Canadian-born and majority-language speaking."[23] More broadly, research documents the racism and discrimination and feelings of social exclusion experienced by recent immigrants.[24]

In sum, the period since the 1980s has given rise to a range of challenges that have led to growing recognition of the need to update the policy foundations of Canada's diversity model. Beginning in the 1990s, the federal government introduced a series of changes to the design and delivery of immigration policy. These changes involve three basic reorientations: first, toward a more holistic policy approach and integrated programming; second, toward more place-based policy that would offer greater flexibility to community-based service provider networks; and third, renewed emphasis on multiculturalism's two-way street to encourage greater integration between immigrants with mainstream organizations such as employer associations, educational institutions, health and housing providers. The next section explores these shifts.

RENOVATING THE MODEL? GOVERNANCE
AND POLICY CHANGE IN THE 1990S AND 2000S

Implementation of these new orientations in federal immigration policy began in the 1990s. Two sets of changes were key, each reflecting a broader view
of the immigrant experience and its policy challenges. On the one hand, the
federal government looked internally to reorganize its policy and programming activity to encourage horizontal integration across departments and
within CIC's various interventions. On the other hand, Ottawa looked out-
ward – or downward – to connect better with other levels of government and
community organizations for vertical coordination that responds to regional
and local variation.

The first horizontal thrust was to engage a variety of federal departments in
issues related to immigrant integration. In addition to CIC, Heritage Canada
has been heavily involved in programs that relate to immigrant integration
and sense of belonging such as the Official Languages Program and the government's anti-racism framework. Since 2008, Heritage Canada's role in immigration policy has diminished as the multiculturalism file was moved to
CIC in a further push for greater horizontality. Other departments playing
important roles include Human Resources and Skill Development Canada in
the critical area of foreign credential recognition, Health Canada in addressing the particular health needs of immigrants and the so-called immigrant
"health effect," the Status of Women focusing on immigrant women, Public
Safety doing work on immigrant youth gangs and the roots of violence, and
the Canada Mortgage and Housing Corporation in housing. Helping to align
these various departmental thrusts has been the Metropolis Project, an ac-
tion-research community, that brings an 'immigrant lens' across government
policy priorities.

Alongside the inter-departmental coordination, CIC has been restructuring
its own settlement and integration programming through what it calls "modernization." Launched in 2008, this approach aims to reduce the silos and
rigidities between the three key CIC programs (ISAP, LINC, Host) to enable
community networks and settlement agencies to combine a "suite of services"
to meet different immigrant needs. In the modernized approach, the federal
programs maintain the same goals, but front-line agencies acquire both greater flexibility in making "community connections," and more accountability
for the results of their service suites.

The same horizontality now informs CIC's evolving relationship with
Francophone minority communities. These developed in 2002 following
amendments to the *Immigration and Refugee Protection Act*. In 2003 these
relationships strengthened with the adoption of the "Action Plan for Official
Languages" which argued for increased federal support for promoting
French-language immigration to francophone minority communities. These

links resulted in large part from the mobilization of non-governmental organizations, and CIC responded by setting up governance structures at the federal and provincial levels. A "Horizontal Management Framework" was established to oversee federal activities and monitor progress. And several of the provincial agreements (British Columbia, Alberta, Manitoba and Ontario) specifically refer to minority francophone communities and their needs in immigrant recruitment and settlement.

In some ways complementing the efforts at horizontal coordination, Ottawa began in the 1990s to decentralize immigration policy through new forms of vertical collaboration. Devolving responsibility to the provinces, it was argued, might better align settlement services with regional priorities and also facilitate immigrant access to the range of social and labour market services necessary for longer term integration. It also provided a partial solution to the large backlog in CIC's permanent resident processing system by allowing provinces to recruit immigrants to meet evolving labour market needs. While the first example of such devolution was conflictual in nature, that between Quebec and the federal government in 1991, the next round of decentralization was initiated by the federal government eager to have provincial governments take over settlement services and play a role in immigrant selection through a new Provincial Nominee Program.

The context, of course, was the intense concern in the mid-1990s about the federal deficit. As part of the 1994 Federal Program Review, settlement services were identified as the most expendable (and expensive) parts of the Department's mandate. In the late 1990s, Manitoba and British Columbia negotiated agreements that included both the nominee program and the full range of federal settlement services with CIC funding transfers. Evaluations of the two devolution experiences reveal both advantages in enabling creative experimentation and local responsiveness and concerns about the loss of national standards and the diversion of settlement funds to non-immigration priorities.[25] Table 1 below illustrates the various arrangements that have evolved between CIC and the provinces. The overall trendline is one of decentralization.

In the mid-2000s a third major example of vertical collaboration came in the Canada-Ontario Immigration Agreement (COIA) that did not pursue decentralization per se but rather tri-level co-management. Negotiated against the backdrop of the Martin government's New Deal for Cities and Communities, the COIA broke new ground in explicitly recognizing a role for municipal governments in immigration policy-making, and also acknowledging the needs and contributions of settlement service providers. The COIA's innovations were expressed in tri-level governance mechanisms and in a substantial infusion of federal funding for settlement services.

Through the COIA several innovative community-based projects were launched such as the placement of settlement workers in schools and in

Table 1
Federal-Provincial Immigrations Agreements, 1991–2010

Type of agreement	Provinces	Date Signed or Renewed
Responsibility for immigrant selection and management of settlement services is devolved to the province	Quebec	1991
Province is responsible for planning and delivering settlement services on behalf of the federal government; compensation provided	Manitoba	(1996) 2003
	British Columbia	(1998) 2010
Planning of settlement services is co-managed by provincial and federal governments, but federal government is responsible for delivery; formal consultation mechanisms exist and partnerships with municipalities are identified as an objective	Ontario	2005
	Alberta	2007
Provincial and federal governments cooperate on immigrant recruitment and planning of settlement services, but without formal consultation mechanisms in place; settlement services are managed and delivered by federal government	Saskatchewan	(1998) 2005
	Nova Scotia	2007
	Prince Edward Island	(2001) 2008
	Yukon	(2001) 2008
Provincial and federal governments cooperate on recruitment only (e.g. nominee program); settlement services managed and delivered by federal government	New Brunswick	(1999) 2005
	Newfoundland and Labrador	(1999) 2006
	Northwest Territories	2009

libraries, and bridge training programs for credential and skills recognition. The most notable of these innovations has been the Local Immigration Partnerships (LIPs) that support multi-sectoral settlement and integration planning councils across the province. A number of experienced immigration policy watchers have expressed their support for the LIPs innovation.[26] The LIPs represent a promising mechanism for progress on some of the challenges that have come to define the immigration field: rooted in the community, they can customize services to diverse local needs; convening multiple stakeholders in the community and across governments, they can integrate different programs; by mandating representation from both mainstream organizations, settlement agencies, and newcomer representatives, they promise to increase the traffic on Canada's multicultural two-way street; and finally, their province-wide geographic coverage offers a new focal point for immigration beyond the dominant Greater Toronto Area. In March 2010, the federal parliament's Standing Committee on Citizenship and Immigration endorsed the LIPs model, recommending its extension to other provinces.[27]

Of course, all of this horizontal and vertical governance activity to modernize and improve CIC policy was introduced by the Chretien and Martin Liberal governments. Since coming to power in 2006, the Conservatives have worked hard to place their own stamp on immigration policy. The next section turns to a consideration of the Harper immigration agenda.

THE CONSERVATIVE IMMIGRATION AGENDA: CHANGE AND CONTINUITY

The Harper Conservatives clearly view immigration policy as a strategic policy field integral to their progression from minority to majority government status. Reflecting on the electoral problems confronting his party in urban Canada, Prime Minister Harper explained the issue "is not that there are more Liberals [in cities] but that conservatives don't vote Conservative, especially new Canadians."[28] In its first term in office, the Conservative government undertook several high profile and targeted initiatives: an apology for the Chinese head tax; the introduction of lower landing fees for immigrants; acknowledgement of the Armenian genocide of the early 20th century; and restoring the Veterans' Allowance for veterans living in Canada who fought with the allies during World War II. All of these mostly symbolic measures can be seen as part of the Conservative Party's strategy to rid itself of a lingering anti-immigration, anti-multiculturalism image.[29]

A high priority for the Harper government has been to reach out to immigrant communities, making the case for common ground with ethno-cultural communities based on conservative themes such as 'entrepreneurship and family values'. Indeed, CIC Minister Jason Kenney has been "inexhaustible" in his attendance at immigrant community events and celebrations to re-brand the Conservatives with new Canadians.[30] In an article titled "A Road Map to a Majority," Tom Flanagan, a high profile Conservative Party advisor, argued that the Harper government should end its electoral courtship of Quebec and instead "woo" new Canadians. Flanagan outlined what he saw as the Conservative opportunity: "Ethnic voters don't rally to fashionable causes of the left, such as gay marriage, carbon neutrality and the 100–mile diet; and they don't make any demands except to be accepted as good Canadians. What they want is exactly what the Conservative Party has on offer – lower taxes, a favourable business climate and safe streets."[31]

Against this electoral-strategic backdrop, we can discern three policy orientations that seem fundamental to the Conservative immigration agenda. First, it is clear that the Conservatives operate within a multiculturalism framework that emphasizes integration and traditional Canadian values more than diversity. CIC Minister Jason Kenney, who also now oversees the multiculturalism program, has captured the government's thinking: "I want to see an integrated society based on active and engaged citizens, not a series of separated ethnocultural silos. I want Canadians, whether they've been here for a few months or all of their lives, to embrace our shared values, our shared history and institutions. I want newcomers to integrate into our proud and democratic Canadian society."[32]

A second distinguishing feature of the Conservative approach is an emphasis on what CIC now terms "community connections" in its modernization approach. The 2010 Speech from the Throne elaborated the broad rationale, asserting that "the best solutions to the diverse challenges confronting Canada's communities are often found locally [and the government] will take steps to support communities in their efforts to tackle local challenges."[33] Finally, the overall Conservative policy agenda – including immigration – is framed by a larger vision of what has been termed "open federalism." Guided by this vision of constitutional clarity and more respectful jurisdictional relations, Prime Minister Harper has been critical of his Liberal predecessors: "Ottawa has stuck its nose into provincial and local matters ... our roles and responsibilities in our respective areas of jurisdiction have become muddled."[34]

Surveying key Conservative immigration initiatives over the past four years, it is apparent that each of these orientations – the integrationist philosophy, the community-driven programming, and the provincializing open federalism – has found policy expression. In fact, what's striking is that each involves a quite different governance logic, moving from a rather centralized or top-down recasting of multiculturalism toward integration, to a co-management partnership with local communities, and finally, a decentralized hand-off to the provinces to lead in immigration policy.

The recentralizing thrust involves a strong assertion of federal priorities framed by a more conservative ideological vision of the Canadian society. One controversial example came with the redesigning of the immigrant examination material and the Canadian citizenship guide. Greater emphasis was placed on the responsibilities of citizenship, and traditional institutions such as the monarchy and the military. Much less attention was paid to concerns about the environment and health care, and broader expressions of diversity such as same-sex marriage were removed.

A similar centralizing approach is evident in the wide grant of Ministerial authority to fast-track temporary foreign workers into Canada, responding to the views of employers while giving short shrift to concerns from human rights organizations and settlement agencies about working conditions, the rights of migrant workers and their lack of access to federal settlement services.[35] It is not hard to see the same 'strong' approach in the government's response to the recent arrival of two boats with Tamil refugees on the shores of British Columbia. With several government Ministers emphasizing the security threats for Canada more than global human rights, Minister Kenney rapidly introduced legislation to "crack down" on human smuggling. However, the scope of the proposals has raised concerns from refugee advocates and immigration lawyers about breaches of refugee claimant rights guaranteed under United Nations convention.[36]

At the same time, the Conservative government has continued along the provincial decentralization and community partnership paths. Strong federal support exists for the provincial nominee program which has greatly expanded in recent years, and Ottawa has welcomed the innovations in settlement and integration services accompanying the Manitoba and British Columbia agreements. The Conservatives have also continued with implementation of the LIPs under the COIA, and indeed, appear set to complete negotiations with Ontario on a renewed agreement starting in 2011. The LIPs involve the federal government in a form of co-management relationship with municipalities and community organizations, and the degree of variation and autonomy in the local planning processes suggests an approach very different from both the top-down recentralization or provincial control that inform other key federal initiatives.[37] Indeed, the federal government has rejected Ontario's overtures for greater provincial control through the renegotiated COIA.

In sum, the Harper Conservatives, when acting on their highly strategic conception of immigration issues, exhibit a number of competing policy and governance tendencies. Critics, perceiving more confusion than coherence, argue that "the national purpose for immigration is lost."[38] Perhaps with these concerns in mind, Ottawa has recently launched a round of negotiations with the provinces and territories to develop common approaches in specific policy bottlenecks such as foreign credential recognition, and more broadly, a national framework for identifying good outcomes in settlement and integration policy and common reporting templates.[39] Such pan-Canadian governance arrangements are new in immigration policy, and suggest an emerging style of federal leadership and coordination. We close our discussion with reflections on these governance trends.

CONCLUSION: TOWARDS FEDERAL METAGOVERNANCE?

This chapter has argued that immigration represents a policy field of particular significance and complexity in Canada. It speaks to central questions about the country's national identity as well as its prospects for economic and social development. Its design and delivery is truly a multi-level, collaborative undertaking with policy performance relying on the combined and aligned efforts of all levels of government, settlement sector agencies, mainstream organizations, business associations, and newcomers themselves. And the 'politics of immigration policy' have become a major axis of federal electoral competition.

Policy fields of such complexity and significance are likely also to feature daunting tasks of coordination and continuity. Simply put, they pose major governance challenges. As we have documented, Canadian immigration policy is replete with these challenges and problems. Scholars of public administration offer the concept of metagovernance to capture how central governments manage devolved policy systems through framing multiple deliberations and steering diffuse interactions. Overall direction, Guy B. Peters argues, comes from identifying broad policy goals and common political values, flanked by deft use of network management tools such as convening, visioning, and learning. As Peters further observes while "the center can always pull power back and impose more direct controls …the initial efforts at meta-governing could be more indirect."[40] Metagovernance thus involves governments tackling complex policy problems and decision processes through combinations of tools quite removed from the traditional reliance on hierarchy *or* networks *or* markets. When governments confront complexity, "it's the mix that matters," rather than the application of a single governance logic or pure policy instrument

The concept of metagovernance is particularly well-suited to interpreting the multi-faceted dynamics of Canadian immigration policy. It helps make sense of the Conservative government's simultaneous mix of values-based centralization as reflected in the revamped citizenship guide; the open federalism decentralization that frames the provincial nominee program; and the community-driven devolution now inspiring the LIPs implementation. In all of this activity, the Conservatives are "steering at a distance," bringing a variety of governance logics to bear on the different elements of their overall immigration agenda.[41]

Along the same lines, the recent moves to seek macro-level policy coordination through pan-Canadian federal-provincial-territorial framework agreements represent another form of metagovernance focused on broad goals and values. "The more strategic approach," Peters concludes, "would continue to emphasize coordination among the actors, but would do so around the principal goals for the political system and the society as a whole … in contrast to beginning with the limited, disparate goals of the individual organizations and programs, and attempting to build coherent policies from them."[42]

Overall, the chapter shows clearly that immigration remains today what it has always been – a federal 'policy field unlike the others'. Shaped by a rich history of shared responsibility, administrative complexity, and political strategy, Canadian immigration policy may now be central to an era of federal metagovernance in managing complexity across policy fields.

NOTES

1 J. Jenson and M. Papillon, "The 'Canadian Diversity Model': A Repertoire in Search of a Framework," CPRN Discussion Paper, F/19. November 2001.
2 K. Banting, "Is There a Progressive's Dilemma in Canada? Immigration, Multiculturalism and the Welfare State," Presidential Address delivered to Annual Meeting of the Canadian Political Science Association, Montreal, June 2, 2010.

3 J.Biles, M. Burstein and J. Frideres., eds. *Immigration and Integration in Canada in the Twenty-first Century* (Kingston: Metropolis, 2008), 6.

4 On the concept of metagovernance and its applications see, L. Meuleman, *Public Management and the Metagovernance of Hierarchies, Networks, and Markets: The Feasibilty of Designing and Managing Governance Combinations.* The Hague: Physica-Verlag, 2008; N. Bradford, "The Federal Communities Agenda: Metagovernance for Place-based Policy in Canada," in C. Andrew and K. Graham eds., *Multi-level Governance and the Federal Urban Agenda.* (McGill-Queen's University Press, forthcoming).

5 B. Jessop,"Multi-level Governance and Multi-level Metagovernance," in I. Bache and M. Flinders, eds., *Multilevel Governance.* Oxford: Oxford University Press, 2004, 49–75.

6 G. Peters,"Meta-governance and public management" in S. Osborne, ed. *The New Public Governance? Emerging Perspectives on the Theory and Practice of Public Governance* (London: Routledge, 2010), 37.

7 A. Perry, *On the Edge of Empire: Gender, Race, and the Making of British Columbia, 1849–1871.* (Toronto: University of Toronto Press, 2001); F. Henry and C. Tator, *The Colour of Democracy: Racism in Canadian Society* (Toronto: Nelson, 2005).

8 J. Biles, M. Burstein, and J. Frideres, "Conclusion: Canadian Society : Building Inclusive Communities," in J. Biles et al., eds. *Immigration and Integration in Canada in the Twenty-first Century* (Kingston: Metropolis, 2008), 269.

9 For an insightful discussion of the links and tensions see, R. Omidvar and T. Richmond, "Immigrant Settlement and Social Inclusion in Canada" (Toronto: Laidlaw Foundation, 2003); M.S. Mwarigha, "Towards a Framework for Local Responsibility: Taking Action to End the Current Limbo in Immigrant Settlement." Toronto: Maytree Foundation, 2002.

10 J. Biles, "Integration Policies in English-Speaking Canada," in J. Biles et al., eds., *Immigration and Integration in Canada in the Twenty-first Century.* Kingston: Metropolis, 2008, 139–187.

11 R. Vineburg, *A History of Settlement Services in Canada.* Study prepared for Citizenship and Immigration Canada, 2010.

12 Ibid., 22.

13 G. Anderson and J.Black, "The Political Integration of Newcomers, Minorities, and the Canadian-Born: Perspectives on Naturalization, Participation, and Representation," in J. Biles et al., eds. *Immigration and Integration in Canada in the Twenty-first Century.* Kingston: Metropolis, 2008, 45.

14 K. Banting, "Is there a Progressive's Dilemma in Canada?"

15 K. Graham and S. Phillips. "Another Fine Balance: Managing Diversity in Canadian Cities," in K. Banting, T. Courchene and L. Seidle, eds. *Belonging? Diversity, Recognition and Shared Citizenship in Canada.* Montreal: Institute for Research on Public Policy, 2007, 159–94.

16 A. Sweetman and C. Warren, "Integration, Impact and Responsibility: An Economic Perspective on Canadian Immigration Policy," in J. Biles et al. eds., *Immigration*

and Integration in Canada in the Twenty-first Century. Kingston: Metropolis, 2008, 19–44.

17 United Way of Greater Toronto and Canadian Council on Social Social Development. *Poverty by Postal Code: The Geography of Neighbourhood Poverty, 1981–2001,* 2004.
18 D. Hulchanski, "The Three Cities within Toronto." Research Bulletin 41, University of Toronto, Centre for Urban and Community Studies, 2007.
19 A. Heisz and L. McLeod, "Low Income in Census Metropolitan Areas," in C. Andrew, ed. *Our Diverse Cities* (Ottawa: Metropolis, 2004), 3–70.
20 R. Walks and L.Bourne, "Ghettos in Canada's Cities? Racial Segregation, Ethnic Enclaves and Poverty Concentration in Canadian Urban Areas," *The Canadian Geographer,* 50 (3) 2006: 273–297.
21 L Bourne and J. Simmons, "New Fault Lines? Recent Trends in the Canadian Urban System and their Implications for Planning and Public Policy," *Canadian Journal of Urban Research,* 12(1)2003: 22–47.
22 M. Burstein, "Reconfiguring Settlement and Integration: A Service Provider Strategy for Innovation and Results." Report for Canadian Immigrant Settlement Sector Alliance, March 2010, 7–10.
23 C. Andrew, J. Biles, M. Siemiatycki and E. Tolley, *Electing a Diverse Canada: The Representation of Immigrants, Minorities and Women.* Vancouver: UBC Press, 2008, 18.
24 J. Reitz and R. Banerjee, "Racial Inequality, Social Cohesion, and Policy Issues in Canada-Summary." Montreal: Institute for Research on Public Policy, 2007.
25 L. Seidle, "The Canada-Ontario Immigration Agreement: Assessment and Options for Renewal," Mowat Centre for Policy Innovation, 2010; C. Leo and J. Enns, "Multilevel Governance and Ideological Rigidity: The Failure of Deep Federalism," *Canadian Journal of Political Science,* 42(1), 2009: 93–116.
26 M. Siemiatycki and T. Triadafilopoulos, "International Perspectives on Immigrant Service Provision," Mowat Centre for Policy Innovation, 2010, 16, 23.
27 Standing Committee on Citizenship and Immigration. "Best Practices in Settlement Services." House of Commons, 2010. For the government's response and its endorsement of the LIP model, see Government of Canada, "Government of Canada Response to the Standing Committee on Citizenship and Immigration 2nd Report, *Best Practices in Settlement Services.*" House of Commons Committees, 2010.
28 J. Ivison, "Mission: Immigration," *National Post,* September 11, 2008.
29 L. Martin, *Harperland. The Politics of Control.* (Toronto: Viking, 2010).
30 Ibid., 228.
31 T. Flanagan, "Courting the Fourth Sister." *Globe and Mail,* November 13, 2008.
32 "The Future of Immigration in Canada." Speaking Notes for the Honourable Jason Kenney, P.C., M.P. Minister of Citizenship and Immigration and Multiculturalism, June 9, 2010.
33 Government of Canada. "A Stronger Canada. A Stronger Economy. Now and for the Future." Speech From the Throne to Open the Third Session of the Fortieth Parliament of Canada, March 3, 2010, 11.

34 Harper, Stephen, Right Honourable Prime Minister, "An Address by the Prime Minister on commitments to communities," Montreal, Quebec, June 2, 2006.
35 For these critiques see, K. Flecker, "Building 'The World's Most Flexible Workforce': The Harper government's 'double-doubling' of the Foreign Worker Program," *BriarPatch Magazine*, November 2007; C. Goar, C. "Finley's bill side-swipes Kenney," *Toronto Star*, April 7, 2008; N.Alboim, N. *Adjusting the Balance*. Toronto: Maytree, July 2009.
36 L. Waldman, "New Refugee Legislation Misses the Mark," *Toronto Star*, October 28, 2010.
37 For an overview of the LIPs early implementation see, N. Bradford and C. Andrew. "Local Immigration Partnership Councils: A Promising Canadian Innovation." Report prepared for Citizenship and Immigration Canada, March 2010.
38 T. Kent, "Immigration: For Young Citizens." Ottawa: Caledon Institute of Social Policy, October 2010, 1.
39 "Federal, provincial and territorial governments agree to improve Canada's immigration system." Citizenship and Immigration Canada, News Release, June 15, 2010.
40 Ibid., 45.
41 G. Peters, "The Meta-Governance of policy networks: steering at a distance, but still steering." Working Paper Online Series http://www.uam.es/centros/derecho/cpolitica/papers.htm, 2007.
42 Peters, "Meta-governance and public management," in S. Osborne, ed., *The New Public Governance?*, 45.

14 Embracing a New Relationship with Canadians: Addressing Barriers to New Media Adoption in Canada's Public Service

MARY FRANCOLI

INTRODUCTION

People today have a wealth of information available at their fingertips and the tools to interact with government on a regular basis. They are demonstrating a greater desire to have a voice and to have access to even more information and knowledge, but our politicians and members of the bureaucracy – the guardians of much of our knowledge – often seem uncertain about how to share. This uncertainty stems in part from a tension that exists within the Canadian political and bureaucratic landscape. On the one hand, we have political and bureaucratic rhetoric espousing the benefits of increased access to information and citizen engagement, coupled with the belief that information and communication technology can achieve this. On the other hand, we see a lack of a clear policy and legal framework governing the use of technology for such purposes and a political environment that has not always demonstrated willingness for transparency and the sharing of information.

This chapter explores this tension by highlighting the use of social media within the public service of Canada. It identifies both the potential benefits and barriers to adopting social media as a means of engaging citizens, providing information and delivering services. Ultimately, it argues that social media has become so widely used that it is impossible to ignore and, as such, must be embraced. In order for the public service to maximize the benefits of such technology, three things need to happen. First, a clear policy framework, aimed at both public servants and Canadians, has to be developed and communicated as a means of guiding online conduct and managing the expectations of the different actors who are becoming more engaged and connected.

Second, members of the public service need to better understand social media and be ready and willing to use it properly. Third, broad cultural change is needed within the public service to allow employees greater freedom to engage in direct communication with citizens. This sort of cultural change is difficult and requires high-level support. While this chapter recognizes that implementing such recommendations is not easy, the suggestions offered here are important first steps for the government and public service when it comes to embracing a new and more interactive relationship with Canadians. Such a new relationship has the potential to improve government transparency and strengthen democracy.

Before explaining the advantages and concerns related a more interactive relationship driven by social media and the above recommendations in more depth, it is useful to first define what we mean by social media.

GOVERNMENT AND SOCIAL MEDIA

Identifying examples of social media is relatively easy. Facebook, Twitter and YouTube are among the most commonly recognized. However, it is important to understand exactly what social media means in order to fully grasp its complexities. Social media guru Clay Shirky has argued that social media is a movement.[1] It involves great numbers of people interacting with one another and that interaction has the potential to be very powerful. Danah Boyd provides further insight with her definition of social software. She says it is about: "letting people interact with people and data in a fluid way. It's about recognizing that the web can be more than a broadcast channel; collections of user-generated content can have value."[2] Shirky and Boyd provide a useful point of departure as they highlight the difference between social media and traditional broadcast media, identifying interactivity as a key-defining element.

Interactivity is the defining feature of social media, which is often interchangeably referred to as web 2.0 technologies. Social media and interactive technology, in turn, are the cornerstones of 'government 2.0' – a term that has become increasingly trendy. Government 2.0 can be defined not as a "new kind of government; it is government stripped down to its core, rediscovered and reimagined as if for the first time…it is the use of technology – especially collaborative technologies (like social media) at the heart of Web 2.0 – to better solve collective problems."[3] Collaborative technology, comprising social media, includes wikis, blogs, social networking sites and interactive discussion boards. These are technologies that allow users to gather information and also to post information and to engage in conversation. This differs significantly from traditional broadcast media, which lacks interactivity and is used to simply push a message, or information, at an audience. This growing capacity for interactivity and collaboration has the potential to drastically alter the way that government and the public service operate. Citizens can be more easily engaged in the development of policy and the delivery of government services.

Political and bureaucratic actors in Canada and in many other countries have a history of promoting rhetoric emphasizing the importance of keeping pace with technological developments, such as those that have given shape to government 2.0. In Canada, the October 1999 Speech from the Throne saw the Governor General make the bold statement that Canada should "be known around the world as the government most connected to its citizens, with Canadians able to access all government information and services online at the time and place of their choosing."[4] This marked the beginning of what became known as Government Online (GOL). What followed were a series of government initiatives to bridge the digital divide – the gap between those who have access and the capacity to use technology and those who do not. More emphasis, for example, was put on programs such as the Community Access Program, meant to connect rural and remote communities and groups that were considered to be among the less connected.

GOL marked the push for a real connection between government and citizens through the use of internet technology. In essence, it set the stage for government 2.0 and the use of social media that we are witnessing today. But adapting to evolving technology is not always a simple task for the bureaucratic arm of government. It necessitates widespread change. As Wayne Wouters, Clerk of the Privy Council, recently told a national community of managers "new technologies have an impact on practically every aspect of our [*public service of Canada*] operating environment."[5] One of the main challenges he outlined is keeping pace with changing technology and a changing media environment. All public servants, he said, are being challenged to "support their day jobs with technological systems and business processes that need to be modernized."[6] And, if adapting to technological change was difficult in the early days of GOL, where the primary goal was the broadcast of information and the simple provision of services, the move to government 2.0 and the adaptation to interactive technology, such as social media, is proving to be very complicated, confusing and fraught with difficulty. Some of the concerns and barriers complicating the uptake of social media will be discussed here. However, first it is important to better understand the many benefits that come from using social media for organizations such as the public service.

BENEFITS OF SOCIAL MEDIA IN THE PUBLIC SERVICE

Four main benefits that are particularly noteworthy to the public service can be identified: 1) internal collaboration, 2) citizen engagement, 3) improved service delivery, and 4) transparency. This section will explore these benefits in greater depth and discuss existing practices in today's public service.

To start, let us look at internal collaboration. This may take place vertically or horizontally. That is, internal collaboration can take place both within a government department or agency, or among a number of departments or agencies. Here, social media tools such as blogs, wikis, or social networking sites, can provide public servants with new means of sharing information and interacting in a fluid and coordinated manner. Such connections are invaluable and go a long way toward improving workplace efficiency. As Jeff Braybrook, a former Senior Director at the Chief Information Officer Branch of Treasury Board, notes "there is a lot of value to connecting people across departments. It has the potential to cut down on duplication. People can consult on policy across departments and can simply know what others are working on."[7]

Importantly, improving internal collaboration has the potential to better connect national offices with the regions. Feelings of isolation and disengagement on the part of those working in regional offices are not uncommon and are perhaps to be expected. Decision-making tends to happen at the national offices and filter down. But, with social media, such feelings of separation can be addressed. It enables national and regional offices to share information and communicate in a faster, more dynamic and interactive way than ever before.

In the past this sort of collaboration was exceedingly difficult and, as the public service has grown, it has become more difficult still. The sheer size of the public service today, approximately 250,000 employees if we look at the core public service and approximately 500,000 if we take into consideration crown corporations and other institutions such as parliament and the Royal Canadian Mounted Police, makes collaboration and coordination a monumental task.[8] Without the proper technology, it was impossible to identify who, in other parts of government, might be working on the same or related issues. Departments and agencies, and even groups within those departments and agencies, were accused of working in silos. In many cases, this was not because of some bizarre desire for isolation or desire to retain control over information, but had more to do with lack of access to the technologies needed to break down those silos.

We have seen several examples of social media being used to break down these silos. Perhaps the mostly widely known is GCPEDIA. This is a wiki for federal government employees. It can be used to publish and share information. It allows its users to post, comment and edit documents, making it possible to brainstorm and collaborate without always meeting face-to-face. It was launched in 2008 and as of early 2010 it was being used by close to 13,000 employees and contained approximately 6000 articles on a range of issues affecting the public service.[9]

GCPEDIA is not an isolated example of social media use spanning departments and agencies. We have also seen projects like the Canada@150 initiative. This particular project brought together over 150 early-career public servants from a range of departments during 2008 and 2009, to consider current and future challenges faced by the public service as Canada approaches its 150th anniversary in 2017. While participants did have some opportunities to meet face-to-face, the bulk of the discussion and deliberation took place using social media. In total, the project produced over 3100 documents, over 1600 discussion threads and over 7000 discussion posts.[10]

Such initiatives hold a place of growing importance in today's public service, and we can anticipate that this will continue to be the case. As the Clerk of the Privy Council recently pointed out, "GCpedia and similar wikis are vital to the public service of today and tomorrow."[11] Technology and policy writer David Eaves agrees. He argues that the sort of interactivity facilitated by projects such as GCpedia will only become more relevant in the near future given the aging public service and high rates of retirement. As he states: "There are a lot of people who, at some point in the next 10 years, are going to leave the public service. Indeed, in the nightmare scenario, they all leave within a short period of time, say 1–2 years, and suddenly an enormous amount of knowledge and institutional memory walks out the door with them."[12] To be sure, technologies that make wikis possible and projects like GCPEDIA come to life can serve to share and preserve knowledge, as well as help to retain institutional memory. This has the potential to improve the efficiency and decision-making of the public service in the years to come, as policy issues becoming increasingly complex and inter-related.

Beyond improving internal connections and collaboration, social media has the capability of improving external communication and collaboration – what we often call citizen engagement. Indeed, this is what many proponents of government 2.0 and technophiles get very excited about. Today, departments and agencies have access to new tools that allow them to reach out to citizens, to engage them in discussions about public policy making or program delivery. The Department of Foreign Affairs and International Trade (DFAIT) serves as one of the early and interesting examples of this development. In 2003, DFAIT hosted a Foreign Policy Dialogue that included a series of online, interactive deliberations. Its site received close to 1.5 million hits by more than 62,000 unique users. In total, over 2,000 messages were posted to the discussion forum, and the discussion paper was downloaded over 28,000 times.[13] While discussion moderators have indicated that more attention needed to be paid to summarizing ideas so that they could be more effectively incorporated into the policymaking process, they did note that interactivity was high and discussion among the participants was productive.[14]

More recently, a large-scale consultation was undertaken by Industry Canada, inviting people to comment on Canada's digital economy. As Industry Minister Tony Clement said at the start or the consultation, "all Canadians have a role to play in shaping Canada's digital future. It's crucial everyone becomes engaged."[15] While the policy impact of the consultation was not yet known at the time this chapter was written, we do know that more than 2000 Canadian individuals and organizations registered to share their ideas and submissions between May 10 and July 13, 2010.[16] This is a strong indication that, when people are given the chance to participate, many of them take it.

Related to the idea of citizen engagement is the potential for improved service delivery. Users of services know best what works and what does not. Their input is essential to allow the public service to deliver programs in a way that serves the needs of Canadians and meets their priorities. Social media allows citizens new means of providing feedback about services. It also allows employees within the public service new avenues for responding to those complaints or concerns. The department of Human Resources Skills Development Canada (HRSDC) serves as a good example of how this can happen in practice. It has engaged in 'corrective blogging', in an effort to address concerns and misinformation related to its student loan program. Essentially, corrective blogging entails finding instances where misinformation has been provided on a blog. Then, an employee makes a comment to provide the correct information, as well as a link to HRSDC site where further information can be found. This may seem like a logical and easy step to take, but its power and significance cannot be overlooked. Prior to social media, much of the information found online was broadcast only. There were few methods for commenting publically on published information. It would have been difficult for HRSDC to join conversations or to have the opportunity to provide this sort of clarification.

Canada Post is another interesting case to explore. It has been actively using its Facebook page to monitor and respond to customers. As Brian Beehler, Director of Social Media at Canada Post Corporation points out:

> There are a number of benefits to social networking. It helps Canadians to see what Canada Post is all about. It also provides a means for Canadians to speak with Canada Post that is better than using the 1–800 number. For example, we recently had a case where a grandmother sent a card to her grandson. The card had money in it, but the money was missing when it arrived. The card hadn't been sealed properly when it was being sorted. The policy here is to donate the money to charity. The call centre informed the grandmother of the policy. She posted the story to Facebook. Within one hour her money was refunded and she commented positively about Canada Post on Facebook.[17]

Again, this example may not appear particularly revolutionary, but it has major implications for service delivery and goes a long way toward promoting positive public perceptions of the organization. The grandmother's original post had the potential to be seen by many. If Canada Post had decided not to engage with its customers using Facebook, the complaint would not have been responded to and may have fed negative conversations about the corporation. The fact that the grandmother followed up with a positive comment about Canada Post when her complaint had been resolved is invaluable. It too had a potentially large audience and could go a long way toward promoting a positive image for Canada Post. In short, social media can lead to unprecedented exposure.

We have seen how social media can be easily used to spread knowledge and information. This can improve transparency, which in turn can strengthen our democratic institutions. Transparency is about providing access to a wealth of information. It is something political leaders have paid lip service to. As Prime Minister Harper has stated himself: "Information is the lifeblood of a democracy...without adequate access to key information about government policies and programs, citizens and parliamentarians cannot make informed decisions, and incompetent or corrupt governance can be hidden under a cloak of secrecy."[18]

Of course such rhetoric does not mean that information is always shared as willingly or as openly as it could be. However, social media does provide citizens with a forum where discourse can thrive, identifying gaps in information as well as instances where the government may have refused to provide information. While this in itself does not solve the problem of information disclosure, it does aid in the quest for transparency, as people are better able to identify and discuss issues related to transparency and the provision of information. This provides grounds for groups to develop, organize and to better demand that government responds to requests for information and citizens' demands for transparency.

Each of the potential benefits discussed here should be of interest not only to the Government of Canada, but also to other levels of governments and to liberal democracies in general, as many face concerns regarding a democratic deficit. This has been characterized by growing mistrust between citizens and government, whereby citizens are disengaged and feel as if government is not communicating with or listening to them. The consequences of this are far-reaching, from online and real world activism used to try and capture the attention of government to decreasing numbers when it comes to voter turnout. By and large, the democratic deficit indicates declining levels of confidence in government and its institutions, including the public service. This is quite alarming given that democratic governments are meant to represent the will of the people.

BARRIERS TO SOCIAL MEDIA

While many recognize the benefits of social media, they also point toward a number of barriers or concerns that have the potential to slow or prevent the uptake of the technology. Some of the main barriers include: 1) a political environment not supportive of openness or transparency, 2) a dated policy environment, 3) security and privacy, and 4) the organizational culture of large bureaucracies such as the public service.

Earlier, the potential for transparency was identified as a benefit to social media. While this is the case, it cannot be realized without political support. And, despite the Prime Minister's rhetoric about the importance of openness and transparency, we have not always seen a political environment that supports information sharing. In fact, there appears to be a deep-seeded reluctance. We can perhaps best see this in the fact that, five years after making his plea for more transparency, Stephen Harper and his government have been beset by criticism that it is obsessed with secrecy and control. Take, for example, the charge of Canada's Interim Information Commissioner, Suzanne Legault, who noted that the "amount of information being disclosed under the access law has decreased during Harper's tenure, at the same time that release times have increased."[19]

Legault's criticism is not surprising given the public attention to the Harper government's control over information. It has had a notoriously rocky relationship with the press and has been accused of muzzling ministers, engaging in what some see as excessive spin, and taking longer than necessary times to respond to requests for information.[20] One of the most noteworthy developments of this situation is that, at the same time as we have seen restrictions put on the flow of information, many members of the political executive, including the prime minister himself, have jumped on the social media bandwagon. The Prime Minister, for example, has a presence on a range of social networking sites including Facebook, Twitter, Vimeo, YouTube and Flickr. This sends a confusing and contradictory message, particularly to rank and file public servants, that while social media is useful, it can or should only be used by a select few. As a recent news article notes: "there are different rules for individual public servants."[21] Reinforcing this fact, we see access to much social media being blocked from public servants. And, if access is not blocked, a confusing and dated policy environment can serve as a barrier.

In Canada's public service, employees must comply with the Communication Policy of the Government of Canada. This includes a requirement that federal institutions maintain "a capacity for innovation and stay current with developments in communications practice and technology."[22] At the time of writing, the policy had not been updated since 2006 and even then it was only updated to make some changes regarding opinion research and advertising. The original policy came into being in 2002. While this may not seem particularly old from a policy point of view, consider how much has changed in the communication landscape since 2002. YouTube was not created until three years later. Facebook had not yet been developed. Twitter was a distant dream. The tools used to communicate have grown exponentially since the Government's communication policy was conceived. They have also become easier to use. And Canadians, including public servants, are using them. Facebook, YouTube and Twitter are among the top ten visited sites by Canadians.[23]

The government's communication policy is somewhat complex. Its purpose is to "ensure that communications across the Government of Canada are well coordinated, effectively managed and responsive to the diverse information needs of the public."[24] It draws on, and ties public servants to, a plethora of legislation where there is overlap with issues related to communication and information management, most notably the Official Languages Act, the Privacy Act, the Access to Information Act, and the Federal Identity Program. Such legislation also pre-dates much social media.

The problem is not just that these instruments are dated when it comes to governing today's communication environment, but also that the communication landscape changes rapidly and legislation and policy do not. Public policy changes take a great deal of time and effort. This is good; they require careful consideration and should not be rushed. However, this creates a very difficult dilemma, where it is next to impossible to bridge the gap between public policy direction and technological capability. The seemingly immense size of this gap can leave many public servants wondering how best to use technology, such as social media, while still respecting the existing legislative frameworks. Often they have to make up the rules as they go.

Going hand-in-hand with the issue of dated policy are concerns regarding privacy and security. There is a worry that government information will be misused or abused, that inappropriate information will be inadvertently leaked, or that doing business in the online environment will make the government increasingly vulnerable to online crime, such as hacking. However, studies done with public servants indicate that social media has not brought about these concerns, but rather focused a new light on them. They are in fact longstanding issues for government that are simply manifesting themselves in a new environment.[25] Moreover, it is thought that concerns regarding privacy and security should not deter government from using social media. In effect, it is, as Shirky has argued, a force. It has gained significant momentum and this is likely to continue to grow.[26]

Another barrier to the uptake of social media is the organizational culture of the public service. Its size and hierarchical nature have traditionally meant long approval processes. This can make people nervous about speaking out of turn, or saying something that has not gone through the formal vetting process. As Jeff Braybrook points out, "public servants have a concern or worry that they will inappropriately share information. They legitimately don't want to get in trouble, but are typically passionate about their work and want to serve the public in the most effective way, which may include engaging through social media channels like YouTube, Facebook, Twitter and so on."[27] Moreover, there are potential consequences to be faced by those who have neglected to go through the formal approval process and say something that is deemed undesirable. "Public servants can get a verbal reprimand if they say something inappropriate. Nobody wants this. It goes on their permanent record. But generally people don't get offside on purpose."[28] Intentional or not, this concern over the possibility of saying something that someone in a position of authority may find inappropriate or 'offside' has an important consequence. It slows the process of communication. This sort of a sluggish approach does not fit well with social media, which moves and changes quickly.

Recognizing the benefits and concerns associated with social media, the question then becomes: where do we go from here? Do the benefits outweigh the barriers and concerns? If so, what needs to be done so that social media is used effectively and best serves the interests of the government and Canadians? These are not easy questions to answer, but one thing is clear: doing nothing is not an option. As was noted above, Canadians are using social media. It is where many conversations are taking place. And, perhaps more importantly, there is evidence that they want the government to use it as well. During a 2007 study on the Internet, 87% of Canadians indicated that they believed the government should invest in using web 2.0 technologies.[29] Equally importantly, and concerns aside, the public service is starting to respond.

Within the public service, there has been a groundswell of activity in the use of social media. While the concerns noted above, coupled with the current political environment that has not always supported information sharing and transparency, may have limited the development of this groundswell, it is clear that the Canadian public service is undergoing some important changes. A government 2.0 best practice wiki, run by social media guru Mike Kujawski, shows close to 50 unique instances of social media being used at the federal level alone.[30] This makes it clear that the question is not whether the public service should use social media; it already is. The better question is how it can make further and better use of social media while managing the risks involved. There are many possible recommendations that could be made, but three key points are proposed here. These represent a starting point that will help to allow the benefits of social media to be more fully realized, while acknowledging and addressing the concerns noted above.

RECOMMENDATIONS

These recommendations build on existing research and discussions with public servants. They include (1) adopting and communicating social media policy, (2) using social media properly, and (3) recognizing that cultural change is required if social media is to be used effectively and widely.

Adopt and communicate social media policy

As was noted earlier, the public policy framework governing communications in the Government of Canada is outdated. Updating the communication policy and related policies will not be a quick or easy undertaking. However, direction is needed at present so that employees know how and when best to use social media. Someone needs to take a leadership role to provide this guidance. This point was made by a former employee of the Chief Information Officer Branch of Treasury Board: "Leadership to leverage the potential of the Internet in government is blurry. Defining whether it is an IT tool, a service delivery channel or a communications instrument, as well as the policy centre that will take authority, has yet to be clearly defined As a result, no clear vision has yet to emerge."[31] As a result, what we are witnessing is a somewhat piecemeal approach to social media. "Some departments are proactively promoting their social network presence externally, while hushing their initiatives internally given the gap in leadership on the policy side."[32] This is quite problematic. To be most effective social media requires exposure.

While legislative change may be useful, and is indeed necessary, it is a long-term goal and it is doubtful that it will accurately reflect the communication tools and capacity of the day, given the speed of technological change. A better solution is to develop a clear and concise set of guidelines that would help people to negotiate social media. At the time of writing, the Chief Information Officer Branch at Treasury Board is known to have a draft set of guidelines in the works. While they have yet to materialize, having this sort of a centralized and universally applicable framework across the Government of Canada is useful as it avoids confusion and remains relevant to employees even if they move around within the public service.

It is also useful to consider the development of guidelines that extend to those outside government when talking about citizen engagement or the external use of social media. As Braybrook states, "you need to make terms of engagement clear up front on the site (page or profile) to set expectations of conduct on your page or site."[33] Canada Post, which has embraced social media, offers a good example of such guidelines. It has a clear set of guidelines on its Facebook page outlining when and how it will engage with people as well as the type of behaviour it anticipates from those using its page. This sort of a proactive approach helps all actors using the page to understand the rules of engagement and acceptable use. This is a useful means of managing some of the loss of command and control that characterizes social media and which troubles many in large bureaucratic organizations who may be debating the pros and cons of using the technology.

Informing and training public servants about the effective use of social media, as well as policies and guidelines governing their behavior, is also important. It will help to manage risks related to things like security and privacy.

Proper training and education also has the potential to improve project evaluation so that the goals of social media are clearly identified and the technology is used as it is intended.

Use social media properly

Beyond establishing policy to guide the use of social media, it is important to stress that social media must be used properly. This means that those thinking of using social media must identify their goals and rigorously evaluate whether social media is an appropriate tool for reaching those goals. In short, as one former employee of the Chief Information Officer Branch argues, it must be recognized that:

> It is evident that social networking isn't for everything and anything, anyone and everyone. There is a lack of knowledge about social media. A social media initiative should always be part of a comprehensive approach that combines communications objectives, service needs, as well as internal resource imperatives, including information technology infrastructures. Being trendy on-line isn't enough. Federal institutions must conduct fitting research to better understand their clients' services and information needs, expectations and preferences. Then, they will assess the advantages and disadvantages, opportunities and challenges, and whether social networking meets their institution's needs as well as Canadians' expectations, in a way that provides value-for-money.[34]

It is not uncommon to see social media being used with little apparent thought as to its purpose. Social media and government 2.0 have become somewhat trendy. People are often keen to jump on the social media bandwagon without a clear idea of what they hope to accomplish. A consequence of this is the appearance of things like Twitter accounts, Facebook pages and blogs that are simply being used for traditional broadcast purposes. This, remembering the definitions of Shirky and Boyd offered earlier in this chapter, is fundamentally what social media is not. Moreover, using it as a traditional broadcast technology can be both problematic and risky. People expect interaction when engaging in social media and will take conversation elsewhere if they are not offered the opportunity to engage with the information. Braybrook stated this well when he said:

> You need to allow conversations to happen. You can't manage communication the same way you did in the past, which was using the channel (Web in this case) as a broadcast media only. There is pressure from lobby groups to keep conversations going. For example, if you post something on YouTube but don't allow for conversation a lobby group

might take what you've posted and re-post it somewhere else inviting people to discuss and criticizing you for not allowing the conversation to happen. The perceived and actual risks relate to people disagreeing with your message or position (and whether to allow it) and the risk that conversations will occur on your official presence that are occurring amongst participants that you have not initiated.[35]

While using social media tools has become relatively easy, using them properly is certainly a challenge. To be interactive requires time and necessitates carefully monitoring what people are saying and responding to it when appropriate. It also requires clear mechanisms for monitoring and measuring social media use to determine whether goals are being reached

Recognize that cultural change is required

While the first two recommendations offered here can be challenging, with careful planning they are certainly attainable within a relatively short period of time. The third recommendation – that cultural change is required – is much more of a long-term challenge. Interviews done with public servants highlight three issues related to the idea of cultural change that need to be addressed: trust, perceptions of social media, and leadership. These issues are interconnected.

Trust is something that has been notoriously difficult in the public service as a result of its size and composition. Social media highlights the issue of trust. "Departments have been taking an inconsistent approach to social networks. Some trust their employees to make productive and professional use of this tool, while others prohibit access."[36] Part of this distrust has to do with concerns that employees may knowingly, or unknowingly, publish something that jeopardizes privacy or security. It also unnerves many managers, as the public service is hierarchical in nature and typically information follows a lengthy, and what some may even call tedious, approval process before being disseminated to the public.

Related to the issue of trust are perceptions of social media. It isn't uncommon for managers, particularly those who may not be keen to incorporate social media, to think of the technology as a distraction that will not facilitate productive output from their employees. For the technology to be used effectively, "we need to get passed thinking of sns (social networking sites) as a time waster."[37] Here there may be a simple misunderstanding about how and why social media might be beneficial. In addition, there may be a belief that the concerns outweigh the benefits. However, as noted above, such feelings and concerns need to be challenged and appear increasingly irrelevant in a public service environment that has seen a growing number of experiments using social media. When appropriate, use of social media should be encouraged and rewarded.

Finally, related to the two previous points, the effective use of social media requires leadership: "The culture needs to change. People need to do their best to represent the public service well at all times. The line between personal and professional life becomes blurred. People need to be clear. They shouldn't say bad things about the brand (government of Canada in this case) in public. They should stay within the things they know when commenting online. Managers have to be educated and familiar with new media. They have to figure out the new balance between command and control. They have to let people have a conversation."[38] Leadership is important and not just the leadership provided through healthy employee-manager relationships, but high level leadership as well. A new culture of trust, information sharing and openness requires high-level support. Other countries have received such support in the form of ministerial level positions that focus primarily on digital engagement. In the UK, for example, there is a Minister for Digital Engagement. The US also has an embedded and strongly coordinated leadership for government 2.0 technology. Most recently, the Australian government 2.0 taskforce recommended the development of a similar approach.[39]

In Canada, the Standing Senate Committee on Transport and Communication has studied the issue, though more tangentially. As part of its recent study on the digital society, which began as a study focusing primarily on the mobile market, the committee recommended that "Canada should, in conjunction with the presentation of a strategy for an inclusive digital society, appoint a Minister for Digital Policy, who would take over the oversight of the strategy from the Minister of Industry."[40] However, the recommendation does not appear to have attracted a great deal of attention and did not stem from broader discussions about government 2.0 or the use of social media.

Currently, it is the Clerk of the Privy Council who has taken on the role of advocate of social media/ government 2.0 in the Canadian context. Recently, the Clerk asked that all government departments inform him about their use of social media by February 2011.[41] While this might help to raise awareness, it is far from the coordinated and highly integrated approach taken by governments in other countries. While the Clerk might champion social media, resources prevent him from the ongoing monitoring and advocacy that a dedicated position, such as the British Minister for Digital Engagement, allows for.

CONCLUSIONS

In conclusion, it has been shown that the Canadian public service is at a crossroads. On the one hand, there is a growing pressure within the public service to use social media. It has been shown that citizens want, expect and use it.

There is excitement growing for the potential of the technology to improve transparency and strengthen democracy, thereby addressing the democratic deficit. The public service is increasingly showing a desire to communicate with people via popular means. On the other hand, contradictory messages have been coming out of the political environment that are not always consistent with rhetorical calls for transparency and engagement. This, coupled with a host of concerns about the consequences of social media, including lack of clear policy, security and privacy as well as issues related to the organizational culture of the public service, have led to a reluctance to embrace the new technology fully.

This chapter has argued that there is currently a groundswell of interest and support within the federal public service when it comes to using social media. If this is to continue to grow, barriers and concerns must be addressed. Ignoring social media would be naïve. To avoid this and to truly show that the stated commitment to transparency has real meaning, today's government must better understand social media and its approach must be coordinated if the technology is to be beneficial to both government and society. Among the many suggestions that could be considered in this regard, the three key recommendations examined – developing a clear policy framework that is well communicated; ensuring social media is used properly; and working toward organizational change built on trust and leadership – all move the public service towards a new relationship with the Canadian people.

NOTES

1 Clay Shirky, *Here Comes Everybody: The Power of Organizing Without Organizations.* New York: Penguin Press 2008.
2 Danah Boyd, "The Significance of Social Software," in *BlogTalks Reloaded: Social Software Research & Cases,* Thomas N. Burg and Jan Schmidt, eds. Norderstedt 2007, 17.
3 Daniel Lathrop and Laurel Ruma eds., *Open Government: Collaboration, Transparency and Participation in Practice.* Sebastopol: O'Reilly 2010, 12.
4 October 1999, Speech from the Throne.
5 Wayne Wouters, Address to the National Managers Community Forum, May 2010, http://clerk.gc.ca/eng/feature.asp?pageId=137, accessed October 28, 2010.
6 Wayne Wouters, Address to the National Managers Community Forum, May 2010, http://clerk.gc.ca/eng/feature.asp?pageId=137, accessed October 28, 2010.
7 Personal Interview with Jeff Braybrook, Former Senior Director, Chief Information Officer Branch, March 26, 2010.
8 Ian Green, Katherine Baird and Kate Fawkes, *Canada's Public Service in the 21st Century.* Ottawa: Public Policy Forum 2007.
9 Wayne Wouters, Address to the National Managers Community Forum, May 2010, http://clerk.gc.ca/eng/feature.asp?pageId=137, accessed October 28, 2010.

10 Canada@150 final report, http://www.recherchepolitique.gc.ca/doclib/can150_
rp-eng.pdf, accessed October 20, 2010

11 Wayne Wouters, Address to the National Managers Community Forum, May 2010,
http://clerk.gc.ca/eng/feature.asp?pageId=137, accessed October 28, 2010.

12 David Eaves, 'How GCPEDIA will Save the Public Service', http://eaves.ca/2009/03/12/
how-gcpedia-will-save-the-public-service/, accessed October 20, 2010.

13 L. Jeffrey, *Dialogue on Foreign Policy: Report on econsultation* (Toronto: Electronic
Commons 2003).

14 Christie Hurrell, 'Civility in Online Discussion: The Case of the Foreign Policy
Dialogue,' *Canadian Journal of Communication*, V.30, N. 4, 2005.

15 CBC news, 'Clement invites input on digital economy', May 10, 2010, http://www.cbc.
ca/technology/story/2010/05/10/digital-economy-tony-clement-consultation.html,
Accessed October 20, 2010.

16 Industry Canada, Digital Economy Consultation, http://de-en.gc.ca/en/home/,
Accessed, October 30, 2010.

17 Personal Interview with Brian Beehler, Director of Social Media, Canada Post
Corporation, June 18, 2010.

18 Stephen Harper, Op Ed, *Montreal Gazette*, 2005.

19 Cited in David Pugliese, 'Stephen Harper's promise to lift the cloak of secrecy from
government, failing critics say' *Calgary Herald*, May 7, 2010, http://www2.dose.ca/
news/india+warns+danger+from+pakistan+militants/story.html?id=3003637&p=1,
Accessed August 9, 2010.

20 Kristen Shane, 'Prime Minister Harper Benefits From Unprecedented Tight Message
Control,' *The Hill Times*, June 21, 2010.

21 Stephanie Levitz, 'Bureaucratic masters rush to social media, but lock out
their staff,' *The Star*, October 30, 2010, http://www.thestar.com/news/canada/
article/883654--bureaucratic-masters-rush-to-social-media-but-lock-out-their-staff,
accessed October 30,2010.

22 Communication Policy of the Government of Canada, http://www.tbs-sct.gc.ca/pol/
doc-eng.aspx?id=12316&section=text#cha9, Accessed October 27, 2010.

23 Alexa.com, Accessed June 20, 2010.

24 Communication Policy of the Government of Canada, http://www.tbs-sct.gc.ca/pol/
doc-eng.aspx?id=12316&section=text#cha9, Accessed October 27, 2010.

25 Toby Fyfe and Paul Crookall, *Social Media and Public Sector Policy Dilemmas.*
Toronto: IPAC 2010, 9.

26 Toby Fyfe and Paul Crookall, *Social Media and Public Sector Policy Dilemmas.*
Toronto: IPAC 2010, 15.

27 Personal Interview with Jeff Braybrook, Former Senior Director, Chief Information
Officer Branch, March 26, 2010.

28 Personal Interview with Jeff Braybrook, Former Senior Director, Chief Information
Officer Branch, March 26, 2010.

29 Statistics Canada, 'Canadian Internet Survey 2007', http://www.statcan.gc.ca/daily-
quotidien/080612/dq080612b-eng.htm, Accessed June 30, 2010.

30 Mike Kujawski, 'Government 2.0 Best Practices: Canada', http://government20 bestpractices.pbworks.com/Canada, Accessed October 30, 2010.
31 Personal Interview with former Chief Information Office Branch employee, May 31, 2010.
32 Personal Interview with former Chief Information Officer Branch employee, May 31, 2010.
33 Personal Interview with Jeff Braybrook, Former Senior Director, Chief Information Officer Branch, March 26, 2010.
34 Personal Interview with former Chief Information Officer Branch employee, May 31, 2010.
35 Personal Interview with Jeff Braybrook, Former Senior Director, Chief Information Officer Branch, March 26, 2010.
36 Personal Interview with former Chief Information Officer Branch employee, May 31, 2010.
37 Personal Interview with Jeff Braybrook, Former Senior Director, Chief Information Officer Branch, March 26, 2010.
38 Personal Interview with Jeff Braybrook, Former Senior Director, Chief Information Officer Branch, March 26, 2010.
39 Government of Australia, 'Government 2.0 Taskforce report', http://www.finance. gov.au/publications/gov20taskforcereport/doc/Government20TaskforceReport.pdf, accessed October 30, 2010.
40 Standing Senate Committee on Transport and Communication, *Plan for a Digital Canada* (Ottawa: Parliament of Canada June 2010), Page 12.
41 Stephanie Levitz, 'Bureaucratic masters rush to social media, but lock out their staff,' *The Star*, October 30, 2010, http://www.thestar.com/news/canada/ article/883654--bureaucratic-masters-rush-to-social-media-but-lock-out-their-staff, accessed October 30, 2010.

APPENDIX A
Canadian Political Facts and Trends

JUNE 8, 2010

Prime Minister Stephen Harper sought to defend the estimated $1billion costs of the G8 and G20 summit in Toronto, especially the criticism of the $2 million "fake lake" being built at the summit's media centre in Toronto. He said that the summit is a classic attempt for us to be able to market the country.

JUNE 8, 2010

Citizenship and Immigration Minister Jason Kenney announced plans to choose a new regulator for immigration consultants as well as legislation to crack down on unethical "ghost" consultants.

JUNE 11, 2010

The opposition Liberals and NPD accuse the Harper government of reneging on a past promise to hold a competition on its $16 billion purchase of new fighter jets. The opposition parties argued that not only was this more costly but also that there would be a missed opportunity to obtain maximum economic benefits to Canada.

JUNE 18, 2010

The spring session of Parliament ended an otherwise very fractious partisan session with agreements and laws on some contentious issues. These included: an agreed mechanism for reviewing documents related to the treatment of Afghan detainees; and a negotiated consensus on the reform of the refugee system.

JUNE 22, 2010
Parliamentary Budget Officer Kevin Page publishes a report which assesses federal new prison costs in the wake of the federal government's longer sentencing law, a key element of the Conservative's tough-on-crime agenda. The federal costs alone will be an additional $5.1 billion by 2016, a much larger figure than any given to date by the government.

JUNE 23, 2010
Just prior to the G20 Toronto summit, Environment Minister Jim Prentice announces that Canada will make a $400 million contribution to the $10 billion (U.S.) international climate change fund for poor countries and also that Canada will gradually phase out coal-burning electricity at home.

JUNE 27, 2010
At the G20 Summit in Toronto, Prime Minister Harper and other G20 leaders agreed to submit their domestic economic programs to peer review within the G20. By the next November G20 summit in Seoul, member countries have promised to explain in some detail how their domestic policies are helping to achieve the G20's goal of reducing the excessive mismatches in spending and saving that exacerbated the financial crisis. Aided by IMF modelling, other G20 members will assess and discuss whether each partner is doing enough.

JULY 16, 2010
The federal government's austerity program element called the Administrative Services Review has begun, headed by PCO Deputy Minister Daniel Jean. The review process involving senior managers from across the federal departments is tasked to find savings in federal overhead costs. Department budgets are already being frozen for two years and this means any new spending for new priorities will have to funded by reallocated savings.

JULY 21, 2010
Munir Sheikh, Canada's Chief Statistician and head of Statistics Canada announces his resignation because of his opposition to the government's decision to scrap the long form census. He argued that in terms of statistical validity, the Conservative government's decision to replace the compulsory census questionnaire with a voluntary survey would not work. The federal position garnered massive opposition from groups across the political spectrum and from the provinces and business groups.

AUGUST 8, 2010
Government House Leader John Baird says that the federal government will not target public servants in the coming deficit reduction austerity program.

He said that he does not see the massive cuts to the public service that happened under the mid-1990s Liberal government program review.

AUGUST 17, 2010
It is announced that the Canadian nuclear reactor at Chalk River is back in service after a 15 month shutdown. The AECL reactor produces up to a third of the world's medical isotopes. The Harper government at an earlier controversial stage when he fired the head of Canada's nuclear regulatory agency, had announced that the government wants to get out of the medical isotope business.

AUGUST 18, 2010
The Senate Committee on Energy, Environment and Natural Resources reported that there was no need to prevent companies from drilling for oil in Canadian coastal waters. It did however say that there is a need to examine the structure of regulatory boards to determine if there is a "material conflict" between their roles as promoters of development and environmental stewards.

SEPTEMBER 3, 2010
Liberal Leader Michael Ignatieff says that the Liberals will defend universal health care and that Canadians would rather see their tax dollars spent on health care than on more prisons and air force planes, areas of announced Conservative spending, despite the recession.

SEPTEMBER 9, 2010
Prime Minister Harper indicates that he is not ruling out federal support for a new hockey arena in Quebec City that would help with a bid to bring back the Quebec Nordiques. He linked this to other similar requests regarding facilities that might come from other parts of Canada. His comments were immediately criticized by media commentators and also by key Quebec MP, Maxime Bernier, his former Industry Minister.

SEPTEMBER 10, 2010
The Conservatives announce that they will create 26 new Tory caucus advisory committees. Their mandate is to have caucus members involved in both advice and related forms of trouble-shooting so as to better flag issues that might create problems for the government.

SEPTEMBER 14, 2010
Kevin Page, the Parliamentary Budget Officer announces that he will not seek reappointment in 2013 when his current term ends. His reports had been critical of the Harper federal government which had created the office as a part of its 2006 accountability strategy.

SEPTEMBER 22, 2010

A Conservative MP's private members bill calling for the scrapping of the controversial long-gun registry is narrowly defeated in the House of Commons.

SEPTEMBER 30, 2010

Environment Minister Jim Prentice announces that an oil sands advisory panel has been established to look into the state of environmental research and monitoring in the oil sands areas of Alberta. The six scientists on the panel will report in 60 days and their report will be made public.

OCTOBER 5, 2010

Public Safety Minister announces $155 million expenditure for 576 new cells at six prisons in Kingston and Montreal. It is a part of an estimated $2 billion expansion by the federal government of the prison system, a figure which the Parliamentary Budget Officer says is too low. The announcement (as with the larger plan) is immediately criticized by the opposition parties as being wasteful and unnecessary given that the overall crime rate is down 17 percent from a decade ago.

OCTOBER 6, 2010

Nigel Wright, a senior Bay Street executive with Onex Corporation is announced as the new chief of staff to Prime Minister Stephen Harper. He replaces Guy Giorno who was seen by many as being hyper-partisan.

OCTOBER 12, 2010

Canada announces its withdrawal from the final vote in the race for a seat on the Security Council of the United Nations. It is the first time ever that Canada had not won a seat and became an immediate and highly visible international and national embarrassment for the Harper Conservative government.

OCTOBER 13, 2010

Maxime Bernier, a former senior Harper Cabinet Minister, and likely future leadership candidate to succeed Harper, proposes in a speech that the federal government's $40 billion in social and health transfer spending to the provinces should be ended and replaced by federal tax cuts to create fiscal room for the provinces to assume their jurisdictional responsibilities without federal control.

OCTOBER 18, 2010

The Professional Institute of the Public Service of Canada, the union that represents federal government scientists, has created a website that will give voice to the work of its members. It follows actions under the Harper Government to require prior approval for any direct communication between the media and federal government scientists.

OCTOBER 18, 2010
Finance Minister Jim Flaherty presents his fall fiscal update. It projected a higher fiscal deficit of $56 billion in 2010–2011 and stressed that while Canada was doing well compared to most countries, the Canadian economy was nonetheless fragile and that caution is therefore required.

OCTOBER 26, 2010
Auditor General Sheila Fraser gives a broadly supportive initial audit report on the federal stimulus program. She concluded that it had adequately managed the programs audited by putting into place appropriate management practices. She also expressed some concern about whether the government had improperly exempted some programs from environmental assessments that would have delayed their starting date.

NOVEMBER 4, 2010
Conservative Environment Minister Jim Prentice announces his resignation from the Harper Cabinet and from politics to take up a senior job the Canadian Imperial Bank of Commerce.

NOVEMBER 5, 2010
The Liberals charge the Harper Conservatives with negligence after it was revealed on November 4th, that it will cost $300 million to close Camp Mirage in the United Arab Emirates which Canada used as a logistics base for Canadian troops in Afghanistan. The federal government had been forced to close the base because of a dispute with the UAE over landing rights at Canadian airports for its commercial airlines.

The Harper Conservative government announces that it will review the Investment Canada Act. The review will be conducted by the Industry Committee of the House of Commons. The review was announced immediately after Industry Minister Tony Clement had turned down the Australian firm BHP Bilton Ltd's $38.6 billion (US) takeover bid of Potash Corporation. The bid had failed to meet the net benefit test but was also the first takeover in years to be so rejected. The decision pitted the Harper Tories stated belief in free markets against strong Saskatchewan and Western Canadian opposition that threatened the electoral survival of its Saskatchewan Members of Parliament.

NOVEMBER 7, 2010

Defense Minister Peter Mackay announced that Canada may extend its military presence in Afghanistan with up to 1,000 Canadian troops remaining to continue training Afghan troops. The non-combat extension would likely last from 2011 to 2014. Harper decides not to seek parliamentary approval for the extension.

NOVEMBER 8, 2010

In a speech at the International Anti-Semitism Conference, Harper said he is willing to stand up for Israel and speak out against anti-Israeli rhetoric at all costs.

NOVEMBER 11, 12, 2010

Harper attends the G20 Summit in Seoul, South Korea. No agreement was reached on any major issues. Canada and India are appointed as co-chairs to a taskforce assigned to help work out a deal among the G20 countries addressing such policy issues as currency. Harper announced free trade negotiations with Indian Prime Minister, Manmohan Singh.

NOVEMBER 12, 2010

Harper attends the APEC Economic Summit with a platform to address human smuggling.

NOVEMBER 16, 2010

Foreign Affairs Minister Lawrence Cannon confirmed that 950 Canadian soldiers will remain in Afghanistan to train Afghan troops at a cost of $7 million per year. The Liberal party did not challenge Harper's choice to not seek parliamentary approval.

Conservative senators voted down the Climate Change Accountability Act, Bill C-311, 43–32. The bill was passed in May by the House and went to Senate for final approval. In response, both the Liberals and the NPD criticized the Harper government for being undemocratic.

NOVEMBER 18, 2010

The Harper government asked for opposition support to speed approval of a bill that would limit senators to eight-year terms.

NOVEMBER 19, 2010

Stephen Harper praised the proceedings at the NATO Lisbon Summit as the most successful summit he has attended since becoming Prime Minister saying that strong and united allies emerged and important decisions were made. Among the decisions arrived at was a consensus to gradually hand over security responsibilities in Afghanistan to Afghan forces by 2014. Both NATO Secretary General Anders Fogh Rasmussen and U.S. President Barack Obama praised Canada's commitment to provide training and aid until 2014.

NOVEMBER 22, 2010

Jim Flaherty confirms that the federal government will move ahead with plans to reduce taxes for small and medium-sized businesses in 2011. In his speech, the Finance Minister said, "We will not make significant new government spending commitments this year that would trigger bigger deficits and higher taxes".

NOVEMBER 24, 2010

According to a CBC news story, the federal government has been silent about leasing Russian MI-17 "Hip" helicopters that Canadian pilots have been secretly using to fly troops into combat in Afghanistan. The government refuses to provide any details of their procurement. The cost of buying an American made Chinook is about $80 million compared with $17 million for a Russian helicopter. Defense Minister Peter MacKay did not go into any details citing reasons of security.

NOVEMBER 29, 2010

Former Ontario Provincial Police commissioner, Julian Fantino beat out Liberal Tony Genco in the Toronto-area riding of Vaughan making a gain for the Conservatives in suburban Toronto. Conservative Robert Sopuck won the Manitoba riding of Dauphin-Swan River-Marquette and Liberal Kevin Lamoureux beat out the NPD candidate in Winnipeg North. The by-election results allow the Conservatives to add one seat to their total in Parliament.
Health Minister Leona Aglukkaq announced that the federal government is cutting permissible lead levels in children's toys by 85%. The new regulations will target toys produced for kids under the age of three and will stop products from being imported and sold in Canada in the first place.

DECEMBER 1, 2010

Liberal Leader Michael Ignatieff announced his party will not support the Conservatives' human smuggling legislation, Bill C-49, because it violates the Canadian Charter of Human Rights. The legislation is criticized for punishing victims instead of criminals.

DECEMBER 2, 2010

Steven Harper announced that the federal government is extending the deadline for the completion of infrastructure projects under its Economic Action Plan until October 31, 2011.

DECEMBER 6, 2010

The federal government quietly postponed the implementation of gun tracing regulations created by the previous Liberal government until late 2012 to allow more consultation time on the rules.

DECEMBER 7, 2010

Public Safety Minister Vic Toews and Citizenship Minister Jason Kenney unveiled the Terrorism Action Plan in response to the 1985 Air India Flight disaster. The plan aims to strengthen security at airports, provide better federal witness protection, and put more resources towards the combat against extremist group financing. Critics complain that the plan is short on details and does not mention payment to families of the victims.

Canada Environment Minister John Baird attended the UN Climate Conference in Cancun, Mexico. Baird challenged China to take more action in meeting the targets set by the Kyoto accord. Baird also called for a new international binding agreement that will see emissions first stabilize and then decline to replace the Kyoto accord, which is to expire in 2012.

DECEMBER 9, 2010

Auditor General Sheila Fraser released a report finding that allegations of wrongdoing against former integrity commissioner Christiane Ouimet are justified. Ouimet resigned from the Public Service Integrity Commission in October. Of the 228 disclosures of wrongdoing or complaints of reprisal received by the PSIC between 2007 and 2010 only 5 resulted in investigations and none resulted in a finding or a wrongdoing. Fraser's report casts doubt on these results.

DECEMBER 10, 2010

Stephen Harper announced that the federal government will provide $19 million over three months through the Enterprise Cape Breton Corporation to deepen the harbour in Sydney, Nova Scotia. The project will open up trade opportunities for Canadian businesses and turn the harbour into a world-class port.

DECEMBER 14, 2010

The Conservative government will spend only half of the $30 million earmarked to encourage Canadians to fill out the 2011 new voluntary survey on initiatives to actually promote participation. Roughly $5 million will be spent instead on extra printing and postage costs incurred because the number of households receiving the survey has increased from one-fifth to one-third. Another $10 million will be spent on adding two extra questions on language to the short census.

Industry Minister Tony Clement denies a media report that the federal government was influenced by politics to reject the takeover bid by BHP Billiton of Potash Corporation of Saskatchewan.

DECEMBER 16, 2010
The Conservative government pitched a private pooled pension plan for small businesses, employees and the self-employed in order to encourage retirement savings.

DECEMBER 17, 2010
The federal government posted a $4.1 billion deficit in October bringing the total over seven months to $21.5 billion compared with $31.9 billion in the same period during 2009. Government revenues for October increased by 0.4% to $100 million and public debt charges increased by $100 million.

DECEMBER 18, 2010
Stephen Harper told CTV News in a year-end interview that he will not trigger an election in 2011 maintaining that his government is committed to governing.

DECEMBER 20, 2010
Stephen Harper named former CFL commissioner Larry Smith and Toronto clergyman Don Meredith as the Conservative party's new senators. The additions bring the Conservatives to 54 seats in the upper chamber while the Liberals have 49.

After a finance ministers meeting in Kananaskis, Alberta, Jim Flaherty reiterated that now is not the time for increase premiums to the Canada Pension Plan. He announced that the provincial and territorial ministers agreed on the "implementation of a framework" to create the private pooled pension plan announced the week prior.

DECEMBER 21, 2010
Environment Minister John Baird announced that he will move quickly to set up an environmental monitoring system for the Alberta oil sands after a high-level advisory panel announced that there was a lack of credible data on the environmental impact of the oil sands.

The Ontario Court of Appeal "unanimously ruled that the Conservative Fund Canada cannot change its spending reports from the 2004 and 2006 elections to reflect GST rebates totalling almost $600,000." The appeal court said that the "spending limits are the primary tool used to promote Canada's 'egalitarian model of elections." Allowing the change in spending reports would raise party spending limits and would unfairly impact smaller political parties. At issue is a "rebate double dipping" where political parties receive rebates from Elections Canada for 50 per cent of all campaign related expenses and an additional 50 per cent rebate from the Canada Revenue Agency for GST payments that are part of the initial campaign total. (The Canadian Press)

JANUARY 4, 2011
The Prime Minister started the New Year off with a cabinet shuffle appointing Peter Kent as the Minister of the Environment, Julian Fantino as Minister of State for Seniors, Tom Menzies to the junior post of Minister for State of Finance, and Diane Albonczy, former Minister of State for Seniors, as the Minister of State for the Americas.

JANUARY 6, 2011
Stephen Harper announced a $24.8 million investment in Domtar, a paper mill in Quebec.

Senator Leader Marjory LeBreton called for an expense rules review in response to reports revealing that Quebec Senator Raymond Lavigne continues to charge more than $10,000 a month in expenses despite being suspended since 2007.

JANUARY 7, 2011
Prime Minister Stephen Harper announced that he intended to continue with corporate tax cuts in order to attract new business and investment.

JANUARY 9, 2011
A study released by University College of London ranked Canada last in freedom of information citing Canada's measures as outdated. The survey highlights the Conservative government's failure to deliver on its 2006 election promise to dramatically reform the Access to Information Act.

JANUARY 10, 2011
Defense Minister Peter MacKay started a four-day visit to Israel, the West Bank, and Jordan. Mackay met with Israeli Defence Minister Ehud Barak to discuss increased military co-operation and thank Israel for their technological support in the mission in Afghanistan.

The Department of Public Safety announced details of federal spending on prison expansions across Canada. Quebec will receive $73 million for 288 beds, Alberta and Saskatchewan will receive $55 million for 196 beds, and Ontario will receive $30 million for 100 beds. The government will spend $2 billion over 5 years on the prison system in response to stiffer sentencing provisions. Critics suggest that the government should be spending money to fix existing problems in the prisons including added support for mental health.

JANUARY 11, 2011
Canada's Minister of International Co-operation Beverley Oda announced a group of new projects, totalling $93 million, which will be directed at the Haitian recovery efforts. The projects include the rebuilding of Haiti's midwifery school including new maternity beds and a paediatrics ward, and a project to provide three million people with free basic health services.

JANUARY 12, 2011
Liberal Leader Michael Ignatieff, NPD Leader Jack Layton, and Bloc Leader Gilles Duceppe each kicked off multi-riding tours in Canada. Ignatieff intends to visit 20 ridings held by rival parties in 11 days asking the question "are you better off?" Duceppe announced that unless the next budget included $2 billion to compensate Quebec for the harmonization of the provincial sales tax and the GST, his party would vote against it.

JANUARY 13, 2011
While unveiling a "red tape reduction commission" mentioned in last year's budget, Prime Minister Stephen Harper announced that the elimination of taxpayer subsidies to political parties would be a conservative campaign pledge in the next federal election.

JANUARY 14, 2011
CBC News reported that Bruce Power Corp, the most likely bidder in the Conservative Government's effort to sell Atomic Energy of Canada Ltd., has backed out. The federal government put AECL on auction in 2009 and has had only two bidders: Bruce Power Corp and SNC-Lavalin Group. AECL has not sold a reactor since the 1990's and cost taxpayers more than $800 million last year alone. The failed sale affects more than 30,000 Ontarian jobs.

In a speech at the University of Ottawa, NPD leader Jack Layton outlined a strategy for Canada's involvement in Afghanistan that focused on development and diplomacy and contained no military component. He criticized the Conservatives and Liberals for brokering backroom deals and for possibly training future Taliban insurgents citing a NATO statistic that 1 in 5 soldiers who quit the Afghan National Army each year later join the Taliban.

JANUARY 15, 2011
In a CBC Radio interview, Finance Minister Jim Flaherty stated that there would be no HST compensation deal of Quebec in the next budget. He also said that he did not believe the issue would be a sticking point in talks with

Quebec and that the province needs to meet several conditions before harmonization will become a reality.

JANUARY 17, 2011

Finance Minister Jim Flaherty announced three changes to existing mortgage rules in an attempt to address high Canadian household debt. The maximum number of years eligible for government – backed mortgage insurance was lowered to 30 from 35. Canadians can now borrow 85 per cent against their home equity instead of 90 per cent. Government insurance backing on home equity lines of credit has also been removed.

JANUARY 18, 2011

The federal government announced that it will place new restrictions on the use of six phthalates in children's toys and products imported, sold, or advertized in Canada.

JANUARY 21, 2011

The Bloc Quebecois released a statement promising to take up the issue of banning the kirpan, a religious Sikh dagger, to the House of Commons. Both the NPD and Liberals have publicly announced they do not support the proposal. The Conservatives have refused to take a position directing the media to seek out the sergeant-at-arms for questions on the security of the House of Commons. The debate arose after Quebec's national assembly denied entry to a group of four Sikhs scheduled to make a presentation earlier in the week. A report by Parliamentary Budget Officer Kevin Page says new cuts are inevitable and that the Federal Government will not be able to meet their targets for reducing the size of the federal bureaucracy. Page criticized the Government's lack of transparency with the fiscal plan. The latest budget projected federal program cuts amounting to $6.8 billion over five years including annual attrition of 11,000 public service jobs. According to Page's report, the public service will see a reduction of 1,000 over three years when the more than 4,000 jobs at Correctional Services Canada are taken into account. Page also reported that the lack of human resource plans by most of the major departments sheds doubt on the government's targets. Page also questioned the Conservatives' goal of eliminating the deficit within five years projecting that Canada's deficit will be $11 billion in 2015 instead of the $2.6 billion surplus that Jim Flaherty predicts. The federal liberals released attack ads on the conservatives.

JANUARY 23, 2011

Stephen Harper celebrated 5 years as Prime Minister.

JANUARY 24, 2011

The NPD unveil their new campaign headquarters.

JANUARY 26, 2011

The conservative government planned events at 6 locations across Canada in defense of corporate tax cuts referring to them as "tax relief for job creators". At an auto systems plant, Finance Minister Jim Flaherty also addressed concerns about using funds in the PPP Canada Corporation to build arenas in Quebec City and Regina. It is speculated that the Bloc could support Flaherty's March budget and prevent an election if Quebec receives the funding.

Harper is in Geneva to co-host a UN commission for transparency and accountability of a $40 billion maternal health initiative. During his visit, Harper also commented that Canada supports democratic transitions in Tunisia and Egypt in a peaceful and non-violent way.

JANUARY 28, 2011

Health Minister Leona Aglukkaq announced that the federal government will fund $8.6 million in new research on Alzheimer's disease. The funding will support 44 research projects approved by the Canada Institute of Health Research. Julian Fantino, the new Minister of State for Seniors, also announced another $160,000 for an international Alzheimer's disease conference held in Toronto in March.

FEBRUARY 1, 2011

The Department of National Defence announced that they will cut off benefit payments offered to military personnel and their next of kin while it reviews the benefit assessment and payment process. The decision to cut payments was made after an internal review determined DND officials mistakenly interpreted eligibility rules for payments resulting in unauthorized payments totalling tens of millions of dollars. The military is now seeking permission from the Treasury Board for these costs.

FEBRUARY 2, 2011

Liberal foreign affairs critic Bob Rae called an emergency debate on the crisis in Egypt.

Public Safety Minister Vic Toews proposed that the government increase the fees for pardons from $150 (last raised in December 2010) to $631 to make criminals pay for the administrative costs of pardon applications. He has asked the Parole Board of Canada to begin consultations on the proposal within the month. The proposal comes in response to the parole board's request for more staff, training, and funds required because of a recently passed law requiring behavioural assessments of each pardon applicant.

FEBRUARY 3, 2011

Industry Minister Tony Clement announced that the CRTC will have to reverse its decision that ends the unlimited internet access plans offered by smaller internet providers or the federal government will intervene.

FEBRUARY 4, 2011

The Prime Minister's Office announced that RCMP Commissioner William Elliott will step down in the summer. William Elliott was the first civilian leader appointed to the position and has been criticized for his temper.

FEBRUARY 14, 2011

According to CBC, the federal government is planning to reduce overall immigration next year by five per cent. The reduced immigration targets affect family reunification visas as well as those applying under the federal skilled worker program.

FEBRUARY 15, 2011

The opposition demanded the resignation of International Co-operation Minister Bev Oda who admitted that she misled a committee and ordered changes to an email that denied $7 million in funding to faith based global aid group, KAIROS.

FEBRUARY 17, 2011

Parliamentary Budget Officer Kevin Page says there has not been "sufficient fiscal transparency" needed for evaluating the cost of the conservative government's anti-crime legislation. According to the federal government the cost over five years due to stiffer sentencing provisions will be $2 billion. According to Page, already one piece of legislation eliminating credit for time already served prior to sentencing will cost $5 billion over 5 years.

The opposition has requested that House Speaker Peter Milliken investigate Bev Oda for breach of parliamentary privilege.

Stephen Harper unveiled amendments to the citizens arrest legislation. The proposed change expands the rights of those making a citizen's arrest and who are trying to protect their property. Stephen Harper assured the public that despite the growing importance of cybersecurity, the federal government has a strategy in place for anticipating potential attacks. The announcement came after a series of cyber attacks on federal computers targeted the Treasury Board, Finance Department, and Defence Research and Development Canada.

FEBRUARY 22, 2011
Health Minister Leona Aglukkaq announced that the federal government will use $39.5 million from the Pan-Canadian Health Human Resources Strategy towards training more than 100 new doctors in rural areas across Canada.

FEBRUARY 24, 2011
Elections Canada laid administrative charges regarding alleged campaign misspending against the Conservative party and four party members including senators Doug Finley and Irving Gerstein and party officials Susan Kehoe and Michael Donison. The charges are part of an ongoing campaign financing case against the Conservative party from the 2006 election involving $1.3 million moved between local ridings and national party accounts for advertising purposes.

FEBRUARY 27, 2011
Stephen Harper announced that the federal government is freezing the assets held by the Libyan government and imposing a ban on financial transactions with Libya's government, institutions, and agencies. Harper's announcement was aligned with a vote at the UN which agreed to an asset freeze and a travel ban.

MARCH 1, 2011
The federal government will send frigate HMCS Charlottetown to Libya on Wednesday to assist in the evacuation of foreigners. The federal government has been criticized for its slow response to the violent situation in Libya and its evacuation efforts of Canadians.

Fiscal Facts and Trends

Figure B.1
Sources of Federal Revenue as a Percentage of Total, 2009–10

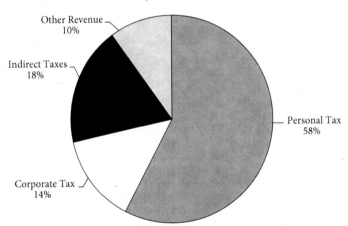

Other Revenue
10%

Indirect Taxes
18%

Personal Tax
58%

Corporate Tax
14%

Source: Department of Finance, *Fiscal Reference Tables 2010*, Table 3.

Figure B.2
Federal Expenditures by Ministry 2010–11 Estimates

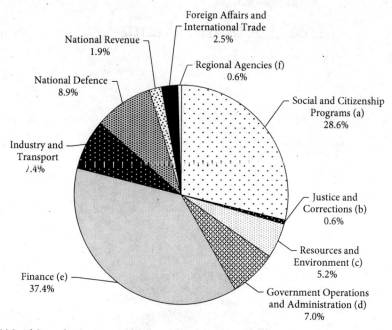

(a) Social Citizenship programs include departmental spending from Canadian Heritage, Citizenship and Immigration, Human Resources and Social Development, Veterans Affairs, Health, and Indian Affairs and Northern Affairs
(b) Justice and Corrections includes spending from the Department of Justice
(c) Resources and Environment includes departmental spending from Agriculture and Agri-Food, Environment, Fisheries and Oceans, and Natural Resources
(d) Government Operations and Administration Spending includes that from Public Works and Government Services, the Governor General, Parliament, the Privy Council, and the Treasury Board
(e) Finance expenditures include but are not limited to, spending on public interest charges and major transfers to the provinces.
(f) Regional Agencies includes Western Economic Diversification, the Atlantic Canada Opportunities Agency and the Economic Development Agency of Canada for the Regions of Quebec
Source: Treasury Board Secretariat, *Main Estimates, Budgetary Main Estimates by Standard Object of Expenditure*, Part II, 2010–2011

Figure B.3
Federal Budgetary Expenses by Type of Payment 1999–2000 to 2009–10

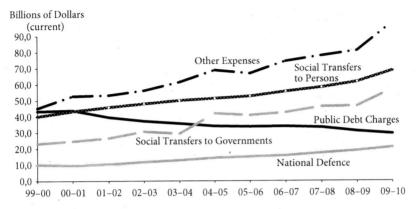

Source: Department of Finance, *Fiscal Reference Tables 2010*, Table 7.

Figure B.4
Federal Revenue, Program Spending, and Deficit as Percentages of GDP 2000–2001 to 2010–11

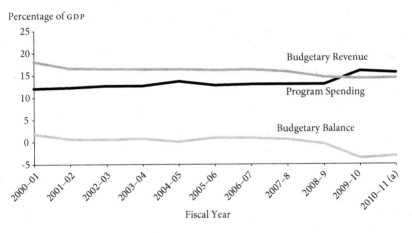

Source: Department of Finance, *Fiscal Reference Tables 2010*, Table 2; Department of Finance, *Budget Plan 2010*.
Note: Budgetary revenue and program spending are based upon fiscal years, while GDP is based on the calendar year. Revenues, program spending, and the deficit are on a net basis. Program spending does not include public interest charges. GDP is nominal GDP.
(a) Figures for this year are estimates.

Figure B.5
Federal Revenue, Expenditures and the Deficit 2000–01 to 2010–11

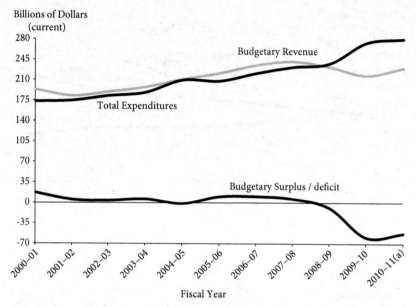

Source: Department of Finance, *Fiscal Reference Tables 2010*, Tables 1 and 7; Department of Finance, *Budget Plan 2010*.

Note: Expenditures include program spending and public interest charges on the debt.

(a) Figures for this year are estimates.

Figure B.6
Growth in Real GDP 1999–2009

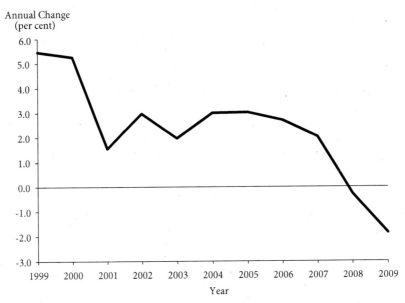

Source: Statistics Canada, CANSIM, Table 380–0017: Gross Domestic Product (GDP), expenditure-based, annual (Constant 2002 Prices).

Figure B.7
Rate of Unemployment and Employment Growth 1999–2009

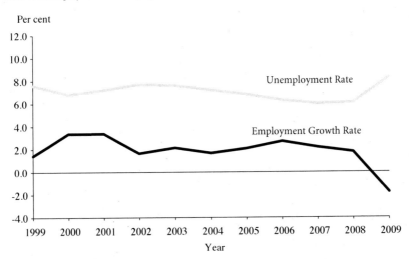

Source: Statistics Canada, CANSIM, Tables 109–5004, 109–5304, 281–0023.
Note: Employment growth rate and the unemployment rate apply to both sexes, 15 years and older.

Figure B.8
Interest Rates and the Consumer Price Index (CPI) 1999–2009

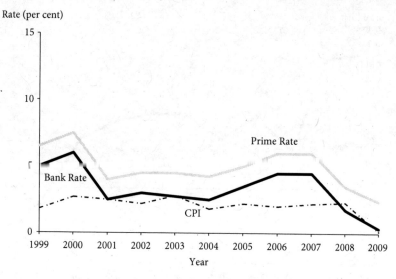

Source: Bank of Canada, *Bank of Canada Review, Banking and Financial Statistics*, Table F1, various years; Statistics Canada, *CANSIM*, Table 326-0021.

Note: The Prime Rate refers to the prime business interest rate charged by chartered bank, and the Bank Rate refers to the rate charged by the Bank of Canada on any loans to commercial banks.

Note: The Prime Rate and Bank Rate are rates effective at year end.

Note: The Trend line for the CPI shows annual percentage change in the index.

Figure B.9
Productivity and Costs 1999–2009

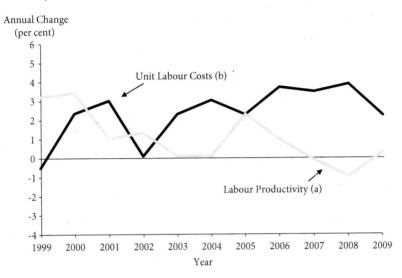

Source: Statistics Canada, CANSIM, Table 383–0008
(a) Labour Productivity is the ratio between real value added and hours worked in the business sector.
This trend shows the annual percentage change in the index.
(b) This is a measure of the cost of labour input required to produce one unit of output, and is equal to labour
compensation in current dollars divided by real output. This trend shows the annual percentage change in
the index.

Figure B.10
Balance of Payments (Current Account) 1999–2009

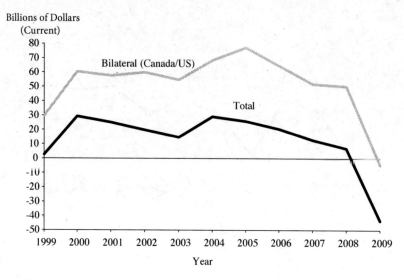

Billions of Dollars
(Current)

Source: Statistics Canada, cat.# 67– 001, various years.

Figure B.11
Growth in Real GDP Canada and Selected Countries 1998–2012

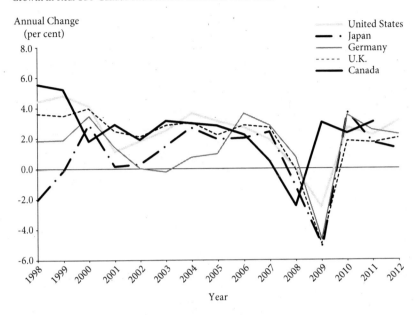

Source: Organization for Economic Cooperation and Development (OECD), *Economic Outlook,* no. 88, issue 2, Nov. 2010, Annex Table 1.

Figure B.12

Standardized Unemployment Rates: Canada and Selected Countries 1998–2012

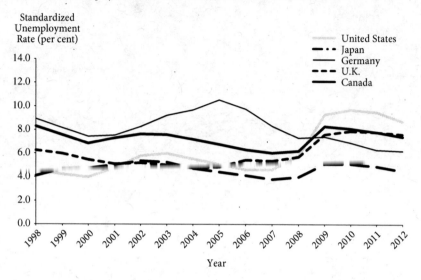

Source: Organization for Economic Cooperation and Development (OECD), *Economic Outlook*, no. 88, Nov. 2010, Annex Table 13.

Figure B.13
Annual Inflation Rates Canada and Selected Countries 1998–2012

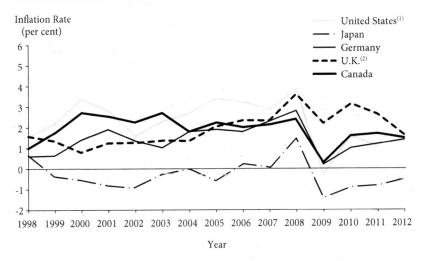

Source: Organization for Economic Cooperation and Development (OECD), *Economic Outlook*, no. 88, Nov. 2010, Annex Table 18.

(1) The methodology for calculating the Consumer Price Index has changed considerably over the past years, lowering measured inflation substantially.

(2) Known as the CPI in the United Kingdom.

Figure B.14
Labour Productivity Canada and Selected Countries 1998–2012

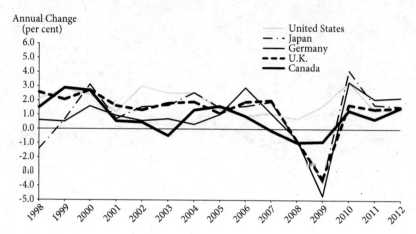

Source: Organization for Economic Cooperation and Development (OECD), *Economic Outlook*, no. 88, Nov. 2010, Annex Table 12.

Note: Labour productivity is defined as output per unit of labour input.

Table B.1
Federal Revenue by Source 1999–00 to 2009–10

			As a Percentage of Total			
Fiscal Year	Personal Tax[a]	Corporate Tax	Indirect Taxes[b]	Other Revenue[c]	Total Revenue	Annual Change (%)
1999–00	60.3	12.5	18.9	8.3	100	6.6
2000–01	58.8	14.6	18.4	8.2	100	10.2
2001–02	58.5	13.2	20.2	8.2	100	-5.4
2002–03	58.1	11.7	21.7	8.6	100	3.6
2003–04	57.2	13.8	20.8	8.1	100	4.2
2004–05	56.4	14.1	20.2	9.3	100	6.7
2005–06	56.1	14.3	20.8	8.8	100	4.8
2006–07	56	16	19.2	8.8	100	6.2
2007–08	55.7	16.8	18.2	9.2	100	2.7
2008–09	59.7	12.6	17.1	10.6	100	-3.8
2009–10	57.7	13.9	18.6	9.9	100	-6.2

Source: Department of Finance, *Fiscal Reference Tables 2010*, Table 3 and 5. Revenue by Source is on a net basis.

(a) Employment Insurance and other income taxes are included in the total.
(b) Consists of total excise taxes and duties.
(c) Consists of non-tax and other tax revenue

Table B.2
Federal Deficit/Surplus 2000–01 to 2010–11 in millions of dollars (current)

Fiscal Year	Budgetary Revenue	Total Expenditures	Budgetary Deficit/Surplus	As % of GDP
2000–01	194,3	174,5	19,9	1.8
2001–02	183,9	175,9	8,0	0.7
2002–03	190,6	183,9	6,6	0.6
2003–04	198,6	189,4	9,1	0.8
2004–05	211,9	210,5	1,5	0.1
2005–06	222,2	209,0	13,2	1.0
2006–07	236,0	222,2	13,8	0.9
2007–08	242,4	232,8	9,6	0.6
2008–09	233,1	238,8	-5,8	-0.4
2009–10	218,6	274,2	-55,6	-3.6
2010–11[a]	231,3	280,5	-49,2	-3.1

Source: Department of Finance, Fiscal Reference Tables 2010, Tables 1, 2, and 7; Department of Finance, Budget Plan, 2010.
Note: While revenue, expenditures, and deficit categories refer to fiscal years, nominal GDP is based upon a calendar year. Total expenditures include program spending and public debt charges.
a) Figures for this year are estimates.

Table B.3
International Comparisons 1998–2012, Percentage Change from Previous Period

	1998	1999	2000	2001	2002	2003	2004	2005	2006	2007	2008	2009	2010	2011	2012
Growth in Real GDP															
Canada	4.1	5.5	5.2	1.8	2.9	1.9	3.1	3.0	2.8	2.2	0.5	-2.5	3.0	2.3	3.0
U.S.	4.4	4.8	4.1	1.1	1.8	2.5	3.6	3.1	2.7	1.9	0.0	-2.6	2.7	2.2	3.1
Japan	-2.0	-0.1	2.9	0.2	0.3	1.4	2.7	1.9	2.0	2.4	-1.2	-5.2	3.7	1.7	1.3
Germany	1.8	1.9	3.5	1.4	0.0	-0.2	0.7	0.9	3.6	3.8	0.7	-4.7	3.5	2.5	2.2
U.K.	3.6	3.5	3.9	2.5	2.1	2.8	3.0	2.2	2.8	2.7	-0.1	-5.0	1.8	1.7	2.0
Unemployment Rates															
Canada	8.3	7.6	6.8	7.3	7.6	7.6	7.2	6.8	6.3	6.0	6.2	8.3	8.1	7.8	7.4
U.S.	4.5	4.2	4.0	4.8	5.8	6.0	5.5	5.1	4.6	4.6	5.8	9.3	9.7	9.5	8.7
Japan	4.1	4.7	4.7	5.0	5.4	5.3	4.7	4.4	4.1	3.8	4.0	5.1	5.1	4.9	4.5
Germany	8.9	8.2	7.4	7.5	8.3	9.2	9.7	10.5	9.8	8.3	7.3	7.4	6.9	6.3	6.2
U.K.	6.3	6.0	5.5	5.1	5.2	5.0	4.8	4.8	5.4	5.4	5.7	7.6	7.9	7.8	7.6
Labour Productivity															
Canada	1.5	2.9	2.7	0.6	0.5	-0.5	1.3	1.6	0.9	-0.1	-1.0	-0.9	1.3	0.7	1.5
U.S.	2.1	2.8	2.4	1.2	3.0	2.5	2.5	1.4	0.9	1.1	0.7	1.6	3.3	1.3	1.4
Japan	-1.4	0.7	3.1	0.7	1.5	1.6	2.5	1.5	1.6	1.9	-0.8	-3.7	4.1	1.7	1.6
Germany	0.6	0.5	1.6	0.9	0.6	0.7	0.3	1.0	2.9	1.1	-0.7	-4.7	3.3	2.1	2.2
U.K.	2.6	2.1	2.7	1.6	1.3	1.8	1.9	1.1	1.9	2.0	-0.8	-3.5	1.7	1.4	1.5

Source: Organization for Economic Cooperation and Development (OECD), *Economic Outlook*, no. 88, Nov. 2010, Annex Tables 1, 12, 13.

Contributors

FRANCES ABELE is professor in the School of Public Policy and Administration at Carleton University.

CAROLINE ANDREW is Professor Emeritus in the School of Political Studies, University of Ottawa and Director of its Centre on Governance.

VANDNA BHATIA is assistant professor in the Department of Political Science at Carleton University

NEIL BRADFORD is an associate professor, Department of Political Science, Huron College, University of Western Ontario.

FRANCOIS BREGHA is an associate and co-founder of Statos who as a consultant, advisor and author has published widely on sustainable development policy and institutions.

DAVID CASTLE is chair of Innovation in the Life Sciences, ESRC Innogen Centre at the University of Edinburgh

G. BRUCE DOERN is professor in the School of Public Policy and Administration at Carleton University and in the Politics Department at the University of Exeter in the UK.

NICK FAVRO is a doctoral student in the School of Public Administration and Public Policy at Carleton University.

MARY FRANCOLI is an assistant professor in the School of Journalism and Communication at Carleton University.

RUTH HUBBARD is senior fellow of the University of Ottawa's Graduate School of Public and International Affairs, and also its Centre on Governance.

DEREK IRELAND has worked as an economist, policy analyst and manager in the Canadian public and private sectors for over four decades. He is currently president of his own consulting firm in Ottawa. He also teaches at the Arthur Leroeger College at Carleton University.

JAMES LAHEY is director of the Centre on Public Management and Policy at the University of Ottawa.

DOUGLAS MACDONALD is senior lecturer and an associate member of graduate faculty, Centre for Environment, University of Toronto.

ERIC MILLIGAN is president of the Regulatory Consulting Group Inc in Ottawa.

LESLIE A. PAL is Chancellors Professor in the School of Public Policy and Administration at Carleton University.

GILLES PAQUET is Professor Emeritus at the University of Ottawa, a senior research fellow with its Centre on Governance, and an associate with its Graduate School of Public and International Affairs.

PETER W.B. PHILLIPS is professor in the Johnson-Shoyama Graduate School of Public Policy, *University of Saskatchewan.*

RICHARD SCHULTZ is professor in the Department of Political Science at McGill University.

CHRISTOPHER STONEY is professor in the School of Public Policy and Administration at Carleton University and Director, Centre of Urban Research and Education (CURE).

KERNAGHAN WEBB is associate professor, Faculty of Business, at Ryerson University. He has published extensively on policy implementation and legal issues. Prior to joining Ryerson, he was Senior Legal Policy Advisor and Chief of Research at the Office of Consumer Affairs, Industry Canada, and

Adjunct Research Professor in Carleton University's School of Public Policy and Administration, and Department of Law.

WEI XIE is a doctoral student in the School of Public Policy and Public Administration at Carleton University.